HILLFORTS

of the Iron Age in England and Wales

A SURVEY OF THE SURFACE EVIDENCE

FOR MY WIFE

By the same author
NEOLITHIC CULTURES OF NORTH AFRICA
Liverpool University Press
HISTORY FROM THE EARTH
Phaidon Press

1. Cley Hill, Wiltshire

HILLFORTS

of the Iron Age in England and Wales

A SURVEY OF THE SURFACE EVIDENCE

J. Forde-Johnston M.A., F.S.A.

Keeper of Ethnology, Manchester Museum

ROWMAN AND LITTLEFIELD

First published in the United States 1976 by
ROWMAN AND LITTLEFIELD, Totowa, New Jersey

First published 1976

Printed and bound in Great Britain
by Hazell Watson & Viney Ltd
Aylesbury, Bucks

Library of Congress Cataloging in Publication Data

Forde-Johnston, James L
    Hillforts of the iron age in England and Wales.

    Bibliography: p.
    Includes index.
    1. Iron age—Great Britain. 2. Fortification,
Primitive—Great Britain. 3. Great Britain—
Antiquities. I. Title.
GN780.22.G7F67 1976   936.2   75-42095
ISBN 0-87471-802-3

Preface

The work on which this volume is based began some fifteen years ago as a general survey of Iron Age forts in England and Wales, attempting to take account of both surface and excavation evidence. It soon became clear that this was too large an undertaking and attention was confined thereafter to a survey of the surface evidence, of which this volume is the eventual outcome. The underlying aim of the survey was to gather together all the surface evidence that could be gleaned from published sources and from an extended field sample (about thirty per cent) in order to make a series of comprehensive statements about the different aspects of Iron Age forts. It is certainly not an attempt to deal with all the problems which exist; ultimately this can be done only by excavation evidence. It is rather an attempt to provide, among other things, sound evidence for the formulation of questions, because unless we ask the right questions, about what to dig, for example, we cannot expect the right answers to come out of the resultant excavations. If it succeeds in this, and in nothing else, it will have performed a useful service in Iron Age studies.

In any such long-term undertaking indebtedness for help received is inevitably very considerable, and is a pleasure to acknowledge here. Without the substantial support of the Leverhulme Trust and the University of Manchester the fieldwork required in such a survey could never have been carried out. The Leverhulme Trust provided generous financial support which enabled fieldwork to be carried on over a period of years. With equal generosity the University of Manchester, through the medium of the Museum Committee, allowed me the very frequent leave of absence which the survey called for, and my heartfelt thanks are due to the then Chairman of the Museum Committee, Professor R. E. Dennell, and the Museum Director, Dr. David Owen, who so cheerfully and patiently bore with my regular absences from the museum. A special expression of gratitude must go to Collin Bowen of the Royal Commission on Historical Monuments for England who first taught me what fieldwork was about, and under whose guidance this work was first conceived, during my service with the Commission (1956–8). For frequent and stimulating discussion, most frequently as his guest at lunch, and much good advice, I have to thank most warmly a staunch friend and former teacher, Professor Terence Powell of Liverpool University. My sincere thanks are due also to friends and colleagues in the University of Manchester and the Hillfort Study Group for many wide-ranging discussions and much invaluable information on sites of which they had particular knowledge. During the preparation of the work for publication I benefited greatly from assistance generously given by members of the museum staff: the secretarial staff, particularly Mrs. C. Higginbottom, who typed, and uncomplainingly retyped, the earlier chapters; my Assistant Keeper, Mrs. Kathleen Hunt, who equally cheerfully typed and retyped, sometimes for a second time, the later chapters of the book; and my technician Mr. George Bridge who brought his skill as a draughtsman to the preparation of the regional maps in Chapter II.

Many of the photographs which illustrate the text were provided by Dr. J. K. S. St. Joseph, Professor of Aerial Photographic Studies in the University of Cambridge, who gave his time most generously to this end. To the landowners and tenants, too numerous to name, who allowed me access to monuments not normally open to the public, I am also grateful. Their ready understanding of what I was trying to do greatly eased my task. To those, less numerous, landowners and tenants whose permission I was unable to obtain, or sometimes at the end of a long day frankly did not seek, I also extend my thanks, and my apologies for surreptitiously venturing on to their property. As the work proceeded to publication, I have been most ably helped by John O'Kane and Mark Holland of Liverpool University Press whose professional skills were always at my disposal. For meticulous work on the index it is a pleasure to express my thanks to Mrs. Ann Morley, whose contribution is a quite invaluable part of the volume.

Finally, and very particularly, I want to express my grateful thanks to my wife who has lived with hillforts for the whole of our married life, who has cheerfully endured field trips in all weathers and conditions, who has read all versions of the text with unfailing interest, and who so arranged our domestic life that I was able to give to the preparation of the final report the time which it called for. Without her constant interest and support I doubt if the work would ever have reached completion.

ADDENDUM

Since I completed work on the text, Dr. D. W. Harding has published *The Iron Age in Lowland Britain* (Routledge & Kegan Paul, 1974), which includes a chapter entitled 'House types: round and rectangular'. The appearance of this chapter calls for some adjustment of the views expressed here on p. 283, particularly the unqualified reference to 'the Continental tradition of rectangular huts'. As Harding points out, 'statements concerning the Continental tradition of rectangular building really refer to the Central European convention, rather than one which has been adequately demonstrated in those areas which border on the Atlantic or the Channel'. He also quotes the literary evidence of Strabo as to the large, circular, plank-built houses of the Gauls, and the sculptured evidence of the column of Marcus Aurelius which indicates that circular huts were common in the Upper Danube region. This and other evidence quoted make it difficult to argue with Harding's conclusion that 'we can no longer doubt that such a tradition was much more widespread in France and the Netherlands than British prehistorians have hitherto been prepared to admit. In consequence, the contrast in building practice between Britain and north-western Europe has been more apparent than real, and its importance in the invasion controversy has been much exaggerated.'

Complementing this evidence of West European round houses there is now some evidence of rectangular houses in Britain, most notably from the hillfort on Crickley Hill, Gloucestershire, but also from Croft Ambrey, Herefordshire (Stanford, 1974), and one or two other sites. The number of sites involved is, and probably always will be, small, but the exclusively round character of British Iron Age houses can no longer be maintained. In Harding's words:

This contrasting pattern now being qualified, on the one hand by the discovery of circular buildings on the Continent and on the other by a re-appraisal of the evidence for rectangular houses in Britain, we must now also question the inference that Iron Age settlements in Britain stemmed from solely insular origins. That the tradition of circular building was already well established in Britain at the outset of the Iron Age is not in doubt. But we can no longer argue conversely against the invasion hypothesis on the grounds that immigrants would necessarily have brought with them their characteristic rectangular buildings, since they could well have come from parts of the Continent where both circular and rectangular houses were in use.

Acknowledgements

I wish to record my gratitude to those friends and colleagues who have so readily given me permission to use the information shown on their original published plans: Mr. J. R. Boyden for Fig. 95; Lady (Aileen) Fox for Figs. 94, 101, 112, and 113; Mrs. W. F. Grimes (Audrey Williams) for Fig. 118; Mr. A. H. A. Hogg for Figs. 87, 88, and 116; Mr. R. W. McDowall, Secretary of the Royal Commission on Historical Monuments (England) for Figs. 21a, 22b, 30b, 34a, 44b, 47, 50, 51a, 51b, 53, 64, 81, 104, 131, and 136; Mr. H. G. Ramm for Fig. 80; Mr. P. Smith, Secretary of the Royal Commission on Ancient Monuments (Wales and Monmouthshire) for Figs. 20, 55, 56, 98, 99, 100, 111, 117, and 127; Mr. J. G. Spurgeon for Fig. 108; Sir Mortimer Wheeler for Figs. 43c and 140; and Mrs. A. Young and Miss K. M. Richardson for Fig. 143. All these figures have been redrawn for the present publication.

The regional maps (Figs. 12–18) are based upon the Ordnance Survey maps with the sanction of the Controller of Her Majesty's Stationery Office, Crown copyright reserved. I also wish to acknowledge permission to use information drawn from various sheets of the Ordnance Survey, which has been used in many of the site plans which appear throughout this work.

Permission to reproduce plates is acknowledged as follows: the University of Cambridge for Plates 1, 5–8, 10, 12, 14–21, 23–25, 27–30, 33, 38–41, 43, and 45–51; the Ashmolean Museum, Oxford, for Plates 26 and 52; and H. Wingham Esq. for Plate 9. Copyright in all these photographs is reserved, as it is in the case of the remaining photographs, which were taken by the author.

Contents

ix

CONTENTS

List of illustrations

PLATES

xi

TEXT-FIGURES

xii

xiii

xiv

CHAPTER I

An introduction to Iron Age forts

Of all the earthworks that are such a notable feature of the landscape in England and Wales few are more prominent or more striking than the hillforts built during the centuries before the Roman conquest (A.D. 43). 'Hillforts are at once among the most impressive and informative of our prehistoric antiquities. They impress by their mere size, by the height of their ramparts, by the depth of their ditches, by the extent of the areas they enclose, and frequently by their commanding position.'[1] They impress also by their sheer number and in many cases by the great complexity of their defences and entrances. They are eloquent testimony of the technical ability and social organization of the Iron Age peoples of southern Britain.

For the purposes of this survey England and Wales is interpreted as the area covered by the south sheet of the Ordnance Survey's 10 miles to the inch maps; that is, the whole of Wales, and England south of the Lake District and the north Yorkshire moors. The Isle of Man is excluded since the sites there could probably be dealt with more intelligibly in the context of the Scottish hillforts. Also excluded, and for the same reason, are the hillforts of north-eastern England, although these are in any case outside the area of the south sheet. The

Fig.1

remaining hillforts of England and Wales, some 1,350 in number, form a single coherent group and clearly demand treatment as a single phenomenon. The examination of this phenomenon in its different aspects forms the subject of this volume.

Fig.2

Hillforts are not distributed evenly throughout the area defined above. The majority of them are to be found in southern England, the Welsh Marches, and Wales, particularly south Wales. They are noticeably scarce in the eastern counties of England. In the south and west there are large numbers in the western extremities, Pembrokeshire and Cornwall, albeit of very small size. Most of the sites in the survey lie to the south and west of a line from the Mersey to the mouth of the Thames. Within this area there are regional and typological groups which will be considered in greater detail in later chapters.

In the preceding paragraphs the term 'hillfort' has been used as the general designation of all the sites under review. That this can be misleading in one respect will become clear when the whole question of siting is dealt with in Chapter III. Not all hillforts are situated on hills, and the term 'fort', moreover,

1. Clark, *Prehistoric England* (1948), 80.

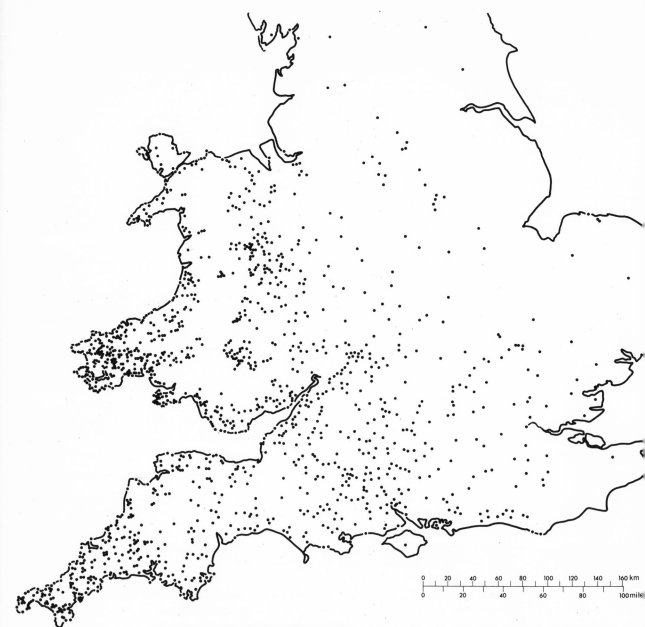

Fig. 1. Over-all distribution of Iron Age forts.

Fig. 2. Number of forts per county.

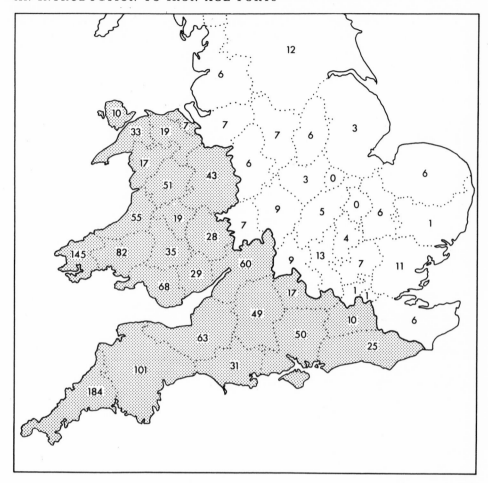

has implications which are not entirely appropriate in a prehistoric context. It is, however, much easier to point out the shortcomings of the existing terminology than to suggest suitable alternatives. The term 'camp', used on earlier Ordnance Survey maps, is even less satisfactory. 'Defensive enclosure' is free of the implications of both 'hillfort' and 'camp' and is, in fact, an objective, if limited, description of these sites. Unfortunately, its objectivity is not confined to defensive enclosures of the Iron Age period only; it can be applied to a wide range of sites of very different periods. In any case it is rather too cumbersome for general use.

In the circumstances the most realistic solution is to bow to existing usage to the extent of retaining the word fort as the general title for all the sites in the survey, and dropping the word hill, except where forts actually sited on hills are being discussed. All the sites under consideration will thus be termed Iron Age forts, or simply forts, the word in this usage meaning a defensive enclosure of the Iron Age, with no other implications. Something along these lines has already

3

been suggested by the Ordnance Survey.[2] Even so, the reservations made above should be kept in mind and the term should be regarded as a very general label for a group of sites which display great variety in their size, shape, and situation.

While the term 'fort' has been adopted for general use the more cumbersome 'defensive enclosure' makes a better starting-point for a brief description of these sites. In any such description the defensive aspect needs to be emphasized. A clear understanding of it is essential for any appreciation of the nature and function of Iron Age forts. 'Their defensive character cannot be stressed too often. In this respect they offer a complete contrast to the outposts of an advancing imperialism. Whereas the typical Roman fort was but a forward post of an organized system, connected by road and sea with a definite base, the prehistoric hillfort, although not without some relation to its neighbours, stood alone as an entity.'[3] Whatever else they mean, the concentrations of forts in certain areas do not imply any over-all strategy. Their existence can probably best be explained in terms of local needs and conditions. They were for the most part independent of each other, and in this independence lay the seeds of their downfall at the hands of the numerically smaller Roman army.

These enclosures vary considerably in size. More than half the sites in England and Wales enclose areas of less than 1 ha (3 acres). At the other end of the scale there are sites enclosing 20 ha (50 acres), 40 ha (100 acres), and, in one or two cases, more than 80 ha (200 acres). These, however, are exceptional. The majority of the remaining sites enclose areas between 1 ha (3 acres) and 12 ha (30 acres).

Fig.3

Fig.4a

Fig.4b

Most Iron Age forts consist of a single enclosure. In a number of cases, however, and particularly in south Wales and south-west England, the interior of the fort consists of two, three, and sometimes more, separate enclosures linked to each other in various ways. In some cases the arrangements can be described as concentric, a larger enclosure completely embracing a smaller one. In other cases the additional enclosures take the form of annexes attached to one side of the main enclosure. Such variations in layout will be considered in more detail in Chapter VI.

The defences which define the enclosed areas are of two kinds, natural and man-made. The natural defences consist of cliffs or very steep slopes which need no additional fortification, together with lesser slopes and such other obstacles as lakes, rivers, and the sea. The man-made defences consist of one or more banks accompanied normally, but not invariably, by external ditches. The banks are triangular in cross-section with a flattened top and the ditches are, broadly speaking, an inverted version of the same shape. These features vary considerably in size. In a relatively small number of cases the banks even now stand over 4.5 m (15 ft) above the level of the interior and up to 12 m (40 ft) above the existing ditch bottom, with over-all widths for a single bank and ditch of 30 m (100 ft) and more. Allowing for the effects of erosion and silting these are quite clearly the remains of considerable structures. For most sites, however, these dimensions are reduced to less than half, and in some cases con-

2. *Field Archaeology*, O.S. Professional Papers, N.S., no. 13 (1963), 68.   3. Clark, loc. cit.

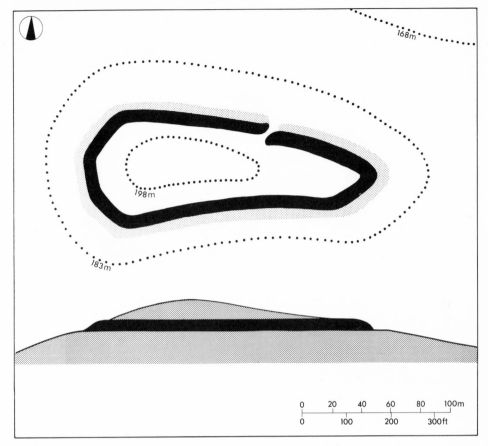

Fig.3. A contour fort.

siderably less. The average bank stands 1·5 or 2 m (5 or 6 ft) above the interior and 3 or 3·5 m (10 or 12 ft) above the ditch bottom, but there are sites where the defences are on an even smaller scale. Banks which rise only 60 or 90 cm (2 or 3 ft) above the interior and fall only 1·5 or 2 m (5 or 6 ft) to the ditch bottom are by no means rare. A detailed analysis of man-made defences will form the subject of Chapter V.

The general nature and typology of Iron Age forts can be illustrated by considering the terminology currently in use to describe them. Since most of the terms involved will be in regular use throughout this work it is convenient to introduce them at an early stage. This basic terminology will be extended as and when required by the more detailed examination of the subject to be undertaken in later chapters.

The majority of Iron Age forts are placed at the moment in one or other of two broad categories, 'contour' forts and 'promontory' forts. Two other smaller categories, 'hill-slope' forts and 'plateau' forts, account for most of the remaining sites. Without anticipating the contents of Chapter III, it can be stated that the sites grouped under these headings show a degree of variety which makes

5

Fig.4a A concentric fort; 4b an annexe fort.

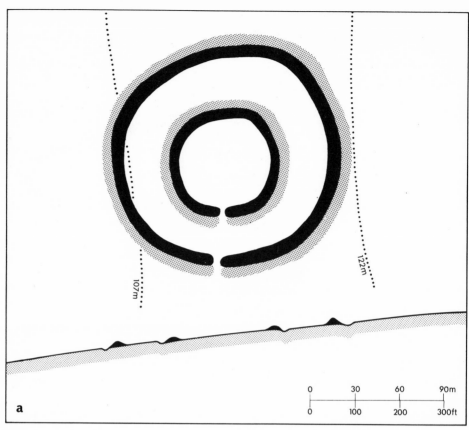

107m

122m

0   30   60   90m
0   100   200   300ft

a

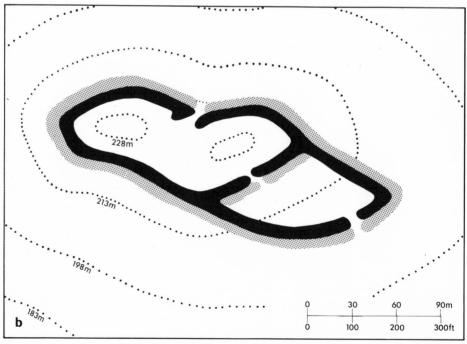

228m

213m

198m

183m

0   30   60   90m
0   100   200   300ft

b

Fig.5. A
promontory fort.

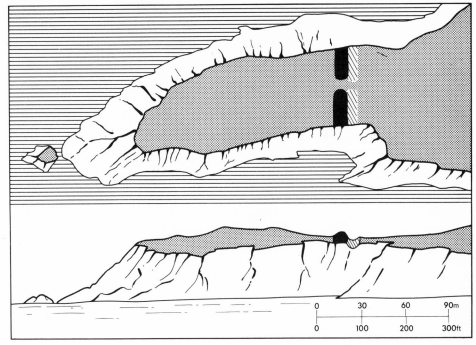

further subdivision a necessity, in the interests of both convenience and accuracy.

A contour fort is one in which the defences cut off the upper portion of a hill from the ground below by following, more or less, the line of the contours encircling it. It follows from this that the shape of the fort in plan will be very much the shape of the hill at that level, and this explains the great variation in the shape of contour forts. The defences are normally placed somewhere on the shoulder of the hill with the main slope below, while the crown of the hill, within the defences, forms the enclosure.

Promontory forts are to some extent self-explanatory. A promontory may be defined for present purposes as an area to which the approach is limited, to a greater or lesser extent, by natural features such as cliffs, very steep slopes, rivers, etc. Where such features exist little or nothing in the way of man-made fortification is required. The main defences needed are on the side from which the promontory can be approached. It will be clear from this that on suitable sites considerable enclosures can be produced by the construction of relatively short lengths of ramparts. It would be wrong to assume that all promontory forts are coastal. While there are, indeed, many sites on the coast, particularly in the west and south-west, there are also many inland promontory forts. A promontory, in fact, provides a very economical way of producing a defended enclosure, and that this was clear to the Iron Age population is apparent from the number of such sites.

The last two categories account for a much smaller number of forts. Hill-slope

Fig.3

Fig.5

7

forts, instead of enclosing the hilltop in the manner of contour forts, are situated on the sloping ground on one side of it, overlooked by the crest. This is quite clearly not a good defensive position and the choice of such a situation must be one of the topics to be considered later. Plateau forts have always been something of a contradiction in the context of existing terminology. Some of them are indeed on plateaux, but their essential feature is that they face level ground on all sides, regardless of their elevation above sea-level. The whole of their defence is based on man-made ramparts, and they are completely lacking in any of the natural advantages mentioned earlier.

All Iron Age forts can for the moment be placed in one or other of these four categories. The names given to the various categories are descriptive, in however generalized a form, of the situation of the enclosures in relation to their surroundings. The same sites can, however, be grouped in an entirely different way which cuts right across this system. The basis of this alternative classification is the number of ramparts by which the sites are defended.

In many of the early accounts the terms 'vallum' and 'fosse' were used to describe rampart and ditch. The latter has now gone out of use, at least with reference to Iron Age forts, but the former survives in various adjectival forms: univallate, bivallate, and multivallate. A terminology based on Roman usage seems inappropriate in a prehistoric context, but there are no really suitable alternatives. Single-, double-, and multiple-rampart are accurate but rather cumbersome for general use. Consequently, the terms 'univallate' and 'multivallate' will be used in this work. 'Bivallate' will not be used since it is embraced by multivallate and has, in any case, never been a satisfactory designation. It has in the past been applied to sites which, on the basis of the definitions below, are in some cases univallate and in others multivallate. All Iron Age forts can thus be placed in one or other of two categories, univallate and multivallate, on the basis of their defences.

Fig.6

A univallate fort is one in which the man-made defences consist of a single rampart, either with or without an outer ditch. The ditch is a regular feature in most of England and the Welsh Marches, but is less common in Wales and south-west England. In a number of cases there is a smaller bank on the outer edge of the ditch, a counterscarp bank, and such sites are among those described by the now discarded term 'bivallate'. Except in a very few cases, however, this counterscarp bank is a minor feature, an obstacle rather than a rampart, and the term bivallate is misleading. For most sites the criterion for a second rampart is the existence of a second ditch. It should be pointed out here that there are sites where the outer bank, even when accompanied by its own ditch, is on such a small scale that it is little more than a minor obstacle. The classification of such sites, and of those in which the counterscarp bank is on a very large scale, is a matter which will need to be discussed later.

A multivallate fort, then, is one which has two or more ramparts, the critical test for most sites being the presence of two or more ditches. This test, however, can only apply to sites where ditches form a part of the defence system. Where the ramparts are unaccompanied by ditches then these cannot form the basis of classification. On the other hand, since there are no ditches there can be no

Fig.6. Univallate
defences: present
form.

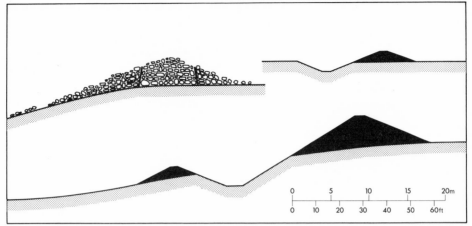

counterscarp banks and therefore no confusion on that score. In such cases the matter can be decided simply on the basis of the number of banks or ramparts, two or more constituting a multivallate fort.

Many of the multivallate sites which have been excavated have been shown to have more than one structural phase. In most cases the first phase consisted of a univallate fort followed by a phase, or phases, in which the addition of extra ramparts transformed the site into a multivallate fort. In other words, multi-vallate sites can be assumed with a fair degree of confidence to have had more than one structural phase. The exceptions to this are certain sites in south Wales and the south-west which appear to have been built from the start in the multi-vallate style.

It will be clear that of the two, the multivallate class is the more likely to be susceptible of subdivision, and this brief outline of terminology can be con-cluded by considering the names of these subsidiary classes. One possible basis of classification, the number of ramparts by which the fort is defended, is likely to reflect the strength or weakness of the defences rather than any more funda-mental difference. In fact, the defences of most multivallate forts are based on two-ditch systems, sites with three and more ditches constituting a relatively small class. A more significant division is based on the disposition of the ram-parts in relation to each other.

Fig.7a

In the majority of multivallate sites the various features, banks, ditches, etc., that make up the defences are set close together, so that one bank and ditch is succeeded immediately by the next, with no interspace. Such sites have been described as having closely set ramparts. The term 'compact' is here proposed and will be used hereafter to describe multivallate defences of this type. Such sites are among those referred to earlier as consisting of a single enclosure, the other single-enclosure sites being, of course, the univallate forts.

Fig.7c

In addition to compact multivallate forts there are others in which the defence features are separated from each other, often by considerable distances. Sites of this type are currently described as having wide-spaced ramparts: the term

9

Fig.7.
Multivallate
defences:
7a compact;
7b separated;
7c dispersed.

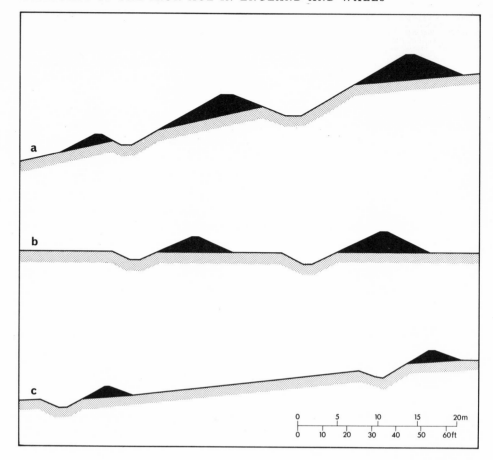

proposed here is 'dispersed'. However, it is possible that this emphasis on the disposition of the ramparts is misplaced. Multivallate forts of this type constitute the class mentioned earlier as consisting of more than one enclosure, and it may well be that the provision of a number of separate enclosures occupied a higher place in the minds of the builders than a particular system of defence. Wide-spaced or dispersed defences may be simply a by-product in forts where more than one enclosure was considered necessary, and a terminology reflecting this aspect rather than the one of defence would perhaps be more appropriate. This will be dealt with in Chapter VI. While it is likely that the enclosure aspect is more often than not the dominant one, both aspects should be kept in mind when considering this class of multivallate fort.

Fig.7b

Finally, there are multivallate defences which are intermediate between the compact type and the dispersed type. The space between the ramparts is too small to constitute an enclosure and must be regarded simply as a means of giving added depth to the defences. This space or berm can be anything from a few metres to as much as 12 or 15 m (40 or 50 ft). Beyond this the space can be regarded as a separate enclosure, with all the problems of emphasis mentioned

Fig.8. Numbers
of univallate and
multivallate
forts.

Columns	1	2	3	4	5	6	7	8
Size	Large		Medium		Small		Totals	
Multivallate forts	64		189		213		466 = 34%	
Univallate forts	81		270		549		900 = 66%	
Totals	145 = 10½%		459 = 33½%		762 = 56%		1366 = 100%	

in the previous paragraph. The defences under discussion can be described as 'separated'. It is unlikely that there is any significant difference between compact and separated multivallate defences. The two arrangements are quite often found in the same site.

Fig.8

A brief analysis of Iron Age forts, based on their defences (univallate/multi-vallate) and on their size, will serve to fill in some of the details in the very general picture drawn so far. This analysis is based on the index of the Ordnance Survey's *Map of Southern Britain in the Iron Age* (1962). The total number of sites listed there, excluding the Isle of Man, is 1,366. Of these, 465, or 34 per cent, are multivallate and the remaining 901, or 66 per cent, univallate. In other words, roughly one-third of the Iron Age forts in England and Wales have multivallate defences, the remaining two-thirds being univallate.

Fig.9

The analysis on the basis of size cuts across this division. For the purposes of the Iron Age map all sites were placed in one or other of three groups, according to the areas enclosed by their innermost ramparts. The first group embraced sites with inner enclosures greater than 6 ha (15 acres) in area, the second those with enclosures between 1 and 6 ha (3 and 15 acres), and the third those with enclosures of less than 1 ha (3 acres). For convenience these three groups may be distinguished as Large, Medium, and Small. It should be pointed out that the areas used as the basis of classification have no particular archaeological significance, but they have, in fact, proved to be a very convenient means of handling the large numbers of sites involved. Of the total of 1,366 sites, 145 or 10½ per cent are in the Large class, 459 (33½ per cent) are in the Medium class, and 762 (56 per cent) are in the Small class. Thus more than half the sites in

Fig.9. Numbers
of Large,
Medium, and
Small forts.

Type	No.	Univallate	Multivallate	Multivallate (per cent)
Large forts	145	81	64	44
Medium forts	459	270	189	41
Small forts	762	549	213	28

England and Wales enclose less than 1 ha (3 acres) each. Stated another way, out of every 10 Iron Age forts 1 is Large, 3 are Medium, and 6 are Small.

The combination of these two analyses produces the following result: of the Large sites 44 per cent (64) are multivallate and there is a comparable percentage for the Medium sites, 41 per cent (189). The percentage of multivallate Small sites is 28 per cent (213). There is a noticeable difference between the percentages for Large and Medium sites on the one hand and Small sites on the other. It looks as if the tendency was to refortify the larger forts, if that is what multivallation means, rather than those at the lower end of the scale. It is possible that this pattern is to be explained at least in part on geographical grounds, since the Large and Small sites are to a large extent exclusive of each other. The size of the sites involved may be only one of a number of factors with a bearing on this problem.

So far the man-made defences of Iron Age forts have been described simply as banks and ditches, that is in terms of their present appearance. In order to understand how this appearance came about and to appreciate what lies beneath the existing remains it is necessary to know something about the defences as originally constructed. The ramparts which lie beneath the banks of Iron Age forts are of two basic types, 'revetted' and 'glacis'.

Fig.10a,b

A revetted rampart is one which presents a vertical or near-vertical outer face to the enemy. This outer face or revetment is normally of timber or dry stone walling, or a combination of the two, and serves to retain the core of earth, chalk, clay, etc., derived in most cases from the outer ditch. In the simplest arrangement the material forming the core slopes down to ground-level at the back so that in cross-section the rampart is wedge-shaped. A timber revetment normally consists of a series of uprights behind which horizontal timbers are placed to retain the core. The stone ramparts consist of a dry-built wall retaining a core, as above, or else they are a solid mass of stones brought to a fair face externally, with no separately distinguishable revetment wall. In a number of cases the rear of the stone ramparts descends to ground-level in a series of steps.

Fig.10c

Fig.10d,e

In more elaborate ramparts there is a revetment at the back as well as at the front, producing a rectangular cross-section. These are usually referred to as box ramparts. In some cases there is a wedge-shaped ramp at the rear which acts as a buttress for the back revetment. The average box rampart is between 3 and 6 m (10 and 20 ft) wide, without the ramp, which can add another 4·5 m (15 ft). The front-revetted types are normally between 6 and 12 m (20 and 40 ft) wide. Heights probably varied between 2 and 3·5 m (6 and 12 ft) without a breastwork, which might add another 1 m (4 ft).

A rampart of this type can be the only defence of an Iron Age fort, although in nearly every case the ramparts so used are of the stone-revetted type. More frequently, however, the rampart is accompanied by an outer ditch from which the material for the core is derived. Normally there is a space or berm between the rampart and the ditch to prevent the front revetment from being undermined by erosion. The ditches of Iron Age forts are usually described as V-shaped, but this term covers a very wide variety of shapes, some of which are

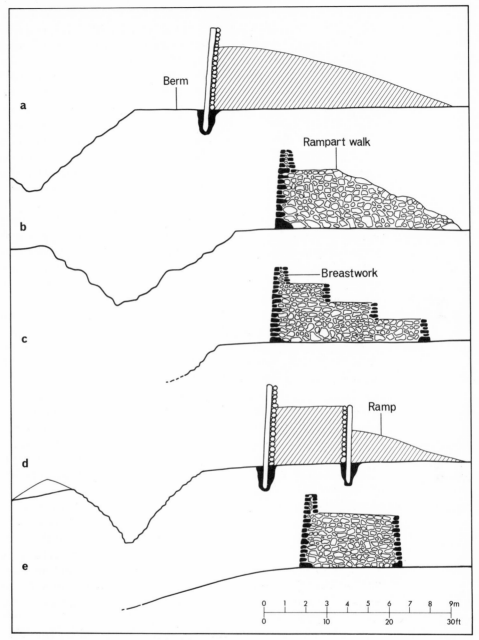

Fig. 10. Revetted ramparts: original form.

due to the type of ground in which they are dug; chalk, clay, sand, gravel, limestone, etc. Dimensions vary considerably but the average ditch is between 6 and 9 m (20 and 30 ft) wide and between 2 and 3·5 m (6 and 12 ft) deep.

Fig.11a

Ramparts of the glacis type involve a different principle of defence. They are usually triangular in cross-section and at their simplest consist of a simple dump of the material excavated from the ditch, with no other structural feature. This rampart stands on the edge of the ditch so that there is a single slope from ditch bottom to rampart crest and it is this slope that constitutes the principal defence; the original angle was probably between 30° and 40°. The average glacis rampart is between 9 and 12 m (30 and 40 ft) wide and about 3 m (10 ft) high, although there are one or two cases where these dimensions are more than doubled.

One advantage of glacis ramparts is that they do not require the elaborate timber or stone work of the revetted types, at least in the simpler versions. All the materials required can, in most cases, be derived from the accompanying ditch. A disadvantage is that there is nothing to prevent the rampart material from being washed back into the ditch. In addition to simple dump construction there are a few ramparts with revetments at the back. The most elaborate of

Fig.11b
Fig.10d

these are found at Maiden Castle (Dorset)[4] and Sudbrook Camp (Mon.).[5]

One other feature may be mentioned here, the counterscarp bank. In most cases this is of simple dump construction, 3 or 4·5 m (10 or 15 ft) wide and a metre or so high. It is placed at the head of the outer slope (the counterscarp) of the ditch, hence the name.

Fig.11c

Apart from revetted and glacis ramparts there is a third, intermediate type, of which a few examples are known. It consists, for the most part, of a revetted rampart built on the remains of an earlier rampart which, whatever its original form, assumes a glacis shape in its collapsed state. Thus externally it has both the slope of the glacis rampart and the vertical face of the revetted rampart forming a single feature. Only a few examples of this type of rampart are known at present but it seems reasonable to assume that it was of not infrequent occurrence.[6]

The various features, ramparts, berms, ditches, and counterscarp banks, may be regarded as the basic units from which most Iron Age fort defence systems were constructed. The simplest arrangement, a rampart alone, has already been mentioned. Most other univallate forts have either a revetted rampart, a berm, and a ditch, or a glacis rampart and ditch, and may be accompanied by a counterscarp bank.

The defence systems of multivallate forts involve the multiplication of some or all of these basic units, the majority of systems being based on two ramparts,

---

4. Wheeler, *Maiden Castle, Dorset* (1943), 101–2 and pl. ix.

5. *Arch. Camb.* 94 (1939), 47–48 and fig. 2.

6. Examples of this type of rampart are known from the following sites: Poundbury (Dorset), *Antiq. J.* 20 (1940), 432–4 and pl. lxxi; Hod Hill (Dorset), Richmond, *Hod Hill*, vol. ii; Oldbury (Kent), *Archaeologia*, 90 (1944), 137–8 and pl. xxxi; Caynham Camp (Salop), *Trans. Shropshire Arch. Soc.* 56. 3 (1960), 218–27.

Fig.11. Glacis
ramparts:
original form.

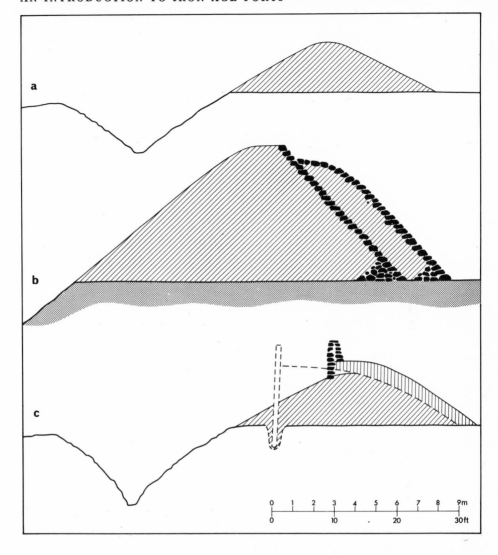

either with or without ditches. Systems with three or more ramparts are much less common. Many two- and three-ditch systems are of the compact type, but in others there are small interspaces, perhaps 4·5 or 6 m (15 or 20 ft) wide, which give added depth to the whole system. Where the fort is of the multiple-enclosure type the defences are virtually a series of separate systems which may take any of the forms mentioned above.

In their original state many Iron Age forts must have been imposing monuments by reason of their size, complexity, and siting, and these qualities survive to a certain extent in the existing remains. The existence of such earthworks inevitably gives rise to the question of the identity of the people who built them. This question can best be answered by giving a brief outline of the Late Bronze

15

Age/Iron Age period in western Europe, the background against which the forts must be seen.

Of the greatest importance in any such survey are the Celts, in Powell's words 'the first great nation north of the Alps whose name we know'.[7] The main roots of Celtic civilization are to be found among the Bronze Age populations of Switzerland and southern Germany in the period between 1200 and 800 B.C. 'It is this total population of the so-called "North Alpine Urnfield Province" ... that demands special scrutiny in relation to the coming into existence of the Celts.'[8] 'The relevance of all these considerations now comes into a clearer light because the pattern in rural settlement and economy, in material culture, and partly in burial ritual, established in the North Alpine Urnfield province, is found to be continuous, however variously enriched, into and throughout the span of the historical Celts.'[9] But the Urnfield people were still not Celts nor did their culture yet contain all the elements which at a later stage and in a more developed form, were to characterize Celtic civilization.

The new elements added to the now well-developed Urnfield culture involved a relatively small number of people, chieftains, or warrior aristocrats. There was no substantial change in the bulk of the settled farming population. 'There are, however, new phenomena which seem to point to new intrusions from the east.'[1] The evidence for these intrusions takes the form of bronze horse trappings very similar to types found in the steppe-lands and in Caucasia and Iran. These bronzes seem to represent the equipment of warrior horsemen who ranged over vast areas from western Asia to the North Alpine area. Shortly after their appearance in this area there is clear archaeological evidence, in the form of elaborate burials, of the emergence of a group of important warriors who must be regarded as the royal chiefs or princes of the North Alpine area. The same social and economic circumstances which brought the royal chiefs into being also gave rise to what can now be called Celtic civilization. One of the most fundamental changes was an economic one, the introduction of the use of iron. The Celts stand thus at the beginning of the Iron Age period in this part of Europe. This iron-using successor to the Urnfield culture is known as the Hallstatt culture, from the name of a site in Austria.

The beginnings of Hallstatt culture can be placed at around 700 B.C. During the two following centuries Hallstatt culture expanded until eventually it embraced a large area of northern and western Europe, from Austria to Portugal in one direction and from the Alps to the Channel in the other, and including at a late stage much of southern and eastern England. The Hallstatt culture is important in any study of the British Iron Age since people at this stage of development first brought an iron-using economy to these shores. The migration to Britain appears to have taken place at a late stage in the Hallstatt culture and may have been brought about by the expansion of the culture which succeeded it, around 500 B.C.

'On the Continent, the reorganization of power and wealth at the end of Hallstatt times, in the fifth century B.C., gave rise to new fashions in material

7. Powell, *The Celts* (1959), 13.   8. Ibid. 39.   9. Ibid. 43–44.   1. Ibid. 44.

culture, and gave birth to a remarkable decorative art. The same populations were involved, and presumably the same ruling or aristocratic families. Archaeologically, the new trends are classified as of the La Tène culture, or of the La Tène art style.'[2] Like the Hallstatt culture before it the La Tène culture went through a process of expansion during some two centuries (450–250 B.C.). As far as Britain is concerned it is the expansion to the north and west, to the Atlantic and Channel coasts, which is the most important. This process seems to have caused the migration, noted above, of Hallstatt people to Britain. It left the coastal areas facing southern and eastern England firmly in the grip of a La Tène culture. In such a situation La Tène influence, either by migration or trade, or both, was likely to follow before long. The nature, extent, and in some cases the date of La Tène influence or movement are still not very clear, but they seem to have given rise either to a second phase of the British Iron Age or a modification of the first phase.

The La Tène expansion brings the story of the Iron Age in northern and western Europe down to about 250 B.C. In fact, the La Tène culture persisted in Gaul until the Roman conquest, so that there and in the North Alpine area generally until the first century B.C. it may be regarded as the typical Iron Age culture, to which the Hallstatt phase served as a prelude. One other development in Europe with some effect on the British Iron Age remains to be described.

During the second century B.C., there developed in north-eastern Gaul a confederation of La Tène tribes under the leadership of the Belgae. This confederation occupied one of the three parts of Gaul distinguished by Caesar: *Aquitania* in the south-west, *Gallia Celtica* in the main part of Gaul, and *Gallia Belgica* in the north-east, the area of the Belgic confederation. Belgic territory lay between the Rhine, the Seine, and the Marne. From about 150 B.C. onwards this area was subject to strong tribal movements from across the Rhine, and while this probably contributed to the mixed composition of the Belgic confederation, 'subsequent analogies would lead us to expect an exodus of Celts from Belgic Gaul and an influx of refugees to Britain at the time of or shortly after the German invasions across the Rhine'.[3] During the second century the use of coinage, derived from Macedonia via the Danube, had developed in this part of Gaul, and much of the evidence of Belgic movement into south-eastern England is based on coins and coin distributions. Germanic pressure on the Belgic confederation may have led to the arrival here of a third element in the composition of the British Iron Age.

This succession, Urnfield, Hallstatt, La Tène, Belgic, is the continental background against which the British Late Bronze Age and Iron Age must be seen.

The Iron Age in Britain is at the moment almost universally described in terms of the system devised by Hawkes, the ABC system,[4] in which Iron Age A, B, and C cultures here are not so much equivalent to Hallstatt, La Tène, and Belgic culture as representative of their effects on Britain. Doubts have been cast on the validity of this system both as originally propounded (1931)[5] and as

2. Ibid. 56–57.   3. Allen, in Frere (ed.), *Problems of the Iron Age in Southern Britain* (1961), 102.

4. Kendrick and Hawkes, *Archaeology in England and Wales, 1914–1931* (1932), chap. x.

5. Daniel, *The Three Ages* (1943), 38, 43; *Arch. J.* 106 (1949), Supp. 66.

more recently revised (1958),[6] but since virtually everything on the Iron Age is written in terms of the ABC system, this will be brought into the account of the period to be given now. However, an alternative chronology will be considered in Chapter X.

According to the ABC system the main Hallstatt migration to Britain, *c.* 500 B.C. onwards, was preceded by more sporadic movements, the evidence for which takes the form of certain items of warrior equipment which are widespread in Britain and Ireland. Whatever the explanation of these Hallstatt military trappings, it is quite certain that 'from the early part of the fifth century B.C., Southern and Eastern Britain received colonists from the Low Countries and Northern France before whom, numerically and economically, earlier invaders pale to insignificance'.[7]

The arrival of these colonists marks the beginning of the Iron Age proper in Britain. Coming as they did from the continental fringe they brought with them a somewhat provincial version of Hallstatt culture, but they were none the less Celts in the full sense of the word. The impetus to their migration at this particular time was given in part at least by the expansion of Celtic tribes following on the growth of the La Tène culture in the heart of the North Alpine region. Because of this some La Tène influence is evident in the groups crossing over to Britain. Whatever its degree it is quite clear that the term Hallstatt is inappropriate in Britain, and in the Hawkes scheme the culture is accordingly labelled Iron Age A.

The arrival of Hallstatt colonists at various points along the southern and eastern coasts was spread over a long period, starting early in the fifth century B.C. From these areas of initial settlement there was a gradual expansion to the west and north until eventually Iron Age culture 'was established almost everywhere south and east of a line from Cornwall and the Cotswolds to the Humber and north Yorkshire, with scattered outposts beyond'.[8] This whole process seems to have occupied roughly two centuries, being more or less completed by about 350 B.C. 'While it brought into being a distinctively Celtic Britain . . . it would be a mistake to envisage it as either an organised or a warlike invasion. The newcomers seem to have consisted of small groups, many of them refugees from the social upheaval now evident on the continent, and although a few hillforts are attributable to this early period most of their settlements, planted in territory that was but thinly populated, were peaceful in character'.[9]

The second phase of the British Iron Age involves the superimposition of La Tène elements on the existing Iron Age A population in certain areas of southern Britain. In other areas the Iron Age A culture continued undisturbed. As pointed out above some degree of La Tène influence is evident during part, if not all, of the A period, having been absorbed on the continent and brought over by the Hallstatt migrants. This may have been added to from *c.* 350 B.C. onwards by trade with the still expanding La Tène culture. At a later stage

6. *Antiquity*, 34 (1960), 138–40; *Proc. Prehis. Soc.* 28 (1962) 152–4.
7. Powell, op. cit. 55.
8. *Map of Southern Britain in the Iron Age* (O.S. 1962), Introduction, 9.
9. Allen, loc. cit. But see also Birchall, *Proc. Prehist. Soc.*, 31 (1965), 290.

again there seem to have been actual movements of La Tène people, although on nothing like the scale of the Hallstatt migration, and it is the arrival of these later migrants which gives rise to the Iron Age B cultures of the Hawkes's scheme. These movements presumably followed on the expansion of La Tène culture to the Channel and Atlantic coasts, and seem to have been spread over about two centuries, from 350 to 150 B.C.

If the distribution of Iron Age forts in England and Wales is indicative of the extent of Iron Age culture, then eventually the Iron Age A and/or B cultures must have entered the Welsh Marches and Wales. The spread of Iron Age A culture to these regions may have been a natural continuance of the process noted already in the years down to 350 B.C. It may, on the other hand, have been occasioned by the arrival of the B-culture groups which, as on the continent, tended to displace earlier peoples, in this case with a culture of the A type. The B cultures of the same area may be partly a result of expansion from an initial settlement area somewhere in the south-west and partly a result, again, of displacement caused by the arrival in the south-east of the third element in the composition of the British Iron Age, the Iron Age C culture of the Hawkes's scheme, the continental background to which has been described already.

Until fairly recently it was thought that the earliest Belgic movements into southern Britain were around 75 B.C., but more recent evidence has suggested that a date at least twenty-five years earlier would be more accurate.[8] The Catuvellauni of the Marne region were one of the tribes in the Belgic confederation mentioned earlier. In 55 B.C., the time of Julius Caesar's first incursion, a tribe bearing this name was in possession of a large part of south-eastern England, and it is likely that they were the dominant element in the peoples who had crossed over from north-eastern Gaul in the latter part of the second century B.C. Eventually the kingdom of the Catuvellauni, with its capital first at Wheathampstead and later at St. Albans (*Verulamium*), embraced Kent, Middlesex, Essex, Hertfordshire, part of Cambridgeshire, and Northamptonshire. This, however, was not the only movement of Belgic tribes into Britain.

After Caesar's conquest of Gaul there was a rebellion in the Belgic homeland about 50 B.C. The tribe involved was that of the Atrebates and the tribal chief, Commius, fled with his followers to southern England and landed probably in Sussex. There he founded a new kingdom and later his sons established a tribal capital at Silchester (*Calleva Atrebatum*) in Hampshire. Eventually the kingdom founded by Commius embraced Hampshire, Berkshire, part of Wiltshire, part of Kent, at least for a time, and part of Sussex. There was no love lost between the Catuvellauni and descendants of Commius whose kingdoms between them embraced the greater part of south-eastern England. Eventually it was the bitter rivalry between these two factions which provided the occasion for the Roman invasion by Claudius in A.D. 43.

So far nothing has been said about the position of forts in the ABC system. Iron Age C can be dealt with very quickly since forts of the type to be considered here played little or no part in its culture, although its arrival in the south-east must have stimulated the construction, or at least the reconstruction, of forts in the surrounding areas. It is to the A and B cultures that virtually all forts are attributed. Since, however, these two cultures persisted until the time of the Roman conquest this still allows a period of some 550 years for the construction and use of this type of fortification. In the ABC system Iron Age forts are not placed in the earliest part of the A culture. Their construction is thought to have begun between 400 and 300 B.C.; Iron Age A forts are of univallate type. Multivallate forts are attributed to the B cultures, which in Wessex at least began *c.* 150 B.C. In southern and south-eastern England generally the arrival and expansion of the Belgae from *c.* 100 B.C. probably led to further reconstruction of Iron Age forts in the surrounding areas. Finally, the Roman invasion and advance from A.D. 43 onwards must have stimulated even greater activity among the native population who probably made the final structural additions to their forts at this time.

Forts of the type under survey are not confined to southern Britain, and are found in most parts of central and western Europe. To the south there are forts in France and the Low Countries which are important in the context of origins since it is from this general area that migration into southern Britain is likely to have taken place. Equally important, in the context of the Atlantic coast route to western Britain, are the forts of north-western Spain and northern Portugal. There are further concentrations of forts in Germany and in central Europe generally, with possible links via the Rhine, the mouth of which faces the eastern flank of southern Britain. Finally, to the north, in southern and south-western Scotland, there is another large group of forts of the same general type as those in England and Wales.

CHAPTER II

A regional survey

For the purposes of the general survey in this chapter the area involved has been divided into seven regions, each of which will be considered separately. The seven regions are: the South-east; Wessex; the South-west; the Cotswolds; the Welsh Marches; South and West Wales; and the Chilterns, the Midlands and the North.

THE SOUTH-EAST

Fig.12

The south-eastern region consists of Surrey, Sussex, Kent, a small area of Berkshire, and the Lower Thames valley on the north side of the river. The structure of the region is fairly simple. The broad chalk ridges of the North and South Downs enclose the sands and clays of the Weald. The clays are low-lying but the sands take the form of a series of ridges, mainly at the centre and northern edge of the Weald, and rise to heights of about 244 m (800 ft), similar to those of the downland ridges. Most of the rivers in the area rise in the Weald and flow either north to the Thames or south to the coast, dividing the North and South Downs into distinct blocks of territory.

The south-eastern region contains about 50 Iron Age forts, which fall into four fairly distinct groups. Nearly half the sites are strung out along the South Downs from the Sussex/Hampshire border to Beachy Head. About 16 km (10 miles) to the north there is a small group in the centre of the Weald, and the third group occupies the northern edge of the Weald and the North Downs ridge. The last group is found in the low-lying area of the Lower Thames valley and the south-east Essex coast.

The 20 sites strung out along the 80-km (50-mile) stretch of the South Downs include Large (5), Medium (10), and Small sites (5). This represents a much higher proportion of Large and Medium sites than the average for England and Wales. More interesting than the size, however, is the fact that nearly all the sites involved are univallate. The two exceptions are Goose Hill Camp and The Caburn. In the latter the outer rampart appears to have superseded the inner, so that the site was probably never multivallate in use. It seems, in fact, to have involved two univallate forts, one succeeding and containing the other. Goose

Fig.95

Hill Camp is unusual in having wide-spaced ramparts which are more at home in the south-west than the south-east. One or two such sites are known in Wessex, and these and Goose Hill may be outliers from the main distribution

21

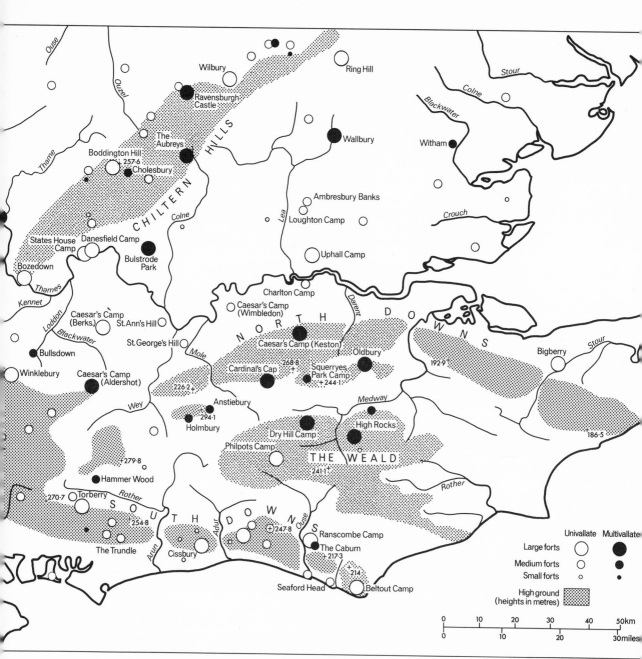

Fig. 12. The South-east.

further to the west. Discounting Goose Hill it can be said that the typical South Downs fort is univallate, and this probably includes The Caburn as well. The most striking aspect of this is the contrast with the north Weald/North Downs area where multivallate sites are the rule.

Although they extend from Beachy Head to the Sussex border the South Downs sites cannot be said to be evenly spaced out. They tend to occur in groups with relatively large intervals between. The Devil's Dyke, Wolstonbury, Ditchling Beacon, and Hollingbury form one such group and Court Hill Camp, The Trundle, and Halnaker Hill another. The intervals between the sites in each group are noticeably smaller than those between the group as a whole and neighbouring groups. Cissbury, the largest site on the South Downs, is surrounded by 3 Small sites, and these 4 account for all the Iron Age defence works in the territory between the Adur and the Arun. Of the remaining sites, Torberry and Harting Beacon stand fairly close together, as do Ranscombe and The Caburn. These groupings account for 15 out of the 20 sites in the area, and leave some quite extensive stretches of downland with no visible defence works.

The rivers flowing southwards from the Weald divide the South Downs into five sections. In the one between Beachy Head and the Cuckmere River, Beltout Camp appears now as a coastal site, but this is almost certainly due to coastal erosion. As originally built it probably stood several kilometres inland in a hilltop situation. The same is true of Seaford in the next section which also contains Ranscombe and The Caburn about 13 km (8 miles) to the north-west. In between there is an isolated block of downland about 8 km (5 miles) long with no forts at all. In the next section there are no sites for about 10 km (6 miles) beyond the Ouse, and then the group of 4 mentioned above. There is a similar gap beyond the Arun as far as Halnaker Hill and Court Hill Camp. A number of sites take advantage of the higher, northern edge of the downs overlooking the wide expanse of the Weald, but the majority are situated on the gentler southern slopes.

The small group of sites at the centre of the Weald consists of both univallate (2) and multivallate forts (3). It may be significant that the 2 univallate sites are in the southern part of the central area, accessible from the South Downs, while the 3 multivallate sites, High Rocks, Dry Hill, and Castle Hill are in the northern part, in the area embraced by the rivers Eden, Medway, and their tributaries, flowing ultimately into the Thames. These 3 multivallate sites look across the Eden/Medway valley to the multivallate sites of the north Weald/North Downs area. The clays surrounding the centre of the Weald must have supported a heavy vegetation, so that the rivers would have formed the best means of communication. At the western end of the Weald the Small site of Piper's Copse, on a tributary of the Arun, may be explained in the same way as Philpots Camp and Saxonbury.

The 6 multivallate forts which form the north Weald/North Downs group are much more widely spaced than the sites in the South Downs. Only Holmbury and Anstiebury stand fairly close together, on Leith Hill, and they are separated from the others by the valley of the Mole. Of the remaining sites only Cardinal's Cap stands on the higher, southern edge of the North Downs. Oldbury and

Fig.58

Fig.26b

Fig.24c

Fig.33b

23

Squerryes Park are on the northern edge of the Ragstone range, facing the southern flank of the downs, and like Holmbury and Anstiebury, are Wealden sites. The one remaining site, Caesar's Camp (Kent) is further north on the lower northern fringe of the downland ridge. Together with the 3 multivallate sites in the centre of the Weald these north Weald/North Downs forts form a group of 9 uniformly multivallate sites covering a wide area of western Kent and east Surrey. Six of these are linked by the network of rivers formed by the Medway, the Eden, and their tributaries. The group includes no less than 5 Large forts, a very high proportion; the other 4 sites are Medium in size. There are no Small sites.

Hascombe Camp stands at the northern edge of the Weald in a position similar to Holmbury and Anstiebury but further to the west. Unlike these, however, it is univallate. It is possibly to be associated with Piper's Copse, Philpots Camp, and Saxonbury, and perhaps all 4 are to be related to the South Downs region. Similarly Hammer Wood, a multivallate site only a few kilometres north of the South Downs, may be an outlier from the north Weald/North Downs area. Caesar's Camp (Surrey), also multivallate, may be another outlier from the same area.

The last of the four south-eastern groups is closely associated with the Thames, its tributaries, and the rivers emptying on to the Essex coast. With one exception (Witham), all the sites involved are univallate. Charlton Camp, Caesar's Camp (Wimbledon), St. George's Hill, and St. Ann's Hill are all within a few kilo-

Fig.44a

metres of the Thames itself, on the southern flank. Caesar's Camp (Berks) and Bigberry (Kent), the latter over 48 km (30 miles) from any other fort, may be part of the same pattern. On the north side of the river, opposite Charlton Camp, there is a group of five sites standing on rivers flowing south to the Thames. The remaining sites are on rivers flowing south-eastwards to the coast through Essex. They include the site at Witham, which appears to have had wide-spaced ramparts rather like Goose Hill Camp in the South Downs group.

The four groups of Iron Age forts in the south-east can be seen to form three quite distinct bands running in an east/west direction. The northern and southern bands are univallate and most of the sites are of Medium size, with smaller numbers of Large and Small sites. The middle band is multivallate with Large sites predominating. There are no Small sites involved. For the southern band arrival via the south coast seems quite certain; for the central and northern bands the Thames would appear to have been the means of access. Assuming that multiple ramparts indicate more than one structural phase the factors responsible for multivallation seem to have arrived via the Thames. The South Downs region was virtually unaffected, and so was the Thames valley. The answer may be that the Medway provided the main route from the Thames estuary. Together with the Eden and the upper reaches of the Mole it could account for the distribution pattern of most of the multivallate sites.

There is a marked contrast between the North and South Downs. In the south the latter appears to be the favoured area for occupation. In the north the Weald and the Thames valley seem to have attracted more sites than the North Downs which, in fact, have only three sites, to the west of the Darent. To the

24

east of the river, for 80 km (50 miles) to the coast, there is not a single Iron Age fort on the downland ridge. The answer may be that the deposits overlying the chalk (clay with flints) supported a much heavier vegetation than the chalk alone. Such deposits appear to be much more widespread on the North Downs, hence the difference in the density of sites between the two chalk ridges.

WESSEX

Fig.13

The Wessex region will be interpreted as covering Dorset, Wiltshire, Hampshire, Berkshire, and a small part of south-eastern Somerset. The region is dominated by the chalk downland which covers an area of about 5,180 sq km (2,000 sq miles) that is, slightly less than half the total area of the four counties (11,771 sq km : 4,545 sq miles). To the south and north-east of the chalk there are low-lying areas, mainly of heathland. To the north and west there are deposits of clay separating the chalk from the limestone. The chalk provides most of the elevated areas of Wessex, with heights generally between 122 and 244 m (400 and 800 ft). The greater part of the region is drained by rivers which flow mainly south and/or south-east, reaching the coast between Southampton Water and Poole Harbour. The northern part of Wessex is drained by rivers flowing east and north-east to the Thames.

The Wessex region as defined above contains about 150 Iron Age forts. Because of structural differences between the two areas they fall less easily into distinct groups than the forts of the south-eastern region, but certain broad trends are observable. There are many more sites in the south and west of the region than there are in the north and east. In Hampshire east of the Test, Iron Age forts are widely scattered. Between the Test and the Avon/Bourne they occur more frequently, while to the west of the Bourne they are numerous, particularly Large sites. In the northern part of the region, in north Wiltshire and Berkshire, sites are more widely scattered, although they still include a high proportion of Large sites. Not unnaturally a large number of Wessex sites are situated on the chalk. There are, however about 35 sites (out of the total of 150) in the non-chalk regions. About 20 of these are on the generally low-lying heathland south of the chalk and the remainder are to be found in another relatively low-lying area between the chalk and the Thames to the north.

The Wessex region contains a very high proportion of Large sites (47, or 31 per cent), three times the average for England and Wales as a whole. In the Medium class the percentage (58 per cent, 88 sites) is nearly twice as high as the over-all average. Small sites, however, account for only 16 (11 per cent) of the Wessex forts. They are all univallate and they would not appear to represent a very important element in the Iron Age defence works of the region. The Large sites are scattered widely throughout Wessex with a more even distribution than the Medium forts. In southern Wessex the two are mixed more or less in the proportions indicated above, but in the north, apart from the lower-lying areas adjacent to the Thames, the Large fort appears to be dominant. In a triangular area defined by Segsbury, Bury Hill, and Cley Hill (40 × 48 × 69 km : 25 × 30 × 43 miles) there are 15 Large forts but only 4 of the

Pl.1

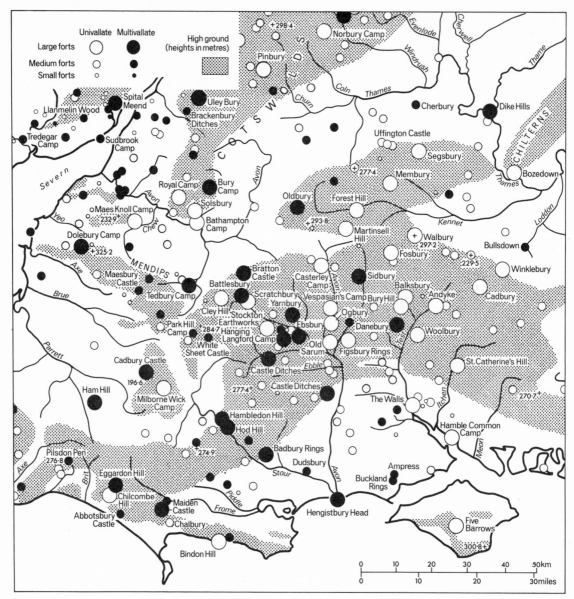

Fig. 13. Wessex.

Medium and 3 of the Small type. To the north and east between the chalk and the Thames only Medium sites occur.

Less than one-third (42, or 28 per cent) of the Wessex sites are multivallate. This is lower than the over-all average (34 per cent) for England and Wales. As indicated above, however, multivallation affected only the Large and Medium sites. Of these 40 per cent (19) of the Large forts and 26 per cent (23) of the Medium forts are multivallate. Assuming that all the multivallate forts in the region were originally univallate, it looks as if conditions in Wessex led to the refortification of many more Large than Medium sites, and to refortification in both of these classes to the exclusion of the Small forts. This may indicate some fundamental difference between the Small sites and the two other categories.

The distribution pattern of multivallate forts in Wessex is fairly clear. To the east of the Test there are no multivallate forts at all. Between the Test and the Avon/Bourne there is a scatter, mainly of Medium size. The main concentration of multivallate forts, however, lies to the west of the Avon/Bourne line and includes no less than 16 Large and 13 Medium sites. Most of these occur in a band running north-east–south-west from the area where the five rivers converge on Salisbury to west Dorset. In the northern half of Wessex multivallate sites occur far less frequently. North of a line from Bratton Castle through Sidbury there are only 8 multivallate forts and most of these are within the area which drains north and east to the Thames.

Pl.38
Pl.5

In the eastern part of Wessex the main rivers, the Meon, the Itchen, and the Test, drain into Southampton Water. Related to these and their tributaries is a series of about 30 sites which are mainly univallate but which include 3 multivallate forts. There is only a single site, Old Winchester Hill, within the curve of the Meon at the western end of a 16-km (10-mile) stretch of chalk downland. Beyond the Meon there is another 16-km (10-mile) stretch of downland before the next site, St. Catherine's Hill, standing above the Itchen. To the north and north-east of this 32-km (20-mile) stretch of downland there is a great area of chalk where Iron Age forts are equally rare. In fact, in an area of about 777 sq km (300 sq miles) to the west of the Weald there are only 3, relatively unimportant, Medium univallate sites. This sparsely occupied area forms something of a natural break between the south-eastern and Wessex regions.

Fig.63

Fig.21c

Many of the remaining sites are closely related to the Test. Most of its tributaries join it from the west and it is noticeable that the greater number of sites is on this side. The main line of the river is marked by a string of Large univallate forts; The Walls, Woolbury, The Andyke, and Cadbury, while the main tributary from the east is marked by Tidbury and Norsebury Rings to the east of The Andyke. The half-dozen tributaries which join the Test from the west are each marked by 1 or 2 sites; these include the 3 multivallate sites. Two other multivallate sites, Buckland Rings and Ampress, stand on the Lymington river, which drains into the Solent. These are the only multivallate forts to the east of the Avon/Bourne line in Wessex.

Fig.119

The main artery of the Wessex river system is the Avon. Its major tributaries form a quarter-circle between the Bourne and the Ebble, with a radius of about 40 km (25 miles), containing many of the most important sites in Wessex. Apart from its lower reaches, where it runs through low-lying heathland, the course of the Avon is marked by a series of univallate sites as far north as Martinsell, nearly 80 km (50 miles) from the sea. The course of the Bourne is also closely marked, but by sites which include 2 multivallate forts, Boscombe and Sidbury. The only other multivallate site which could be included, Whitsbury Castle Ditches, is 4·8 km (3 miles) to the west of the Avon.

The sites encompassed by the quarter-circle noted above fall into two groups, inner and outer. The inner group, within a radius of about 19 km (12 miles), forms a dense concentration with a high proportion of Large sites. These include 4 of the multivallate type. The only other multivallate forts are 2 out of the 10 Medium sites.[1] Beyond this inner quarter-circle to the west, north-west, and north there are wide areas of chalk downland where Iron Age forts are rare or non-existent. To the west of Codford Circle, Stockton Earthworks, and Tisbury Castle Ditches there is an area of more than 259 sq km (100 sq miles) without a single Iron Age fort. There is another complete absence of forts in an even larger area to the north, defined by Oldbury, Bratton Castle, Scratchbury, and Vespasian's Camp. The lack of sites in these two areas is the more marked in view of the dense concentration to the south and east. Of the sites in the outer group the most prominent are the 6 Large sites: Battlesbury, Scratchbury, Cley Hill, Bratton Castle, Casterley, and Sidbury.

Wessex to the west of the Avon is divided diagonally by the Stour, which flows from north-west to south-east. On the chalk downland between the two rivers there is only a scatter of sites. This area can, in fact, be linked with the two blank areas mentioned above to form a great semicircular band from the Avon back to the Avon where Iron Age forts are very rare and entirely univallate. The south-western edge of this band is formed by the sites associated with the Stour. The course of the river is marked by a string of multivallate sites consisting of 4 Large and 2 Medium, from Hengistbury Head to Hambledon Hill.[2] Apart from Hengistbury these are all on the north-eastern side of the river. There are only 3 sites on the south-west side and all are univallate and of Medium size.

To the south-west and west of these 3 sites is the main block of the Dorset downland. It is noticeable once again that there is an extensive area where Iron Age forts do not occur. Apart from a scatter of mainly univallate sites on and near its northern edge the downland area is free of forts in an area some 40 km (25 miles) long and 11 km (7 miles) wide. The sites on the northern edge stand above tributaries which flow north and north-east to the Stour.

In south Dorset, associated with the Frome, the Trent, and their tributaries, is a series of sites a high proportion of which are multivallate. They show a clear tendency to group together in twos, threes, and fours, leaving wide areas be-

Pl.5

Pl.28;Fig.89

Pl.33;Fig.79
Pl.38
Pls.24,28;
Figs.30c,49a
Pls.1,38,5;Fig.43b

Pl.20;Fig.30b

1. *Large multivallate:* Yarnbury, Ebsbury, Hanging Langford Camp, and Castle Ditches, Tisbury. *Large univallate:* Old Sarum, Figsbury Rings, Ogbury, Vespasian's Camp, and Stockton Earthworks. *Medium multivallate:* Boscombe Down and Bilbury Rings.   *Medium univallate:* Codford Circle, Grovely Castle, Wick Ball, Chiselbury, Great Woodbury, Winkelbury, Odstock Copse, and Clearbury Ring. *Small univallate:* East Castle.

2. The six sites from south-east to north-west are: Hengistbury Head, Dudsbury, Badbury Rings, Buzbury Rings, Hod Hill, and Hambledon Hill.

Pl.6

tween unrepresented.[3] Four sites are closely associated with the coast,[4] although the position of Flower's Barrow is similar to that of Seaford in Sussex and is to be ascribed to coastal erosion. Originally it was a hilltop site, probably a little inland from the coast. Beyond the Brit in the extreme west of Dorset there are another 3 sites, once again forming a fairly compact group. Beyond these again is the valley of the Axe and the beginning of the south-western region.

The distributions considered so far have not extended any further north than the source of the Avon and Martinsell Hill. In northern Wessex, however, the rivers drain in an easterly direction and the distribution pattern is somewhat different. The sites involved fall into three main groups. There are about 14 sites, including 3 multivallate,[5] surrounding the valleys of the Lambourn, the Kennet, the Enborne, and the Loddon. To the north and west of this group there is an arc of chalk downland about 40 km (25 miles) long and 8 km (5 miles) wide where Iron Age forts are conspicuously absent. The outer edge of this arc, at or near the edge of the chalk escarpment, is occupied by the second group of sites. These are again mainly univallate, with just 2 multivallate forts.[6] The third group forms another arc following closely the course of the Thames. The 7 sites involved include 3 multivallate forts;[7] all seven are Medium in size. They occupy low hills or level areas in the Thames valley. Nash Hill, in the Avon valley, extends the arc by another 24 km (15 miles).

One or two other sites in the north-western part of Wessex could equally well be related to rivers flowing generally westwards to the Bristol Channel. The 3 Large sites in Somerset (two multivallate) which form part of the Wessex group are closely related to the Parrett, Yeo, and their tributaries.[8] They are somewhat isolated from the other sites in the region. To the north-east of these another

Pl.39

small group, Park Hill Camp, Castle Wood Camp, and White Sheet Castle, could be related to the Cale, which flows south-east to the Stour, or equally well to the Brue, which flows north-west to the Bristol Channel.

Perhaps the most interesting aspect of the distribution pattern in Wessex is the absence of sites from very wide areas of chalk downland in all four counties. For the most part the many sites which can be said to be on the chalk are, in fact, on the edge of the chalk, in most cases within a kilometre or two of one of the major rivers or its principal tributaries. From this point of view the rivers must be regarded as environmental factors and not simply as highways. Where the rivers are absent, so for the most part are Iron Age forts. This, however, is not true in reverse. The Dorset downland west of the Stour has a close network of rivers but no sites except at its northern edge.

For the southern half of Wessex it is difficult to suggest arrival other than across the south coast and up the principal rivers on a front some 113 km (70 miles) wide from the Brit to the Meon. If multivallate sites are the results of a

---

3. Weatherby, Woodbury, Bulbury, and Woolsbarrow from one such group and Maiden Castle and Poundbury another. Eggardon, Chilcombe Hill, and Shipton Hill which form another group about 16 km (10 miles) further west are probably part of the same pattern.
4. Abbotsbury, Chalbury, Bindon, and Flowers' Barrow.
5. Bullsdown, Bussocks, and Chisbury.   6. Oldbury and Barbury.
7. Ringsbury, Castle Hill, and Cherbury.
8. Ham Hill, Cadbury Castle, and Milborne Wick Camp.

second wave of immigrants, then this wave seems to have confined itself for the most part to the western half of Wessex, beyond the Avon, leaving the eastern part as the province of the univallate site. The sites in north Wessex are explicable in terms of arrival via the Thames although it is probable that a spread northwards from the southern half of the region is involved as well. On the western and north-western sides of Wessex a few sites are related to rivers emptying into the Bristol Channel and arrival by this route is another possibility. Apart from the rivers the principal overland routes of southern Britain are focused on the Wessex region and may well have played a part in producing the existing distribution pattern.

THE SOUTH-WEST

Fig.14

The south-west region includes the whole of Devon and Cornwall and the portion of Somerset to the west of the river Parrett. Structurally, the dominant features are the high moorland areas of Dartmoor, Exmoor, and Bodmin Moor, together with a number of less extensive areas, all of which rise above the general level of the south-western plateau. These high moorland areas supply most of the water for the highly developed river system of the region. Dartmoor in particular is at the heart of a pattern of rivers which radiate in all directions. One of the effects of this river system on the south-western plateau is to produce many valleys which are narrow, steep-sided, and sheltered as compared with those of the chalk regions. The edges of the plateau produce the high rugged cliffs which are such a characteristic feature of the south-western coasts. Many of the rivers end in deep inlets, particularly on the south coast. The underlying rocks of the region belong to the older, harder series which are characteristic of northern and western Britain.

The south-west region contains just over 300 sites. With the exception of 7 widely scattered Large sites[9] the forts involved are of the Medium or Small variety. In Devon the majority of sites are in the southern and south-eastern part of the county. They are to be found in a coastal strip between 16 and 24 km (10 and 15 miles) wide from the Axe to the Tamar, skirting Dartmoor to the south and east. Beyond Dartmoor to the north and north-west sites are few and far between except in the areas adjacent to the coast. To the west of the Tamar, where the north and south coasts converge, sites are fairly evenly spread over the whole area with, if anything, a slight emphasis on the north coast. It is on this coast that the greater number of promontory forts occur.

Of the 300 or so Medium and Small sites about one-third (98) are Medium. Most of these are to be found in the area from Bridgwater Bay south to Lyme Bay, in the coastal area of southern and south-eastern Devon, and on and near the north-west coast, from Land's End to Hartland Point. Elsewhere Small forts predominate. These are found wherever forts occur in the south-west, but the main concentrations are to the west of the Tamar and in north Devon between Bideford Bay and the Tone.

9. *Large multivallate:* Carn Brea, Dodman Point, and Hillsborough. *Large univallate:* Rame Head, Tremayne Camp, Bolt Tail, and Cranmore Castle.

Plates 2–17

2 Mam Tor, Derbyshire, a large roughly triangular univallate fort situated at the end of a narrow ridgeway. View looking north along the western rampart.

3 Old Oswestry, Shropshire, showing the multivallate defences on the northern side of a roughly rectangular site.

4 Moel Arthur, Flintshire, one of the group of six sites on the Clwydian range in north-east Wales. The fort has excellent natural defences on the south and west, multivallate defences and a well-designed entrance on the east and north-east. View from the south.

5 Sidbury, Wiltshire, one of the major multivallate sites of Wessex, viewed from the north. The rectangular box-like outworks form a strong barbican entrance.

6 Flower's Barrow, Dorset, originally an inland semi-contour site, now in process of erosion by the sea. View from the east.

7 Castle-an-Dinas, St. Columb Major, Cornwall, a concentric site with clear surface evidence of the development of additional ramparts in the space between the inner and outer lines of defence. View from the north-east.

8 Clovelly Dykes, Devon, one of the most complex of all multiple-enclosure sites, viewed from the south-east. There are two concentric inner enclosures and a series of outer enclosures of the annexe type.

9 Kimsbury, Gloucestershire, a multivallate single-enclosure site in a semi-contour situation. View from the south-west.

10 Crickley Hill, Gloucestershire, a promontory fort in the Cotswolds, defended by a single bank and ditch. Within the existing defences there is clear surface evidence of a smaller, earlier promontory fort. View from the south-east.

11 Uley Bury, Gloucestershire, a very large site in the Cotswolds. The defences consist of a wide inner quarry ditch, a rampart, a ditch and a counterscarp bank. View from the north-east.

12 Caer Caradoc, Church Stretton, Shropshire, occupies one of the most spectacular sites of all the Welsh Marcher forts. Its defences consist for the most part of an inner quarry ditch and a bank, separated by a sloping space from a ditch with a counterscarp bank. View from the south-west.

13 Caer Caradoc, Church Stretton, Shropshire, showing the main entrance and a section of the eastern defences.

14 Old Oswestry, Shropshire. The complex system of defences on either side of the entrance on the western side can be clearly seen.

15 Castle Rings, Cannock, Staffordshire. This large multivallate site has a complex defence system involving five banks on the vulnerable eastern side. View from the north.

16 Pen Dinas, Aberystwyth, Cardiganshire, a multiple-enclosure site with the subsidiary enclosure, of the annexe type, to the north. The main fort has multivallate defences except on the west where there were strong natural defences.

17 The Bulwark, Cheriton, Glamorgan, a multiple-enclosure site, with two concentric inner enclosures and outer enclosures of the crossbank type. View from the east.

2. Mam Tor,
Derbyshire

3. Old Oswestry,
Shropshire

4. Moel Arthur,
Flintshire

5. Sidbury,
Wiltshire

6. Flower's
Barrow, Dorset

7. Castle-an-
Dinas, St.
Columb Major,
Cornwall

8. Clovelly
Dykes, Devon

9. Kimsbury,
Gloucestershire

10. Crickley Hill,
Gloucestershire

11. Uley Bury,
Gloucestershire

12. Caer
Caradoc,
Church
Stretton,
Shropshire

13. Caer
Caradoc,
Church
Stretton,
Shropshire
(detail)

14. Old
Oswestry,
Shropshire

15. Castle Ring,
Cannock,
Staffordshire

16. Pen Dinas,
Aberystwyth,
Cardiganshire

17. The
Bulwark,
Cheriton,
Glamorganshire

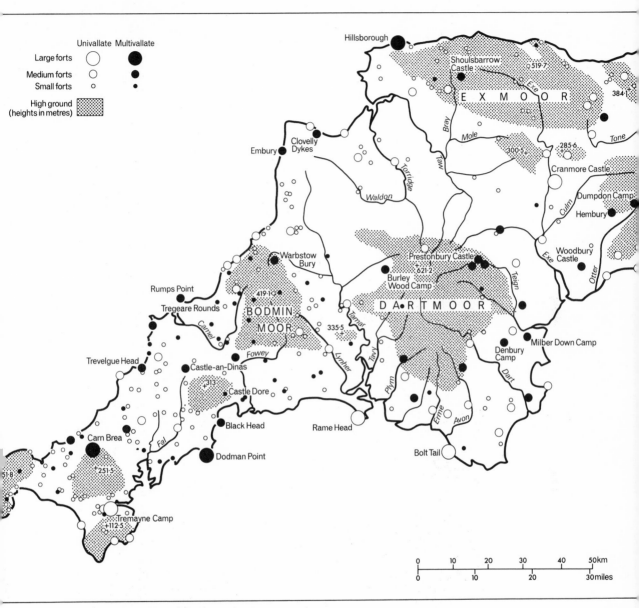

Fig. 14. The South-west.

Apart from 3 Large multivallate sites the multivallate forts are fairly evenly divided between the Medium (37) and Small categories (44), although these figures represent quite different percentages in their respective groups (38 and 21 per cent). In many parts of the south-west univallate and multivallate are fairly evenly mixed with no particular pattern to be seen. There are, however, a number of areas where one or other predominates. In the Land's End district and in the area around the Camel there are noticeable concentrations of multivallate sites. Adjacent to these are areas where univallate sites predominate. In another wide area in north Devon and Somerset there is a scatter of multivallate sites in a region occupied mainly by univallate sites, from Bideford Bay to the Parrett. The lack of a really clear-cut distribution pattern may be due to the existence of two types of multivallate fort, for in the south-west are found both the compact and wide-spaced multivallate defences mentioned previously in Chapter I.

At the eastern end of the South-west region there are two fairly distinct groups, one on the north coast between the Tone and the Parrett, and one on the south coast between the Clyst and the Axe. The Clyst/Axe group (14 sites) consists mainly of Medium forts, 5 of them multivallate.[1] Eight sites are strung out from east to west on, or very close to, the coast. The remaining 5 form another east–west band parallel to, but about 11 km (7 miles) further north than, the coastal group. All of these sites are related to a series of rivers which flow south to the coast from the Blackdown Hills. Horse Pool Camp and Castle Neroche are the only sites in the area, about 622 sq km (240 sq miles), between the two groups. The northern group of 12 sites includes only 2 multivallate forts. It is noticeable that 3 of the 4 Small sites form a single, very compact group. Most of the other sites are in the eastern fringes of the Brendon Hills and the eastern edge of the Quantocks. They are related to the Tone and its tributaries and to a series of tributaries flowing east to the Parrett.

To the west and south-west of the Clyst three important rivers, the Exe, Teign, and Dart, provide access from deep coastal inlets north and north-west into Devon. Related to these rivers and their tributaries are about 24 sites, mostly within 16 or 24 km (10 or 15 miles) of the coast. The general course of the Exe is north–south, rising very close to the north coast. Associated with it are about 12 sites, mostly univallate, many of them in the Small category.[2] The Teign group, on the other hand, includes a high proportion of multivallate sites (7 out of 10), mostly of Medium size.[3] A tendency for sites to be grouped in twos and threes can be observed. Most of the sites in the Dart group are on the upper reaches of the river on the south-eastern fringe of Dartmoor.

The south Devon distribution is completed by a series of sites between the

---

1. *Medium multivallate:* Woodbury Castle, Seaton Down, Musbury Castle, Hembury, Dumpdon Camp. *Medium univallate:* High Peak, Sidbury Castle, Berry Cliff Camp, Hawkesdown Camp, Blackbury Castle, Stockland Great Camp, Membury Castle. *Small univallate:* Stockland Little Camp and Belbury Castle.

2. Apart from the small univallate forts the remaining sites include Cranmore Castle (*Large univallate*); Castle Close, Huntsham Castle, and Stokehill Camp (*Medium univallate*); Posbury Camp (*Medium multivallate*); and Cadbury Castle (*Small multivallate*).

3. The multivallate sites are Milber Down Camp, Denbury Camp, Castle Dyke (Ugbrook), Cranbrook Castle, Prestonbury Castle, and Wooston Castle (*Medium*), and Hunter's Tor (*Small*).

Dart and the Tamar, most of them within 8 or 10 km (5 or 6 miles) of the coast. They are closely related to a series of rivers rising on Dartmoor and flowing generally south to the coast. There is a noticeable increase in the number of Small sites, of which 3 are multivallate. There is also a high proportion of Small sites in north Devon. It looks very much as if the build-up of Small sites in the south-west began to the west of a north–south line from Start Bay to Porlock Bay. Most of the north Devon sites are on or within a few kilometres of the coast.

To the west of the Tamar the north and south coasts converge to such an extent that it is not possible to distinguish specifically north and south coast groups. Forts are spread fairly evenly over the whole of Cornwall, except for the moorland areas. Over 80 per cent of the sites involved are in the Small category, more than one-third of them being multivallate. The Medium sites, 31 in number, also include a high proportion of multivallate forts (13):[4] the concentrations of multivallate sites in Land's End and around the Camel have already been mentioned. More than half of the Medium sites, both univallate and multivallate, stand on the coast. On the other hand, only 6 of the much more numerous Small sites are similarly located. The vast majority are inland sites, although there are a few, particularly on the north coast, which are only a kilometre or two from the sea. It is worth noting that 3 out of the 4 Large sites are also on the coast.

The distribution pattern in the south-west may be summarized as follows. East of the Tamar Iron Age forts can be divided into northern and southern groups with a considerable gap between them. This intermediate zone coincides roughly with the area of the Millstone Grit. Where forts are more numerous the underlying formations are generally of the Old Red or Devonian Sandstone. West of the Tamar there is a very high proportion of Small sites, most of which are located inland. The coastal sites are generally larger, although this may not be particularly significant. The size may be dictated by the nature of the promontories available rather than the desire or need to enclose a larger area. In terms of numbers and of multivallate sites the north coast of Cornwall appears to be rather more important than the south.

THE COTSWOLDS

Fig.15

The Cotswold region is interpreted here as including Somerset north-east of the Parrett, the greater part of Gloucestershire, and parts of the counties of Worcester, Oxford, Warwick, and Northampton. The area involved is about 160 km (100 miles) long and 40 km (25 miles) wide and runs in a north-east–south-west direction. Structurally the greater part of the region is dominated by the limestone which provides elevations generally comparable with those of the chalk country. The higher, steeper edge of the Cotswolds is on the north-west, flanking the Severn and the Avon at a distance of 8 or 9 km (5 or 6 miles). The drainage of the region is either north and west into these two rivers or south and east to

4. Kendijack Castle, Treryn Dinas, Bosigran Castle, Trereen Dinas, Crane Castle, Bovisack Camp, Trevelgue Head, Castle-an-Dinas, Black Head, Castle Canyke, Rumps Point, Warbstow Bury, and Warren Camp.

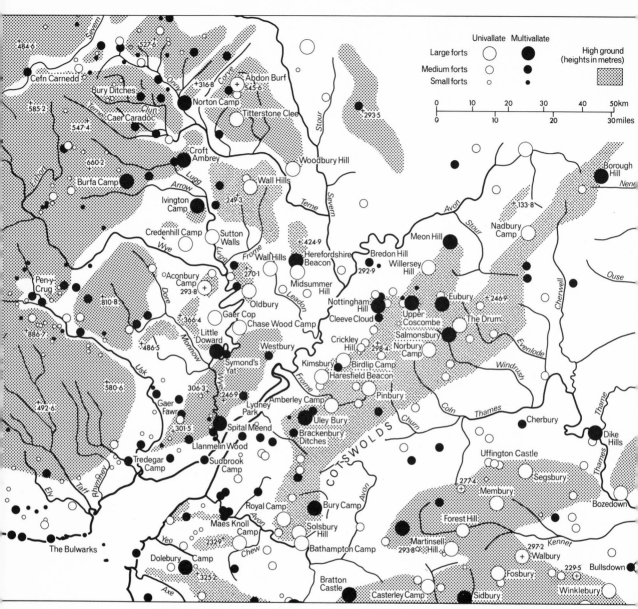

Fig.15. The Cotswolds and southern Marches.

the Upper Thames. In the south-western part of the region the main features (the Bristol Avon and the Mendips) are at right angles to the long axis of the Cotswolds.

The Cotswold region as defined above contains just over 100 sites. In the south-west there are only 1 or 2 forts in the low-lying area between the Parrett and the Mendips. The effective distribution starts in the latter and continues north-east for about 113 km (70 miles). Beyond Willersey Hill and The Roundabout there is only a scatter of sites. In the Cotswolds proper the majority of forts are on or near the north-west escarpment. There is a long line of sites, some 30 in number, from Little Down Camp to Meon Hill nearly 100 km (60 miles) away, which define in very striking fashion the north-western edge of the Cotswold range. Beyond this edge there are no sites except towards the south-west where the main escarpment swings away from the line of the Severn. Here on a series of low hills there is a spread of about 12 sites.

On the gentler, south-eastern side of the Cotswolds sites are more widely scattered, and most of them are related to tributaries flowing south-east to the Thames. To the south-west, in the 32 km (20 miles) between Trewsbury and Bury Camp, there are no sites on the south-eastern side of the range. The distribution in the region is completed by about 24 sites in the rectangular area defined by the Bristol Avon and the Mendips. It is noticeable that the Mendip sites are absent from the highest part of the range and occur for the most part near its edges.

Fig.26c;Pl.11 The over-all distribution pattern in the Cotswold region can be likened to an hour-glass with its base in the Mendips. From here it narrows gradually to its middle, at Uley Bury, where, in fact, it is virtually only one site wide. Beyond, it broadens out again to match the south-western half. In the latter there is a fairly even distribution of sites. In the north-eastern sector the concentration on the Severn/Avon side is much greater than on the Thames side.

Half of the 16 Small sites in the region are found in the restricted area southwest of the Bristol Avon. In the greater part of the region Small sites play a relatively unimportant role. The forts in the largest group are of Medium size (64 in number). They occur more or less evenly throughout the region. The Large sites, which form nearly a quarter of the total, are not quite so evenly spread. Although many of them stand alone others show a tendency to form small groups, e.g. Bury, Royal and Bathampton Camps, and Solsbury Hill. This group accounts for all the Large forts between the Bristol Avon and Pl.11 Uley Bury.

The 100 or so sites in the Cotswold region include 42 multivallate forts (41 per cent). Only 4 of the 16 Small sites are involved. The percentages of multivallate forts in the Medium and Large classes are strikingly similar (43·7 and 43·4 per cent respectively), and suggest that these two categories underwent the same experience with regard to multivallation. They also suggest again a difference between Large and Medium sites on the one hand and Small sites on the other. The distribution pattern is made up of areas where univallate forts virtually exclude all else, and other areas where univallate and multivallate are mixed, with the latter predominating.

37

At the south-western end of the region there is something of a concentration of multivallate sites in and around the Mendips.[5] This is flanked to the north by an east–west band of univallate sites from the coast to the upper part of the Avon and its tributaries. Around the mouth of the Avon there is another, small concentration of multivallate sites. North of this again, opposite the mouth of the Wye, is another small spread of univallate sites, and still further north another concentration of multivallate sites, from The Toots to Nympsfield. The pattern in the upper part of the hour-glass is relatively simple. There is, in fact,

Fig.43a

a single main concentration of multivallate forts in the area surrounding Nottingham Hill and Eubury. Elsewhere univallate sites account for the greater part of the distribution of Iron Age forts.

In the south-western part of the region the most considerable group of sites occupies the area embraced by the Bristol Avon and its tributaries. For the most part the sites involved on the lower reaches are multivallate. Including Cadbury Camp there are 8 multivallate sites, all Medium in size.[6] Higher up the river the sites are mainly univallate, both Large and Medium in size. On the north side of the Avon there is a single multivallate site, Bury Camp, among the univallate forts. On the south side the 3 multivallate sites associated with tributaries of the Avon are situated in a line to the south-west of the univallate forts, on the fringes of the Mendips. There are very few sites associated with the upper course of the Avon. There are, however, a number of tributaries which drain the north-west edge of Wessex and which may have some significance for the distribution of sites in that area. The sites on the south side of the Mendips, both univallate and multivallate, are related to the Axe, the Brue, and their tributaries. Between the Axe and the Avon there is a scatter of sites on or within a few kilometres of the coast.

Beyond the Avon the most striking aspect of the distribution is the proximity of Iron Age forts to the north-west edge of the Cotswolds. The sites involved are of all types, Large, Medium, and Small, univallate and multivallate.[7] This pattern is in part a result of the north-western escarpment cutting across the various univallate and multivallate groups distinguished above. Most of the rivers in this part of the region are quite short, rising only on the north-west side of the Cotswold range and flowing a few kilometres north-west to the Severn. Where there is a longer river, for example the Frome, rising in the heart of the Cotswolds, it is noticeable that there are sites behind the escarpment. On the whole, however, the sites on the broad top of the range are greatly outnumbered by those on the north-western edge.

5. Worlebury, Dolebury, Brent Knoll, Maesbury, Blacker's Hill, Small Down Camp, Tedbury Camp, and Burledge Hill.

6. Blaise Castle Camp, King's Weston Down, Bury Hill Camp, Little Sodbury Camp, Stokeleigh Camp, Clifton Camp, Burgh Walls, and Cadbury Camp.

7. *Large multivallate:* Uley Bury, Nottingham Hill and Meon Hill. *Large univallate:* Royal Camp, Haresfield Beacon, High Brotheridge, Willersey Hill. *Medium multivallate:* Little Sodbury Camp, Brackenbury Ditches, Nympsfield, Kimsbury, Cleeve Cloud, and Dixton Hill. *Medium univallate:* Little Down Camp, Dyrham Camp, Horton Camp, Hawkesbury Knoll, Randwick Wood, Crickley Hill, Leckhampton, Battledown Camp, The Knolls, Langley Hill, Toddington Camp, and Beckbury Camp. *Small multivallate:* Drakestone Point, Hailes Wood, and Shenberrow Camp. *Small univallate:* Birdlip Camp.

Many of the sites on the south-eastern side of the Cotswolds are related to a series of rivers flowing generally south and/or east to the Upper Thames. They are mainly univallate but include 1 or 2 multivallate forts. They should be considered in relation to the sites in the Thames valley on the northern fringe of the Wessex region mentioned earlier.

The obvious means of access to the region is the Severn, which forms the north-west flank, and it is difficult to regard it as anything other than a very important route by which Iron Age forts arrived in the Cotswolds. In the south-western part of the region river valleys penetrate more deeply than further north and the distributions are in consequence broader and more evenly spread. Some of the balance is restored by the sites associated with the tributaries of the Upper Thames and access from this direction is probably a factor in the distributions of the area. Both the Thames and the Bristol Avon provide links with Wessex and the possibility of interchange between the two regions must be kept in mind.

As in Wessex there are fairly extensive elevated areas in which forts are rare. Just as many downland sites followed the edge of the chalk so in more striking fashion do the Cotswold sites seek the edge of the limestone. It is noticeable again that there are very few sites at any distance from a river. The multivallate sites are more strikingly associated with the Severn than the group as a whole. Most of them lie to the north-west of a line drawn through the centre of the region from north-east to south-west. If univallate and multivallate sites represent two waves of migration, then the second wave would seem likely to have come via the Bristol Channel and the western sea route. The Bristol Channel and the Severn provide access also to the Welsh Marches, the next region to be considered, and one which, on this basis, would be likely to have close connections with the Cotswold region.

THE WELSH MARCHES

Figs. 15, 16

The Marcher region is defined here as the territory to the west of the Severn and the Dee as far as the Conway valley in the north and the Usk in the south. This area is about 201 km (125 miles) long and about 72 km (45 miles) wide. Since the eastern parts of Radnorshire and Montgomeryshire are an integral part of the region the scatter of sites in their western parts will also be dealt with here, as will the sites in eastern Merionethshire. The western parts of Merionethshire, however, will be considered in the next section (South and West Wales). In the northern part of the region the small group of sites in Cheshire will also be dealt with.

Geologically the southern part of the region consists almost entirely of Old Red Sandstone. Further north, in south Shropshire, the picture is more complex, but the main formations are Silurian limestones and shales. Basalts and volcanic rocks provide some of the outstanding features of the landscape; the Clee Hills, the Wrekin, etc. There are also restricted areas of Old Red Sandstone. In north Wales the Silurian shales and sandstones are accompanied by outcrops of carboniferous limestone flanking the Clwyd valley to east and west. The river

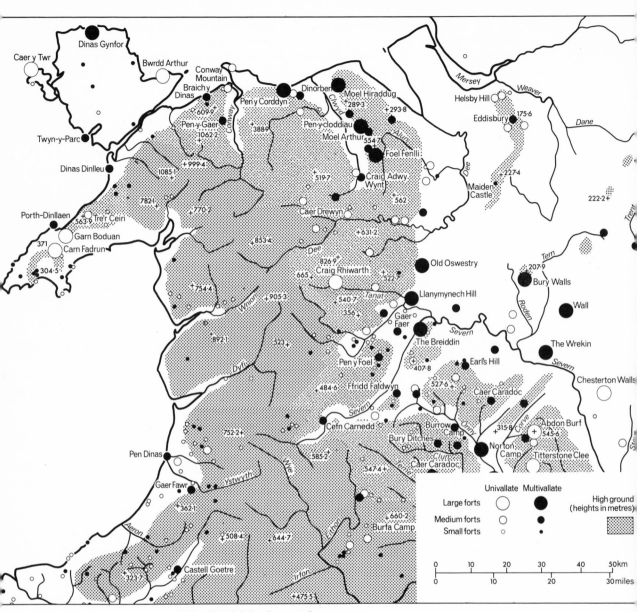

Fig.16. The Welsh Marches, northern sector.

system embraces five main rivers: about a quarter of the region in the north is drained by the Clwyd, the Dee, and a network of tributaries, the direction of flow being generally east and/or north; the remainder of the region, from Shropshire southwards, is drained by the Severn, the Wye, and the Usk and an involved network of major and minor tributaries, all emptying ultimately into the Bristol Channel, the direction of flow being generally east and south.

Broadly speaking the Marcher region provides a terrain intermediate between the low-lying areas to the east and the high chain of the Cambrian mountains to the west. It is an area of mostly moderate elevations divided up into fairly restricted zones by the complex pattern of rivers. In the north the valleys tend to be deeper and narrower than in the south, and the elevations somewhat greater. There is no striking change anywhere; the trend is a gradual one from south to north. Some of the terrain is not dissimilar to parts of the south-west, particularly Devon. Geologically the two regions have a good deal in common.

The Marcher sites consist of 31 (12 per cent) Large forts, 99 (39 per cent) Medium forts, and 122 (49 per cent) Small forts. These figures represent a considerable decrease in the percentages of Large and Medium sites as compared with Wessex and the Cotswolds, but a big increase in the percentage of Small sites. Large sites are fairly well scattered throughout the region from Spital Meend in the south to Pen-y-Corddyn in the north. In Herefordshire they represent a very high proportion (46.5 per cent) of all Iron Age forts in the county. In the central sector Large sites fall into two groups, one in north Herefordshire and south Shropshire and the other in north Shropshire and eastern Montgomeryshire. About 32 km (20 miles) to the north, beyond the Berwyns, there is another small group related to the Clwyd valley.

There is something of a concentration of Medium sites on and between the Wye and the Usk. Further north, however, Medium sites are comparatively rare until the central sector is reached. From here as far as the north Wales coast there is a more or less continuous and fairly even spread, with a single site reducing the gap formed by the Berwyns.

The distribution of Small sites is much more restricted than those of the other two categories. In the north most of them are located in eastern Montgomeryshire and the adjacent area of Shropshire. There are only a few Small sites in the rest of Shropshire and only two in the whole of Herefordshire. In the southern part of the region there is something of a concentration on the upper reaches of the Usk in Breconshire, about 25 sites, and another group, about 15, in the lower Usk/lower Wye area mentioned above. In north Wales Small sites are rare in the Clwyd valley area but there is a small scatter to the south on the upper Dee and its tributaries.

Of the 252 sites in the Marcher region 117 (46 per cent) are multivallate. This is higher than the percentage for the Cotswold region (42 per cent), and considerably higher than that for Wessex (28 per cent). The percentages for Large and Medium sites are virtually the same (57 and 56 per cent), but the figure for Small multivallate sites is only 35 per cent. This suggests once again that with regard to multivallation the experience of the Large and Medium sites differed from that of the Small sites.

Multivallate forts are found in three main areas. At the southern end of the Marcher region multivallate forts predominate in the triangular area defined by the Usk and the Severn, and there is another considerable group to the north-west in Brecon. For more than 32 km (20 miles) to the north of Little Doward Camp there is a wide area, including the greater part of Herefordshire, where multivallate forts are very much in a minority, the Large univallate fort being the dominant type. North of this again, in the central sector of the Marches, sites fall into three fairly clear-cut zones. The eastern strip is entirely univallate as far north as the Severn. Immediately to the west of this, in an area defined roughly by The Ditches, Risbury Camp, Burfa Camp, and Bury Ditches, there is a concentration of multivallate sites relieved by only one univallate fort. North and west of this in the remainder of the central sector there is a spread of mixed univallate and multivallate sites. Most of the univallate forts are in the Small category.

Fig.86

To the north-west of the central sector there is another spread of mainly univallate sites in the upper Dee valley, and beyond that again, in the Clwyd valley area, another concentration of multivallate sites relieved by only a handful of univallate forts.

At the southern end of the Marcher region there is a scatter of sites along the Usk for about 24 km (15 miles), beyond which there is a long gap, separating it from the Brecon group.[8] There is a similar situation on the Wye, except that the sites involved are confined to the first 8 or 10 km (5 or 6 miles), with a 16-km (10-mile) gap before the next sites occur. Apart from a small group of sites on a tributary, most of the remaining forts stand on a series of short rivers between and on either side of the Wye and the Usk.[9]

Beyond the 16-km (10-mile) gap the main Marcher distribution follows the course of the Wye and then the Lugg, and it is noticeable that most sites are within a few kilometres of the river.[1] To the west there are a few sites on the Dore and the Troddi but otherwise the area between the Wye/Lugg group and the Brecon group is a blank. Similarly, to the east, apart from a small group in and around the Malverns,[2] the large area between the Lugg and Wye valleys and the Severn is virtually free of Iron Age forts. Sites on or near the Severn are rare until Shropshire is reached. The middle section of the Wye, where it flows generally east, is another blank as far as forts are concerned. On the upper reaches, however, there is a small group of about 12 sites, very much isolated from the main Marcher distribution.

8. The main sites in the Brecon group are Pen-y-Crug, Slwch Tump, Hillis Camp, Pendre Camp, Castell Dinas, and Penmyarth (all *Medium multivallate*).

9. Sites in the lower Wye/lower Usk area include Tredegar Camp, Lodge Wood Camp, Wilcrick Hill, Sudbrook Camp, Llanmelin, and Lydney Park (all *Medium multivallate*), and Spital Meend (*Large multivallate*).

1. The Wye/Lugg group includes 21 sites. *Large multivallate:* Little Doward, Ivington Camp, Croft Ambrey, and Burfa Camp. *Large univallate:* Chase Wood Camp, Gaer Cop, Aconbury Camp, Oldbury, Credenhill Camp, and Sutton Walls. *Medium multivallate:* Symond's Yat, Capler Camp, Cherry Hill, Backbury Camp, Risbury Camp, Bach Camp, Pyon Wood, and Wapley Camp. *Medium univallate:* Dinedor Camp. In addition there are two *Small univallate* sites (Castle Ring and Glog Camp) on the upper reaches of the Lugg.

2. *Large multivallate:* Herefordshire Beacon. *Large univallate:* Midsummer Hill. *Medium univallate:* Haffield Camp and Gadbury Bank.

Fig.23a

To the north of the Lugg there is a considerable group of sites associated with the Teme, the main tributary of the Severn on its western side.[3] It is noticeable that the Teme's tributaries, with one minor exception, join it from the north and form a closely set pattern of rivers defining an area about 48 km (30 miles) from east to west and 24 km (15 miles) from north to south. Within this area there is a fairly dense concentration of sites of all types. Together with the adjacent Lugg group it accounts for most of the sites in the southern half of the central Marcher region. To the east of the Teme group there is once again an extensive area where Iron Age forts do not occur. In the territory between the lower Teme, the Severn, and the Clee Hills, an area of about 518 sq km (200 sq miles), there is only one site, Woodbury Hill.

Only in the northern half of Shropshire, where the river flows north-east and then east across the county, is there any considerable number of forts associated with the Severn. In this area and in north-east Montgomeryshire sites are well spaced out and include mainly Large and Medium forts,[4] a high proportion of them multivallate. To the west and south-west, around the uppermost reaches of the Severn and its tributaries, the sites are mostly of the Medium and Small type and again include a high proportion of multivallate sites.

Beyond the Berwyns the rivers drain in a different direction. There are about 12 sites, mostly univallate and forming an L-shaped pattern, associated with the Dee. There is an east–west group along the line of the upper Dee. Where the river turns north into flat country the sites are associated with the tributaries which join it from the high ground to the west. The most northerly Marcher group is based on the Clwyd valley. The most striking are the 6 forts which stand on the top of the Clwydian range, with a wide prospect over the valley below. Together with 3 other sites to the east of the river they form a group of 9 multivallate sites (3 Large, 6 Medium).[5] There are fewer sites to the west of the river, and only 2 of them are multivallate. Beyond the Clwyd group there are no sites at all as far as the Conway valley, the western limit of the northern Marcher region.

In summary it can be seen that the bulk of the Marcher sites are associated with the generally southward-flowing river system and it would be difficult to suggest any other route by which they could have arrived. In the southern part of the region the Wye accounts for much of the distribution and is obviously both a means of access and an important environmental factor. The same is true of the Usk. The lower Severn, running through flat country, is virtually deserted as far as Iron Age forts are concerned. On the other hand, the greatest concentration of sites, in the central sector, is associated with the Teme, its principal tributary, and its own upper reaches in Shropshire and Montgomeryshire. This

3. The Teme group consists of about two dozen sites, many of them multivallate. These include Caynham Camp, Nordy Bank, The Ditches, Caer Caradoc (Church Stretton), Caer Caradoc (Clun), Coxall Knoll, Burrow Camp, Bury Ditches, and Billings Ring (all *Medium*), and Norton Camp (*Large*).

4. *Large multivallate:* The Wrekin, Wall, Bury Walls, Old Oswestry, Llanymynech Hill, and The Breiddin. *Medium multivallate:* The Burgs, Oliver's Point, Earl's Hill, and Gaer Fawr.

5. *Large multivallate:* Moel Hiraddug, Pen-y-cloddiau, and Foel Fenlli. *Medium multivallate:* Moel-y-Gaer (Bodfari), Moel Arthur, Moel y Gaer (Llanbedr), Moel y Gaer (Rhosesmor), Craigadwy Wynt, and Dinas.

suggests the possibility of the lower Severn and the Teme as an important route, one through which the whole of the central sector could be reached. It is more likely, however, that it was used in conjunction with a route following the main line of the Severn north and then west through Shropshire. In the northern part of the region the Clwydian sites and those on the central ridge of Cheshire suggest the possibility of arrival from an entirely different direction.

With regard to multivallate sites, it is noticeable that the southern group faces a corresponding group of multivallate sites across the Severn, in the Cotswold region. It is also noticeable that beyond each group is an area of univallate forts. Multivallate forts are rare north of Symond's Yat. It may be that the multivallate sites in north Herefordshire arrived via the Severn–Teme route and then spread south to the Lugg. The area of virtually unrelieved multivallate sites mentioned earlier covers the Teme, its tributaries, and the northern section of the Lugg, and it is feasible to suggest a single event to explain them. A similar event needs to be invoked for the unbroken chain of multivallate sites east of the Clwyd.

Small sites occur in two main areas. In the Monmouth/Brecon area they are part of the general pattern of such sites covering south Wales. The Shropshire/Montgomeryshire group is more isolated and it is just possible that the sites in it are the result of movement across the Welsh mountains from the Cardigan Bay area where Small forts predominate. There is a scatter of sites between the two areas to lend some support to this suggestion.

SOUTH AND WEST WALES

Figs.16,17   This region covers the whole area to the west of the Marches and includes all the counties of Wales except Flint, Denbigh, Montgomery, Radnor, and Brecon, which have been dealt with already. Structurally the southern part is dominated by the south Wales coal measures. These are flanked to the south and west by limestone areas in south Glamorgan, Gower, and Pembrokeshire. In mid Wales, as in much of Shropshire and the northern Marches, the main formations are the Silurian shales and limestones. In north-west Wales the igneous rocks provide some of the highest ranges and most rugged scenery of the region. The trend of most of the geological formations is north-east–south-west, and this is the direction of most of the rivers, except in the extreme north.

Although much of the region consists of a high plateau there are considerable areas where elevations are more modest. There is a broad band of such territory across south Wales, from the Vale of Glamorgan to St. Bride's Bay, and in the north-west in and around the Lleyn peninsula. Many of the river valleys, the Tywi for example, must be included as part of this zone, forming considerable salients into the Welsh massif.

There are just over 400 sites in the region as defined above, the bulk of them being in the southern counties. In the north sites are much more widely scattered except for one or two restricted areas. There is a fairly distinct group in Glamorgan in the southern, relatively low-lying, part of the county. To the west, apart from a marked concentration in the Gower peninsula, there is a noticeable

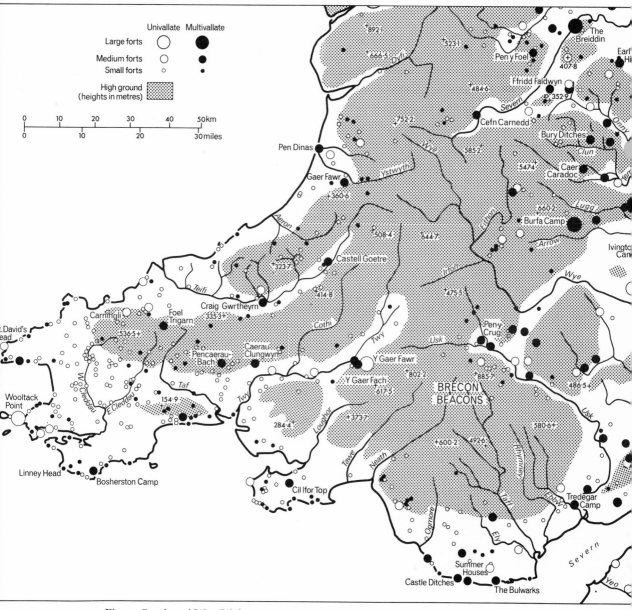

Fig. 17. South and West Wales.

scarcity of sites until the Tywi valley is reached. There the course of the river is marked by a series of sites which are rarely more than a few kilometres from its banks. The whole group extends north-east for over 48 km (30 miles) but is rarely more than 8 or 10 km (5 or 6 miles) wide.

To the west of the Tywi, in western Carmarthenshire and in Pembrokeshire, there is a very large number of sites spread more or less evenly over the whole area. To the north and north-east sites follow the Teifi valley in much the same way as they followed the Tywi. There is a scatter of sites along the coasts of Cardigan Bay and up the series of short rivers, but no very great numbers except perhaps in the region of Aberystwyth where there is a group of about 12. In north-west Wales the only considerable spread of forts is in the Lleyn peninsula.

Large sites are very rare in the region; only 7 are known, and of these 5 are in two adjacent counties, Anglesey and Caernarvonshire, in the north. Even the Medium sites represent only a small proportion, less than 12 per cent, of the total. Most of them are located in the southern counties, Glamorgan, Carmarthenshire, and Pembrokeshire. In the northern part of the region Medium sites are inevitably widely scattered. The greatest part of the distribution pattern is formed by Small sites, of which there are about 350. Since they form such a high proportion of the total their distribution is virtually the same as the overall distribution described above and will not be repeated here.

Roughly one-third of all the sites in the region are multivallate. These include only one of the Large sites, so that attention can be confined to the other two categories. The percentages of multivallate sites in these are markedly different. Nearly 60 per cent of the Medium sites are multivallate, while only 30 per cent of the Small sites take this form. In Glamorgan, adjacent to the Marcher region, the proportion of multivallate sites is somewhat higher than elsewhere. Further west there is a tendency for multivallate sites to be on or near the coast. Inland sites, particularly in Pembrokeshire, tend to be univallate, although some multivallate sites do occur. Around Cardigan Bay multivallate sites are fairly evenly, though widely, scattered throughout the area. In north-west Wales the proportion of multivallate sites is roughly the same as in Glamorgan. There is something of a concentration, mostly of Small sites, at the south-west end of the Lleyn peninsula, all of them on or near the coast.

In south Wales the sites in Glamorgan are virtually confined to the broad tongue of land between the Rhymney and the Neath, and to the Gower peninsula. In the former area there are about 48 sites.[6] Apart from 9 Medium sites, 6 of them multivallate, all the sites are of Small size. Eleven of these are multivallate. The multivallate sites, both Medium and Small, tend to be on or within a few kilometres of the coast. Univallate sites occur both in the coastal zone, where they are in a minority, and further inland where multivallate sites are rare or non-existent.

In the much smaller area of the Gower peninsula there are about 24 sites. Except for 2 Medium sites all the forts involved are Small. Once again a high

6. The Glamorgan sites include The Bulwarks, Summer Houses, Castle Ditches, Dunraven, Llanbethian Hill, and Caerau (all *Medium multivallate*), and Llanquian Wood, Maendy Camp, Caer Cwm Phillip, Caer Blaen y Cwm, Bwlwarcau, and Y Gaer (all *Small multivallate*).

proportion of them are on or very close to the coast. There is a marked concentration along the south-west coast. About half the Gower sites are multivallate.

Apart from the Gower group there are very few sites between the Neath and the Tywi some 40 km (25 miles) away. Following the course of the latter is a group of about 30 sites. Some are in the low-lying area close to the river while others take advantage of the heights which flank it on either side. Still others stand above tributaries a few kilometres from the main course. Most of the sites are Small, but there are 5 Medium sites and a rare Large site, Gaer Fawr, one of the largest Iron Age forts in Wales.[7] The Tywi group, lying generally north-east–south-west, forms a long salient into an area which is otherwise without Iron Age forts. To the north-west, north-east, and south-east is a no-man's-land, in most cases at least 16 km (10 miles) wide, between the Tywi and neighbouring groups.

To the west of a line from the mouth of the Tywi to the mouth of the Teifi, that is, in western Carmarthenshire and the whole of Pembrokeshire, there is a very large spread of Small Iron Age forts. There are only 11 Medium sites and 1 Large site in the same area,[8] as compared with over 170 Small forts. The distribution consists of areas where only univallate sites occur, areas where univallate and multivallate are mixed, and one area where multivallate forts predominate. This is the area between the Taf and the southern coast, where there is a noticeable concentration of multivallate sites. Most of the Taf's tributaries join it from the north, and in the roughly rectangular area which they define there is a spread of mainly univallate Small forts, about 20 in number. Among these is a scatter of multivallate forts.

On and close to the south coast of Pembrokeshire is a spread of about 12 mixed univallate and multivallate forts. There are only a few sites in the northern part of this area which forms the southern flank of Milford Haven. On the north side of Milford Haven and between it and St. Bride's Bay there is a triangular group (about 20), about half of which are coastal sites. There is a matching group on the peninsula on the north side of St. Bride's Bay. These include an even higher proportion of coastal sites. In fact, there are only 3 sites away from the coast and even these are only a kilometre or so inland.

This coastal pattern is continued north-eastwards up to and beyond Strumble Head. In the large area to the east and north-east of St. Bride's Bay there is a very wide spread of Small sites, virtually all of them univallate, many of them related to the West Cleddau and its tributaries. To the east of this area, in the neighbourhood of the East Cleddau and the upper part of the Taf, there is an area where univallate and multivallate sites are mixed. In the northern part of the region in the triangular area between the coast, the Teifi, and the Prescelly mountains, there is a group of about 15 sites, most of them univallate, including 4 Medium sites.

---

7. *Large univallate:* Gaer Fawr. *Medium multivallate:* Gaer Fach, Llwyn Du, and Caerau Clungwyn. *Medium univallate:* Grongaer and Merlin's Hill.

8. *Large univallate:* Wooltack Point. *Medium multivallate:* Castle Penpleidiau, Bosherston, Bignen Earthworks, Pencaerau-Bach, Foel Trigarn. *Medium univallate:* St. David's Head, Dale Point, Great Castle Head, Carningli, Castell Mawr, and Castelltreruffydd.

Outside the areas described so far there are only two or three clearly defined groups of forts. One of them defines the valley of the Teifi; about 30 sites are involved, all but 3 of Small size. There are only 1 or 2 sites on the lower 24 km (15 miles) of the river. From this point on the sites follow the river for over 48 km (30 miles), although the bulk of them are in the middle section, between 24 and 56 km (15 and 35 miles) from its mouth. About one-third of the group are multivallate and they are scattered throughout the area, so that no particular pattern is observable.[9]

The Teifi group is parallel to and about 16 km (10 miles) from the coast and seems to have attracted many more sites than the latter. In the 97-km (60-mile) stretch of coast between the Teifi and the Wnion there are less than 10 sites on or near the coast. To these may be added a small scatter of sites up the series of short rivers draining on to the coast. The only concentration occurs to the north of the Teifi group in the neighbourhood of Aberystwyth. About 20 sites are involved, both Medium and Small, univallate and multivallate. Apart from Pen Dinas all are away from the coast mostly on or very close to the rivers flowing west to Cardigan Bay.

Fig.106

North of the Dyfi sites of any sort are rare as far round as the end of the Lleyn peninsula. In the 40-km (25-mile) length of the latter there are about twenty sites, Large, Medium, and Small, univallate and multivallate.[1] With one exception all the latter are of Small size and nearly all are concentrated in the extreme end of the peninsula. To the north-east there is a scatter of mixed univallate and multivallate sites along or very close to the Caernarvonshire coast as far as the Conway valley. It is noticeable that apart from one site about 10 km (6 miles) from its mouth the latter is entirely lacking in Iron Age forts. The same is true of the mountainous inland areas of Caernarvonshire. The last area to be considered is Anglesey, where there are 10 sites widely distributed over the whole island. They include 3 Large sites, all on or near the coast, and a Medium site also coastal.[2] The Small sites are mainly inland. Six out of the 10 Anglesey sites are multivallate.

Perhaps the most significant aspect of the region is that fact that it contains nearly one-third of all the Iron Age forts in England and Wales, considerably more than any other regional group. Also significant is the fact that the majority of them are of Small size. Large and Medium sites, particularly the former, are very much in a minority and in some parts of the region are completely absent. Apart from the great concentration in Pembrokeshire and the adjacent area of Carmarthenshire, most of the sites in the region fall into a relatively small number of clearly defined groups, separated from each other by wide areas where no forts occur. Six such groups were distinguished: south Glamorgan, Gower, Tywi, Teifi, and the smaller groups near Aberystwyth and in the Lleyn

9. *Medium multivallate*: Craig-Gwrtheyrn and Castell Goetre. *Medium univallate*: Pencoed-y-Foel.
1. *Large univallate*: Garn Boduan and Carn Fadrun. *Medium multivallate*: Dinas Dinlleu and Porth-Dinllaen. *Medium univallate*: Tre'r Ceiri. *Small multivallate*: Craig-y-Dinas, Foel (Clynnog), Caer Engan, Bwlch-Clawdd, Conion, Castell Caeron, Pen-y-Gaer (Llanengan), Bodwrog. *Small univallate*: Creigiau Gwineu, Garn Saethon, Castell Pared Mawr, and Pen-y-Gaer (Llanaelhaiarn).
2. *Large multivallate*: Dinas Gynfor. *Large univallate*: Caer y Twr and Bwrdd Arthur. *Medium multivallate*: Twyn-y-Parc.

peninsula. It is noticeable that the four main groups are all in the southern half of Wales. In the north, apart from the two small groups just mentioned, there is only a scatter of sites.

The distribution pattern leaves about half of the region unoccupied. This is the area of mountain and high moorland which runs down the centre of Wales from the north coast of Caernarvonshire to the south Wales coalfield and forms the natural division between the Marcher sites on the one hand and those of south and west Wales on the other. There are multivallate sites throughout the area, although they tend to occur on or near the coast in many parts of the region.

THE CHILTERNS, THE MIDLANDS AND THE NORTH

Under this heading will be considered all the areas not covered by the six regions dealt with already. About 80 sites are involved, forming four or five quite separate groups, the largest being in the Chilterns area.

In the north-west there is a small scattered group in the north Lancashire area. Three of the sites are located on the three sides of Morecambe Bay, while the other 3 are on tributaries of the rivers Lune and Ribble which provide access from the Lancashire coast. A single site in the southern part of the county, close to the Mersey, probably needs to be considered in conjunction with the Cheshire sites, although these too may be interpreted as part of the process which brought about the distribution in north Lancashire.

Fig.18

The largest group outside the Chilterns in this context is in the south Pennine area where there is a scatter of about 20 sites,[3] three-quarters of them of the Small type. Nearly all the sites in the group are on the eastern side of the Pennines, and with one exception they are related to rivers which flow ulti- mately to the east coast. The sites in the northern part of the group stand on tributaries of the Aire and the Don, and those in the southern part on tributaries of the Trent. All three rivers drain into the Humber. The lower-lying sites on the eastern side of the group tend to be univallate. The sites to the west in the more elevated parts of the Pennines tend to be multivallate, and indeed the western flank of the group consists of a roughly north–south line of multivallate forts. The larger sites occur in the same general area, with the eastern, lower-lying area occupied mainly by Small sites. Three other scattered sites, Boltby Scar, Grimthorpe, and Castleberg, which are outside this group, may be considered here. All are related to rivers which flow into the Humber and are probably to be associated with the south Pennine group.

Between the south Pennine group and the Chilterns there is nothing which can strictly be called a group. In the roughly triangular area between the Severn, the Avon, and the Trent there are about 20 widely scattered sites. In the western part, in Staffordshire, Worcestershire, and Warwickshire, there are about 10 sites in the angle between the Marcher and Cotswold groups, which are

3. The south Pennine group include the following: *Large univallate*: Mam Tor. *Medium multivallate*: Fin Cop and Almondbury. *Medium univallate*: Burr Tor, Brierley Common, and Markland Grips. *Small multivallate*: Combs Moss, Whinny Hill, and Gilbert Hill.

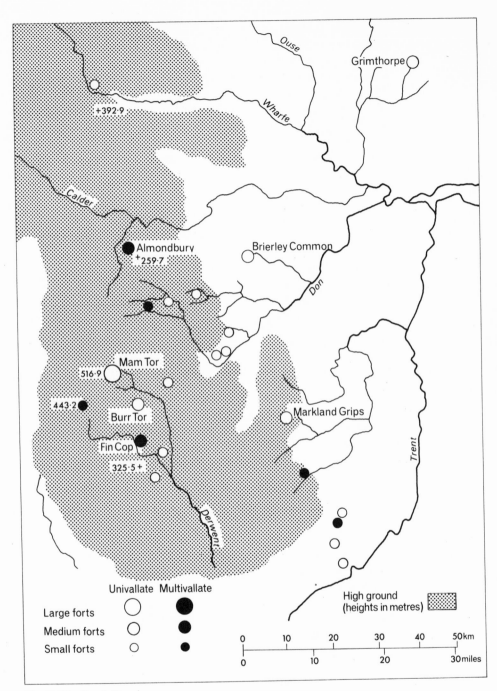

Fig. 18. The South Pennines.

probably best interpreted as outliers from these two regions. In the eastern part sites are again related to rivers flowing generally eastwards and may for this reason be associated with the sites of the south Pennine group. Further east again there is a small group of 4 sites on the north coast of Norfolk, and a single Large and very much isolated site in the southern part of the county.

Fig.12

The largest and most important group in this section is situated in and around the Chilterns, which run in a north-east–south-west direction. The higher edge of the range is on the north-west side, as in the Cotswolds. Geologically the Chilterns, an area of chalk upland, belong with Wessex and the North and South Downs and form part of the great stretch of chalk which occupies so much of southern and eastern England. Much of the drainage is to the south-east, emptying into the Thames. On the northern and much of the north-western flank the rivers drain in the opposite direction, generally north or north-east, emptying finally into the Wash. On the remainder of the north-western side the drainage is to the west and south-west, emptying once again into the Thames. The latter forms a clear boundary to the south-west marking off, but not necessarily isolating, the Chiltern area from Wessex.

Of the 30 or so sites involved a high proportion (11) are Large. This is in keeping with the pattern in the two adjacent chalk regions. The remaining sites include both Medium (15) and Small forts (6). Most of the Large sites are in the south-western half of the area, most of the Medium sites in the north-eastern. About one-third of the sites are multivallate. Once again the emphasis in this respect is on the Large sites of which 5 are multivallate; there are only 3 Medium and 2 Small multivallate sites. No particular pattern is observable in the distribution of the two types of site.

At the south-western end of the area there are 4 Large sites closely associated with the Thames.[4] To the north-east along the high north-west edge of the Chilterns there is a string of sites following, or close to, the Icknield Way. About 12 sites are involved, Large, Medium, and Small, univallate and multivallate.[5] Roughly parallel to this group, to the south-east, is a scatter of sites on or close to rivers draining south to the Thames. They include 3 Large multivallate sites.[6] The remaining forts are scattered beyond the Chilterns to the north-west on isolated hills and low-lying land.

The most interesting aspect of the Chiltern group is the close association between some of the sites and the Icknield Way, one of the natural highways of prehistoric times. Such a route would have facilitated movement in either direction, north-east or south-west. The river system would have supplemented this and permitted approach from virtually all directions. The sites not on the north-west edge of the chalk are related to rivers flowing south and east to the Thames and to others flowing north and east to the Wash.

---

4. *Large multivallate*: Dike Hills. *Large univallate*: Bozedown, States House Camp, and Danesfield Camp.

5. *Large multivallate*: Ravensburgh Castle. *Large univallate*: Boddington Hill and Wilbury. *Medium multivallate*: Hoy's Farm. *Medium univallate*: Ragpit Hill, Ivinghoe Beacon, Maiden Bower, Arbury Banks, Limlow Hill, and Hyde Farm. *Small multivallate*: Pulpit Hill and Whitely Hill.

6. Bulstrode Park, the Aubreys, and Wallbury.

CHAPTER III

The siting of Iron Age forts

The terms currently used to describe the siting of Iron Age forts were defined briefly in Chapter I. While these are useful for the purpose of general discussion, they do not adequately describe the wide range of situations which actually exist. Quite clearly additional terms are required to define the various situations more precisely. These and the sort of terminology required can best be understood by considering the question of siting theoretically.

Fig.19a
Fig.19g

What may be termed basic situations are shown on p. 53. They range from a hilltop situation with the ground falling away from the defences on all sides, to a low-lying situation, in which the ground outside the defences is quite flat. These and the situations in between summarize the whole range of positions in which Iron Age forts are found. In all of them it is assumed for the moment that the ground is flat, except where indicated otherwise by contour lines. The latter represent a range of slopes from the very steep—in some cases sheer cliffs—to the very shallow which afford only slight supplementary support to the defences.

Fig.19a

In the first situation shown the approaches to the enclosure are equally steep on all sides. There is no one direction from which approach is easier than any other. This, of course, is the basic pattern of a contour fort.

Fig.19b

In the next situation, on the other hand, the natural defences exist on only three sides of the site, with a level approach to the defences on the fourth. This is the basic pattern of a promontory fort although, as will be seen later, other situations are also represented by this pattern. In yet other situations the site is approachable on two adjacent sides with natural defences on the two remaining sides. Between them these patterns represent the siting of a very large number of Iron Age forts, probably over three-quarters of the total in England and Wales.

Fig.19c

The number of sites represented by the remaining situations illustrated is comparatively small. In the first of these the site is again approachable from two directions. In this case, however, the directions are opposite to each other, so that the situation is basically that of a ridge-top. In the second the sides with natural defences are reduced to one, so that in some cases the term cliff-edge is appropriate. In the situations covered by the third the site lies on sloping ground. The basic characteristic of the situations covered by the final illustration is that they have no elevation whatsoever above their immediate surroundings.

Fig.19d

Fig.19e

Fig.19f

Fig.19g

The situations represented here provide a framework within which the siting

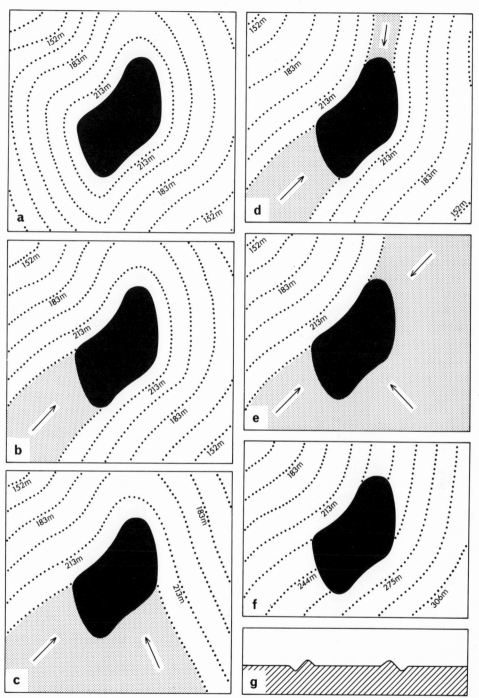

Fig. 19. Basic situations.

of all Iron Age forts can be considered in the main part of this chapter. Sites will be dealt with in seven groups (I–VII), each group based on one of the seven situations illustrated.

Before dealing with the various types of situation in more detail one other topic, that of elevation, can be considered. Absolute height, i.e. height above sea-level, is of less importance as a tactical factor than relative height, i.e. height above the immediate surroundings), but it does indicate, when all sites are taken into account, the sort of elevations at which Iron Age people built defensive works and at which they were prepared to live, at least for limited periods. For the purpose of this section elevation will be interpreted as the highest point reached by any part of a fort, of either defences or interior.

Fig.13(map)

Fig.12(map)

The lowest elevations are, not surprisingly, on or close to the coast. In southern Hampshire, Hamble Common Camp, Ampress Camp, and Tourner-bury are all below the 8-m (25-ft) contour and can be regarded as being virtually at sea-level. In the same county The Walls and Lower Exbury are very slightly higher, but still well below the 15-m (50-ft) contour. In East Anglia few of the very scattered forts in the area are at any great height above sea-level. Holkham Camp (Norf.) is below the 8-m (25-ft) contour and like some of the Hampshire sites can be regarded as being at sea-level. Camphill and Warham Camp, also in Norfolk, and Grove Field Camp, Asheldham Camp, and Witham Camp (all in Essex) are very little higher, rising to c. 23 m (c. 75 ft) above sea-level. There is another small group of low-lying sites in the Lower Severn/Bristol Channel area. Sudbrook (Mon.) and The Toots (Glos.) both stand between the 8-m and 15-m (25-ft and 50-ft) contours. One or two other sites in the same general area are slightly higher but still below the 30-m (100-ft) contour. Apart from these three groups, in Hampshire, East Anglia, and the Bristol Channel region, and one or two sites in north-west Wales the majority of Iron Age forts are situated at considerably higher elevations.

Pl.18;Fig.15(map)

Figs.16,17(maps)

The highest elevations are found mainly in Wales and the Welsh Marches. The highest fort in southern Britain, however, appears to be Ingleborough (Yorks), which rises at its highest point to 716 m (2,350 ft). The remaining sites are all below 610 m (2,000 ft). They include Abdon Burf (Salop), Craig Rhiwarth (Montg.), and Titterstone Clee (Salop), which rise to 545·6 m (1,790 ft), 533·4 m (1,750 ft), and 533 m (1,749 ft) respectively. Clee Burf, between Abdon Burf and Titterstone Clee, rises to 502·9 m (1,650 ft), and Foel Fenlli (Denb.) to 510·8 m (1,676 ft). Three other sites, Moel-y-Gaer, Llantysilio (Denb.), Mam Tor (Derby.), and Castell Rhyfel (Card.) complete a group of only 9 sites with elevations above 488 m (1,600 ft).

Fig.54
Pl.2;Fig.66

Between 396 and 488 m (1,300 and 1,600 ft) there is a group of about 20 sites spread fairly evenly through this 91-m (300-ft) range. Two of the forts involved, Whit Tor, 465·4 m (1,527 ft), and Shoulsbarrow, 457·2 m (1,500 ft), are in Devon. The remainder are in Wales and the Marcher region: they include the two Caer Caradocs in Shropshire, one near Clun and the other near Church Stretton, at 396·2 m (1,300 ft) and 459 m (1,506 ft) respectively. They also include another 2 of the 6 Clwydian forts, Moel Arthur (Flint.), 455·3 m (1,494 ft), and Pen-y-cloddiau (Flint) 439·5 m (1,442 ft), in addition to the one

Fig.14 (map)
Pls.12,13,25;
Figs.31,71
Pl.4

Pl.30

mentioned already, Foel Fenlli. The Welsh sites are mostly in the eastern part of the country. The only sites involved in the west are Castell Rhyfel, mentioned already, and Tre'r Ceiri (Caer.) which rises at its highest to 484·9 m (1,591 ft).

The sites mentioned above account for the highest situations in which Iron Age forts occur. Bracketed between them and sea-level are all the remaining sites in England and Wales, at elevations varying according to the different regions. Quite clearly a much greater range of elevations is available in the north and west than in the south and east where the highest point of the chalk is below 305 m (1,000 ft). On the other hand, in the south and east sites occur at every level, from sea-level to the highest point of the chalk, Walbury (Berks), 297 m (975 ft), which is occupied by an Iron Age fort. In the north and west the highest site of all, Ingleborough, is still well below the level of the highest elevations in Wales.

Figs.12,13(maps)

In Wessex and the south-east, there are about a dozen sites above the 244-m (800-ft) contour and a rather larger number below the 122 m (400 ft), but the bulk of the 200 or so sites in the area fall somewhere between the two. The higher sites, apart from Walbury (Berks) include Liddington Castle (Wilts.),

Fig.69;Pl.52
Fig.52;Pl.29

277·3 m (910 ft), Pilsdon Pen (Dorset), 277 m (909 ft), Uffington Castle (Berks), 260·9 m (856 ft), Beacon Hill (Hants), 261·5 m (858 ft), and Ditchling Beacon (Sussex), 247·8 m (813 ft).

Fig.15 (map)
Fig.77

To the north-west, in the Cotswold region, the highest point of the limestone (Cleeve Cloud, 330·1 m: 1,083 ft) is about 30 m (100 ft) above the highest part of the chalk (297·2 m: 975 ft), and some of this difference is reflected in the general range of heights. The region includes some low-lying sites, but it also includes at least 12 sites situated above the 274-m (900-ft) contour and a considerable group in the 122-m (400-ft) zone between the latter and 152 m (500 ft). The higher forts include Bredon Hill (Worcs), 289·5 m (950 ft), and

Fig.114

Leckhampton, 294·7 m (967 ft), High Brotheridge, 282·5 m (927 ft), and Nottingham Hill, 278·9 m (915 ft), all in Gloucestershire.

Fig.43a

The south-west region includes 2 of the elevated sites mentioned earlier (Whit Tor, 465·4 m: 1,527 ft, and Shoulsbarrow, 457·2 m: 1,500 ft), but very few others above the 305-m (1,000-ft) contour. There are about 12 such out of a total of over 300 sites in the south-west as a whole. They include Dowsborough (Som.), 333·1 m (1,093 ft), Stowe's Pound (Corn.) 381 m (1,250 ft), and Cranbrook Castle (Devon) 320 m (1,050 ft). In the south-west generally, however, Iron Age forts are peripheral to the higher areas (the moorlands), so that most sites are found at lower elevations. In the eastern part of the region there are

Fig.14(map)

Fig.30a

sites at heights generally similar to those in Wessex, such as Hembury, 269·7 m: 885 ft, for example, but in the western part the general run of sites is considerably lower. While there are sites standing above 213 m (700 ft)—Carn Brea, 224·9 m: 738 ft, Castle-an-Dinas, 233·1 m: 765 ft—the majority of sites are situated between 61 and 122 m (200 and 400 ft) above sea-level.

Pl.7

Figs.16,17

In Wales and the Marches there is a range of elevations from sea-level to 545·6 m (1,790 ft) at Abdon Burf. The region includes nearly all of the higher sites mentioned earlier. There are, in fact, about 100 sites above the 305-m (1,000-ft) contour and another 50 or 60 between 244 and 305 m (800 and 1,000 ft). These represent roughly a quarter of all the sites in the region: about 650. There is another considerable group situated between the 152- and 244-m (500- and 800-ft) contours. In the Marches and north Wales elevations are generally higher than in south and west Wales where sites above 152 and 183 m (500 or 600 ft) are comparatively few.

The many different situations in which Iron Age forts occur can now be considered in more detail, on the lines indicated earlier.

GROUP I: HILL-TOP SITUATIONS

Group I includes all those sites which can, broadly speaking, be said to occupy the tops of hills and which thus receive some protection on all sides from sloping ground. The defences of such sites follow the main trend of the contours although the two do not always coincide. Sites in which only part of the summit is enclosed belong to groups which will be considered later.

In certain Group I situations an appreciable portion of the site is defended by cliffs or very steep slopes which need no further fortification. Complementary to these are man-made defences which follow the contours on the less steep sides. One of the most striking examples of this type of situation is The Breiddin (Montg.). On the north, north-west, and west it is defended by cliffs and very steep slopes which form a natural barrier more than 183 m (600 ft) high. Viewed from the north-west where it appears to rise sheer from the plain it could well be a natural stronghold. On the southern and south-eastern sides, however, the slopes are much less steep and supplement a system of wide-spaced ramparts. Between them the natural and man-made defences define a hilltop situation. A similar pattern can be seen at Earl's Hill (Salop), where the north-eastern sides of both the main enclosure and the annexe are defended by natural slopes falling some 122 m (400 ft) to the river below. Other sites which appear to conform to this pattern are Pen-y-Gaer and Conway Mountain (Caer.) and Dinas Bran (Denb.). In southern England the geological conditions which give rise to such situations are less common, but the huge site at Bindon above Lulworth Cove (Dorset) appears to belong to this category, as do Ditchling Beacon (Sussex) and Cley Hill (Wilts.).

At Coxall Knoll (Here.) most of the southern defences, standing above the steepest slopes, consist of a scarp and ledge, quite clearly the remains of comparatively slight defences. On the north side the slopes are much less steep and the defences are correspondingly stronger, consisting of three banks and two ditches defending the main enclosure, with a wide-spaced arrangement elsewhere. There is a similar marked difference in the man-made defences at Hod Hill (Dorset). The western defences, standing above the steep slopes to the River Stour, consist of a simple bank and ditch. On the north, east, and south the natural slopes are much less steep and the man-made defences are again stronger, consisting for the most part of two banks, two ditches, and a counter-scarp bank. Other examples of the same sort of situation occur at Poundbury (Dorset), Croft Ambrey and Capler Camp (Here.), and Bury Ditches and Burrow Camp (Salop).

Fig.105

Fig.20

Pl.1
Fig.104

Fig.21a
Pl.23

Fig.86

56

Fig.20. Pen-y-
Gaer,
Caernarvonshire.

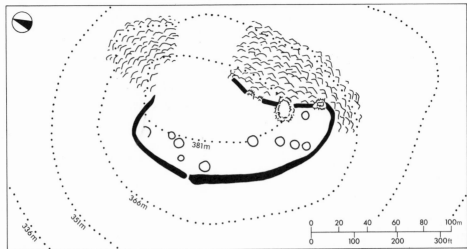

In most hilltop situations some variation from the strict contour principle is involved, leaving true contour forts as a comparatively small group. For this reason it is not proposed to interpret the term contour fort too strictly. Any hilltop site in which the greater part of the defences follows the trend of the contours fairly closely will be termed a contour fort, without further qualification.

Fig.21b

An excellent example of a contour fort is provided by Sidbury (Devon). Its shape, that of an elongated pear, is almost exactly that of the 183-m (600-ft) contour above which the defences stand. The ground falls steeply to the 152-m (500-ft) contour and less steeply to the 122-m (400-ft) contour on all sides except the north-west, where there is a narrow saddle about 30 m (100 ft) below the fort. This sort of feature is fairly common with any hill forming part of a larger range. At Credenhill (Here.), enclosing 20 ha (49 acres), the ramparts follow the 183-m (600-ft) and 190-m (625-ft) contours fairly closely, so that the shape of the hill is reflected in the plan of the site. The interior is domed, rising to 219.4 m (720 ft) near the southern end. Externally the ground falls steeply for over 61 m (200 ft) except at the northern end where the slopes are somewhat less steep. Unlike Sidbury, which has a saddle to the north-west, Credenhill is an isolated hill. At Gadbury Bank (Worcs.) the ramparts are in the region of the 46-m (150-ft) contour and the interior is domed. Externally the ground falls only to the region of the 30-m (100-ft) contour and the slopes are not particularly steep, but the site is nevertheless a true contour fort. In Yorkshire, Almondbury derives its regular oval plan from the shape of the hill on which it stands. The outer defences, situated well beyond the inner rampart, also follow the lower contours of the hill closely. Other sites in the contour category include Ivinghoe Beacon (Bucks), The Trundle (Sussex), Cefn-y-Castell (Montg.), Cadsonbury (Corn.), and Bryn Dinas (Denb.). There are, of course, many other examples of contour siting which cannot be dealt with here.

Fig.22

Adherence to the contours, however strict, does not necessarily guarantee any

57

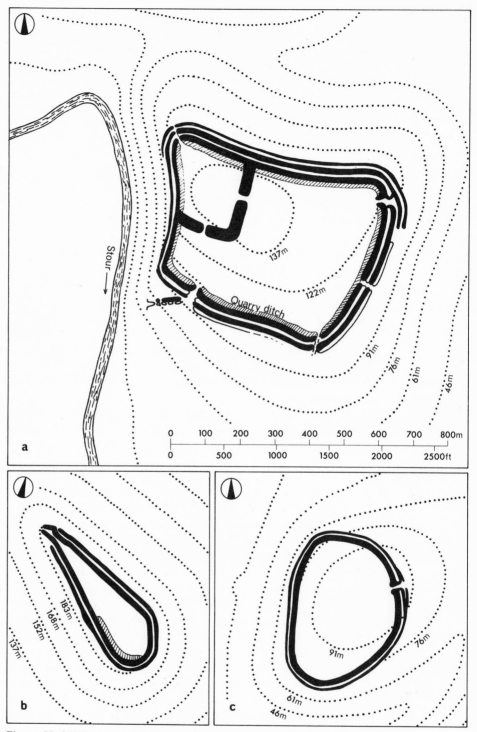

Fig.21a Hod Hill, Dorset; 21b Sidbury, Devon; 21c St. Catherine's Hill, Hampshire.

Fig.84
Pl.43

marked degree of elevation above the surrounding territory. At Badbury Rings (Dorset) the multivallate defences of three banks and three ditches follow the contours defining the lower slopes of a knoll fairly closely, but the outermost bank and ditch still face more or less level ground in all directions. These outer features are probably later additions, so that the inner defences, and particularly the inner bank and ditch which may be earlier again than the middle bank and ditch, would have enjoyed some command over their surroundings. This could never have been very great, however, and this may explain the strength of the man-made defences. In Hampshire, Dunwood and Tatchbury occupy the summits of low hills which stand only about 9 m (30 ft) above the level of the surrounding terrain. In spite of their low elevation, however, these sites quite clearly belong in Group I.

In most of the sites just considered the hills involved were generally round-topped, so that the interiors, to a greater or lesser degree, were domed. In a number of cases, however, the geological conditions are such that the hills are, or at least now appear to be, flat-topped, so that there is a clearly defined shoulder which more or less dictates where the ramparts are to be situated.

One of the best examples of a contour site on a flat-topped hill is Solsbury Hill (Som.). The interior is quite flat, although the accumulation of material behind the rampart may have contributed to this appearance to some extent. Externally the sides of the hill slope down steeply for about 91 m (300 ft). The shape of the hill is such that there is only one practicable place for the ramparts. Since the flat top of the hill is in the horizontal plane the result of placing the ramparts on the shoulder is a contour-site. The site stands about 183 m (600 ft) above sea-level.

At a much lower level in relation to its surroundings is Sutton Walls (Here.), where the ramparts follow the 100-m (330-ft) contour very closely. The interior is now quite flat. The sides of the hill slope down for about 9 m (30 ft) and then the ground more or less levels off. Ham Hill (Som.) is another flat-topped hill, in this case on an enormous scale, covering some 85 ha (210 acres). The ramparts, some 5 km (3 miles) in length, stand above the 107-m (350-ft) contour and the hill rises to about 46 m (150 ft) above its surroundings.

In addition to such sites there are others in which the flat top is tipped over in one direction so that the defences, placed on the shoulder of the hill, cannot follow a single contour and the sites cannot be strictly described as true contour sites, although the nature of their siting is the same as those already described.

A classic example of this type of situation is Bwrdd Arthur (Anglesey). The summit, 6·8 ha (17 acres) in area, is absolutely flat but slopes down from south to north. The enclosure is surrounded by a wall of limestone blocks which follows the clearly defined shoulder of the hill. Beyond the rampart there are good
Fig.76
Pls.3,14;Fig.91
natural slopes in all directions. Other less striking examples are Eddisbury (Ches.), Old Oswestry (Salop), and Madmarston (Oxon.). In all three the enclosed area is markedly flat, but in each case it is tipped over in one direction with the ramparts following the shoulder rather than the contours.

There are sites which appear to be tipped over in one direction for other than
Fig.21c
geological reasons. An excellent example is provided by St. Catherine's Hill

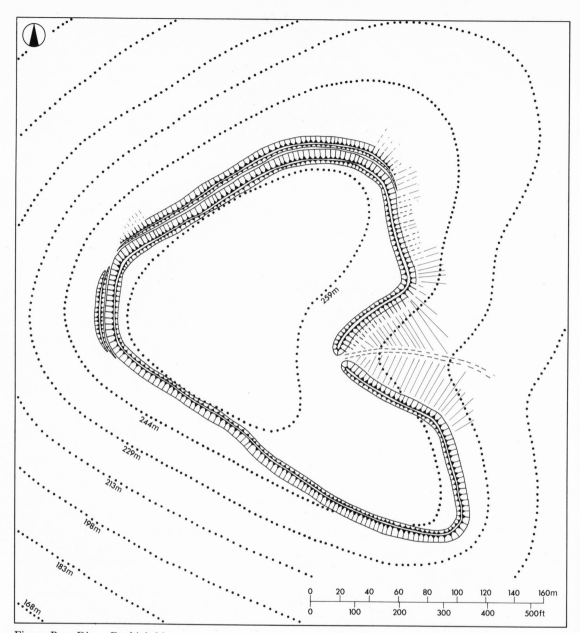

Fig. 22. Bryn Dinas, Denbighshire.

(Hants). The situation is a round-topped hill rising to 99·9 m (328 ft) and standing some 61 m (200 ft) above its surroundings to the west, north-west, and south-west. On the east and north-east, however, it is connected to the adjacent hill by a saddle which is only about 23 m (75 ft) below the summit. Had the ramparts been placed so as to follow the contours absolutely the result would have been to leave the north-eastern and eastern defences with little or no elevation above the ground in front. By tipping the whole site over it was possible to provide a good supplementary slope below this section of the defences without materially affecting the strength of the remainder.

Fig.54

There is a generally similar saddle to the east of Foel Fenlli (Denb.). To make maximum use of the slope the multivallate defences are placed high on the side of the saddle, just taking in the highest point of the hill. The defences at this, the eastern end of the site, are at a considerably higher level than those at the western end. The position of the ramparts in the western half of the site is dictated, however, by the shoulder of the hill, which is fairly sharply defined. Towards the eastern end the shoulder is less clear-cut and the defences swing diagonally up the slope to take in the highest point of the hill, overlooking the saddle which links it to the adjacent hill.

This survey of Group I situations can be concluded by considering one or two hilltop sites in which the contours are ignored, if only for a short distance, in ways other than those outlined above. Quarley Hill (Hants), for example, is situated in a hilltop position, but does not fully occupy the summit. On the south, south-east, and north-west the bank, ditch, and counterscarp bank follow the contours closely, but on the west and north-east they swing away, leaving the triangular ends of the hill outside the defences. This was done, presumably, to restrict the enclosure to a given size. To have followed the contour principle would have involved the construction of an additional 366 m (1,200 ft) of bank, ditch, and counterscarp bank.

Fig.23a

At Woodbury (Worcs) the univallate defences follow the contours fairly closely on three sides. On the fourth side the contours swing in, narrowing the hill to an hour-glass shape. The defences, however, ignore this and instead sweep down into the coomb thus formed and up out of the other side to resume their position on the contour. Strict adherence to the contours would have produced a stronger, if smaller, enclosure. Presumably it was felt that the reduction in tactical strength was compensated for by the increased space available for the function of the fort.

Fig.23b

The last site to be considered in Group I occupies two hills, Midsummer Hill and Hollybush Hill (Here.). The univallate defences follow the main trend of the contours on the western half of Midsummer Hill. They do not, however, run around the eastern half of the hill to enclose the summit in the normal contour manner. Instead, the defences run down the eastern slopes of the hill into the saddle between it and Hollybush Hill and then take up a line approximately on the 229-m (750-ft) contour which defines the latter on three sides. The defences on the western side of Midsummer Hill stand, at their highest, on the 274-m (900-ft) contour.

The number of sites covered by Group I is difficult to estimate but it is

Fig.23a
Woodbury,
Worcestershire;
23b Midsummer
Hill,
Herefordshire.

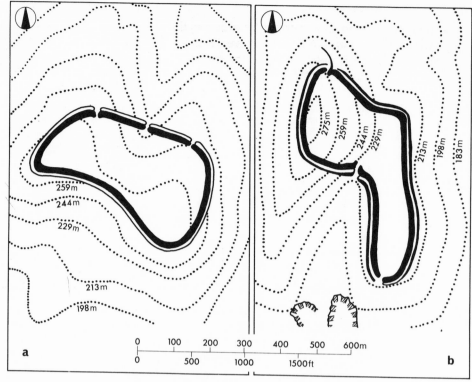

probably in the region of 500, or rather less than 40 per cent of the total of all Iron Age forts.

GROUP II: PROMONTORY AND SEMI-CONTOUR SITUATIONS

Group II includes all those sites in which there is an easy, or relatively easy, approach on one side, the other three sides being defended either completely or in part by nature. The natural defences range from sheer cliffs to slopes which afford only slight supplementary support to man-made ramparts. The defences facing the easy approach form a more or less straight line.

In many Group II situations the natural defences are such that they provide complete security on three sides. Man-made defences are required only on the fourth, approach, side. This, of course, is the pattern of a promontory fort. It will be clear that the conditions which give rise to such sites occur frequently in coastal regions, but it should be made equally clear that by no means all promontory forts are on the coast: they occur in almost equal numbers inland. The geological structure of southern Britain is such that conditions suitable for coastal promontory forts occur mainly on the western side of the region. In fact, the bulk of them are found in only two counties, Cornwall and Pembrokeshire,

62

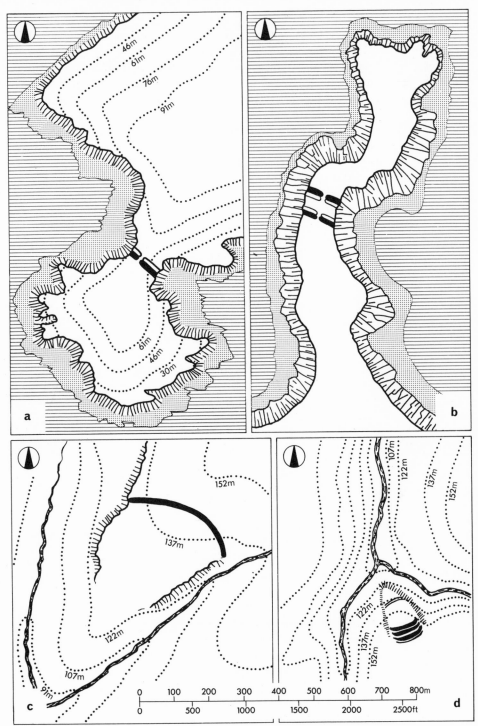

Fig.24a Rame Head, Cornwall; 24b Porth Dinllaen, Caernarvonshire;
24c Philpots Camp, Sussex; 24d Caer Blaen Minog, Carmarthenshire.

with smaller numbers in Caernarvonshire, Anglesey, Glamorgan, and Devon. There are very few coastal promontory forts outside these regions.

Fig.24a

In a number of Group II coastal sites the plan is almost that of an island. Rame Head (Corn.), for example, is connected to the mainland by a causeway, across the narrowest part of which a single bank and ditch, with great economy, converts the site into a fortress. The approach to the defences is downhill; beyond them the enclosed area takes the form of a cone-shaped hill with fairly even slopes down to the water's edge on all sides. In this case, at least, the term promontory fort is not entirely appropriate and the term pseudo-island may be suggested. A generally similar pattern obtains at Rumps Point (Corn.). Again, the approach is downhill, in this case to multivallate defences. Beyond them the whole site broadens out and the ground rises, although less steeply than at Rame Head.

In many of the remaining Group II coastal promontory forts the approach to the defences is quite level, so that whatever the height of the promontory above the sea the man-made defences have no elevations above their landward surroundings and in this sense are virtually low-lying. The advantages of the sites arise, as it were, out of their plan rather than their elevation, and on this basis they may be compared with some of the low-lying sites in Group VII.

Fig.24b

Porth-Dinllaen (Caer.) stands on a promontory which projects northwards from the main line of the coast for about 1 km ($\frac{2}{3}$ mile). The defences are situated about 457 m (1,500 ft) from the outer end, cutting off an area of about 6 ha (14 acres). The approach to the site, along the inner part of the promontory, is flat. The multivallate defences are situated on a slight slope, so that the interior of the fort is at a slightly higher level than the approach, in the form of a step. At Twyn-y-Parc (Anglesey) the defences are situated at the root of the promontory where it joins the main land mass, so that they face an approach extending through 180°. The promontory is about 427 m (1,400 ft) long and between 91 and 122 m (300 and 400 ft) wide. The defences are multivallate and the area enclosed is about 3 ha (8 acres).

At Wooltack Point (Pemb.) three sides, north, west, and south, are defended by cliffs. The univallate defences, facing east, are supplemented by a natural gully which runs north–south across the neck of the promontory and fills the function of an enormous ditch, with the man-made defences for the most part standing high on its western edge. The much smaller site at Linney Head is more typical of the Pembrokeshire coastal forts. The multivallate defences, 2 banks and 2 ditches with a 6-m (20-ft) space between, defend an area of about 40 ares (1 acre) standing some 61 m (200 ft) above sea-level, with a more or less level approach from the north. The site at Dinas Mawr is even smaller with a usable area of only about 24 × 27 m (80 × 90 ft); the multivallate defences face squarely uphill. The crest of the inner bank is level with the outer edge of its ditch and about 3 m (10 ft) below the crest of the outer bank which is some 21 m (70 ft) beyond.

Fig.25

The defences at Trereen Dinas (Corn.) also face uphill. The inner rampart of its multivallate system is some 6 m (20 ft) lower than the outermost ditch. The promontory is triangular in cross-section. Its western side is steep and rocky and of no practical use; its eastern side is only slightly less steep but provides the only

Fig.25. Linney
Head,
Pembrokeshire.

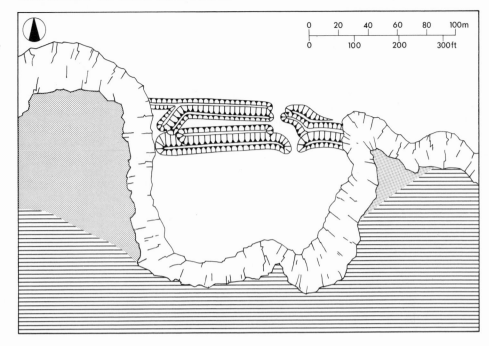

usable area. The defences are at the root of the promontory, which projects some 335 m (1,100 ft) northwards from the coast and rises to about 61 m (200 ft). The over-all area is about 4 ha (9 acres).

Dodman Point (Corn.) is a large promontory fort enclosing about 22 ha (55 acres). It stands about 107 m (350 ft) above the level of the sea below. The defences, a bank, ditch, and counterscarp bank, stand above sloping ground so that the site has the advantage of both promontory and contour siting. At Red-cliff Castle in the same county the area enclosed is only 54·8 m (180 ft) long and 21·3 m (70 ft) wide, although this is probably the result of erosion. The more or less level approach is defended by a compact arrangement of 2 banks and 2 rock-cut ditches.

As mentioned earlier, promontory forts are not confined to the coast: there are many in inland areas. Philpots Camp (Sussex) makes use of a triangular promontory defined by the junction of two rivers. The western and south-eastern sides are defended by low cliffs which are set back some distance from the rivers. The third side which faces more or less level ground to the north-east is defended by a single bank and ditch. The area enclosed is about 6 ha (15 acres). In the case of Castell Pyr (Carm.) the rivers, the Teifi and a small tributary, are immediately at the foot of the promontory slopes. The approach to the site, and the interior, slope downwards towards the promontory end. The defences are multivallate, having 2 banks and 2 ditches, and the area enclosed is about 40 ares (1 acre). Caer Blaen Minog in the same county, defended by 3 banks and 3 ditches, is in a similar situation.

The promontory fort at Bishopston (Glam.) is defined by a U-shaped bend

Fig.24c

Fig.73

Fig.24d

Fig.26a

65

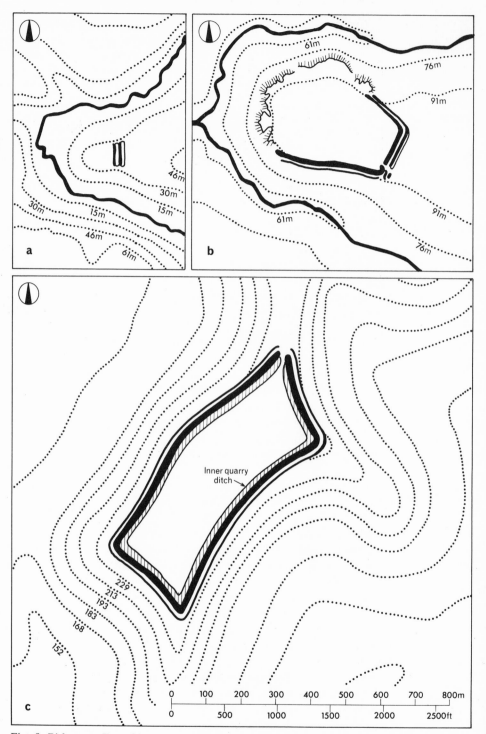

Fig.26a Bishopston Fort, Glamorgan; 26b High Rocks, Sussex; 26c Uley Bury, Gloucestershire.

Fig.27

in the Bishopston stream, which isolates a small promontory about 30 m (100 ft) above the water-level. The site faces rising ground to the east and is defended by 2 banks and 2 ditches. The area enclosed is only 10 ares ($\frac{1}{4}$ acre) and is about 37 m (120 ft) long and 30 m (100 ft) wide. Caerbre (Salop) is likewise situated in a U-shaped river bend. Symond's Yat and Spital Meend (both Glos) are associated with very big loops of the River Wye which define large oval areas. The neck of each loop is occupied by a defended promontory which prevents any access from the landward side.

Fig.28
Pl.10

Crickley Hill Camp (Glos) is situated on a promontory which projects westwards from the main Cotswold range. It is roughly triangular in plan with a limestone cliff on the south-west side, a steep slope on the north and a level approach from the east. It is defended by a single bank and ditch and the area enclosed is about 2·4 ha (6 acres). Within the enclosure there are the remains of another, much slighter bank, cutting off a smaller part of the promontory, presumably the remains of an earlier promontory fort. Little Down Camp (Som.) occupies the end of a westward projection of Lansdown Hill. The ground falls very steeply on the north-western and south-western sides. It is defended on the east by a curving bank and ditch which face rising ground. Other Group II inland promontory forts which can only be mentioned here are Combs Moss (Derby.), Carl Wark (Yorks), Bosherston (Pemb), and Henllan (Card.).

Pl.37;Fig.87

In a number of Group II sites the natural defences are surmounted by man-made defences of a minor character compared with those defending the approach side. These lesser defences often take the form of scarping. The site at Bodbury (Salop) stands at the end of a steep-sided spur projecting into Cardingmill Valley. On the approach side, facing level ground, it is defended by a single bank and ditch of modest dimensions. On the other three sides the upper 3 m (10 ft) or so of the natural slope has been scarped to produce a steeper slope, with a ledge about 1 m (4 ft) wide at the foot. The same sort of arrangement is found at Hafod Camp (Carm.). The site is roughly triangular with a substantial bank and ditch facing north-west, and scarped slopes on the eastern and south-western sides. The area enclosed is about 50 ares ($1\frac{1}{4}$ acres).

Fig.29

Fig.117

Fig.60

Bury Walls (Salop) is a Group II site in which the minor defences take the form of a single bank. On the approach side, from the north, the site is defended by two massive banks and ditches, but around the promontory edge there is only a small bank, 3–4 m (10–15 ft) wide, standing at the head of the steep natural slope. The material for this bank is presumably derived from an inner quarry ditch, although there is now no surface indication of this. The area enclosed is about 8 ha (21 acres). Other sites in which the minor defences take more or less the same form are Lydney Park (Glos), where the derivation of the material from the interior was confirmed by excavation, Okehampton (Devon), and Craig-y-Dinas (Caer.), situated in a U-bend of a river with multivallate defences on the approach side.

In a large number of sites in Group II the slopes are reduced to the point where full-scale man-made defences are necessary. Since the defences follow the contours on three sides they may be termed semi-contour sites. The approach is on a front which corresponds more or less to the width of the site. There are

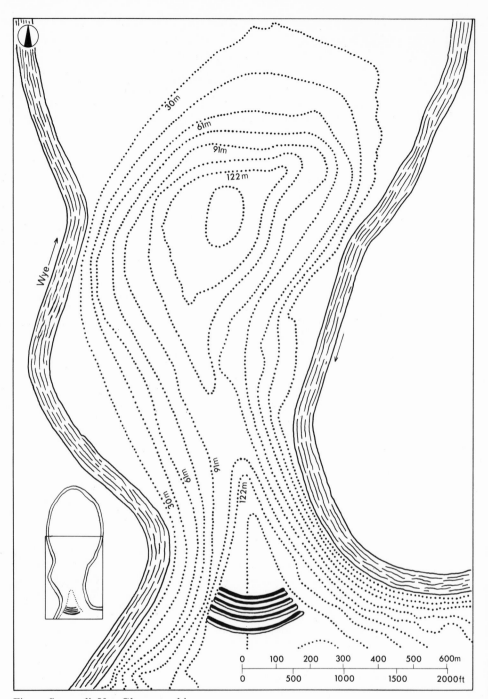

Fig.27. Symond's Yat, Gloucestershire.

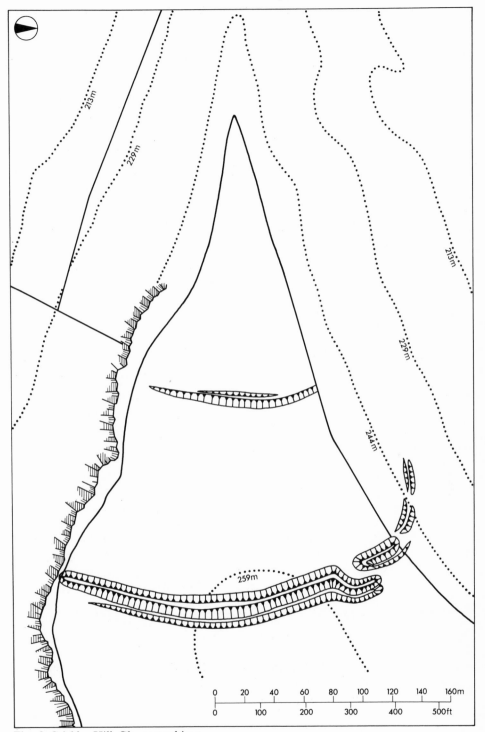

Fig.28. Crickley Hill, Gloucestershire.

Fig.29. Bodbury
Ring, Shropshire.

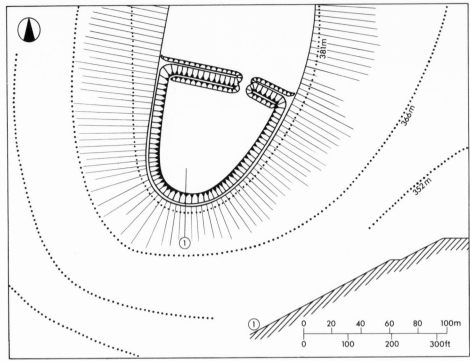

however, certain sites in which the approach is very much narrower and which come very close to being contour sites.

Fig.26c
Pl.11

At Uley Bury (Glos), for example, the ground falls away on all sides except for a very short section on the north where there is a narrow neck of land at the same level as the fort, linking it to the adjacent plateau. To describe such sites the term pseudo-contour can be used. Similar situations exist at Rawlsbury (Dorset) and Old Sarum (Wilts.). At Wall Hills, Ledbury (Here.), the defences

Pl.40

follow the contours closely to the north, east, south, and south-west. Only on the north-west is the contour principle ignored. There a narrow neck of ground, defined by the 122-m (400-ft) contour, stands at the same level as the enclosure

Fig.66

and provides easy access to it. Mam Tor (Derby.) also belongs to the pseudo-

Pl.2

contour group. The eastern and north-western slopes converge to define a ridge running generally north-east, which provides a relatively easy approach to the site.

Fig.30a

Apart from pseudo-contour sites, the remaining Group II sites conform more or less to the pattern illustrated. Semi-contour sites, in fact, account for a very

Pls.36,20,24;

large number of Iron Age forts. In southern England they include Hembury

Figs.43e,30b,c

(Devon), Dolebury (Som.), Pilsdon Pen and Hambledon (Dorset), Battlesbury

Figs.119,63

and Martinsell (Wilts.), Buckland Rings and Old Winchester Hill (Hants), the

Figs.58,44a

Devil's Dyke (Sussex), Squerryes Park (Kent), Caesar's Camp (Berks), and

Pl.9;Fig.62

many others. In the counties outside southern England they include Kimsbury

Pl.25;Figs.81,50,31

(Glos), Wapley and Ivington Camps (Here.), Caer Caradoc, Clun (Salop),

70

Bury Bank and Berry Ring (Staffs), Borough Hill (Northants), and Borough Hill (Leics.).

In many semi-contour forts the existence of an easy approach on one side is indicated by larger or more complex defences than elsewhere on the site. At Hembury (Devon), for example, the defences on the north side, facing the level approach, consist of three banks and three ditches. At Pilsdon Pen (Dorset) there is a similar indication of an easy approach, again from the north, in the form of multivallate defences more complex than elsewhere on the site.

The multivallate semi-contour site at Dolebury stands at the western end of a long ridge with a level approach from the east. Immediately inside the eastern defences, however, the ground falls to the west and the whole site is tipped over in this direction, with a difference of some 30 m (100 ft) in the elevation of the eastern and western defences. The position of the northern, southern and western defences is dictated by the shape of the ridge, and that of the eastern defences by the need to provide an unobstructed view to the east along the ridge. Similar situations exist at Squerryes Park (Kent) and Boddington Hill (Bucks).

Although the level approach in Group II situations frequently produces multivallate defences, this is by no means universal. Martinsell (Wilts.), for example, occupies the eastern half of a large flat-topped hill. On three sides the univallate defences follow the contours; on the fourth, western, side, however, they cut squarely across the top of the hill facing level ground to the west. In spite of this the western defences are still only univallate. At the Devil's Dyke (Sussex) the western, univallate defences also face more or less level ground, but in this case they are more massive than the rest of the defences. States House (Bucks) also belongs to this category: as at Dolebury the whole site is tipped down towards the end of the spur.

Multivallate defences in a semi-contour situation appear in striking form at Hambledon Hill (Dorset), which projects north-west from the main mass of the Dorset downland. The ground falls on all sides except the south-east, where there is a slightly downhill approach on a front about 122 m (400 ft) wide. The ease of this approach is reflected in the strength of the defences, which occupy some 122 m (400 ft) from front to back and consist of an inner bank, ditch, and counterscarp bank with an outer system of 2 banks and 2 ditches about 37 m (120 ft) beyond. Other Group II sites in southern England with multivallate defences on the approach side include Abbotsbury (Dorset) and Battlesbury (Wilts.).

In Herefordshire Ivington Camp has an easy approach from the east on a front some 213 m (700 ft) wide, where it is defended by inner and outer banks with accompanying ditches. Beyond these defences the site broadens out to form a roughly L-shaped enclosure with the defences, basically bank, ditch, and counterscarp bank, following the contours very closely. The inner enclosure takes advantage of the contours on only two sides and faces level ground on the two remaining sides; in this respect it belongs to Group III.

In Shropshire at Caer Caradoc, Clun, the western defences cut squarely across the top of the hill and face level ground. They are in consequence more

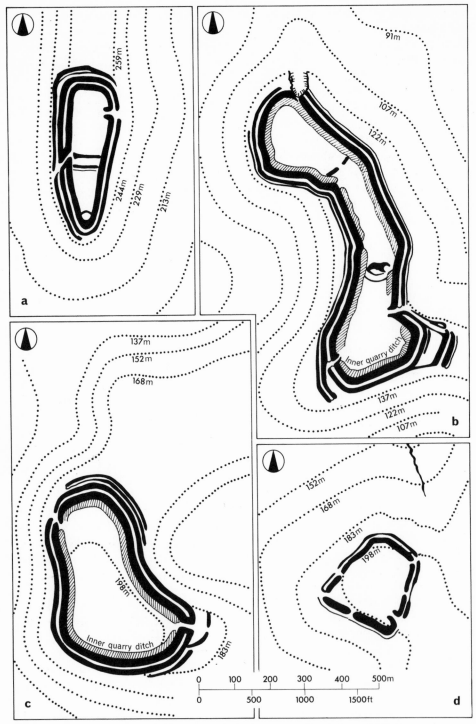

Fig.30a Hembury, Devon; 30b Hambledon Hill, Dorset; 30c Battlesbury, Wiltshire;
30d Borough Hill, Leicestershire.

complex than elsewhere on the site and consist of a bank, ditch, and counterscarp bank, another bank and ditch immediately beyond, and a third bank, ditch, and counterscarp bank separated from the others by a space about 12 m (40 ft) wide. The total depth of this sytem from front to back is about 85 m (280 ft).

In north Wales Pen-y-cloddiau is probably to be included in this category. The complex northern defences swing across the contours, just taking in the highest point of the hill. Although they stand on a slope they actually face level ground immediately outside the outermost ditch.

Fig.26b

A number of sites in Group II have what may be termed mixed characteristics. At High Rocks (Sussex) part of the site is defended by cliffs, giving it a promontory aspect, and part by slopes supplementing man-made defences, giving it a semi-contour aspect. Caesar's Camp (Surrey) and Piercefield Great Camp (Mon.) likewise display mixed characteristics and fall somewhere between the promontory and semi-contour categories.

Group II accounts for probably between 400 and 450 sites, between 30 and 35 per cent of the total.

GROUP III: PROMONTORY AND SEMI-CONTOUR SITUATIONS

In Group III situations the approach to the site is on a front which accounts for roughly half the total circuit. There is, of course, no sharp line between Groups II and III, and in certain cases it is difficult to decide in which group a site should be placed. However, an excellent example of a Group III situation is provided by Warton Crag (Lancs). On the south and west it is defended by a combination of rock scarps and steep slopes, and on the north and east by three ramparts without ditches, spaced out at roughly 61-m (200-ft) intervals. For the most part the outer rampart faces level or near-level ground. It will be clear from this site alone on what a wide front such forts can be approached as compared with the promontory forts of Group II.

Fig.114

Bredon Hill (Worcs) also belongs to the Group III promontory type. It is defended on the north and west by very steep natural slopes falling in all some 213 m (700 ft) to the plain below. On the two remaining sides it is defended by a wide-spaced multivallate system. Beyond the outer defences the ground slopes away gently to the south and east with the defences following the trend of the contours, so that to this extent the site has a contour aspect. The dominant aspect is not in doubt, however, and the location of the site was quite clearly

Fig.65

dictated by the natural slopes on the north and west. At Kinver Edge (Staffs) the defences consist of a single bank and ditch defending the south-eastern and south-western sides, with natural defences on the two remaining sides. The flat top of the hill is tipped over north-west to south-east, so that the south-western defences run downhill while the south-eastern defences follow the general line of the contours and stand at the head of an appreciable slope.

In Caernarvonshire Pen-y-Gaer, Llanbedrog, stands at the edge of level ground on the east of a steep-sided valley; it is defended on the west and south

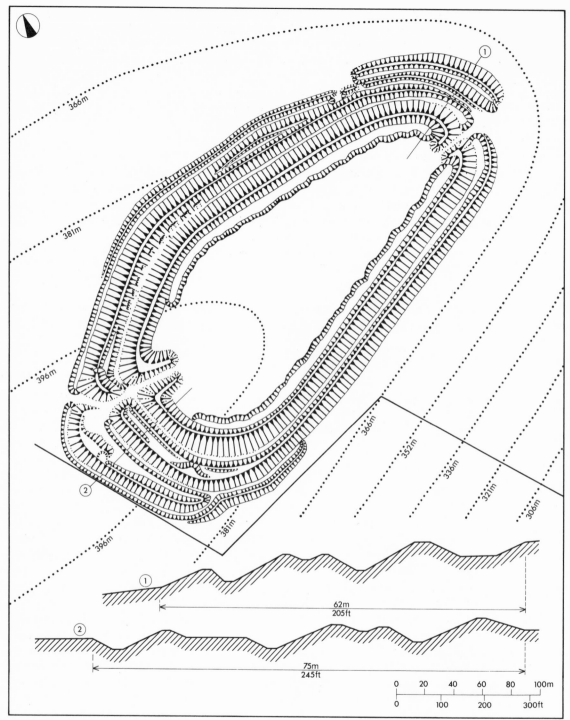

Fig.31. Caer Caradoc (Clun), Shropshire.

Fig.32. Maiden
Castle, Cheshire.

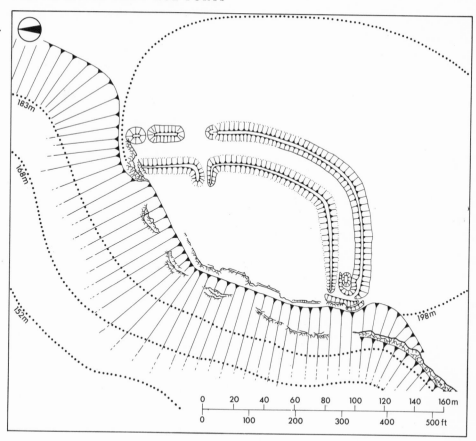

by steep cliffs. On the other two sides, the east and north-east, a system of three
banks cuts off an area about 76 m (250 ft) from north to south and about 61 m
(200 ft) from east to west. Other sites of the Group III promontory type are
Maiden Castle and Helsby (Ches.), Fin Cop (Derby.), Leckhampton (Glos),
and Llandewi Gaer and Great Treffgarne Rocks in Pembrokeshire.

Figs.32,70
Figs.82,33a
Fig.33b

Holmbury (Surrey) is a Group III site which is defended on the west and
north by ramparts and on the south and east by natural slopes augmented by
scarping. The western defences face level ground while those on the north run
downhill, west to east, dropping down a pronounced step in the ground-level
which runs north–south at right angles to the rampart.

In the largest category of sites in Group III the sloping sides, while still useful
as a defensive feature, are not sufficiently strong to stand alone. They are surmounted by conventional, man-made defences comparable with the defences
facing the easy approach on the other two sides, although the two are not
always of equal strength. They are the Group III version of the semi-contour
site.

The unfinished site of Ladle Hill (Hants) is a good example of this type of
situation. On the north and west the defences are supported by natural slopes

75

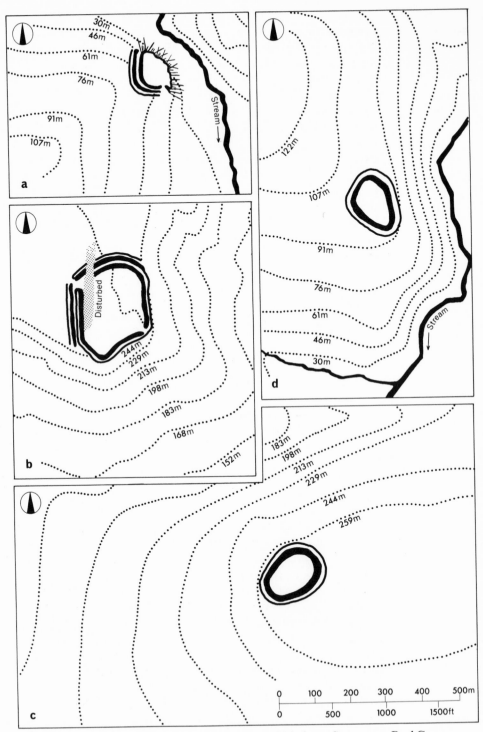

Fig.33a Great Treffgarne Rocks, Pembrokeshire; 33b Holmbury, Surrey; 33c Roel Camp, Gloucestershire; 33d Dunmere Camp, Cornwall.

Fig.114

but on the other two sides the approach is comparatively easy. In fact, as at Bredon Hill, there is a slight contour aspect, the southern and eastern ramparts following the gentle contours on these sides. As at Bredon Hill, however, the dominant aspect is not in doubt and the site is quite clearly a Group III semi-contour fort.

Fig.141

Llanmelin (Mon.) and Boro Wood (Corn.) fall somewhere between Group II and Group III in plan view. Llanmelin stands at the western end of a triangular tongue of land which falls between 30 and 46 m (100 and 150 ft) on the north-western and south-western sides. On the other sides (north-east, east, and south-east) the approach is more or less level. The annexe, a complex of earthworks blocking direct approach to the entrance, may, at least in part, be an acknow-ledgement of the easy approach from the east. At Boro Wood, a univallate site, the defences on the north-east and east run at the head of slopes which fall between 61 and 91 m (200 and 300 ft). Along the south-west side the defences and the natural slope diverge so that the site is approachable on most of this side as well as from the west, thus qualifying for inclusion in Group III. In fact, the approach from the west is downhill, the whole site lying on sloping ground with the top of the hill, above the 244-m (800-ft) contour, some distance to the west.

Fig.33d

Dunmere Camp (Corn.) is a more clear-cut example of this type of situation. It is located to the south-east of the summit at a point where the contours broaden out to form a sloping platform or ledge with steeper slopes on two sides. In this case the ledge is defined on the west and south by the 91-m (300-ft) contour, below which the ground falls away for about 61 m (200 ft). Above this contour the ground slopes gently upwards, north-westwards, towards the crest of the hill. A site placed on the crest would have had only very slight slopes all round. By taking advantage of the sloping shoulder good natural defences were gained on two sides at the price of a slightly downhill approach on the two remaining sides.

Pl.34

Two other Group III sites, The Ditches (Salop) and Spettisbury (Dorset), are likewise on sloping ground but so placed that they have a level approach on one side. At Spettisbury the western rampart is placed where the ground begins to fall from the plateau level, so that to the west the ground is level, while to the east, behind the rampart, the interior slopes downhill towards the river. The southern rampart runs squarely across the contours so that approach from this side, although across sloping ground, is comparatively easy. The Ditches is placed at the northern angle of a section of Wenlock Edge. The multivallate defences follow the general line of the contours on the north-western and north-eastern sides where there are good slopes to the valley below. The defences on one of the other sides face level ground externally but have sloping ground im-mediately inside. On the fourth side the defences run downhill, south-east to north-west, but the slope is less than that at Spettisbury and the approach is correspondingly easier.

Fig.33c

An excellent example of a Group III site in which the ground is flat except on the two contour sides is provided by Roel Camp (Glos). It stands at the outer end of a broad, flat-topped spur of the Cotswolds, and utilizes one corner of the spur to supplement its defences on the north and west. On the other two sides the southern and eastern defences face a level approach. There are probably between 80 and 100 forts that occupy Group III situations (6 or 7 per cent of the total).

GROUP IV: RIDGE-TOP SITUATIONS

Like Group III, Group IV embraces sites in which there is an easy or relatively easy approach on two sides. In this case, however, the two sides are opposite and not adjacent to each other, so that the general situation is that of a ridge-top.

Fig. 34c   In some Group IV sites the slopes involved are comparatively slight, so that the ridge-top aspect cannot always be said to be dominant. At Segsbury (Berks), for example, the eastern and western defences face level ground along a ridge which is defined by the 213-m (700 ft) contour. The ground to north and south, however, slopes away only gently and the supplementary support which it provides is of no great significance.

Fig. 143   The same is true at Blackbury Castle (Devon). The ridge on which it stands runs east and west and its top is defined by the 152-m (500-ft) contour. The approach to the eastern and western defences is level and the approach to those on the north and south up only a gentle slope. Both Segsbury and Blackbury quite clearly belong to Group IV, but the slopes defining the ridge are so slight that they can almost be regarded as plateau forts.

Fig. 78   By definition Group IV must include such sites as Walbury (Berks) and Oldbury (Wilts.), being sites which can be approached from two opposite directions. Walbury, standing on the highest point of the chalk in England (297·2 m: 975 ft), is a very large, sub-rectangular site enclosing about 33 ha (82 acres). The ground falls steeply all round except at the diagonally opposite north-western and south-eastern corners where there are narrow necks of land at the same ground-level as the site. This is the Group IV equivalent of the narrow-

Pl. 33   neck pseudo-contour sites of Group II. At Oldbury the approach from one direction, the west, is likewise along a narrow neck of land, but the approach from the north-east is on a much wider front. On the south-eastern and south-western sides the multivallate defences follow the contours, as do the simpler defences, the bank, ditch, and counterscarp bank on the much steeper north-western side.

Pl. 29; Fig. 52   Beacon Hill (Hants) falls somewhere between Group IV and those sites in Group I—Quarley Hill, for example—that do not fully occupy the summit of a hill but that must nevertheless be classed as a hilltop situation. It is approachable from the north-west and the south along what must be classed as ridges, at least in the immediate vicinity of the defences. These, however, are actually long spurs projecting north-west and south respectively from the main part of the hill which it would not have been economical to incorporate in the defences. To this extent Beacon Hill is approachable from two directions in the Group IV manner, but beyond a certain distance from the defences the approach to the ridges themselves is uphill.

Pl. 22; Fig. 34a   Eggardon (Dorset) is situated on a spur about 1 km ($\frac{3}{4}$ mile) long projecting

78

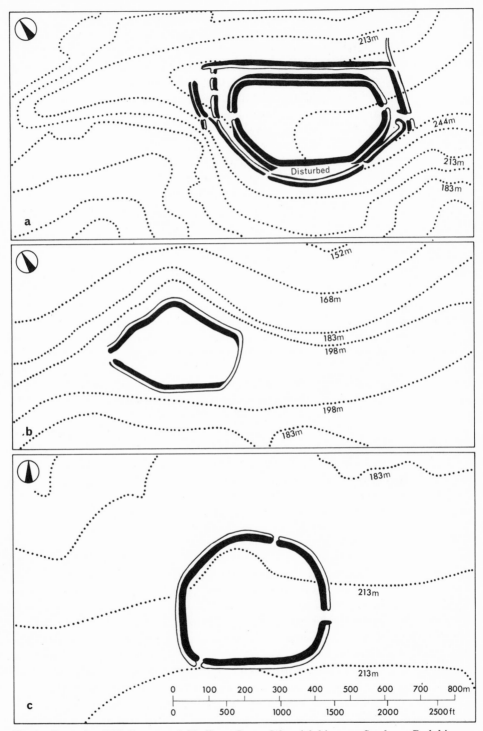

Fig.34a Eggardon Hill, Dorset; 34b Nadbury Camp, Warwickshire; 34c Segsbury, Berkshire.

north-westwards from a block of chalk downland. The enclosure occupies less than half this distance, so that it is approachable from both north-west and south-east. The spur slopes gently downhill from south-east to north-west towards its outer end. Park Hill Camp (Wilts.) occupies a similar position, on a spur projecting south-east from a section of the Wiltshire downland.

Chanctonbury (Sussex) and Chiselbury (Wilts.) are both situated on the northern edges of stretches of chalk downland where the ground drops away steeply, defining one side of the situation. In both cases the other side is provided by the head of a dry valley running in from the south. Both sites occupy knolls on the ridges but the dominant aspects are the easy approaches from directions which are generally opposite.

Fig.34b

Fig.44b

Other ridge-top situations include Lawley (Salop), Craig y Tyddyn (Caer.), Nadbury (War), and a series of sites in Hampshire including Woolbury, Chilworth Ring, Malwood, and Norsebury Ring. The (presumed) first phase at the Herefordshire Beacon also belongs to this group. The full site is of the contour type with the defences following the shape of a long, narrow, and somewhat irregular hill. The smaller enclosure which apparently preceded this occupies a knoll more or less midway along the hill, so that it had much easier approaches on two sides (south and north-east) and thus would qualify for inclusion in Group IV on the same basis as Chiselbury and Chanctonbury.

Group IV situations account for far fewer sites than the groups considered so far and include probably only about 30 sites or 2 per cent of the total.

GROUP V: CLIFF-EDGE AND PLATEAU-EDGE SITUATIONS

Group V covers all those sites in which there is a level, or at least an easy, approach on three sides with natural defences only on the fourth side. These natural defences range from sheer cliffs, in true cliff-edge sites, to slopes which provide only supplementary support for man-made defences in plateau-edge sites.

Sites such as Seaford and Beltout (Sussex) and Flower's Barrow (Dorset) now look like good examples of cliff-edge situations, but their present appearance is due to the erosion of the coast. As originally built they were inland sites of the contour or semi-contour type. Seaford is now triangular in plan with a single bank and ditch on the east and north-west and a steep chalk cliff on the south-west. The man-made defences follow the main trend of the contours and in its original state, prior to the erosion which produced the cliffs, Seaford was probably a contour site. At Flower's Barrow the northern and western defences follow the contours but those on the east cut across the top of the hill in the semi-contour style.

Pl.6

Fig.35a

The site at Boltby Scar (Yorks) is D-shaped in plan with the straight side of the D formed by a sheer cliff on the west. On the north, east, and south it is defended by a bank and ditch which face more or less level ground. The area enclosed is about 1 ha (2½ acres). Pen-y-Gaer, Trevor (Denb.), is roughly rectangular in plan with the southern side formed by a cliff standing above the

Fig.35a Boltby
Scar, Yorkshire;
35b Dudsbury,
Dorset.
35c Norton
Camp,
Shropshire;

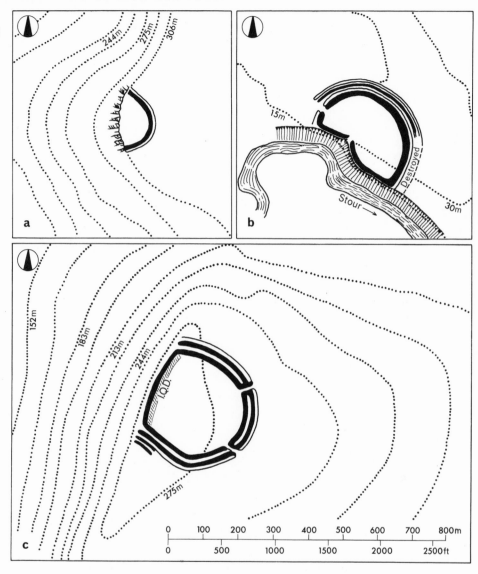

Dee valley. The cliff top is tipped over from west to east, so that the western defences face uphill and those on the east downhill. The northern defences run downhill in conformity with the cliff-edge.

Fig.36   At Craigadwy Wynt (Denb.) two separate enclosures are involved, upper and lower. The upper, larger, enclosure is based on a sheer limestone cliff about 12 m (40 ft) high which runs generally north and south. The bow-shaped defences face level ground to the north, east, and south. About 61 m (200 ft) beyond the foot of the 12-m (40-ft) cliff there is a second cliff forming a second step. This is utilized as a lower enclosure by means of crossbanks at the northern and southern ends, so that the whole site forms a double cliff-edge situation.

81

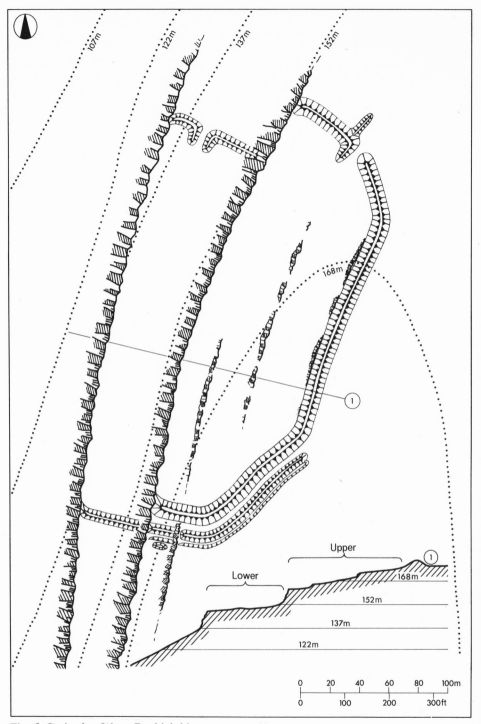

Fig.36. Craigadwy Wynt, Denbighshire.

Figs.35b,c

The remaining Group V sites can all be included under the heading of plateau-edge situations. Among those that have fairly steep slopes on one side are Norton Camp (Salop), Little Sodbury (Glos), and Dudsbury (Dorset). Norton is circular in plan except on the north-west, where it follows the head of the natural slope. On this side it is defended by a simple bank derived from an inner quarry ditch. On the remaining sides the defences consist of two substantial banks with ditches. These defences face ground which slopes down generally from north-west to south-east, but the slope is gentle and the essential plateau-edge nature of the site is not in doubt.

Little Sodbury (Glos) is almost a classic example of this type of situation. It is rectangular in plan and has double banks and ditches facing virtually level ground to the north, east, and south. On the west is has simpler defences standing at the head of a natural slope which falls to the plain below. At Dudsbury the south-western side of the enclosure is formed by the head of a steep slope which forms the northern bank of the River Stour flowing about 30 m (100 ft) below. The approach on the three remaining sides is virtually level.

Among the sites in which the natural slopes on one side are such that full-scale defences are required are Caesar's Camp, Wimbledon (Surrey), and Woodbury (Devon). Caesar's Camp is almost identical in plan with Norton, described above, with in this case only a gentle slope to the north-west. The man-made defences are uniform on all sides and consist of a single bank and ditch; on the sides other than the north-west the approach is level. Although the site can still be described as plateau-edge it is very much closer to a full plateau site than Norton Camp or Dudsbury.

Woodbury is a more complex site than Caesar's Camp and consists of inner and outer enclosures. Strictly speaking only the inner enclosure is plateau-edge, but since the outer enclosure appears to be unfinished, presumably the inner existed first as a separate entity and can thus be considered here. The inner enclosure stands on level ground with its western defences at the head of sloping ground. These defences do not follow a straight line because they incorporate an entrance which involves pulling once section of the defences back from the plateau-edge. On the other three sides the massive bank, the ditch, and the counterscarp bank face more or less level ground.

Group V accounts for rather more sites than Group IV, probably in the region of 50 or 60 (about 4 per cent of the total).

GROUP VI: HILL-SLOPE SITUATIONS

Fig.43e
Pl.36

Group VI embraces those sites which are situated on sloping ground, generally termed hill-slope forts. It will be clear from what has been said already, however, that some of the sites in the groups considered already also stand on sloping ground, so that some more precise definition is required. In some of the sites in Group II, Dolebury (Som.) for example, the whole interior slopes down quite steeply from east to west, but Dolebury is not a hill-slope fort in the generally accepted meaning of the term. Broadly speaking true hill-slope forts can be defined as sites which stand squarely on sloping ground, facing uphill on

Fig.37.
Tregeare
Rounds,
Cornwall.

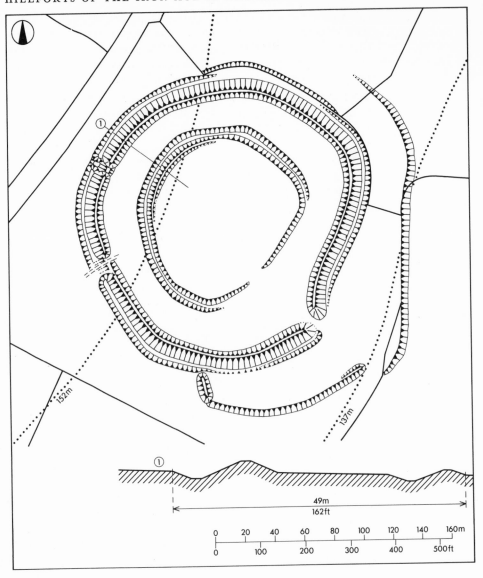

one side, downhill on the opposite side, and across the slope on the two remaining sides. In such situations the contour lines are straight, broadly speaking parallel, and evenly spaced. A classic example of such a situation is provided by Tregeare Rounds (Corn.).   Before dealing with this something must be said about Lady Fox's work on hill-slope forts and related earthworks.

Fig.37

The four classes (I–IV) distinguished by Lady Fox[1] were based not only on situation but also on defences, two aspects which are considered separately in

1. 'Hill-slope Forts and Related Earthworks in South-West England and South Wales', *Arch. J.* 109 (1952), 1–22.

84

this work. This means that forts designated by her as Class III (multivallate with wide-spaced lines of defence on plateau sites) will be considered, as far as siting is concerned, in Group VII. The same sites will, of course, be considered also in Chapter VI on the basis of their multiple enclosures. Similarly, her Class IV forts (multivallate with wide-spaced lines of defence on promontory sites) belongs by definition to Groups II and III, considered already. Again the multiple-enclosure aspect will be dealt with in Chapter VI. This leaves Classes I and II, which embrace hill-slope forts of univallate and multivallate type respectively. This distinction, based on defences, is irrelevant in the present context because sites are being considered purely on the basis of their situation.

Tregeare Rounds is a true hill-slope fort as defined earlier, situated on ground which slopes down evenly from west to east, the contour lines running generally north and south. The site straddles the 145- and 152-m (475- and 500-ft) contours. The ground rises beyond the western defences, which were thus at a positive disadvantage, facing uphill with dead ground a couple of hundred metres away beyond the crest of the hill. The northern and southern defences look out on ground sloping across their fronts, while the eastern defences are in the best position with some supplementary support from the slope below. The fort could have been moved for a couple of hundred metres in any direction without altering the nature of the siting in any way. Tregeare Rounds belongs to a clear-cut type of Iron Age fort, the circular, concentric, multiple-enclosure site to be considered in detail in Chapter VI.

Fig.38a

An entirely different type of site, Stockland Great Camp (Devon), stands in an exactly similar situation. It is, or was when complete, a univallate, single-enclosure site of irregular shape, like many other Iron Age forts. In this case, however, the shape is not due to the contours and some other reasons must have governed its particular plan. It stands on an even slope which runs down from north to south. It is, if anything, further below the crest of the hill than Tregeare Rounds. It straddles the 191- and 206-m (625- and 675-ft) contours which run east and west in more or less parallel lines.

Fig.92
Pl.50

Warbstow Bury (Corn.) is another concentric site, larger and stronger than Tregeare Rounds but in a generally similar situation, on sloping ground with the crown of the hill to the west. The outer defences do, in fact, follow the trend of contours on the north and east, but the advantage thus gained is slight. The dominant aspect is quite clearly the sloping situation, as at Tregeare Rounds. The same may be true of Carnbargus Castle (Corn.), a Small univallate site. The contour lines are parallel and run generally north and south. To the west, however, they are closer together so that the site stands at the head of a slope, in a sort of sloping plateau-edge position. To the east the ground continues to rise but less steeply than before. The fort is certainly on sloping ground, with the crown of the hill to the east, and is probably to be regarded as of the hill-slope type.

Fig.38b

A number of other Small univallate sites in Cornwall seem to belong to the hill-slope category. Tokenbury, for example, seems to sit squarely on the parallel 206-m, 213-m, and 221-m (675-ft, 700-ft, and 725-ft) contours, with further parallel contour lines, more or less evenly spaced, above and below.

85

Fig.38a
Stockland Great
Camp, Devon;
38b Tokenbury,
Cornwall.

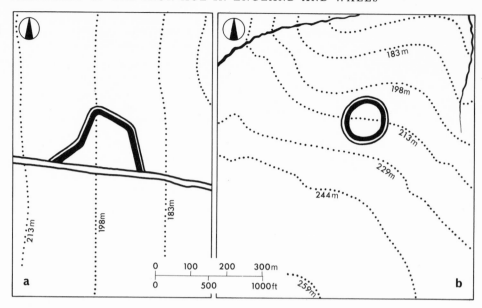

Carthamartha Wood straddles the 46- and 53-m (150- and 175-ft) contours and likewise appears to sit squarely on the sloping ground. Both of these appear to be true hill-slope forts in the sense defined earlier.

There are fairly large numbers of forts in Wales recorded as being in hill-slope positions, many of them of the small, univallate type. These have been listed by Savory,[2] Hogg,[3] and Crossley.[4] The greatest numbers occur in the south-western part of Wales, in Pembrokeshire and Carmarthen, where there are something like 150 sites, most of them of the Small univallate type. Without detailed ground examination it is difficult to say how many of these qualify for inclusion in Group VI under the terms outlined earlier. Some of them may be simply sloping spur sites, in which the sloping situation is secondary to the defence provided by the natural slopes on two or three sides. Accepting the figure of 150 quoted above, Group VI probably accounts for something in the region of 200 sites or about 14 per cent of the total.

GROUP VII: PLATEAU AND LOW-LYING SITUATIONS

Group VII includes all those sites which are more or less level with their immediate surroundings, whatever their elevation in absolute terms.

Fig.119

Ampress Camp (Hants) is defended on two sides (south and west) by a bank, ditch, and counterscarp bank which face a level approach. The two remaining sides have natural defences. Although this is the pattern of a promontory fort,

2. 'List of Hill-forts and other Earthworks in Wales, V; Carmarthenshire', *Bull. Board Celtic Stud.* 16. 1 (1954), 54–67.
3. 'List of Hill-forts in Cardiganshire', ibid. 19.4 (1962), 354–66.
4. 'List of Hill-forts in Pembrokeshire', ibid. 20.2 (1963), 171–203.

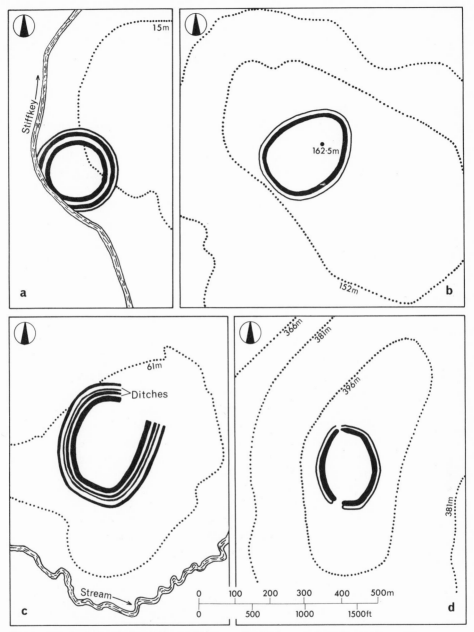

Fig.39a Warham Camp, Norfolk; 39b Badbury, Berkshire; 39c Bullsdown, Hampshire; 39d Beacon Ring, Montgomeryshire.

the site is not in fact a promontory but a low-lying tongue of land standing only 3 m (10 ft) or so above the adjacent mud flats of the Lymington river to the west and a tributary stream to the north. In the same county Hamble Common Camp occupies a tongue of land below the 8-m (25-ft) contour line, in the angle formed by the Hamble river and Southampton Water.

Like Ampress Camp and Hamble Common Camp, a number of other Group VII sites rely on water as part of their defences. Tedbury (Som.), for example, stands in the junction of Mells Stream and Fordbury Water. On the west there is a straight line of multivallate defences running from river to river. River-junction sites have been discussed already under Group II, but in those cases height was the dominant factor and the sites could be described as promontory forts. Tedbury is not a promontory; it is a tongue of land which, while not flat all over, is flat where it counts for classification, around the edges. Without the rivers there would be nothing to define, or defend, the north, east, and south of the enclosure.

Fig.41

Dike Hills, Dorchester (Oxon.), takes advantage of a bend in the River Thames. The western and southern sides are formed where it makes a right-angled bend, turning from a southerly to an easterly course. To the north the ground is absolutely flat and on this side it is defended by two massive banks, about 21 m (70 ft) apart, with a small ditch outside the outer bank. The area enclosed by the defences is about 46 ha (114 acres). About three-quarters of a kilometre ($\frac{1}{2}$ mile) to the south, beyond the river, the high, hilltop position of Sinodun (Berks) is clearly visible.

Fig.40

Oakmere (Ches.) occupies a tongue of land on the eastern side of the mere of the same name. The level of the latter now appears to be somewhat lower than in Iron Age times. The site is triangular with water defences on the south-west and north and a single bank and ditch on the east. The western side of the enclosure is only about 3 m (10 ft) above the level of the mere, although the ground rises gently to the east towards the artificial defences where it is some 6 m (20 ft) higher. The ground outside the defences to the north-east, east, and south-east is more or less level. The area enclosed is about 91 ares ($2\frac{1}{4}$ acres).

Fig.39a

Warham Camp (Norf.) is the Group VII equivalent of the situations embraced by Group V (cliff- and plateau-edge sites). On its south-western side it makes use of the River Stiffkey as its main defence. On the remaining sides it is defended by a compact arrangement of 2 substantial banks and 2 ditches. As they reach the river the 2 ditches and the outer bank die out together, leaving only the inner bank standing above the river, which thus fulfils the function of a wet ditch.

Fig.39b

Many of the remaining sites in Group VII depend entirely on their man-made defences. Badbury (Berks) is defended by a single bank and ditch of no great strength and stands on a hill, the flat top of which is defined by the 152-m (500-ft) contour. From this contour the ground falls away in good slopes in all directions. The flat top of the hill, however, is very much larger than the enclosure, which is set roughly in the middle of it, so that in spite of its general elevation above the surrounding countryside the approach to the defences is level. This constitutes a true plateau site, using the word plateau to define an area which is flat but elevated above its surroundings.

Fig.40. Oakmere,
Cheshire.

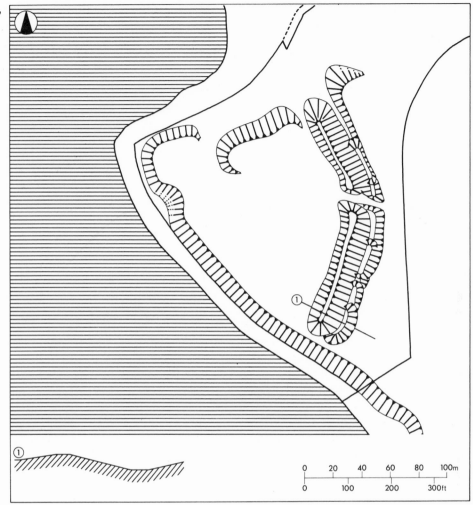

At the Aubreys (Herts) the approach to the ramparts is again level, but it lacks even the advantage of Badbury in that it has no general elevation above the surrounding countryside. It is simply a large enclosure, defended by two banks and two ditches, built on flat ground with no natural advantages whatsoever. In fact, to the north-west and south-east there is a general rise in ground-level, although not in the immediate vicinity of the ramparts.

Castle Close (Devon) follows the same general pattern as Badbury. The generally flat top of the hill on which it stands is defined by the 198-m (650-ft) contour. The top of the hill does, in fact, rise gently towards the centre where the small, circular site is situated, but the essential nature of the situation arises out of the marked discrepancy between the size of the hilltop and the size of the site. Defences following the shoulder of the hill, the 198-m (650-ft) contour, would have produced a very large site. Any site smaller than this would involve level

89

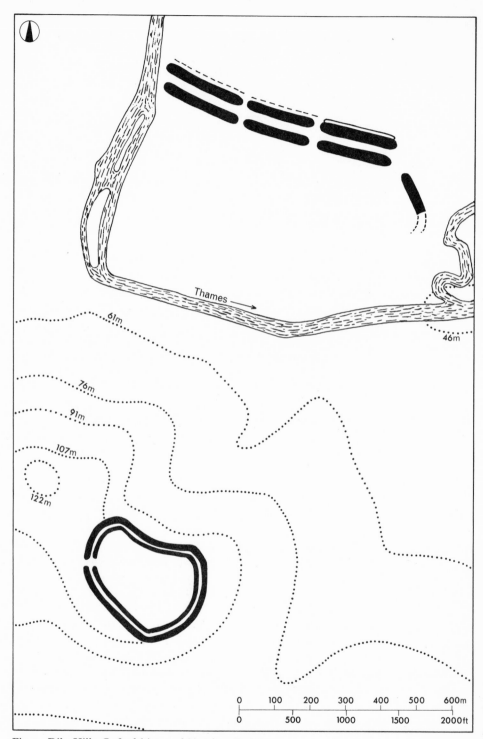

Fig.41. Dike Hills, Oxfordshire, and Sinodun, Berkshire.

approaches on at least one side. A very small site, such as the one actually involved, in which the defences on all sides are withdrawn from the shoulder of the hill, is inevitably of the plateau type.

Fig.39d

Tedbury (Hants) likewise involves a slight rise towards the centre of the hill where the site is situated, but once again the nature of the situation is that of a plateau with slopes on all sides falling from the 107-m (350-ft) contour, except at the north-east where there is a narrow neck at the same level as the hilltop. The defences surround a slight knoll defined by the 114- and 122-m (375- and 400-ft) contours but beyond them the ground levels out until the 107-m (356-ft) contour and the shoulder of the hill is reached. Other examples, if rather less clear-cut, of this type of siting are Banbury and Dogbury (Dorset), Beacon Ring (Montg.), and Cerrig Gwynion (Denb.). The latter is one of the relatively small number of sites which stand at over 457 m (1,500 ft). In spite of this, however, the immediate approach to the modest single bank and ditch is quite easy and the site thus qualifies as a plateau situation in the sense defined earlier.

Because of their relatively small size many of the Cornish rounds fall into this category. With diameters of only 60 or 90 m (200 or 300 ft) it is inevitable that they will be smaller than most of the hilltops on which they stand and the result is a plateau site as defined above. Other rounds, of course, are simply in the low-lying category, with no natural advantages whatsoever.

Fig.39c

Pl.8

Flat or low-lying sites in the manner of the Aubreys (Herts) account for the remaining forts in Group VII. Among these are such sites as Bullsdown (Hants), Cholesbury (Bucks), Windrush and Salmonsbury (Glos), Chastleton (Oxon.), Clovelly Dykes (Devon), and Ambresbury (Essex). Bullsdown has a very gentle slope on one side but so slight as to make little difference to the nature of the siting: on all the other sides the approach is flat. The defences are entirely man-made and consist of an inner bank and ditch with a very slight counterscarp bank. About 5 m (15 ft) beyond is a second slight bank with an outer ditch and a counterscarp bank. The area enclosed is about 4 ha (10 acres).

Fig.42

Cholesbury (Bucks) is of roughly the same size and shape as Bullsdown. It is defended by a bank, ditch, and substantial counterscarp bank, with an outer ditch and counterscarp bank on the southern half of the site. On the south-west, a couple of hundred metres beyond the ramparts, there is a percept-ible fall in the ground but elsewhere the surroundings are entirely flat.

Pl.8

The large multiple-enclosure site of Clovelly Dykes is also entirely on flat ground. It stands about 1·6 km (1 mile) from the coast on what is described as a plateau, about 213 m (700 ft) above sea-level, but it is not a plateau in the restricted sense defined earlier. It is at the same general level as the countryside around it. There is no sharply defined plateau edge as at Badbury or Castle Close, for example, which could have formed a larger site.

In marked contrast to the complexity of Clovelly are the circular sites of Windrush (Glos) and Chastleton (Oxon.). Their only defences are a single rampart without even the additional support of an outer ditch. The rampart at Windrush is about 9 m (30 ft) across and about 1·5 m (5 ft) high above ground-level, which is the same inside and outside the enclosure.

Of the remaining sites mentioned above, Ambresbury is actually on a gentle

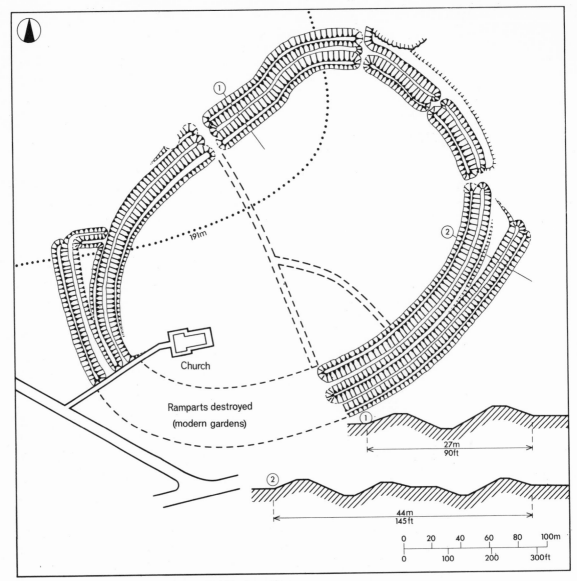

Fig.42. Cholesbury, Buckinghamshire.

slope down, north-west to south-east, but this is so slight that the approaches on all sides can for all practical purposes be classed as level. Salmonsbury has level approaches on all sides and to that extent can be described as relying entirely on man-made defences. However, the site is placed in the broad flat area formed by the junction of two rivers, so that approach from any direction except the north would have been restricted.

Group VII accounts for something between 80 and 100 sites, or about 7 per cent of the total of all Iron Age forts.

CHAPTER IV

Internal features

The interior space of most Iron Age forts consists of a single enclosure, but in a smaller number of cases the interior consists of two, three, and sometimes more separate enclosures, related to each other in various ways (see Chapter VI). Except for the size aspect of multiple-enclosure sites, all interiors, both single- and multiple-enclosures, will be considered here. Although some indication of the areas enclosed was given in Chapter I, they must now be considered in more detail. All areas, noted here and elsewhere, which were measured in acres, are also shown converted to the nearest hectare.

SIZE

It would seem reasonable to assume that the size of the enclosed area bears some relation to the function of the site. On the basis of size alone, however, it would be difficult to suggest different functions for sites of, say 6, 10, and 12 ha (15, 25, and 30 acres). On the other hand, it seems unlikely that sites enclosing 20 ha (50 acres) or more enjoyed precisely the same function as sites in which the defences enclose less than 40 ares (1 acre). Size is quite clearly a factor to be considered in formulating any typology based on surface evidence. Large sites, i.e. those enclosing more than 6 ha (15 acres), will be dealt with first.

The index accompanying the Ordnance Survey's *Map of Southern Britain in the Iron Age* lists 145 sites, both univallate and multivallate, in this category. Some of these, however, involve more than one enclosure and as such will be dealt with in Chapter VI. This leaves something over 130 Large single-enclosure sites. These can be broken down into different size groups with some indication of the numerical content of each group. The sites can be conveniently separated into four groups with dividing lines at 12, 20, and 40 ha (30, 50, and 100 acres).

It will be clear from the size of the group that sites enclosing more than 40 ha (100 acres) are rare. There are, in fact, only 7 sites in this category, of which Bindon (Dorset) appears to be the largest. What may be termed the upper enclosure occupies an area of some 20 ha (50 acres). In addition to this, however, there is a low-lying tongue of land to the south which brings the total area enclosed to about 105 ha (260 acres). This is larger than either Hengistbury Head (Hants) or Ham Hill (Som.). Hengistbury is described by Williams-Freeman[1] as being about 259 ha (640 acres), but it is actually considerably less

1. Williams-Freeman, *An Introduction to Field Archaeology as Illustrated by Hampshire* (1915).

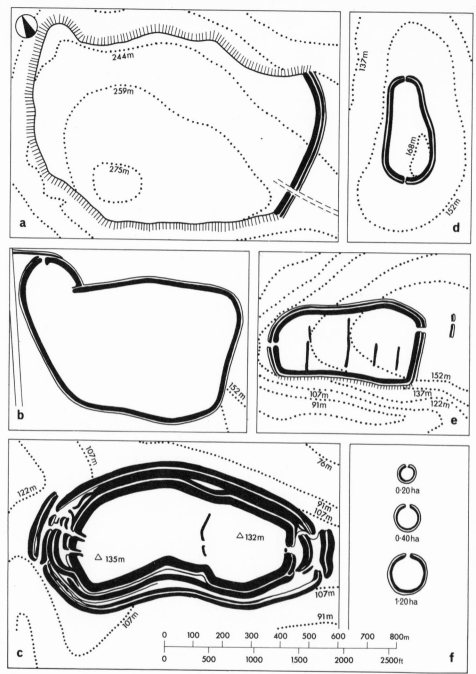

Fig.43a Nottingham Hill, Gloucestershire; 43b Casterley Camp, Wiltshire; 43c Maiden Castle, Dorset; 43d Quarley Hill, Hampshire; 43e Dolebury, Somerset; 43f very small sites.

Plates 18–33

18 Sudbrook Camp, Monmouthshire, one of a small group of Iron Age forts which are situated in low-lying positions. Excavation has shown that its massive inner rampart, of the *glacis* type, had a substantial back revetment of stone in much the same way as the main rampart of Maiden Castle, Dorset. View from the north-west.

19 Flimston Bay, Pembrokeshire, a coastal promontory fort. The main defences consist of a multivallate arrangement of two banks and two ditches. There is also a third bank and ditch transforming the fort into a multiple-enclosure site. View from the north.

20 Hambledon Hill, Dorset, one of the county's most spectacular forts, with multivallate defences standing above steep natural slopes. The narrow, south-eastern side, with an easy approach, was defended by a massive bank, ditch and counterscarp bank with two further substantial banks and ditches beyond. View from the north-west.

21 Eggardon, Dorset, a classic example of ridge-top siting with easy approaches to north and south. The outer eastern and western defences appear originally to have been free-standing cross-ridge dykes, incorporated at a later stage into the fort's defence system. View from the south-east.

22 Eggardon, Dorset. The northern defences. The inner line of defence consists of a bank, ditch, and a massive, and apparently unfinished counterscarp bank. The outer defences consist of a ditch with the spoil thrown outwards to form a rampart along the top of which the present-day track runs.

23 Hod Hill, Dorset, a large multivallate fort of the contour type, with sloping ground below the defences on all four sides. The site is notable for the Roman auxiliary fort which occupied its north-west corner. View from the south-east.

24 Battlesbury, Wiltshire, a large multivallate site with a very wide inner quarry ditch and the remains of a box-like outwork covering the entrance. View from the north.

25 Caer Caradoc, Clun, Shropshire, a semi-contour site with a complex system of defences on the western side where approach is easiest.

26 Yarnbury, Wiltshire. Within the existing multivallate defences, and concentric with them, are the remains of a smaller and earlier univallate fort. View from the north-east.

27 The Herefordshire Beacon, a multiple-enclosure site on the border of Herefordshire and Worcestershire. The central Iron Age enclosure contains a later, medieval work, and there are Iron Age annexes to north and south. View from the south-west.

28 Scratchbury, Wiltshire. Surface evidence within the defences indicates that there were two successive enlargements of an original D-shaped enclosure. View from the west.

29 Beacon Hill, Hampshire, from the south-east. It is one of the small number of Iron Age forts with surface evidence of occupation in the form of hut-circles.

30 Tre'r Ceiri, Caernarvonshire, a stone-walled fort in north-west Wales with clear evidence of occupation in the form of numerous, circular stone-built huts. View from the west.

31 Figsbury, Wiltshire, is unusual in that its inner quarry ditch is set well back from the ramparts. This forms a second, inner enclosure, concentric with the main defences. View from the south.

32 Figsbury, Wiltshire, giving an impression of the space between the rampart (far left) and the inner quarry ditch (centre). View from the south-east.

33 Oldbury, Wiltshire, a multivallate fort with surface evidence of an earlier, smaller stage, viewed from the north.

18. Sudbrook,
Monmouthshire

19. Flimston Bay,
Pembrokeshire

20. Hambledon
Hill, Dorset

21. Eggardon,
Dorset

22. Eggardon,
Dorset: the
northern
defences

23. Hod Hill,
Dorset

24. Battlesbury,
Wiltshire

25. Caer
Caradoc, Clun,
Shropshire

26. Yarnbury,
Wiltshire

27. The
Herefordshire
Beacon

28. Scratchbury,
Wiltshire

29. Beacon Hill,
Hampshire

30. Tre'r Ceiri,
Caernarvonshire

31. Figsbury,
Wiltshire

32. Figsbury,
Wiltshire (detail)

33. Oldbury,
Wiltshire

than this and covers an area of about 81 ha (200 acres). Unlike either Bindon or Hengistbury Head, Ham Hill is completely enclosed by man-made ramparts which define an area of about 85 ha (210 acres). The four remaining sites in this group, Llanymynech Hill (Montg.), Oldbury (Kent), Nottingham Hill (Glos), and Dike Hills (Oxon.) enclose areas of 57, 50, 53, and 46 ha (140, 123, 130, and 114 acres) respectively. These seven sites represent only 5 per cent of the total of all Large single-enclosure sites, and only $\frac{1}{2}$ per cent of the total of all Iron Age forts.

Fig.43a
Fig.41

The sites in the second group have interiors of between 20 and 40 ha (50 and 100 acres). The largest sites in the group appear to be Walbury (Berks) and Bathampton (Som.) at 33 ha (82 acres) each. The remaining sites are grouped between these and Hod Hill (Dorset) which has an interior space of just over 20 ha (50 acres). They include Tedbury (Som.), 29 ha (72 acres) Titterstone Clee (Salop), 28 ha (71 acres), Casterley and Ogbury (Wilts.), 25 ha (62 acres) each, the Andyke (Hants), 24 ha (60 acres), Dodman Point (Corn.), about 22 ha (55 acres), and Pen-y-cloddiau (Flint.), 21 ha (52 acres). This group accounts for about 10 per cent of the Large single-enclosure sites and less than 1 per cent of all Iron Age forts.

Pl.23;Fig.21a
Fig.43b

The third group (interiors between 12 and 20 ha: 30 and 50 acres) is spread fairly evenly throughout the range, from Cranmore (Devon), 13 ha (31 acres), to Credenhill (Here.), 20 ha (49 acres), and includes such sites as Bagsbury (Hants) and Maiden Castle (Dorset), 18 ha (45 acres) each, Vespasian's Camp and Scratchbury (Wilts.), both 15 ha (37 acres), and Membury and Martinsell (Wilts.), 14 and 13 ha (34 and 32 acres) respectively. This group represents about 15 per cent of the total of Large single-enclosure forts. The three groups together, i.e. all sites enclosing more than 12 ha (30 acres), represent about 30 per cent of the total of the sites under consideration, or slightly less than one-third. In relation to Iron Age forts as a whole they account for only $2\frac{1}{2}$ per cent of the total.

Pls.41,42;Fig.43c
Pl.28;Fig.49
Fig.120

The last of the four groups (interiors between 6 and 12 ha: 15 and 30 acres) is by far the largest and accounts for nearly three-quarters of all Large single-enclosure sites. Within this range there appears to be something of a concentration at the lower end. About half the sites in the group, in fact, have interiors of less than 8 ha (20 acres), which means that the group average would be much nearer to 6 ha (15 acres) than to 12 ha (30 acres). The group includes many well-known sites in Wessex, the Marches, and adjacent areas: Yarnbury 11 ha (28 acres), Oldbury 8 ha (20 acres), and Cley Hill 7 ha (17 acres), all in Wiltshire; St. Catherine's Hill 9 ha (23 acres), Winklebury 8·5 ha (19 acres), and Castle Ditches 6·5 ha (16 acres) in Hampshire; Maes Knoll 8·5 ha (19 acres), and Solsbury and Cadbury 7·5 ha (18 acres each) in Somerset; Sutton Walls 12 ha (29½ acres), Wall Hills (Thornbury) 9 ha (23 acres), and Aconbury and Gaer Cop 7 ha (17 acres), in Herefordshire; and Bury Walls and Chesterton Walls 8 ha (21 acres) each, Norton Camp 7 ha (17 acres), and Abdon Burf 6·5 ha (16 acres) in Shropshire. The group represents about 70 per cent (about 95 sites) of the total of Large, single-enclosure forts and about 7 per cent of the total of all Iron Age forts, and would appear to be the upper end of the size range for the bulk of Iron Age forts.

Pl.26
Fig.78
Fig.21c

Fig.43e;Pl.36

Fig.35c

97

Fig.43d

The index of the Iron Age map lists 459 sites with interiors between 1 and 6 ha (3 and 15 acres) in area. As with the Large sites this total includes a certain number of multiple-enclosure sites which will be dealt with in Chapter VI. Their number is difficult to ascertain, but if 15 per cent is allowed, then just under 400 Medium-sized, single-enclosure sites remain for consideration. Unfortunately, there is insufficient evidence available to analyse this number in any detail. If the trends suggested by the pattern of the Large sites are any guide then there would be more sites in the lower half of the scale (1–4 ha: 3–9 acres) than in the upper half, and this receives some sort of confirmation from the further increase in numbers beyond the lower end of the scale, i.e. in the Small category. This, however, involves the assumption that numbers and size vary in inverse proportion to each other throughout the whole range of Iron Age forts. This is not necessarily so and the question of size is discussed further in Chapter VIII (pp. 249–51)

Fig.43f

In the Small category there are 762 sites where the interior is less than 1·20 ha (3 acres) in extent. Allowing about 15 per cent for multiple-enclosure sites leaves about 650 single-enclosure sites to be dealt with here. Because of the large numbers involved and the lack of specific information it is not possible to identify the one site which marks the lower end of the scale of sizes. Nor, indeed, is it necessary to do so. The citing of a number of examples of Small sites will be sufficient to show the striking differences in size which exist between them and the sites considered already, especially those at the upper end of the Large category. Castell Caerau (Caer.), for example, has an interior space only 18 m (60 ft) square which is less than 412 sq m (493 sq yd). In the same county Craig y Tyddyn and a fort near Nantlle have interiors of 674 and 578 sq m (806 and 691 sq yd) respectively. In Pembrokeshire Parc-Robert Camp has an enclosure only 21 m (70 ft) in diameter (337 sq m: 403 sq yd), and in St. Dogwell's parish one of a group of 5 small sites has a diameter of about 23 m (75 ft) or 405 sq m: 484 sq yd.

There are many other forts in the Small category which have interiors of less than 40 ares (1 acre). These include many of the Cornish rounds and similar circular sites in Devon, Somerset, and many parts of Wales with internal diameters between 46 and 61 m (150 and 200 ft), giving areas of between 1,642 and 2,920 sq m (1,964 and 3,492 sq yd). In the same areas there are, of course, other sites between these sizes and the maximum of 1 ha (3 acres).

The most interesting aspect of the Small category is the very large number of sites which it embraces. Something like half of all the Iron Age forts in England and Wales, about 680 out of 1,366, consist of a single enclosure less than 1 ha (3 acres) in extent.

SHAPE

The shape of the interior of an Iron Age fort cannot be regarded as significant where it is dictated by the contours. Contours account in large measure for the great variety in the appearance of Iron Age forts. In some cases a rigid or very close adherence to them has produced a very unusual shape. Possibly the best

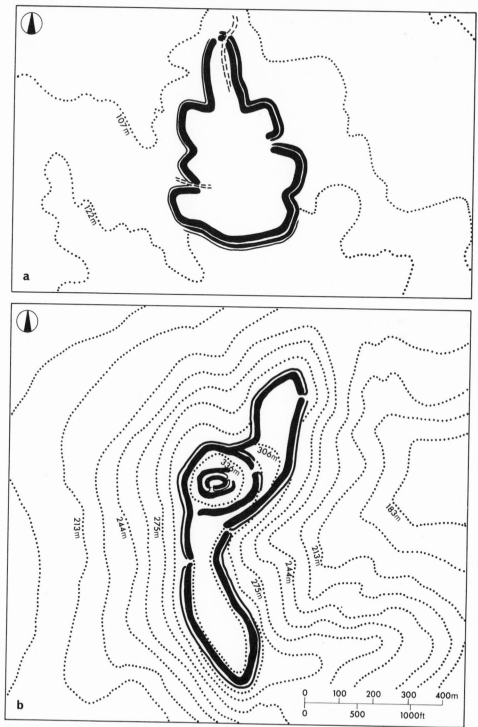

Fig.44a Caesar's Camp, Berkshire; 44b Herefordshire Beacon, Herefordshire.

Fig.44a

Pl.20;Fig.30b

Fig.44b
Pl.27

Figs.35c,39a

Fig.39c
Figs.39d,45

example of this is Caesar's Camp (Berks). The site is a Group II semi-contour type with a straight line of defences facing the easy approach from the south. The three remaining sides of the spur are deeply indented and the defences follow the line of the contours absolutely, producing a most unusual shape. The unusual plans of two other semi-contour sites, Hambledon (Dorset) and Wall Hills, Ledbury (Here.), can be explained in the same way. In Group I the shape of the Herefordshire Beacon can likewise be explained by the very close adherence of the defences to the contours of a hill of unusual shape. The remaining sites in Groups I–V are all affected to a greater or lesser extent by the contours, so that the shape of their interiors cannot be regarded as significant.

Shape does assume some significance, however, when it is clear that it is not dictated by the contours. Presumably in such cases it represents a deliberate choice on the part of the builders. The sites involved are mainly in Groups V and VI. In many such cases the chosen shape is circular. This applies to many of the Small sites in the south-west and in Wales and includes many of the multiple-enclosure sites. Outside these areas Windrush Camp (Glos) and Chastleton (Oxon.) have quite clearly been laid out on a circular plan. A number of other sites, Norton (Salop), Warham (Norf.), and Caesar's Camp, Wimbledon (Surrey), also appear to have been based on a circular layout, even though one side of each site is flattened by the use of a natural feature.

Apart from the circular plan, the other common shape in situations where the contours have little or no effect is an oval. This is well exemplified at sites such as Bullsdown (Hants), and Cherbury (Berks), which are virtually on level ground. Other examples are Beacon Hill (Montg.) and Caster Cliff (Lancs), both of which are elevated but in both of which the contours in the immediate vicinity of the sites are such that they do not dictate any particular shape.

CONTOUR

Pl.26;Figs.35b,143
Pls.31,32;
Figs.39c,42
Fig.26c
Pls.3,14;
Figs.86,60,91

As far as the usefulness of the enclosed area is concerned contour is probably of more significance than shape. An entirely flat interior would almost certainly be of more use than an irregular or sloping one, and many forts do, in fact, have flat interiors. Sites of this type occur in all sorts of situations, hilltop, semi-contour, cliff-edge, low-lying, etc. The following are simply a selection of such sites: Pilsdon Pen and Dudsbury (Dorset), Blackbury Castle (Devon), Yarnbury and Figsbury (Wilts.), Bulldown (Hants), Caesar's Camp (Surrey), Cholesbury and Bulstrode Park (Bucks.), the Aubreys (Herts.), Uley Bury (Glos.), Sutton Walls (Here.), and Bury Ditches, Bury Walls, and Old Oswestry (Salop). These are sites which have noticeably flat interiors. There are many others in which the interior is only very slightly domed so that little or no loss of usefulness occurs. Among the sites just listed is Sutton Walls where it is known from excavation that the flat interior is not an original feature, but is caused mainly by the accumulation of soil behind the ramparts at the expense of the centre of the enclosure. It is possible that other apparently flat interiors were originally domed, although probably not to any marked degree.

Fig.45. Caster
Cliff,
Lancashire.

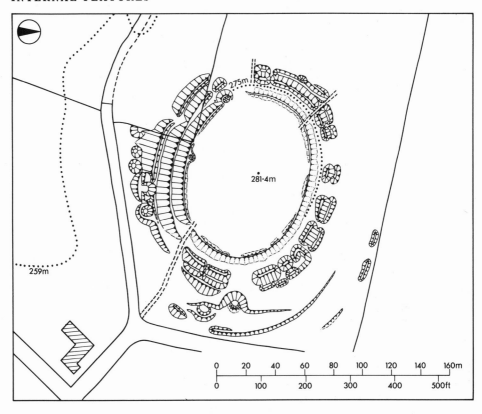

Pl.23;Fig.46a

Fig.46b
Plate 4

Fig.46c

Fig.46d

Pl.1;Fig.46e
Pl.43;Fig.46f

In a number of forts the interior is domed beyond the slight degree mentioned in the last paragraph. One of the effects of such doming is to restrict visibility from one side of the enclosure to the other. At Hod Hill (Dorset), for example, it is impossible to see the southern defences from the top of the rampart on the north side. An example of the same effect on a small scale is provided by Moel Arthur (Flint.) where the whole interior is simply a dome rising above the level of the defences, offering little or no shelter from the elements. The doming at the northern end of Hambledon Hill (Dorset) is even more pronounced, the crest standing some 30 m (100 ft) above the level of the ramparts. At Foel Fenlli (Denb.) the southern half of the enclosure contains some very steep slopes which could not have been put to any practical use. Other sites in which there is a pronounced dome inside are St. Catherine's Hill (Hants), Cley Hill (Wilts.), and Badbury (Dorset).

In one or two promontory sites the contours are such that great restrictions would have been placed on the utilization of the interior space. At Rame Head (Corn.) the enclosure is cone-shaped with the slopes on most sides running down virtually uninterrupted to the water's edge. Only on the southern side is there any break in the pattern, providing one or two more or less level areas. At Gurnard's Head (Corn.) the promontory is triangular in section with the apex of the triangle forming the crest. One side of the triangle is bare rock and too

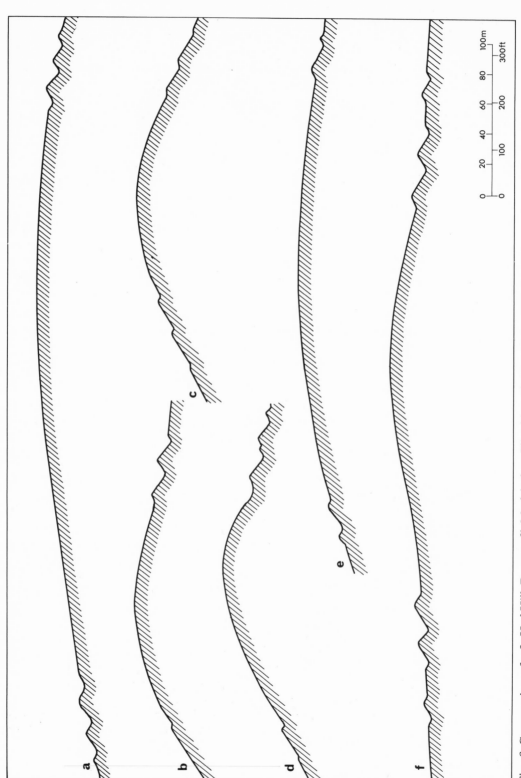

Fig.46. Cross-sections of: 46a Hod Hill, Dorset; 46b Moel Arthur, Flintshire; 46c Hambledon Hill, Dorset; 46d Foel Fenlli, Denbighshire; 46e St. Catherine's Hill, Hampshire; 46f Badbury Rings, Dorset.

steep to be used at all. The other side is only slightly less steep but this provides virtually the whole of the area available for the purposes of the enclosure.

The interior space of most Iron Age forts is now featureless. It does not follow from this, however, that no features ever existed. One of the results of regular ploughing would be to destroy all but the most strongly defined interior features, including the evidence of occupation in the form of hut remains. A number of Iron Age forts are under the plough regularly at the present time: Uley Bury (Glos), Bury Walls (Salop), Berry Ring (Staffs), and Eddisbury (Ches.) to mention only four. There is evidence of ploughing in others in the recent past, particularly during the two wars. It is likely, however, that there was a great deal more ploughing in medieval times, of which there is now no record. How much more it is quite impossible to say. It is, however, highly improbable that the lack of features in every site can be explained by ploughing or similar agencies. In many cases it must simply be that such features never existed, at least not in any form substantial enough to leave surface remains. Such a situation makes any assessment of the extent and nature of occupation as evidenced by surface remains almost meaningless. Many sites with no visible surface remains in the interior have produced, on excavation, abundant evidence of occupation, as for example at Maiden Castle, Dorset, and this must be true of many other sites.

Pl.11

Pls.41,42

PRE-IRON AGE FEATURES

In many Iron Age forts earlier and/or later features, pre- and post-Iron Age, can be seen which have no cultural connection with the Iron Age defence works. By far the commonest of these are the round barrows or cairns of the preceding Bronze Age. The reason for their fairly frequent occurrence inside Iron Age forts arises out of the principle underlying their location. Many Bronze Age barrows appear to have been deliberately placed so that they could be seen in profile against the skyline, on hilltops, ridges, and promontories.[2] These are, of course, the situations in which Iron Age forts occur, so that it is not surprising that the two features should coincide in several dozen cases. It may also be that the existence of the barrow was an additional inducement. It may have been felt that the sacred associations of the burial place would afford protection over and above that provided by the ramparts.

There is as yet insufficient evidence to make a complete statement of all forts which contain Bronze Age barrows. There are probably many yet to be discovered. Most of the known examples are fairly prominent but there are some which are only 30 or 60 cm (1 or 2 ft) high and 6 or 9 m (20 or 30 ft) across, and these can easily be overlooked, particularly if there is any thick cover of vegetation. The examples to be mentioned below are simply a selection of the known sites to illustrate the general nature of this phenomenon. In most cases only 1 or 2 barrows are involved. Numbers greater than this are comparatively rare. St.

2. Grinsell, L. V., *Ancient Burial Mounds of England* (1953), 50–51.

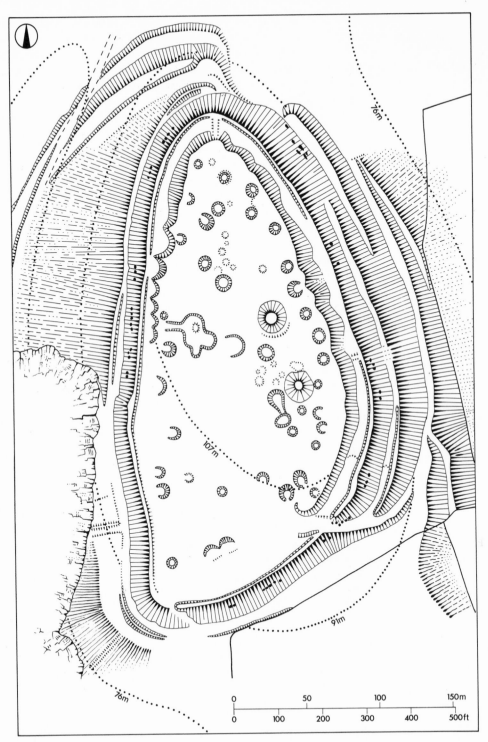

Fig.47. Chalbury, Dorset.

George Gray[3] records 11 round barrows in Small Down Camp (Som.), 7 in Scratchbury, and 6 inside Winkelbury (Wilts.). There are 4 round mounds inside Little Doward Camp (Here.) and 3 inside Midsummer Hill in the same county. There are also 3 each in Braich-y-Dinas (Caer.) and Foel Trigarn (Pemb). The remaining sites to be mentioned have only 1 or 2 barrows each. There are 2 prominent round barrows on the highest part of Chalbury (Dorset) and 2 each in Denbury (Devon) and Cley Hill (Wilts.). Of the 2 mounds at Trevelgue Head (Corn.) 1 is in a very prominent position on the highest part of the promontory and the other now on the cliff-edge on the north side and in process of being eroded. In Wales there are single mounds at the highest points of Foel Fenlli (Denb.) and Tre'r Ceiri (Caer.). Other sites in this category include Embury (Devon), Abbotsbury (Dorset), Hengistbury (Hants), Croft Ambrey (Here.), and Mam Tor (Derby.).

Earlier again than the round barrows just considered, although far less common, are long barrows. The same principle holds good with regard to siting. At Hambledon Hill (Dorset) there is a well-preserved long barrow (about 73 m, 240 ft, long) at the narrowest part of the site in a ridge-top situation where it would have been visible in profile from both east and west. Long mounds of smaller dimensions are recorded at Warbstow Bury (Corn.), Bratton Castle (Wilts.), and Hengistbury Head (Hants).

POST-IRON AGE FEATURES

Perhaps the most interesting of the post-Iron Age features is the Roman fort in the north-west corner of Hod Hill (Dorset). This makes use of the prehistoric defences on the north and west so that additional defences, of Roman construction, were required only on the south and east. There are more examples of the utilization of the Iron Age defences in the succeeding medieval period. One of the most striking is at Old Sarum (Wilts.) where the great Norman motte is roughly concentric with the Iron Age defences. Mottes of smaller dimensions were inserted at the western ends of Hembury, Buckfastleigh, and Loddiswell Rings, both in Devon, at the eastern end of Twm Barlwm (Mon.), the south-western end of Cefnllys Castle (Rad.), and in the central part of the Hereford-shire Beacon. The bailey associated with the motte at Castlestede (Lancs) may originally have been an Iron Age fort. A stone-built castle with a rock-cut ditch was placed within the defences at Dinas Bran above Llangollen (Denb.), and something similar seems to have happened at Dryslwyn Castle (Car.).

ABANDONED DEFENCES

Other surface remains within the defences, where they exist at all, consist for the most part of abandoned defence systems and hut remains. In many cases the abandonment of the original defences, either in part or in whole, arises from the enlargement of the enclosure, so that the old and new defences appear to

3. Gray, H. St. George, 'Excavations at Smalldown Camp, Evercreech'. *Proc. Somerset Nat. Hist. and Arch. Soc.* 50 (1904), 32–49.

Marginal figure references:
Pl.28;Figs.49,103
Fig.23b
Pl.51

Fig.47
Pl.1
Fig.90

Pl.30;Fig.54
Fig.53
Fig.66

Pl.20;Fig.30b

Pls.50,38;Fig.92

Pl.23;Fig.21a

Pl.40

Fig.48

Fig.44b
Pl.27

Fig.48.
Loddiswell
Rings, Devon.

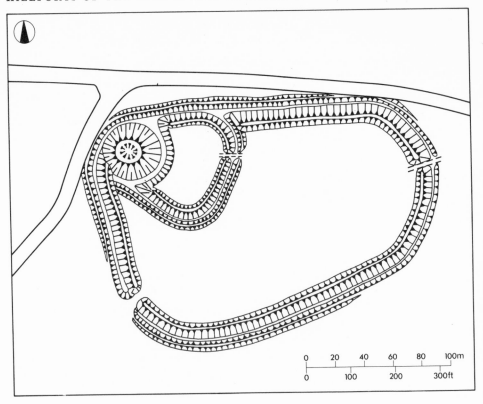

define two separate enclosures. However, these are not strictly two-enclosure sites since it is usually quite clear from the condition of the abandoned defences that they had ceased to have any real function. They are usually very much more eroded than the later defences, and that they exist at all is probably due to the fact that they were not worth the trouble of dismantling.

Pl.26

Yarnbury (Wilts.) is an excellent example of a site with easily distinguishable earlier and later defences which form two more or less concentric circles. The earlier defences consist of a much eroded bank and a ditch. These features are completely dwarfed by the massive later defences which are multivallate. The original fort had an internal diameter of about 183 m (600 ft). When this was abandoned the diameter was increased to about 381 m (1,250 ft), leaving the earlier bank and ditch within the new enclosure. At Caster Cliff (Lancs) the

Fig.45

presumed earlier and later defences are likewise concentric, although in this case there is no space between the two systems and thus no impression of a two-enclosure site. The most prominent defences appear to have been built immediately outside the original rampart, which had no ditch. This rampart is now only about 30 cm (1 ft) or so in height and is overshadowed by the adjacent rampart of the later system which consists of a bank, ditch, and counterscarp bank and appears to be unfinished in places.

Most sites in this category other than Yarnbury and Caster Cliff have

Fig.49.
Scratchbury,
Wiltshire.

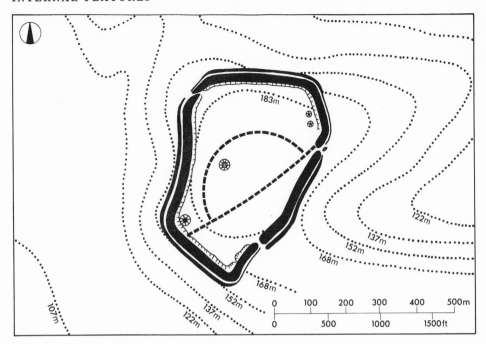

abandoned defences on one side only. Perhaps the best-known example is
Fig.43c
Pl.41
Maiden Castle (Dorset). The original fort occupied only the eastern of two
adjacent knolls. Subsequently the site was extended to take in both knolls and
the abandoned western defences of the original enclosure can still be seen
within the enlarged fort. The existence of the abandoned system suggests, from
surface evidence alone, that there was originally a smaller fort and that it had
univallate defences.

Fig.30b
Pl.20
A generally similar process seems to have taken place at Hambledon Hill in
the same county, although in this case there appear to have been two extensions
and there are therefore two sections of abandoned defences. The original fort
occupied only the outer end of the long spur on which it stands and was, judging
by the remains running across the spur, univallate. At a later stage it was
extended to the south, still apparently in univallate style. At a still later stage it
was extended to occupy the whole of the spur, leaving a second section of
defences across the spur to fall into decay. Another Group II site, the promon-
Fig.27
Pl.10
tory fort at Crickley Hill (Glos), was enlarged in much the same way. The most
prominent defences, a bank and ditch, cut off a roughly triangular area. Within
this space, however, there are the remains of earlier defences cutting off a much
smaller area.

Fig.49
Pl.28
At Scratchbury (Wilts.) the original enclosure was D-shaped. This was later
extended by lengthening the straight side of the D to the position of the existing defences, which presumably cover the other sides of this second enclosure.
At a later stage again the straight side was abandoned in favour of the existing
outer defences: the abandoned inner features are very much flattened although

107

Fig.50. Ivington
Camp,
Herefordshire.

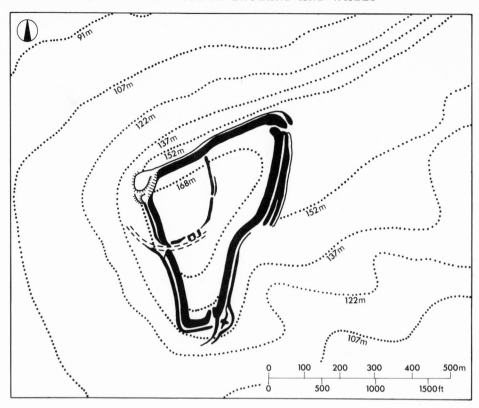

Fig.78
Pl.33

still perceptible. Oldbury (Wilts.) seems to have gone through the second part of this process. Within the enclosure, running more or less parallel to, and about 46 m (150 ft) from, the southern defences, is a bank and ditch which seem to have formed the original univallate southern defences. These appear to have been abandoned in favour of the multivallate defences, which occupy a better defensive position.

Fig.50

In Herefordshire the multivallate defences of Ivington Camp follow the contours on the north, west, and south, and face an easy approach on the east; a Group II semi-contour situation. Within the enclosure thus defined are the remains of earlier, univallate defences facing south and east and following the contours on the two remaining sides; a Group III semi-contour site. At Burrow Camp (Salop) there appears likewise to be an abandoned line of earlier univallate defences a short distance behind the main multivallate system on the southern side. At Ffridd Faldwyn (Montg.) the remains of the smaller earlier fort are very slight as compared with the defences of the larger later fort which enclose them, and had certainly ceased to have any defensive function by the time the latter were completed. Finally, at Bosherston Camp (Pemb) there is

Fig.87

an earlier bank and ditch about 30 m (100 ft) behind the later multivallate system defending the approach to the promontory.

108

HUT PLATFORMS AND HUT CIRCLES

The surface evidence for the occupation of Iron Age forts takes the form of either the collapsed remains of the actual huts or the platforms on which they were built. Evidence of this type, however, exists in a very small number of sites. Only about 5 per cent of all Iron Age forts are recorded as having hut circles or hut platforms within their defences. The remainder, something like 1,300 sites, are, as far as is known at present, completely blank in this respect. Probably this low percentage is to be accounted for, at least in part, by lack of fieldwork in certain areas and by incomplete observation. Hut platforms in particular are easily overlooked, the more so where they exist only in ones and twos and where the vegetation cover is thick. Even allowing for this, however, it is unlikely that the percentage of sites with visible evidence of occupation will ever exceed 15 per cent, and probably 10 per cent would be nearer the true figure. This means that in about 1,200 Iron Age forts the surface evidence of habitations has been removed (by ploughing, for example), or else such habitations never existed. The whole problem of the nature and extent of the occupation of Iron Age forts is one which can be settled only by extensive excavation in the interior of the sites.

The habitation remains which do exist take three main forms. The first two are the collapsed remains of the hut walls, either in earth or in stone. The third is the platform, cut back into a slope, on which the hut was built. These platforms are usually circular or near circular in plan, and as nearly all the known hut remains in the Iron Age forts of England and Wales are circular, it is likely though not inevitable that any huts built on such platforms would take the same form.

Pls.20,23

Pls.51,30

The number of huts or platforms in any one site varies considerably from only one or two, to over one hundred, though there are few of the latter. Among the latter are Hambledon Hill and Hod Hill in Dorset, with about 175 and 250 respectively. Other sites with large numbers of such remains include Carn Brea (Corn.), Foel Trigarn and Carningli (Pemb), and Tre'r Ceiri, Garn Boduan, and Carn Fadrun (Caer.). Braich-y-Dinas (Caer.) is now entirely destroyed but is recorded as having about 90 huts. At Midsummer Hill (Here.) only about 36 hut circles are now visible, but it is recorded that over 200 could be made out as late as 1875. In many other sites the hut remains number 12 or

Fig.57

less. At St. David's Head (Pemb) there are the remains of 6 huts, at Gelli-Gaer (Card.) traces of 3 or 4 huts, while at Dinorwig (Caer.) there is only one, but this is in the only section of the interior which has not been ploughed, and it is possible that there were originally more than one. This could apply to many other sites with only small numbers of huts and, of course, to sites with no huts at all.

Fig.51a
Pl.20

In southern England visible hut remains in the interiors of Iron Age forts are quite rare. The few sites where they are found are mainly in Wessex. At Hambledon Hill (Dorset) the evidence for the 175 or so habitations takes the form of platforms cut back into the sloping surface of the interior. Many of these are of the fairly common, more or less circular, type with a diameter of between 4·5

Fig. 51a Hut
platforms,
Hambledon Hill,
Dorset; 51b Hut
circles, Hod Hill,
Dorset.

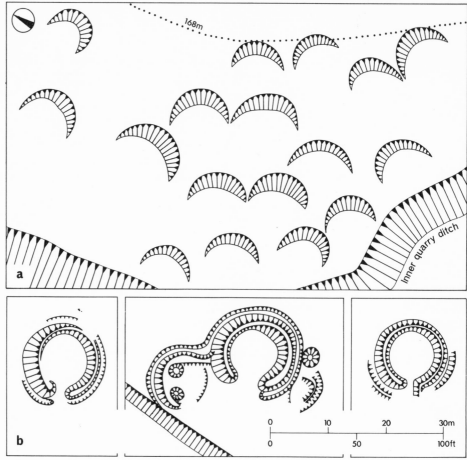

and 9 m (15 and 30 ft), sometimes standing alone, sometimes joined together in twos, threes, and more. Other platforms are oval or elongated and these are quite clearly the setting for something more than a single hut, so that the number of habitations could have been in excess of 175. The platforms are not spread evenly throughout the interior. There is a large concentration at the south-western end of the site just inside the main entrance and another concentration at the north-western end. Very few of the sites are on the crest of the hill, most of them taking advantage of the more sheltered sloping ground which runs down to the inner quarry ditch behind the rampart.

Fig. 51b
Pl. 23

    In the neighbouring fort on Hod Hill the surface evidence suggests an even larger population. Part of the interior has been ploughed in recent times so that it is not possible to be certain of the exact number of habitations, but something between 200 and 300 seems likely. About 50 of these are still well preserved. Unlike Hambledon the remains inside Hod Hill are those of the actual huts and not simply the platforms on which they stood. At their simplest they consist of a low bank, about 2·7 m (9 ft) wide, with a slight outer ditch, defining a circular

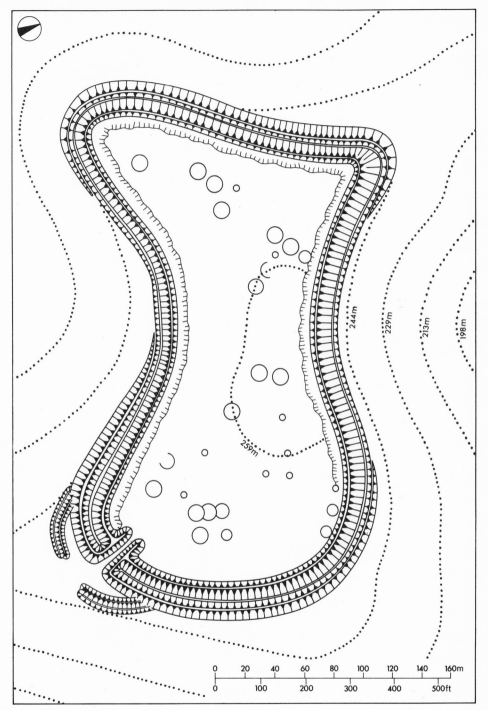

Fig.52. Beacon Hill, Hampshire.

area of from 4·5 to 9 m (15 to 30 ft) in diameter. Added to many of them are more or less semicircular annexes defined in the same way. One hut, probably of this type, stands within a roughly rectangular enclosure, about 23 m (75 ft) square, defined by a shallow ditch.

Pl.29

Fig.52

Fig.47

Fig.53

Two other Wessex sites, Beacon Hill (Hants) and Chalbury (Dorset), have much smaller numbers of hut circles, although it should be noted that the areas available for occupation are also considerably smaller. At Beacon Hill the internal area is about 3·6 ha (9 acres) and there are the remains of about 20 hut-circles scattered throughout the enclosure. Chalbury is of generally similar size, enclosing 4 ha (10 acres), and has some 70 circular depressions or platforms inside. Many of these, however, are very small and are probably the remains of pits rather than huts. About 40, rather more than half, appear to be large enough to be interpreted as huts. At Abbotsbury (Dorset) there is a compact group of 10 hut sites approximately in the middle of the enclosed area. They consist of either hut platforms or circular earth banks.

The only other sites in Wessex which can be mentioned in this context are St. Catherine's Hill, Old Winchester Hill, and Hengistbury Head (Hants), and Scratchbury (Wilts.). At St. Catherine's Hill, according to Williams-Freeman,[4] 'there are numerous deep depressions about 50 ft across, mostly in the eastern half of the area', and 'they seem too big for hut-circles'. At Old Winchester Hill there are a few depressions suggestive of hut circles. At Hengistbury Head there

Pl.28

are 5 possible hut circles. At Scratchbury the remains take the form of platforms cut into the slope and measuring between 6 and 9 m (20 and 30 ft) across. There are about 12 of them just within the north-western entrance.[5]

In the remainder of southern England, i.e. outside Wessex, there appear to be no such sites at all in the south-east and only 2 in the south-west, both in Cornwall. At Carn Brea there are reported to be a large number of hut-circles both inside and outside the defences. At Bury Down several circles are recorded within the enclosure and these may well be hut-circles. Apart from the 11 sites mentioned above there are no other sites known to the writer in southern England where there is surface evidence of occupation in the form of hut-circles or platforms.

Pl.27

The remaining sites in which hut remains occur are located in the Welsh Marches and Wales. At Midsummer Hill (Here.) there are now traces of about 36 hut circles in the form of rounded hollows, but the south-eastern slope of the summit is said to have had a series of 11 terraces on which more than 200 hut sites could be traced as late as 1875. A few of these are still visible, as are traces of the terracing. At the Herefordshire Beacon there are what are described as sinkings but which from the plan are quite clearly platforms cut back into the slope. There is one immediately north-east of the west entrance, two south-west of the north entrance, and a small one about 46 m (150 ft) north-west of the south entrance. According to the plan three of these platforms are quite large, some 15 or 18 m (50 or 60 ft) across.

---

4. Williams-Freeman, *An Introduction to Field Archaeology as Illustrated by Hampshire* (1915).
5. For this information I am indebted to Mr. D. J. Bonney.

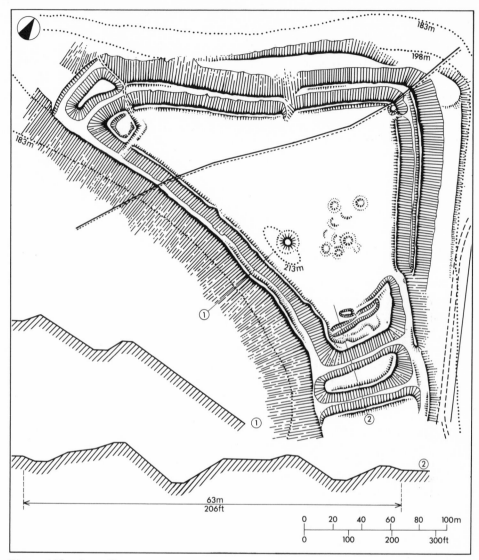

Fig.53. Abbotsbury, Dorset.

In Shropshire there are indications of 3 hut circles near the south-west entrance of The Wrekin. At Abdon Burf and Clee Burf in the same county numerous hollows are reported both inside and outside the enclosures and on the ridge between them. Some of these may be hut circles, but many, possibly all of them, are the remains of workings for coal. At Caer Caradoc, Clun, there are alleged to be 5 hut circles with openings towards the rampart on the north side. It is quite clear, however, that the 5 so-called hut circles are formed by the scalloped edge of the inner quarry ditch at this point. The same explanation would appear to hold good for the 7 hut circles at Norton Camp, although it is

Fig.31
Pl.25

Fig.35c

113

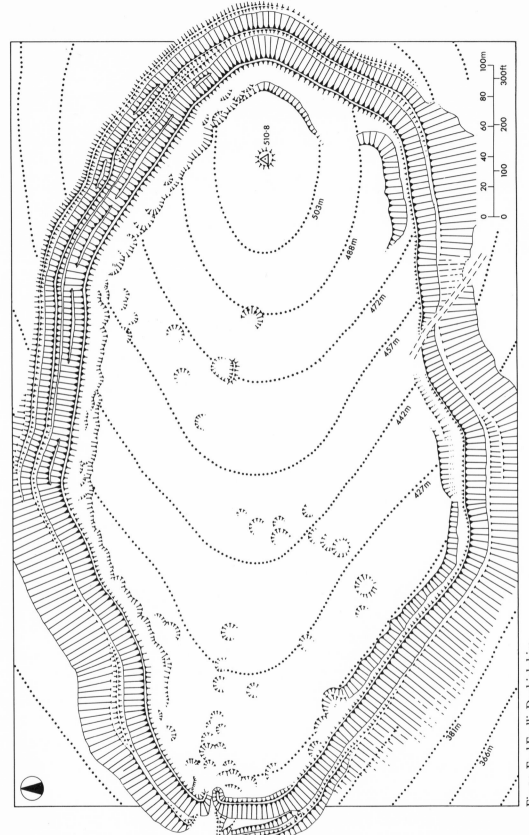

510·8

503m

488m

472m

457m

442m

427m

381m

366m

100m
80
60
40
20
0

300ft
200
100
0

Fig.54. Foel Fenlli, Denbighshire.

stated[6] that there the flat stones of the walls are still standing 60 cm (2 ft) high in one place. It may be that the inner quarry ditch fulfilled a dual purpose. Certainly where it is cut back into sloping ground it provides a series of platforms very similar to those dug specially as hut emplacements, and it may be that in certain cases advantage was taken of this.

In Montgomershire there are hut remains at Craig Rhiwarth, roughly in the middle of the very large enclosure of about 16 ha (40 acres). In this area, usually in sheltered hollows, are numerous round stone house foundations. In some, a smaller inner house has been built within a larger, presumably earlier, ring. Beyond the Marcher region to the north-east there are numerous hut platforms on the steeply sloping north-western side of the enclosure at Mam Tor (Derby.).

Fig.66

In Wales other hut remains are found, particularly in the western parts of the country. In Flintshire there are about 24 hut circles inside Moel Hiraddug, mostly in the northern half of the site on the more sheltered eastern side. As with so many other sites in Wales semicircular scoops inside the rampart may have served a dual purpose, as quarries for rampart material and as suitable settings for huts. There are two such scoops on the north-western side of Moel Arthur in the same county, just inside the inner rampart. At the southern end of the Clwyds, in Denbighshire, Foel Fenlli has about 24 hut platforms dug back into the sloping ground within its defences. The actual platform, i.e. the level circular or sometimes oval area, is usually between 6 and 9 m (20 and 30 ft) in diameter. Most of the platforms are in the south-western quarter of the site. There is a single oval platform immediately adjacent to the inner quarry ditch on the southern side of Moel y Gaer, Llanbedr (Denb.). This could be a hut platform or simply an additional part of the quarry ditch. At Dinorben in the same county there are something like 50 hut platforms scattered over an interior area of about 2 ha (5 acres).

Fig.54

Hut remains, are, or appear to be, more numerous in Caernarvonshire. This may be because the use of stone has led to the survival of a greater number, but it is possible that it is to be accounted for to some extent by more intensive survey. The county includes some of the sites with relatively large numbers of hut remains mentioned earlier. In the fort on Conway Mountain there are in all 58 hut foundations. About 40 of these are between 3 and 5 m (11 and 18 ft) in diameter, with the remainder up to 8 m (26 ft) in diameter. Many of the hut walls consist of two rows of stone slabs on edge, about 1 m (3 ft) apart, with a filling of earth or rubble between, but laid masonry is also found, often in the same hut. About half of the huts are on a shelf immediately inside the southern rampart; the remainder are scattered throughout the enclosed area. The nearby site of Braich-y-Dinas is now entirely destroyed but originally there were, according to Hughes,[7] about 90 huts, either circular or oval in plan, 3–6 m (10–20 ft) in diameter, with walls of coursed masonry some 1·5–2 m (5–6 ft) thick. Only a few of the huts were on the hilltop, the majority being on the eastern slope.

6. Wall, J. C. & Downman, E. A., 1908. The appearance of stone walls may be due to the manner in which the local rock fractures in the rock-cut ditch. A similar effect can be seen in the main ditch at another Shropshire site, Bury Ditches.

7. Hughes, 'Prehistoric Remains on Penmaenmawr', *Arch. Camb.* (1923), 243–68.

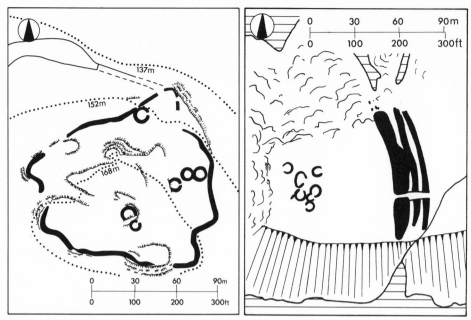

Fig.55. Caer Carreg-y-fran, Caernarvonshire.   Fig.57. St. David's Head, Pembrokeshire.

Pl.30

To the south of, and roughly equidistant from Braich-y-Dinas and Conway Mountain, Pen-y-Gaer, Llanbedr-y-Cennin, has the foundations of 12 huts in the main enclosure. These appear as levelled circular platforms on the hillside, generally surrounded in whole or part by a low wall of earth and stone. There are, in addition, vague hollows in the eastern half of the site which may indicate further huts. Between the middle and inner ramparts there are 8 more huts, similar to the 12 already mentioned.

Apart from Tre'r Ceiri and Garn Boduan, the remaining 9 sites in this category average 7 huts each. The largest number is found in Dinas, Llanfairfechan, where there are traces of 14 circular huts, up to 9 m (30 ft) in internal diameter, scattered over most of the enclosure. At Pen-y-Gaer, Llanaelhaiarn, there are about 12 rather ill-defined terraced platforms, about 6 m (20 ft) in diameter, scattered from one end of the enclosure to the other, but not on the summit of the hill. At Castell Odo there are traces of at least 8 round huts, with perhaps 2 more, averaging about 8 m (25 ft) in diameter.

At Carn Fadrun the huts are between 4·5 and 8 m (15 and 25 ft) in diameter with walls 90 cm to 1 m (3–4 ft) thick, generally faced with laid masonry but sometimes with orthostats. Only 9 or 10 of this type are found in the interior, but there are many more on the slopes outside, especially to the north and northwest. In addition to the circular huts, there are many smaller, sub-rectangular, and irregular huts in the scree and the ruins of the ramparts. There are 6 huts

Fig.55

each at Caer Carreg-y-Fran and Dinas Dinlleu, the former of laid masonry, the latter of overgrown earthen banks, 30–60 cm (1–2 ft) high. There are 3 circular

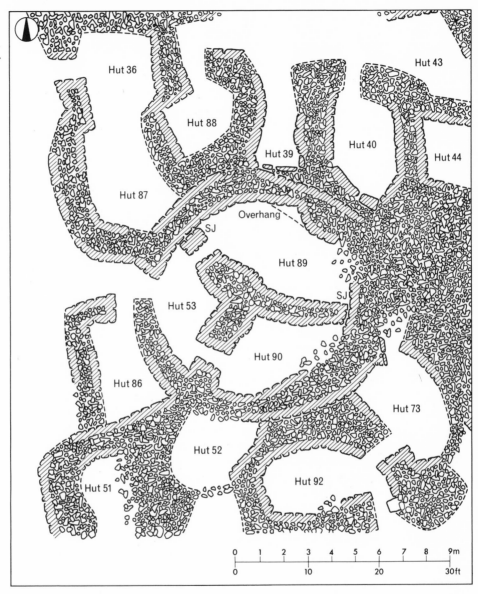

Fig.56. Hut
circles, Tre'r
Ceiri,
Caernarvonshire.

huts, 4·8, 5·5, and 6 m (16, 18, and 20 ft) in diameter, at Creigiau Gwineu and 1
each at Caer Bach and Dinas Dinorwig.

Pl.30

Although both Garn Boduan and Tre'r Ceiri have large numbers of hut
foundations in their enclosures the character of the huts is noticeably different
in the two sites. At Garn Boduan nearly all of the 168 huts are circular or near-
circular in plan. They are between 4·5 and 9 m (15 and 30 ft) in internal
diameter with walls of from 91 cm to 1·5 m (3 to 5 ft) in thickness. The latter
were built in two styles, upright slabs and laid courses, the two sometimes ap-
pearing in the same hut. The hut circles are spread fairly evenly throughout the

Fig.56
Pl.30

main enclosure with something of a concentration at the southern end. Most of them stand free of each other but a number are joined in groups of 2, 3 and, in one or two cases, 4. At Tre'r Ceiri the number of huts is 150, and they differ from those at Garn Boduan. The majority of them can be described as sub-rectangular or irregular, many of them 4·5–6 m (15–20 ft) long and 2·4–3 m (8–10 ft) wide. Less than 30 of the huts are circular in plan and about a third of these have been subdivided by internal, presumably later, walls. The sub-rectangular and irregular huts are probably of Roman date; the circular huts are probably of Iron Age date. The subdivided huts represent two structural phases, the earlier one probably Iron Age, the later Roman.

In Anglesey the interior of the fort at Parciau is filled with shallow circular depressions averaging 8 m (25 ft) in diameter, representing huts. About 20 are shown on the plan in the Welsh Commission's inventory and there are vague traces of many more. At Bwrdd Arthur in the same county there are vague indications of a number of hut sites.

The remaining sites in Wales with surface evidence of occupation are in four counties, Cardigan, Carmarthen, Merioneth, and Pembroke. At Gelli-Gaer (Card.) there are traces of 3 or 4 huts, while at Dinas, Melindwr, there is 1 hut platform near the centre of the enclosure with some suggestion of 3 others. At Daren Camp in the same county there are 2 hut platforms and at Pen-y-Ffrwyd-llwyd one at least, with possibly 2 or 3 others. Finally, at Castell Bwa-Drain there is one doubtful hut platform. In Carmarthen there are traces of hut circles in Gilman Camp and Allt-y-Cnap, and single hut circles in Gaer Fawr and Gaer Fach.

In Merioneth 5 sites can be mentioned, although the evidence in 4 of them is very slight. For example, at Tyddyn-y-coed there is a single depression which may denote a hut dwelling, at Craig-yr-Aderyn possibly 2 hut depressions, and at Foel Offrwm 'hollows which may be the sites of hut dwellings'.[8] At Bryn y Castell there are features which could be interpreted as hut dwellings, 'but it is possible that these are only depressions caused by the excavation of the earth to heighten the banks'.[8] The evidence at the remaining site is a little more positive. At Caer Drewyn there are hut circles in the small annexe adjacent to the north-eastern entrance and one circular hut in the main enclosure just inside the western entrance.

In Pembrokeshire at least 12 sites are recorded as having hut remains, although in most cases only small numbers are involved. At Gribin Camp there are 3 circular hut foundations and at Foxes' Holes, Talbenny, 6 circles, but these are said locally to be the result of surface mining. Cultivation is supposed to have removed all signs of the hut circles which are said to have existed at Castell Gwyn. There are slight traces of hut circles at Dinas Mawr, and there are a few hut circles along the line of the wall at Carn Ffoi. Crossley[9] records evidence of hut remains in 6 other sites in the county, most of them involving only 2 or 3 huts.

Fig.57

At St. David's Head there is a compact group of 6 stone-built huts with an

8. R.C.A.M. *Merionethshire* (1921).

9. Crossley, 'List of Hillforts in Pembrokeshire', *Bull. Board Celtic Stud.* 20.2 (1963), 171–203.

annexe or vestibule attached to one of them. Huts 1–4 and the annexe form a single complex. Huts 5 and 6 are free-standing, each of them about 2·4 m (8 ft) from the central group; hut 4 is oval in plan, 9·7 m (32 ft) long and 6·4 m (21 ft) wide. The remaining huts are circular and between 4·5 and 6 m (15 and 20 ft) in diameter, with walls about 1 m (4 ft) thick.

Pl.51

Very much larger numbers are involved at Foel Trigarn where there are three enclosures. The main enclosure is said to contain 77 hut platforms and the middle enclosure 63. The number for the outer enclosure is not stated, but assuming generally similar numbers to the others a total in the region of 200 is arrived at. There are also many hut platforms on the terrace below the site to the south.

Finally, there are visible hut circles in one site in Glamorgan (Mynydd Bychan) and a single hut circle in one site in Monmouth (Trelleck Gaer).

CHAPTER V

Defences and single-enclosure sites

Fig.43c
Pls.41,42

It will be clear from some of the sites illustrated already that there are not infrequently both univallate and multivallate defences or two different kinds of multivallate defences in the same fort. For this reason it is difficult to deal with the question of defences on the basis of sites, and the method to be adopted here is on the basis of what may be termed 'systems'. A system can be defined as the defences of a site, including the inner quarry ditch, at any one point considered in cross-section. Thus the system on the northern side of Maiden Castle (Dorset) consists of a compact arrangement of two banks, two ditches, and a counterscarp bank, while on the southern side there are, at one point, three ditches and four banks with two intervening spaces. There are further variations in other parts of the same site.

The systems on the northern and southern sides of Maiden Castle belong respectively to the compact and separated multivallate styles as defined in Chapter I. The third multivallate style defined there, dispersed or wide-spaced defences, calls for some comment in the present context. Such sites involve more than one enclosure and, as implied in the chapter heading, they will not be dealt with here. However, for the survey of defences, as opposed to sites, to be complete, the defences which exist in all sites, including those with wide-spaced defences, must be included. For the purposes of this chapter and to cover all contingencies, wide-spaced defences will be treated as single systems, although they will be considered in rather less detail than the compact and separated systems which defend single-enclosure sites.

The original structure of Iron Age defences was described briefly in Chapter I (pp. 12–14). Where only the collapse of the structure and the normal processes of erosion are involved then, broadly speaking, the present remains are a reflection of the original arrangement. This situation, which fortunately embraces the majority of Iron Age forts, makes it possible to discuss the subject of defence systems without recourse to excavation. Where other agencies, e.g. ploughing or deliberate destruction, are involved, the defences are sometimes reduced to a state where it is impossible to discuss the original arrangement.

In any chapter dealing with defences something must be said about those sites where the defences are apparently unfinished. The classic unfinished site is Ladle Hill (Hants), where the evidence for the non-completion of the fort takes three forms. The ditch is in a series of separate lengths with undug causeways between. The next stage would have been the removal of the causeways to

Fig.58. Devil's
Dyke, Sussex.

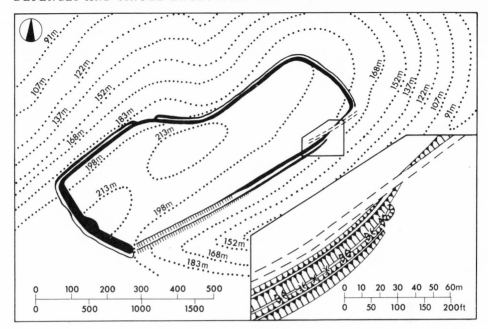

produce a continuous ditch. The separate lengths are usually interpreted as the work of separate gangs. The bank also appears in a series of separate lengths, corresponding roughly to the lengths of ditch. Behind the bank, and roughly at right angles to it, is a series of irregular mounds running in towards the centre of the enclosure, and these are interpreted as dumps of lighter material dug from the upper part of the ditch and put to one side until the heavier material, from the deeper parts of the ditch, had been dumped on its inner edge to form a solid foundation.

Of the three types of evidence present at Ladle Hill only two appear to occur elsewhere. At all the other sites known to the writer the evidence rests in the nature of the bank or the ditch, or both, and in many cases is confined to a relatively small part of the site. At the Devil's Dyke (Sussex), for example, the ditch for a distance of about 76 m (250 ft) takes the form of six or seven separate lengths, with undug causeways between. It may have been felt that the steep natural slope below the south-eastern corner made a continuous ditch unnecessary. There is a generally similar length of ditch with four undug causeways at Pencarrow (Corn.). On the southern side of the inner enclosure there are two banks and two ditches with a third bank and the causewayed ditch immediately beyond, presumably intended to form a compact three-ditch system. Unfortunately, this part of the site is covered with dense undergrowth and the arrangement is difficult to follow. The outer ditch at Moel y Gaer, Rhosesmor (Flint.), likewise has a series of undug causeways on the eastern side, presumably indicating that the outer defences were never completed.

At other sites the evidence is to be found in the nature of the bank, which appears as a series of mounds connected end to end rather than as a continuous

Fig.58

Fig.102

121

Pl.34

bank. These mounds are presumably dumps of material from the ditch, ready to be formed into a rampart. A series of such mounds can be seen at Spettisbury Rings (Dorset), on the eastern side of the site. They cover a distance of about 91 m (300 ft) and the larger mounds are about 21 m (70 ft) long. There is a

Fig.21a
Pl.23

similar feature at the south-western entrance of Hod Hill in the same county. Outside the bank there are the beginnings of a ditch in the form of a series of shallow scoops. At Woodhouses (Ches.), the defences consist of a single bank without a ditch. Along most of the eastern side the bank is very irregular, relatively massive sections alternating with much slighter lengths.

Fig.45

In a number of multivallate sites the unfinished defences appear to represent an attempt to strengthen existing defences. At Caster Cliff (Lancs) the original defences appear to have consisted of a single bank without a ditch, with a bank and ditch and, in places, a counterscarp bank added later. On the northern side of the site, however, these additional defences appear to be unfinished. Instead of a continuous bank and ditch there is a series of short lengths with level ground between that shows no evidence of ever having been disturbed.

Fig.92
Pl.50

Warbstow Bury (Corn.) is a concentric site with inner and outer lines of defence that appear to be complete. In the southern half of the site, however, in the space (*c.* 37 m: 120 ft wide) between the inner and outer lines there is a third line of defence, apparently unfinished. This could be a later insertion but equally well it could be a first attempt to provide an outer defence, abandoned in favour of the present outer defences. At Earl's Hill (Salop) there are two short

Fig.105

lengths of ditch about 27 m (90 ft) long with most of the material thrown out on to the counterscarp. In their present state they make no sense. They must surely have been intended to form part of a continuous bank and ditch and may well have been abandoned in favour of the long bank about 91 m (300 ft) to the west which is in a much better defensive position. Along the southern and

Fig.59

western sides of Woodbury (Devon) there are five separate lengths of bank and ditch, two lengths of bank alone, and a length of ditch alone, covering in all a distance of some 457 m (1,500 ft). On the north-eastern side the continuation of

Fig.103

this outer defence ends on level ground. At Winkelbury (Wilts.) the outer defences seem to have reached a more advanced stage. The southern defence appears to have been originally a cross-ridge dyke and the new eastern and western defences do not quite reach it, leaving considerable gaps at the south-western and south-eastern corners. In addition the ditches are in a series of separate lengths with undug causeways between.

Other apparently unfinished sites include Cranbrook Castle (Devon), Elworthy Barrows (Som.), Golden Camp and Twm Barlwm (Mon.), Allt yr Esgair (Breck.), and Lawley Camp (Salop).

The simplest defences involve only one feature, a bank, but most systems consist of two or more elements, the commonest combination being a bank and ditch. Multivallate systems involve the multiplication of these arrangements. The division into univallate and multivallate types is an obvious first step in classifying defence systems, but the multivallate systems are susceptible of further subdivision. Because of counterscarp banks subdivision according to the number of banks is not practicable. A subdivision based on the number of

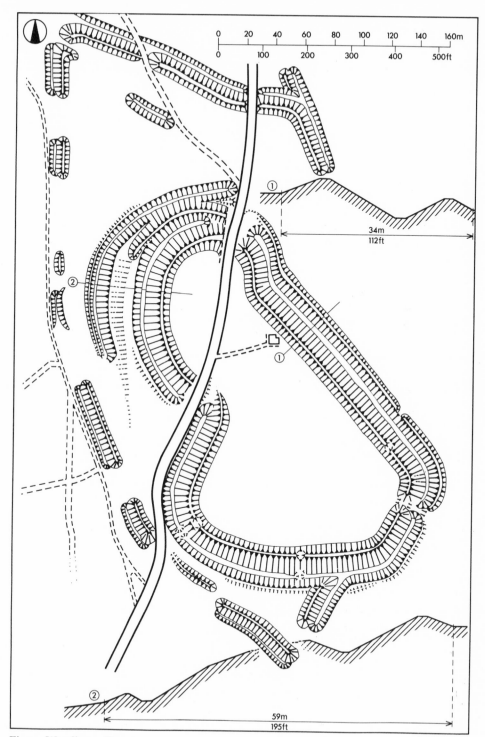

Fig.59. Woodbury, Devon.

Fig.60. Bury
Walls,
Shropshire.

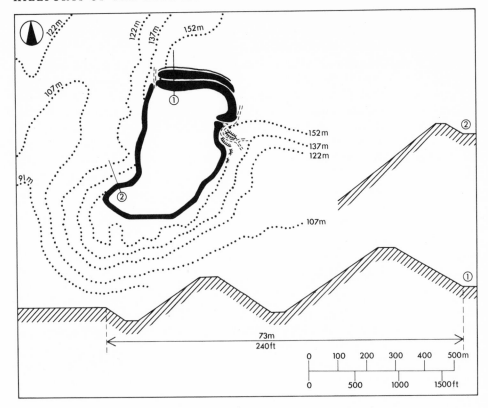

ditches provides a more objective basis. This, of course, cannot apply to systems without ditches, but since in such cases there are no counterscarp banks to complicate the issue the system can then be classified according to the number of banks present. Accordingly, all systems will be placed in one or other of the following four groups:

Group 1. Single-ditch or single-bank systems.
Group 2. Double-ditch or double-bank, or mixed, systems.
Group 3. Triple-ditch or triple-bank, or mixed, systems.
Group 4. Systems with more than three ditches or three banks.

The mixed systems mentioned under Groups 2 and 3 call for some comment, although only small numbers are involved. They consist of arrangements in which one rampart is ditchless while the other has a ditch. To classify this as a single-ditch system would be to defeat any attempt at classification and it has to be placed in Group 2. Instead of being a double-ditch or double-bank system it is, in effect, a half of each and as such is multivallate and appropriate to the second group. The same principle applies to mixed systems in Group 3. Most of the defence systems in England and Wales belong to either Group 1 or Group 2. Groups 3 and 4 account for much smaller numbers of systems.

Before dealing with these four groups there are certain aspects of the features making up the systems that can best be considered separately. One of these is the size of the banks involved. At the upper end of the scale the largest banks are around 6 m (20 ft) in height and between 21 and 30 m (70 and 100 ft) wide.

Fig.60

The ditchless stone-built western rampart at Gaer Fawr (Carm.) is about 30 m (100 ft) wide and about 6 m (20 ft) high. The inner rampart at Bury Walls (Salop) is of the same general dimensions; it forms part of a two-ditch multi-

Fig.50

vallate system. The inner ramparts at Ivington Camp (Here.), Castle Ditches

Fig.30b

(Hants), and Hambledon (Dorset) are of similar heights but are somewhat narrower at the base (about 23 m : 75 ft). Ramparts of comparable dimensions

Pls.41,42;Fig.75a

exist at Cissbury (Sussex), Danebury (Hants), Maiden Castle (Dorset), Yarn-

Pl.18;Figs.76c,61a

bury (Wilts.), Haresfield Beacon (Glos), Credenhill (Here.), Sudbrook (Mon.), Dinorben (Denb.), and a few other places. Ramparts of this size, however, are comparatively few in number.

In most Iron Age forts the banks or ramparts are between 7·6 and 10·6 m

Fig.61b

(25 and 35 ft) wide and between 1·5 and 2 m (5 and 7 ft) in height above present ground-level. These dimensions suggest original ramparts in the region of 2·7 or 3 m (9 or 10 ft) high. In the case of revetted ramparts another 1 m (4 ft) could be added for a breastwork, so that the face presented to the enemy would have been 3·9 or 4·2 m (13 or 14 ft) high. Supplemented by an outer ditch such a rampart would have represented a fairly stiff obstacle to any would-be attacker. Banks of the larger dimensions quoted earlier suggest original ramparts between 6 and 7·6 m (20 and 25 ft) high. Most of these were accompanied by ditches, so that the original height from the top of the rampart to the bottom of the ditch must have been in the region of 12 or 15 m (40 or 50 ft) a formidable obstacle in a defence work of any period.

In their present state most of the banks surrounding Iron Age forts are tri-angular in cross-section, with the apex of the triangle flattened in varying degrees. There are, however, a few sites which show a particular variation from this shape, and they can be noted here. One of the best examples occurs at

Fig.61c

Ivington Camp (Here.), where it can be seen that the rear of the bank consists of two scarps separated by a horizontal ledge or platform. On the eastern side, where the bank is 6 m (20 ft) high, the ledge is 4·2 m (14 ft) above the interior and 1·8 m (6 ft) below the rampart crest. At the southern end the ledge is 1·8 m (6 ft) above the interior and 2·4 m (8 ft) below the crest. There is a similar feature on a smaller scale at the eastern end of Smalldown Camp (Som.). There the ledge is about 1 m (4 ft) above the interior and about 91 cm (3 ft) below the rampart crest. Another site in Somerset, Burrington Camp, is reported as having 'a rampart walk at a height of about 6 ft with a breastwork of about 3 ft.',[1] which must represent the same sort of arrangement. At Abbotsbury

Fig.53

(Dorset) the ledge at the back of the rampart is very much wider than those considered so far (5 m : 17 ft). It stands about 1·8 m (6 ft) above ground-level and is 91 cm (3 ft) below the rampart crest.

Two other sites can be mentioned in this context. At The Trundle (Sussex) the rear of the bank on the western side also consists of two scarps, at different

---

1. Bothamley, 'Ancient Earthworks', *V.C.H. Somerset*, 2 (1911), 467–532.

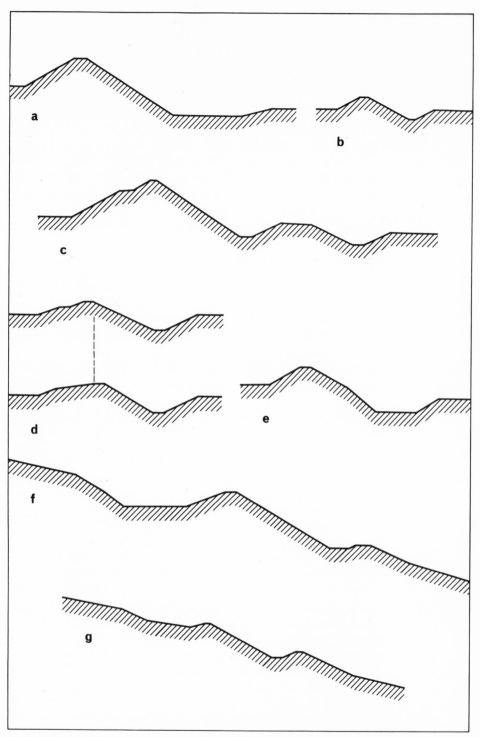

Fig.61. Features of defence systems: 61a Haresfield Beacon, Gloucestershire; 61b Casterley Camp, Wiltshire; 61c Ivington Camp, Herefordshire; 61d Segsbury, Berkshire; 61e Spettisbury Ring, Dorset, 61f Credenhill Camp, Herefordshire; 61g Midsummer Hill, Herefordshire.

Fig.61d

angles, although in this case there is no ledge between. Segsbury (Berks) has a smaller cross-section which, however, alternates with lengths of rampart showing a quite clear ledge, as at the sites mentioned above. It looks as if The Trundle and Segsbury ramparts were of the ledge type, but subject to greater erosion.

The function which these ledges performed has been suggested already for Burrington Camp, that of a rampart walk behind a breastwork. This is feasible for all the sites considered except Ivington Camp. There the dimensions make this interpretation rather more difficult. In places the ledge is 2·4 m (8 ft) below the present crest of the bank and this is much too high for a breastwork. It is possible that the ledge is the lower step of a stepped rampart, with a smaller upper step, now gone, acting as a rampart walk. Another possibility is that it is a structural device designed to give greater stability to the rampart. Steps or ledges are visible also in a number of stone-built ramparts, at Caer Drewyn (Mer.) and Tre'r Ceiri (Caer.) for example, and it may be that the 6 sites considered above are simply the earthen counterparts of these.

In the majority of Iron Age forts the outer scarp of the bank and the inner scarp of the ditch form a single continuous slope, so that it is not possible to see exactly where the bank ends and the ditch begins. In a few cases, however, this transition is indicated by a perceptible break of slope, the inner scarp of the ditch being at a steeper angle than the outer scarp of the rampart. This can be

Fig.61e
Fig.31
Fig.104

seen very clearly on the western side of Spettisbury Rings (Dorset) and on the northern side of Caer Caradoc, Clun (Salop). It appears also at The Trundle (Sussex), Horton Camp (Glos), and Coxall Knoll and Wall Hills, Thornbury (Here.).

The scarp from rampart crest to ditch bottom is sometimes interrupted in another way. In a few cases there is even now surface evidence of a berm

Fig.83f

between the rampart and its accompanying ditch. At Worlebury (Som.) there is a flat berm about 4·5 m (15 ft) wide between the innermost of the six banks and its associated ditch at the eastern end of the site. Berms of varying widths in corresponding positions occur at Maesbury in the same county and at Cranbrook Castle (Devon), Brackenbury Ditches (Glos), Little Doward Camp

Fig.75e

(Here.), Foxcovert (Denb.), and Caer Estyn (Flint.).

Berms in other positions do not necessarily have the same structural implications, i.e. indicating the existence of a revetted rampart, as those considered

Fig.62
Pl.9

above. At Kimsbury (Glos) for example, there is a berm between the middle bank and the outer ditch. The middle bank, however, is simply the counterscarp bank to the main ditch and probably belongs to an earlier structural phase than the outer ditch and bank. This berm has thus no structural implications for the bank behind it. Berms of this type are simply the flat spaces of natural ground which turn compact systems into separated systems, as defined in Chapter I, and their nature will emerge more clearly when the various types of separated system are being considered later in the chapter.

In section most ditches are an inverted version of the flat-topped triangle which is the model for most banks, although the effects of silting tend to make them rather less angular. There are, however, a few ditches which can be

Fig.62.
Kimsbury,
Gloucestershire.

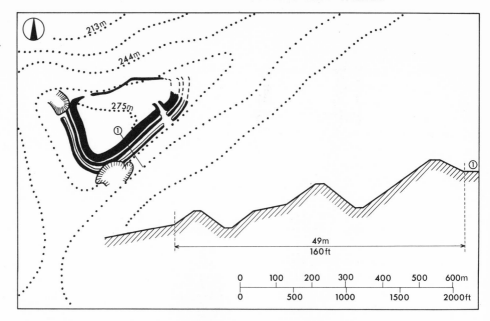

described as flat-bottomed. An excellent example is provided by Spettisbury
Rings (Dorset) where there is a flat-bottomed ditch on the southern, western,
and northern-western sides of the site. On the west the ditch is 6·7 m (22 ft)
wide across the flat bottom and 2 m (7 ft) deep below ground-level. At ground-
level it is in the region of 17 m (55 ft) wide. At Hinton Camp (Glos) the ditch
is about 6 m (20 ft) wide across the bottom, about 11 m (35 ft) wide over-all,
and about 1·5 m (5 ft) deep. At Castle Hill, Blunsdon (Wilts.), the ditch is
even wider across the bottom (9 m: 30 ft). Because of the large counterscarp
bank it is difficult to see the other dimensions clearly, but it is probably in the
region of 1 or 1·5 m (4 or 5 ft) deep and about 14 m (45 ft) wide over-all,
Other flat-bottomed ditches are found at The Caburn (Sussex), Maesbury
(Som.), Sudbrook (Mon.), and Dinas Dinorwig (Caer.). These are discussed
in Chapter X (p. 284).

The last feature to be considered in this section is the inner quarry ditch.
Because it is entirely within the fort and performs no defensive function its
character differs from those ditches which act as both quarry and defence. It is
a feature which is frequently overlooked in field survey, so that its occurrence
may be more widespread than appears from existing published sources. It is
also a feature which is likely to be obscured by later developments such as
ploughing.

In virtually every case the inner quarry ditch where it exists is immediately
behind the rampart for which it supplies the material. Figsbury Rings (Wilts.)
differs from all other sites in that its inner quarry ditch is set back some 30 m
(100 ft) from the rampart, so that it divides the interior into inner and outer
concentric enclosures. This fact, together with the provision of two entrances,

Fig.61e
Pl.34

Pl.31

suggests that the ditch had some function other than that of a mere quarry and the site will be considered again in Chapter VI under multiple enclosures. It may be that the need for more rampart material provided the opportunity of subdividing the interior of the site to suit the needs of the people using it. In its present form the inner quarry ditch is about 9 m (30 ft) wide and about 2·4 m (8 ft) deep.

Pls.20,23,24;
Figs.21a,30b,c
Pl.28;Figs.49,54
Pl.25;Fig.31

Pl.12;Fig.71

The extent of the inner quarry ditch varies considerably from site to site. At some it is virtually continuous, separating the interior area from the defences. This happens at Hod Hill and Hambledon Hill, Dorset, Battlesbury and Scratchbury (Wilts.), Pen-y-cloddiau (Flint.), and Foel Fenlli (Denb.) At Caer Caradoc, Clun (Salop), the inner quarry ditch stops short about 30 m (100 ft) from one side of the western entrance and about 21 m (70 ft) from the other but is otherwise continuous. At the other Caer Caradoc in Shropshire, at Church Stretton, there is no inner quarry ditch at the southern end but on the remainder of the site it is a very prominent feature. At Moel Arthur (Flint.) the inner quarry ditch exists on about two-thirds of the circuit, where the defences stand above the steep natural slope. At Chalbury (Dorset) the inner quarry ditch is prominent on the eastern and western sides, but is missing at the southern end.

Fig.47

Fig.21b

Fig.35c

Fig.75e

Fig.61f

At other sites the inner quarry ditch occupies a relatively small part of the total circuit. At Sidbury (Devon), for example, there is an inner quarry ditch for only about one-fifth of the total circuit. At Norton Camp (Salop) the inner quarry ditch exists only on the straight north-western side, where the defences stand above the steep natural slope. At Foxcovert (Denb.) it appears only behind the very short length of multivallate defences which cross the neck of the promontory. At Credenhill (Here.) there is an inner quarry ditch on the southern and part of the western sides, representing about a quarter of the total circuit.

Pl.20

Pl.4;Fig.46b

Fig.61g,f
Pl.20;Fig.46c

Figs.31,75e,46a

Because they perform no defensive function inner quarry ditches tend to be wide in relation to their depth and they are often considerably wider than the outer ditches. Inner quarry ditches between 9 and 12 m (30 and 40 ft) wide, at Foel Fenlli for example, are of comparatively modest dimensions as compared with the corresponding features at Croft Ambrey and Credenhill (Here.), Pen-y-cloddiau (Flint.), and Hambledon Hill (Dorset), where they are between 21 and 24 m (70 and 80 ft) wide. The depth of the inner quarry ditch below its inner edge can be as much as 3 or 4·5 m (10 or 15 ft), but this does not necessarily represent the depth of material excavated. At Moel Arthur (Flint.), for example, the inner edge is about 3·6 m (12 ft) above the level of the rampart, but this is the result of scraping away no more than 60 or 90 cm (2 or 3 ft) of surface soil from the steep slope of the interior. The same effect is apparent at Pen-y-cloddiau (Flint.), Midsummer Hill, and Credenhill (Here.), and Hambledon Hill (Dorset). Where the interior slopes less steeply or is level then it is possible to get a clearer picture of the depth of the inner quarry ditch. At Caer Caradoc, Clun (Salop), Foxcovert (Denb.), and Hod Hill (Dorset) depths of between 1 and 1·8 m (4 and 6 ft) below present ground-level seem to be general. Allowing for silting they were probably at least half as deep again, about 1·8–3 m (6–10 ft) as originally dug.

GROUP 1: SINGLE BANK OR SINGLE BANK-AND-DITCH SYSTEMS

This group embraces all those systems which defend the 900 or so univallate sites in England and Wales. The commonest arrangement consists of a closely set bank and ditch, sometimes accompanied by a small counterscarp bank. Systems with large counterscarp banks will be considered later. Single bank-and-ditch systems defend between 80 and 90 per cent of all univallate forts. In actual numbers this means something like 750 sites, or more than half the total of all Iron Age forts.

Single bank-and-ditch systems vary considerably in size, size in this context being the vertical measurement from the crest of the existing bank to the bottom of the existing ditch. This vertical measurement will be referred to as the Crest/Ditch vertical, contracted for convenience to C/D vert. Such measurements vary from about 12 m (40 ft) down to only 1 or 1·5 m (4 or 5 ft), and in some cases less. Only a few occur at the upper end of the scale, one being at Wall Hills Camp, Thornbury (Here.), where the system at one point has a C/D vert. of 12 m (40 ft) and an existing width of about 33 m (110 ft). The area enclosed by this system is about 9 ha (23 acres) and the defences themselves occupy a further 2·8 ha (7 acres). Credenhill in the same county has a maximum C/D vert. of 11·5 m (38 ft), at the southern end of the site. The area enclosed is 9 ha (23 acres) with the defences occupying a further 4·8 ha (12 acres). Cissbury in Sussex is in the same class: it has at one point a C/D vert. of 12 m (40 ft), with the crest of the bank standing 6 m (20 ft) above the interior. The area enclosed is some 24 ha (60 acres). Systems of the dimensions just quoted are quite clearly the remains of very strong and imposing defences. Allowing for the erosion of the bank and the silting of the ditch anything between 3 and 6 m (10 and 20 ft) could be added to the figures given above, suggesting original C/D verts. of between 15 and 18 m (50 and 60 ft).

Univallate systems of this size are, however, quite rare. Even systems with C/D verts. of between 6 and 9 m (20 and 30 ft) are comparatively few in number. In Hampshire, a county with a high proportion of univallate forts, there are only two sites with C/D verts. in this range: Old Winchester Hill, 7 m (23 ft) and Frankenbury, 6·4 m (21 ft). The remaining univallate systems in the county have C/D verts. of less than 6 m (20 ft). In England and Wales as a whole univallate systems in the 6–9-m (20–30-ft) range probably account for only 40 or 50 sites at most.

A few examples of such systems can be quoted here. The maximum C/D vert. (6·4 m : 21 ft) at Clearbury Ring (Wilts.) is just within the 6–9-m (20–30-ft) range. The bank rises between 2·4 and 2·7 m (8 and 9 ft) above the interior and the area enclosed is 2 ha (5 acres). Spettisbury (Dorset) is of similar dimensions, its maximum C/D vert. being about 6·7 m (22 ft) and the area enclosed about 2 ha (5 acres). Dungeon Hill in the same county has a C/D vert. of 6·4 m (21 ft) on the eastern side where it is accompanied by a counterscarp bank. Woodbury, Stoke Fleming (Devon), has a maximum C/D vert. of 8·5 m (28 ft), although on the north-east, where the ditch is markedly flat-

Fig.61f

Fig.63

Fig.61e
Pl.34
Fig.64

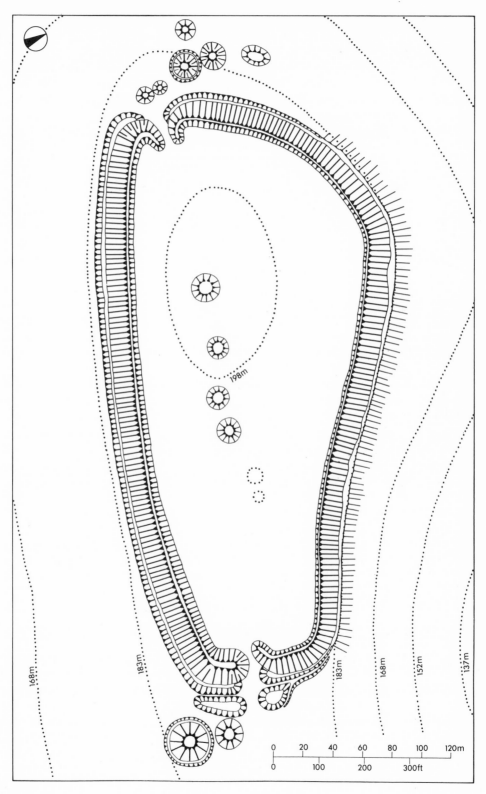

Fig.63. Old Winchester Hill, Hampshire.

198m

168m

183m

183m

168m

152m

137m

| 0 | 20 | 40 | 60 | 80 | 100 | 120m |

| 0 | 100 | 200 | 300ft |

Fig.64.
Dungeon Hill,
Dorset.

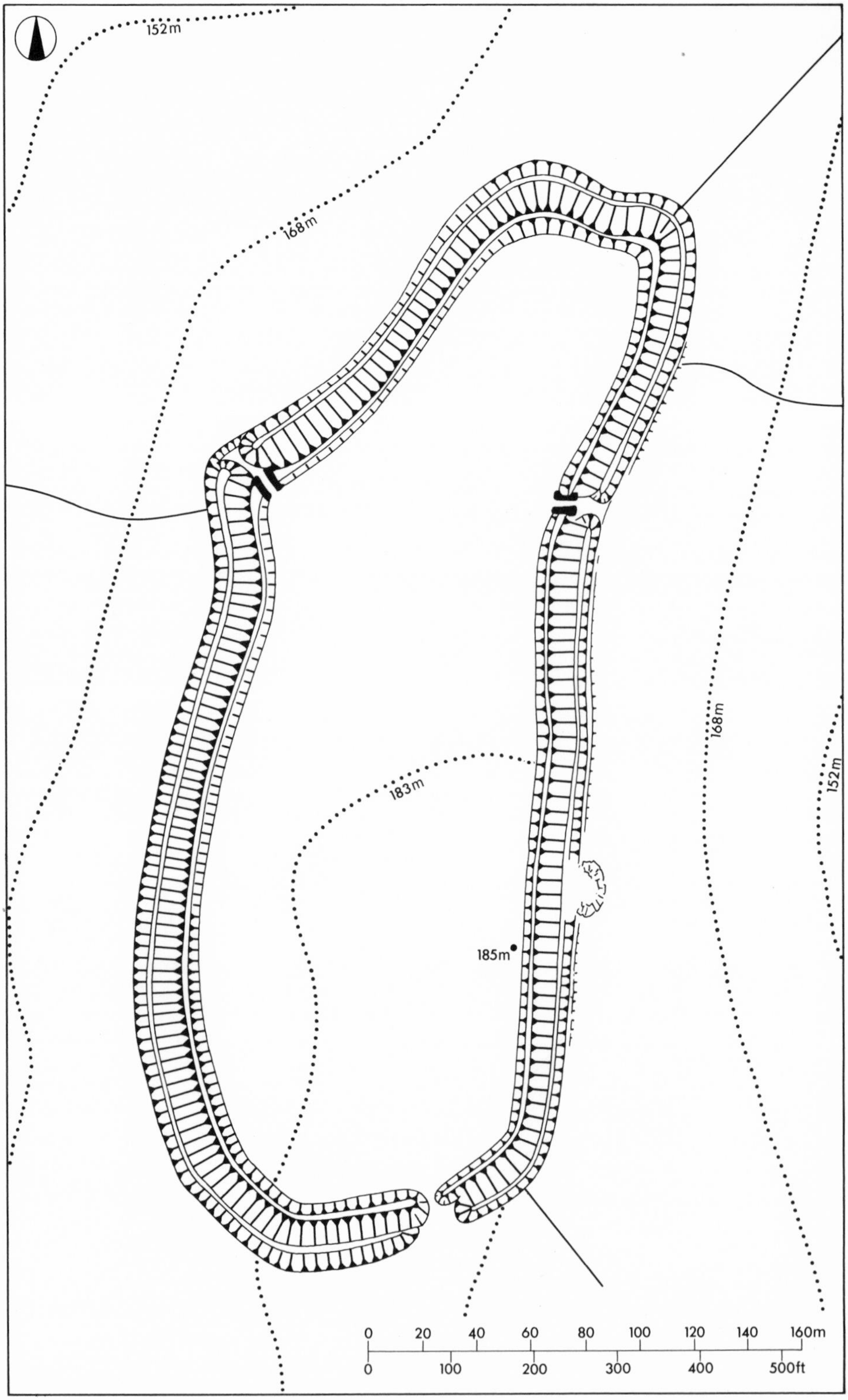

152m

168m

168m

152m

183m

185m

| 0 | 20 | 40 | 60 | 80 | 100 | 120 | 140 | 160m |
| 0 | | 100 | | 200 | | 300 | 400 | 500ft |

Fig.65. Kinver
Edge Camp,
Staffordshire.

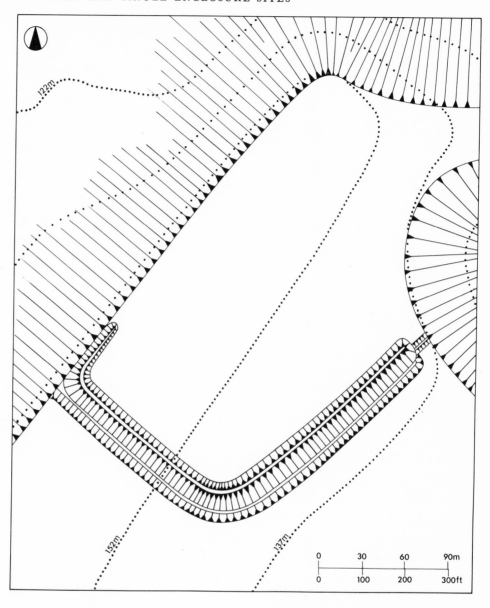

Fig.21b

Fig.61f

bottomed, this is reduced to 4·2 m (14 ft). In the same county Sidbury has a C/D vert. of 6·7 m (22 ft) and encloses an area of about 2·4 ha (6 acres). Cadsonbury (Corn.) comes just within the 6–9-m (20–30-ft) range. The bank rises only a couple of metres above the interior (about 2·8 ha: 7 acres) and the ditch is quite small, so that much of the C/D vert. of just over 6 m (20 ft) must be accounted for by the slope of the ground. The same is true of Sidbury, just mentioned. In Herefordshire Credenhill, mentioned earlier, has a C/D vert. of 7·9 m (26 ft) on the north-east and 7·3 m (24 ft) on the west. In Staffordshire at

133

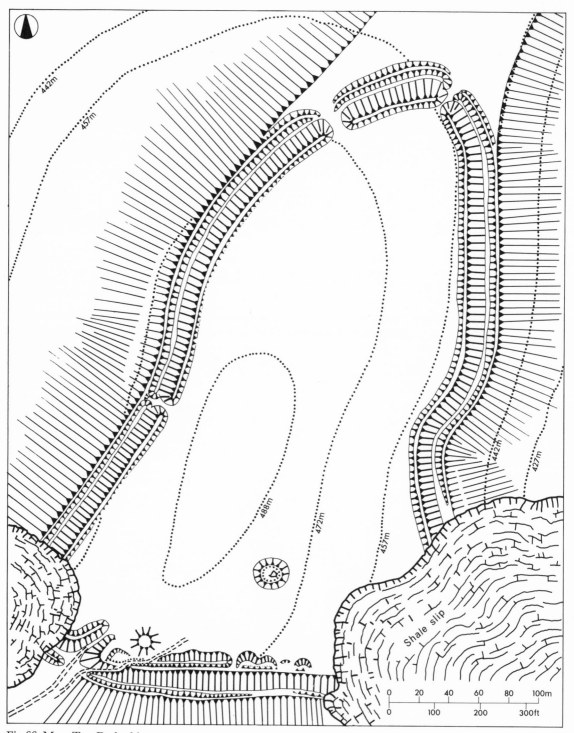

Fig.66. Mam Tor, Derbyshire.

Fig.65

Fig.66
Pl.2

Kinver Edge Camp (about 2·4 ha : 6 acres) the bank rises 2·4–3 m (8–10 ft) above the interior and has a C/D vert. of about 6·7 m (22 ft). Mam Tor (Derby.) encloses a much larger area (6·5 ha : 16 acres). Its defences are situated on sloping ground, which probably accounts for part of its C/D vert. of about 6·4 m (21 ft).

The remaining single bank-and-ditch sites have systems with C/D verts. of less than 6 m (20 ft), many of them in the 1·5–4·5-m (5–15-ft) range. However, since there are between 675 and 700 it is difficult to do more than mention a selection of sites from different regions. In Hampshire St. Catherine's Hill (9·3 ha : 23 acres) and The Andyke (24 ha : 60 acres) have C/D verts. of 5·8 and 5·5 m (19 and 18 ft) respectively, while Rockbourne Knoll (1·6 ha : 4 acres) and The Old Pound (80 ares : 2 acres) have C/D verts. of 1·5 and 1·8 m (5 and
Figs.34c,61d
6 ft) respectively. At Segsbury and Walbury in Berkshire the C/D verts. are in the region of 5 m (17 ft), while the areas enclosed are 10·5 and 33·2 ha (26 and
Fig.43b
82 acres) respectively. In Wiltshire Casterley, another very large site (25 ha : 62 acres), has a C/D vert. of only 2·4 or 2·7 m (8 or 9 ft). In the same county Chiselbury, enclosing 4 ha (10 acres), has a C/D vert. of 3·4 m (11 ft). Chilcombe (Dorset) encloses a large area (7·7 ha : 19 acres) but has a C/D vert. of only 1·98 m (6½ ft).

In the Cotswold region High Brotheridge, Crickley Hill, Leckhampton, and Norbury (Glos) all have C/D verts. within the range under discussion. High Brotheridge and Norbury are both in the Large class of sites, but their C/D verts. are modest, 1·8–2·4 m (6–8 ft). At Crickley Hill the C/D vert. is about
Fig.28
3·6 m (12 ft). To the north and west, in the Marches, Aconbury (Here.) and
Fig.23a
Woodbury (Worcs) have C/D verts. varying between 4·2 and 5·5 m (14 and 18 ft) and enclose areas of 6·8 and 10·5 ha (17 and 26 acres) respectively. In Shropshire the semi-contour site of Nordy Bank has a C/D vert. of 5·8 m (19 ft) and encloses about 2·4 ha (6 acres). The area enclosed at Ebury in the same county is half as big again (3·6 ha: 9 acres), but its C/D vert. is only about 2 m (7 ft). In Montgomeryshire Beacon Hill (about 2 ha : 5 acres) has a C/D vert. of about 3 m (10 ft) and in Denbighshire Cerrig Gwynion, Caer Caradog, and Pen-y-Gaer are all well within this size range with C/D verts. in the region of 2·4 or 3 m (8 or 10 ft).

Single bank-and-ditch sites in the rest of Wales and in south-west England include very few in the Large category. They do, on the other hand, include large numbers of Small forts, (i.e. enclosing less than 1 ha: 3 acres). These include many circular sites, 61–91 m (200–300 ft) in diameter with C/D verts. between 1·5 and 3 m (5 and 10 ft) which form a considerable group in Devon, Cornwall, western Somerset, and southern and western Wales. They include Roborough Castle (Devon), with a C/D vert. of 1·5 m (5 ft) and a diameter of 76 m (250 ft), and Ugborough and Chawleigh, of similar dimensions, in the same county.

Some of the systems described so far have had small banks on the outer edge of the ditch that could never have formed anything more than minor obstacles. In the systems to be considered now these counterscarp banks assume the pro-
Fig.68a
portions of a second rampart. At Old Sarum (Wilts.) the main bank rises some

Fig.67. Small sites with Group 1 defences.

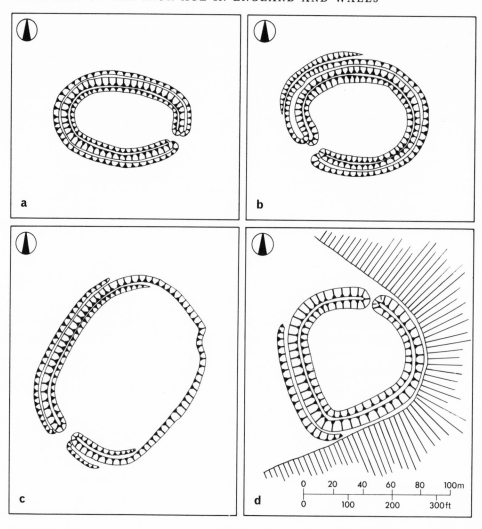

Pl.40

Fig.68b

1·8–2·4 m (6–8 ft) above the interior and falls about 12 m (40 ft) to the ditch bottom. The most notable feature, however, is the enormous bank on the counterscarp. This rises over 6 m (20 ft) above the ditch bottom and stands 7·6 m (25 ft) above the external ground-level. There is a similar system at Sinodun (Berks). There the main rampart rises only a few centimetres above the interior but falls externally 7·6 m (25 ft) to the ditch bottom. The large counterscarp bank stands 3 m (10 ft) above the ditch bottom and 4·5 m (15 ft) above the external ground-level. Its flat top is about 6 m (20 ft) wide and it is some 18–21 m (60–70 ft) wide over-all. Banks of these dimensions, if they are indeed prehistoric, must be regarded as the remains of full-scale ramparts and not the minor obstacles mentioned above. As such they can be regarded as transforming the system from the univallate to the multivallate style. They are, in fact, mixed systems as described for Group 2, i.e. having two ramparts, one

136

Fig.68. Group 1
defence systems:
68a Old Sarum,
Wiltshire;
68b Sinodun,
Berkshire.

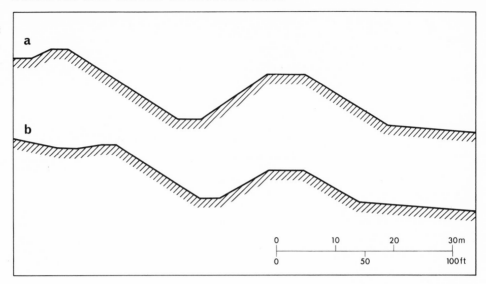

with a ditch and one without. As such they are more appropriate to Group 2 than to the present group. The difficulty arises in trying to decide where a bank ceases to be a conventional counterscarp bank and becomes a rampart.

The outer banks at Old Sarum and Sinodun are exceptionally large and very few others approach their dimensions. There are, however, some 20 or 30 sites where the counterscarp banks are as big, if not bigger, than the main banks of many other sites. Allowing for the effects of erosion they can be seen as major obstacles, if not true ramparts, sufficiently large to raise questions of classification, univallate or multivallate. At Liddington Castle (Wilts.), for example, the counterscarp bank is very much smaller than the two described above, but it is still substantial. On the northern side the main bank rises 90 cm to 1 m (3–4 ft) above the interior and falls about 4·8 m (16 ft) to the ditch bottom. The counterscarp bank rises 3·6 m (12 ft) above this and is 2 m (7 ft) high externally and about 12 m (40 ft) wide. If the existing remains are any guide it is larger than the inner bank, at least at this point. A number of other systems in

Fig.69

Pl.52

Pl.29;Fig.52

Wessex come into this category. They include Grimsbury, Uffington Castle and Caesar's Camp (Berks), Chisbury and Castle Hill, Blunsdon (Wilts.), Beacon Hill and Bury Hill (Hants), and Coney's Castle (Dorset).

In Cornwall the promontory fort at Dodman Point also belongs with this group. Its main bank rises 3 m (10 ft) above the interior and falls about 6 m (20 ft) to the ditch bottom. The counterscarp bank rises 2·7 or 3 m (9 or 10 ft) above this and is about 1·8 m (6 ft) above external ground-level. Other sites

Fig.42

which merit consideration in this context are Cholesbury (Bucks), Wallbury (Essex), Woodbury, Stoke Fleming (Devon), Bat's Castle (Som.), Caer Euni (Mer.), and Mynydd y Gaer (Denb.).

All the Group 1 systems described so far have included ditches. There are, however, univallate systems where the defences consist of a bank alone. A very large example (c. 30 m: 100 ft wide and 6 m: 20 ft high), mentioned earlier,

137

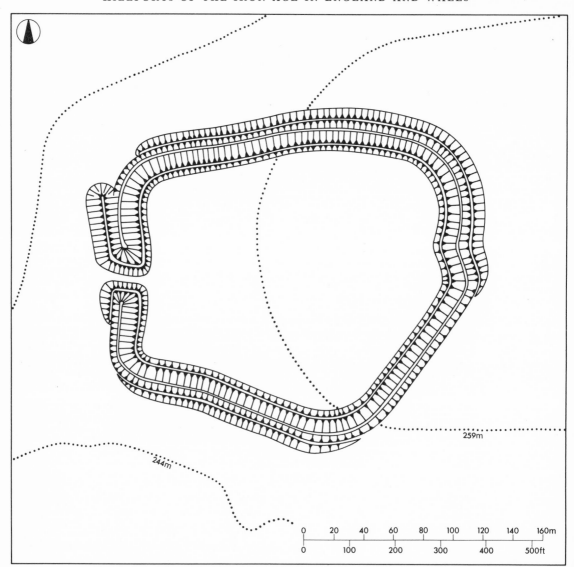

259m

244m

| 0 | 20 | 40 | 60 | 80 | 100 | 120 | 140 | 160m |
| 0 | | 100 | | 200 | | 300 | | 400 | | 500ft |

Fig.69. Uffington Castle, Berkshire.

exists at the western end of Gaer Fawr (Carm.). The remaining defences at the
same site are on a smaller scale (*c.* 12 m: 40 ft wide and 1–1·5 m: 4–5 ft high)
and are much more typical of single-bank systems. The majority of such systems
are as they appear at Gaer Fawr, mounds of loose stones, roughly triangular in
cross-section. There are, however, a number of earthen banks in this category.
They include Windrush Camp (Glos), a small circular site about 122 m (400 ft)
in diameter. The bank which constitutes the only defence is about 9 m (30 ft)
wide and about 1·5 m (5 ft) high. The contour site at The Roveries (Salop) has

138

Fig. 70. Helsby
Hill, Cheshire.

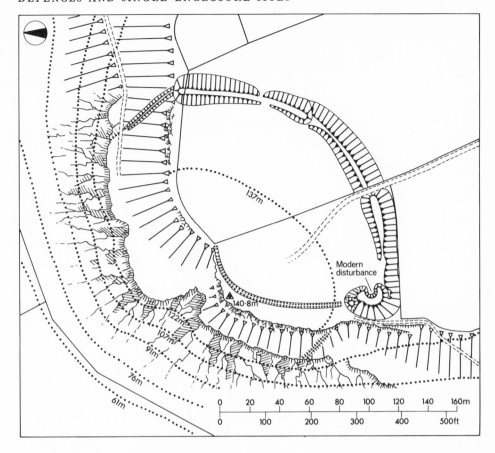

Fig. 70

a similar defence of somewhat larger size (*c.* 12 m: 40 ft wide and 2·4 m: 8 ft high) defending a larger area, and there are defences of the same type at Helsby and Woodhouses (Ches.). At Helsby, a promontory fort of the Group III type, the bank is about 18 m (60 ft) wide and about 2·7 m (9 ft) above the external ground-level. Other earthen single-bank defences which can be mentioned here are Chastleton (Oxon.), Sharpenhoe Clappers (Beds), and parts of Caer Drewyn (Mer.).

The majority of single-bank systems, however, are of the loose-stone type as at Gaer Fawr. In such cases it is sometimes possible to see the original inner or outer, and sometimes both, faces of the rampart. This can be done at Caer Drewyn (Mer.) where it is possible to see on the northern side that the rampart was about 5·5 m (18 ft) thick. Some of the original facing can still be seen at Craigadwy Wynt (Denb.) and Tre'r Ceiri (Caer.). On sloping ground the roughly triangular mound becomes a thick layer of stones spreading down the hillside.

Univallate sites defended by a bank alone account for between 10 and 12 per cent of all univallate forts—around 100 sites. Most of these are located in western regions, from Cornwall to Anglesey, with the emphasis on the north-west rather than the south-west. Among sites which can be mentioned here are Craig Rhiwarth (Montg.), Pen-y-Gaer, Trevor, and Craigadwy Wynt (Denb.). Craig Rhiwarth is a very large site, enclosing about 24 ha (60 acres), defended on the north and west by a stone rampart and on the other two sides by natural slopes. Craigadwy Wynt and Pen-y-Gaer are both of the cliff-edge type. Pen-y-Gaer is a roughly rectangular site enclosing about 1·6 ha (4 acres), with the cliff forming the southern side. At Craigadwy Wynt the bank is about 15 m (50 ft) wide and faces level ground to the east. The upper enclosure covers about 2·8 ha (7 acres).

Stone single-bank systems are more numerous in Caernarvonshire. They include some very small sites with interiors only 21 or 24 m (70 or 80 ft) in diameter. Among these are Castell Caerau and Nantlle Camp. The inner and outer faces are visible in both ramparts which are 3·6 and 2·7 m (12 and 9 ft) thick respectively. The site at Maes y Gaer is larger (122×61 m: 400×200 ft), although the original rampart, the faces of which are visible in the mass of loose stones, was only 2·4 m (8 ft) thick. At Craig-y-Dinas, a promontory fort in a U-bend of the Afon Llyfnwy, the defences around the promontory edge consisted originally of a stone rampart at least 3 m (10 ft) thick. The defences on the approach side, the west, are multivallate, a compact arrangement of three banks and two ditches. Other single stone-bank systems in Caernarvonshire include Pen-y-Gaer, Aberglaslyn, Caer Carreg-y-Fran, Pen-y-Gaer, (Llanaelhaiarn), Tre'r Ceiri, and Conway Mountain.

The material used in the construction of the single-bank systems just described was presumably derived from some adjacent convenient source, but certainly not from an outer ditch. It is possible that in some cases the material came from an inner quarry ditch which has now been completely filled, but in most cases there is no good reason for assuming this. There are, however, a number of cases where the single bank can be seen to have a quarry ditch on its inner side. Such arrangements, termed single out-throw, are usually found where the outer slopes are fairly steep, so that a conventional outer ditch is neither possible nor necessary. An excellent example is provided by Moel Arthur (Flint.), where such a system forms about two-thirds of the circuit. The inner quarry ditch is cut into the sloping shoulder of the hill so that its inner edge is about 3 m (10 ft) above the top of the bank. The crest of the latter is only 30 cm (1 ft) or so above the ditch bottom and its outer scarp merges into the natural slope. There are similar single out-throw arrangements at Pen-y-cloddiau (Flint.), Moel-y-Gaer, Llantysilio (Denb.), and Norton Camp (Salop).

Double out-throw systems also belong to Group 1. They involve both inner quarry ditches and conventional outer ditches. There are normally four features involved: an inner quarry ditch, a main bank, an outer ditch, and a counter-scarp bank. Where these are arranged in compact form, i.e. with no spaces between any of the features, they are no different in appearance from the single-ditch systems already described. Such arrangements occur at Credenhill Camp and Midsummer Hill (Here.), Caer Caradoc, Clun (Salop), Foel Fenlli (Denb.), and Pen-y-cloddiau (Flint.). Uley Bury (Glos.) is usually described as having multivallate defences, but what has been interpreted as the inner line of

Fig.36

Fig.55
Pl.30

Fig.46b
Pl.4

Fig.35c

Fig.61f
Figs.61g,31,54
Fig.26c
Pl.11

defence is surely the inner quarry ditch. The dominant feature of the system is the bank, which rises 1 or 2 m (3 or 6 ft) above the bottom of the inner quarry ditch and falls about 9 m (30 ft) to an almost filled ditch. The same filling presumably masks the existence of the counterscarp bank. The main effect of the outer ditch, dug into a steep natural slope, would have been to produce a high inner scarp. Its outer scarp and the counterscarp bank would have been relatively modest. The counterscarp banks at Credenhill and Midsummer Hill are likewise of modest dimensions. At the other sites mentioned, however, the counterscarp banks are of fairly substantial size and raise again the question of classification, univallate or multivallate. This question arises, anyway, in certain double out-throw systems where a space or berm of natural ground is introduced into the arrangement.

Fig.54   This sort of situation is best exemplified at Foel Fenlli (Denb.) in the area south of the western entrance. About 91 or 122 m (300 or 400 ft) from the entrance there is a compact double out-throw arrangement with a substantial counterscarp bank. Closer to the entrance the outer ditch and the counterscarp bank swing away from the main bank and inner quarry ditch, leaving a flat berm between. Immediately south of the entrance this berm is about 12 m (40 ft) wide. At Pen-y-cloddiau (Flint.), along most of the western side, compact sections alternate with sections in which there is a berm, about 3 m (10 ft) wide, between the main bank and the outer ditch. In other sites the berm is wider, as at Foel Fenlli, and is also sloping. Cefn-y-Castell Hill (Montg.), when viewed from The Breiddin, looks as if it has a single very large rampart with an outer ditch. Ground examination, however, shows that most of this apparent height is due to the natural slope of the ground surface in the space between the main bank and the outer ditch. The complete arrangement is inner quarry ditch, main bank, natural slope, outer ditch, and counterscarp bank. There is a

Fig.71
Pl.12   similar arrangement at Caer Caradoc, Church Stretton (Salop).

The question that arises with regard to such systems is whether they are univallate or multivallate, regardless of the size of the counterscarp bank. In compact form they are undoubtedly univallate. This being so it is questionable whether the same features can be regarded as multivallate simply because a space is introduced in the middle of the arrangement. The result could be described as a wide-spaced univallate system, if that were not a contradiction in terms. Fortunately there are only a few sites with this sort of complication.

The last arrangement to be considered in Group 1 is that of scarp and ledge. This is the system frequently used around the edges of promontories where the natural features do not provide absolute defence. The scarp is produced by the removal of material from a point below the shoulder of the hill, thus increasing the angle of the slope. This scarped slope is, in effect, the outer face of a rampart. The scarp is, inevitably, accompanied by a ledge at its foot. In some cases what appears now to be a ledge may in fact be a filled-in ditch, but this makes no difference to the main principle involved; that of increasing the angle of an existing slope. In any case, the scarp-and-ledge can be regarded as a ditch tipped over at an angle. Any ditch dug into sloping ground will have one scarp higher than the other and the scarp-and-ledge, or scarp-and-ditch, simply

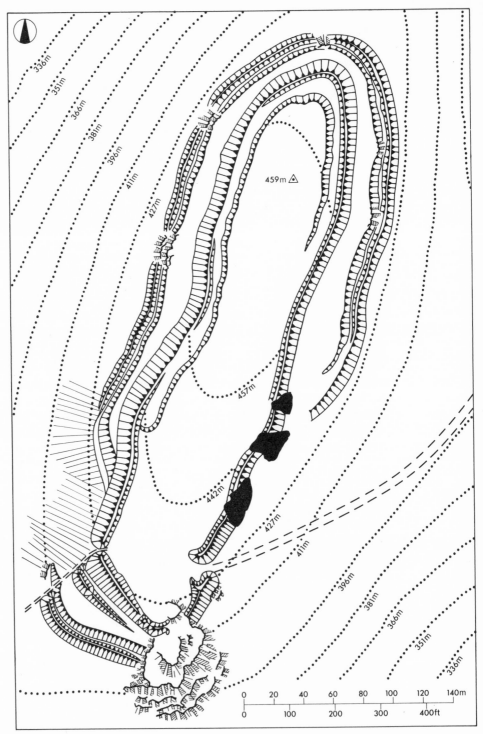

Fig.71. Caer Caradoc (Church Stretton), Shropshire.

Figs.29,117

makes the fullest use of this principle. Good examples of the scarp-and-ledge arrangement are found at Bodbury Ring (Salop), and Hafod Camp (Carm.). In both of these there are conventional bank-and-ditch defences on the approach sides and scarp-and-ledge defences around the promontory edges.

GROUP 2: TWO-DITCH OR TWO-BANK OR MIXED SYSTEMS

Of all the defence systems involving more than one ditch the two-ditch system is by far the commonest. Single-enclosure sites defended in this way probably account for over half of all multivallate forts. The simplest type of two-ditch system is a compact arrangement of two banks and two ditches with no intervening spaces. This system is found in a large number of multivallate sites in England and Wales. It appears also in a variety of sizes. One of the most sub-

Fig.60

stantial stands at the northern end of the promontory fort of Bury Walls (Salop). The inner bank rises no less than 6·4 m (21 ft) above the interior and falls 11·6 m (38 ft) to the bottom of the first ditch. The second bank rises to a height of 4·5 m (15 ft) and falls 4·2 m (14 ft) externally to the bottom of the second ditch, which is 1·8 m (6 ft) deep below external ground-level. The width of the system from front to back is about 73 m (240 ft). It defends the northern end of the site where the approach is relatively easy. On the remaining three sides the defences appear now as a single bank standing at the head of the steep natural slope.

The majority of systems in this category, however, are of more modest

Fig.35b

dimensions. The two-ditch system at Norton Camp in the same county has an over-all width of 57·9 m (190 ft), with the main bank standing about 6 m (20 ft) above the ditch bottom. This system defends three sides of the site, partly in the compact form just described and partly with a berm from 3 to 6 m (10 to 20 ft) wide between the inner ditch and the outer bank. Two-ditch systems of gener-

Fig.43e;Pl.38
Fig.43a
Fig.137

Fig.72
Figs.39a,73
Fig.74

ally similar dimensions are found at Dolebury (Som.) and Bratton Castle(Wilts.) Somewhat smaller systems occur at Nottingham Hill (Glos), defending the easy approach from the east, and at Caesar's Camp (Surrey), again defending the easy approach, in this case from the south-west. Other two-ditch, compact systems are found at Bulstrode Park (Bucks), the Aubreys (Herts), Bussocks (Berks), Warham Camp (Norf.), Portfield (Lancs), Eddisbury (Ches), Borough Hill (Northants.), Craig-y-Dinas (Caer.), and Castell Pyr (Carm.).

Many of the compact two-ditch systems described so far have been on level or nearly level ground. A variation often found on sloping ground involves the addition of a counterscarp bank, making the system one of three banks and two ditches. The existence of the counterscarp bank shows that the out-throw method was used at least in part in digging the outer ditch, and further confirmation that this method was used can be found in the existence of inner quarry ditches in a number of cases. Both of these facts are presumably connected with the sloping nature of the ground in which the system is built.

One of the classic examples of the compact three-bank and two-ditch system

Fig.75a

is supplied by the northern defences of Maiden Castle (Dorset), which have an

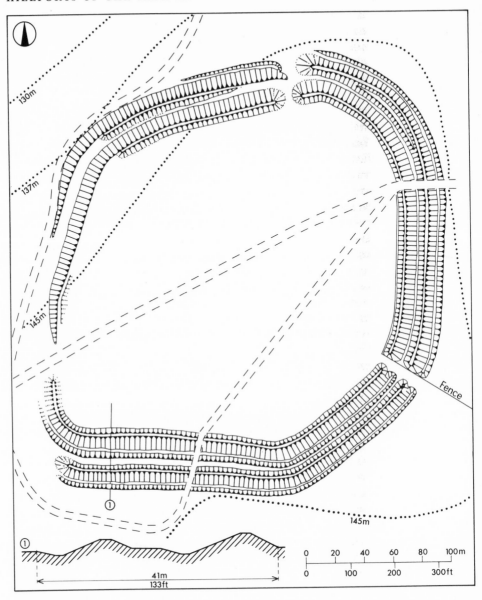

Fig.72. Bussocks, Berkshire.

Pls.41,42

Fig.21a
Pl.23
Fig.54

over-all width of 94·5 m (310 ft). The crest of the inner bank is some 15 m (50 ft) above the bottom of the ditch and 23 m (75 ft) above the level of the ground beyond the counterscarp bank. There is now no surface evidence of an inner quarry ditch but one of considerable size was revealed by excavation. There is a similar system, on a smaller scale, at another Dorset site, Hod Hill. Inside the main rampart there is a large inner quarry ditch. Two other systems with visible inner quarry ditches are found at Foel Fenlli (Denb.) and Croft Ambrey (Here.). The Foel Fenlli system is some 52 m (170 ft) wide and the

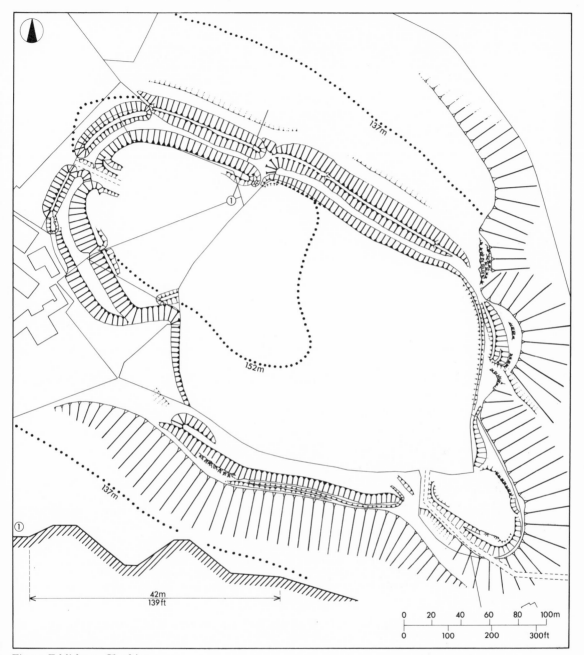

Fig.73. Eddisbury, Cheshire.

Fig.74. Castell
Pyr,
Carmarthenshire

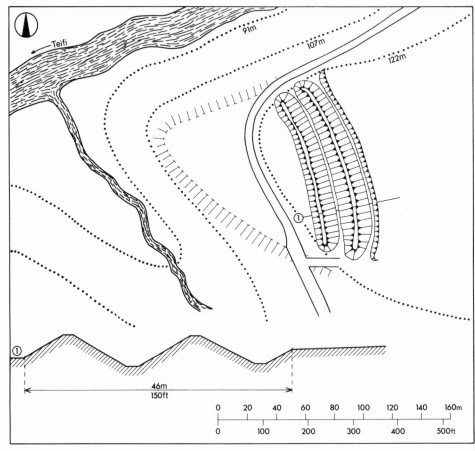

Fig.75b
Pls.38,33;
Figs.30a,78

Croft Ambrey system, defending the inner enclosure, about 64 m (210 ft) wide. Other sites which have compact three-bank and two-ditch systems include Hembury (Devon), Small Down (Som.), Bratton Castle, Oldbury, and Barbury (Wilts.), Whitsbury (Hants), Dry Hill (Surrey), Caesar's Camp, Keston (Kent), Meon Hill (War), Wychbury (Worcs), Walterstone and Backbury (Here.), The Burgs (Salop), and Caerau, Llantrisant (Glam.).

Variations on the two-ditch system are numerous and involve the introduction of berms or flat spaces between various parts of the system, the building of banks additional to the two main banks, and, in a number of cases, the reversal of the outer part of the arrangement so that the outer bank is outside the outer ditch. The simplest variation has a space between the inner ditch and the outer bank. This space varies from 1 or 2 m (3 or 6 ft) to a width great enough to form a separate enclosure. Two-ditch systems with a narrow space between the inner and outer bank and ditch will be considered first.

In the majority of compact systems the platform between the inner and outer ditches is wide enough to accommodate only the outer bank. In most cases this means that there is an even slope from the bottom of the inner ditch to the top

146

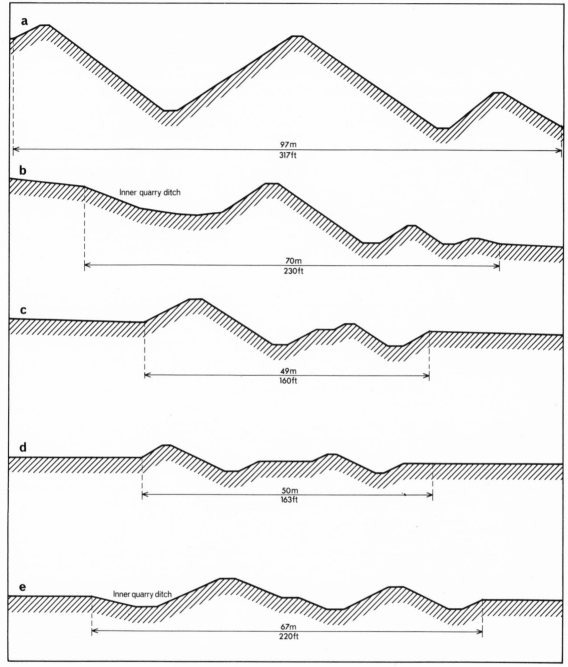

a

97m
317ft

b

Inner quarry ditch

70m
230ft

c

49m
160ft

d

50m
163ft

e

Inner quarry ditch

67m
220ft

Fig.75. Group 2 defence systems: 75a Maiden Castle, Dorset; 75b Croft Ambrey, Herefordshire; 75c Norton Camp, Shropshire; 75d Dumpdon Camp, Devon; 75e Foxcovert, Denbighshire.

of the outer bank. In a few cases, however, there is a noticeable break in this slope, marking the transition from the counterscarp of the ditch to the back slope of the outer bank. This seems to arise from the existence of a relatively wide platform between the two ditches. In the case of Castle Dore (Corn.) this platform is fully occupied by a bank some 3 m (10 ft) wider than the inner bank, but in two other cases the platform appears to be wider than is absolutely necessary to accommodate the outer bank. At Buckland Ring (Hants) there is a very narrow berm between the inner ditch and the middle bank, arising out of the greater width of the platform, and at Bury Hill (Glos) there is what may be termed an incipient berm in a similar position and for the same reasons. In both of these cases the arrangement may be the result of some error or miscalculation in the alignment or capacity of the ditches, but in the cases to be considered below, the berm appears to be an integral part of the system.

Fig.119

At Norton Camp (Salop), mentioned earlier, the greater part of the defences is in a compact arrangement, but to the north of the east entrance there is a berm or space between 3 and 6 m (10 and 20 ft) wide between the inner ditch and the outer bank. At Dumpdon Camp (Devon) the northern defences, facing the fairly easy approach to the promontory, have a corresponding gap, about 8 m (25 ft) wide. The over-all width of the system is about 40 m (130 ft). At Cleeve Cloud (Glos) the gap between the two parts of the system varies between 4·5 and 7·6 m (15 and 25 ft), while the over-all width is about 42·7 m (140 ft). In this system the outer bank and ditch appear to be more massive than the inner. At Pen y Gaer, Llanbyther (Carm.) there is a 5-m (16-ft) space in a system which is only about 20 m (65 ft) wide over-all. There are generally similar gaps between the inner and outer defences at the promontory forts at Great Treffgarne Rocks and Linney Head (Pemb.), although the features are on a larger scale than at Pen y Gaer. Other systems in this category include Bussocks (Berks) and Castle Ring (Staffs).

Fig.75c

Fig.75d

Fig.77

Figs.33a,25

Figs.72,79

In the sites just considered the gap between the inner and outer elements of the system has been sufficiently narrow for it to be regarded simply as a device for adding depth to the defences. In the sites to be dealt with now the gap is wide enough for questions of a second enclosure to arise. Greenaway Camp (Devon) and Killibury (Corn.) can be said to fall somewhere between the two groups. At Greenaway the gap varies between 9 and 15 m (30 and 50 ft) and at Killibury between 7·6 and 21 m (25 and 70 ft). At Cwm Berwyn (Rad.) and Knave and High Penard (Glam.) the gap is in the region of 18 m (60 ft), while at Tregeare Rounds (Corn.) it varies between 15 and 30 m (50 and 100 ft), and at Caerbre (Salop) between 15 and 52 m (50 and 170 ft). At Tregeare Rounds it is noticeable that the outer bank and ditch are bigger than the inner. At Weatherby Castle (Dorset) and Warbstow Bury (Corn.) there are 30-m (100-ft) gaps in places between the inner and outer sections of the system. At Park Hill Camp (Wilts.) there is a gap of between 30 and 36·5 m (100 and 120 ft) on the western side and at Pen y Foel (Montg.) a gap of 46 m (150 ft), also on the western side, facing the easy approach to the promontory. At Bredon Hill (Worcs) the gap varies between 52 and 91 m (170 and 300 ft). There are, of course, many other examples of wide spacing in two-ditch systems but those

Fig.93

Fig.37

Fig.92
Pl.50

Fig.115
Fig.114

mentioned are sufficient to show the sort of range that exists. In any case all such sites will be considered again under the heading of multiple-enclosure sites in Chapter VI.

The remaining variations on the two-ditch arrangement involve only narrow spaces between the various parts of the system, so that the sites are of the single-enclosure type. In a number of sites there is an additional berm between the inner bank and its associated ditch. This appears at Brackenbury Ditches (Glos), Cranbrook Castle (Devon), and Maesbury (Som.). In a number of other sites this berm is the only one in the system, so that the arrangement is otherwise compact. At Foxcovert (Denb.) the arrangement is inner quarry ditch, bank, berm, ditch, bank, and ditch. At Caer Estyn (Flint.) there is a similar arrangement except for the inner quarry ditch. This arrangement appears also at Planes Wood (Lancs) at the north-western end of the site, again without the inner quarry ditch. At two other sites the extra berm is placed between the outer bank and its ditch. In parts of Dudsbury (Dorset) and Moel y Gaer, Rhosesmor (Flint.), the arrangement is bank, ditch, berm, bank, berm, and ditch. In both of these cases the outer bank is very small and could never have constituted a serious obstacle. The existence of a berm in the sites mentioned above suggests that the ramparts involved were of the revetted type.

Further variations on the two-ditch system involve the addition of banks on the counterscarp of one or other, in some cases both, of the ditches. In many cases these extra banks make very little difference to the nature of the system which remains basically that of two banks and two ditches with a relatively narrow interspace. At the north-western end of Pilsdon Pen (Dorset), for example, and at Holmbury and Anstiebury (Surrey) the additional bank is on the counterscarp of the outer ditch and the three systems are otherwise the same as those discussed earlier. In other cases, however, there is a bank on the counterscarp of the inner ditch instead of, or in addition to, the one associated with the outer ditch. In this position the extra bank can, in some cases, give rise to a misinterpretation of the nature of the system.

This is well exemplified by the system on the western side of Yarnbury (Wilts.). Starting from the inside this consists of a massive bank, a ditch, and a substantial counterscarp bank. Immediately beyond the latter is the outer bank and ditch. The space between the counterscarp bank and the outer bank is not, however, a ditch. It is simply the V-shaped space resulting from the juxtaposition of two banks. What appears to be the ditch bottom is simply the natural ground surface. In plan view the arrangement gives the impression of three banks and three ditches, but in section it can be seen to be a two-ditch system. The defences of Burrow Camp (Salop) give a similar impression, but the explanation is the same as for Yarnbury. For most of their length a fourth bank is involved so that the whole system is bank, ditch, and counterscarp bank, with another bank, ditch, and counterscarp bank immediately beyond. Other sites which in plan view give the impression of having three ditches are Sidbury (Wilts.) and Cherbury (Berks), but in each case the arrangement is bank, ditch, and counterscarp bank with an outer bank and ditch immediately beyond, as at Yarnbury.

Fig.76. Group 2
defence systems:
76a Dudsbury,
Dorset;
76b Holmbury,
Surrey;
76c Yarnbury,
Wiltshire;
76d Bullsdown,
Hampshire.

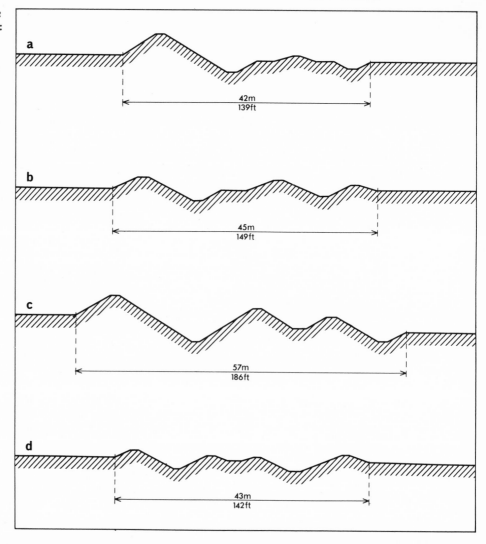

In the variations just described the middle and outer banks have been fairly substantial, hence the impression of a ditch in the space between. In other sites the corresponding banks are comparatively small and sometimes give the impression of a single broad-topped bank. One of the best examples is provided by Bullsdown (Hants). Williams-Freeman[2] describes the middle bank as being 8·8 m (29 ft) wide and shows it as such in the plan. He also describes it as being 'slightly worn down in the middle'. This provides the clue to the arrangement. The broad middle bank, in fact, consists of a slight counterscarp bank to the inner ditch, a flat space about 3 m (10 ft) wide and another slight bank on the

Fig.76d

2. Williams-Freeman, *An Introduction to Field Archaeology as Illustrated by Hampshire* (1915).

Fig.77. Cleeve
Cloud,
Gloucestershire.

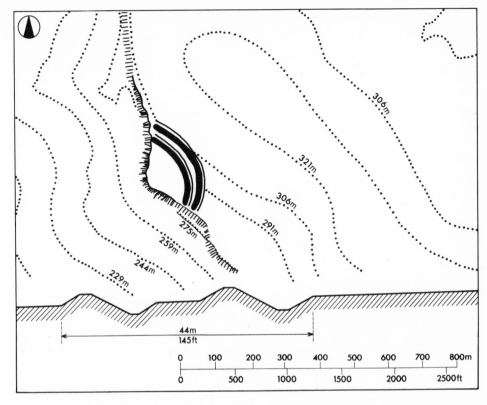

inner edge of the outer ditch. Both banks are so slight that the impression of a
single broad bank is understandable. Beyond the outer ditch is a counterscarp
bank, making four banks in all. The arrangement at Maesbury (Som.) is on the
same lines; on the north and north-east the counterscarp bank to the inner
ditch and the outer bank are clearly distinguishable, but in other places they
merge into one broad-topped bank.

Fig.78
Pl.33

Something similar happens on the eastern side at Oldbury (Wilts.). North of
the main entrance the two banks between the inner and outer ditches are clearly
distinguishable and separated by a space about 3 m (10 ft) wide. South of the
entrance the two are either separated by only a narrow furrow or else form a
single bank. A similar furrow appears in part of the southern defences of

Pl.38

Bratton Castle (Wilts.), and is apparent, in short sections, in a number of other
sites. It appears to be the result of one bank being heaped against another so
that both crests are just visible as separate features. Caer Caradoc, Clun
(Salop), and Foel Fenlli (Denb.) both belong to this general group. At Caer

Fig.31
Pl.25

Caradoc just north of the eastern entrance there is a slight counterscarp bank
to the main ditch and an equally slight bank on the inner edge of the outer
ditch. The space between the two forms a furrow. At this point most of the
material from the outer ditch appears to have been thrown outwards to form an
enormous counterscarp bank. Inside the main rampart there is a well-defined

151

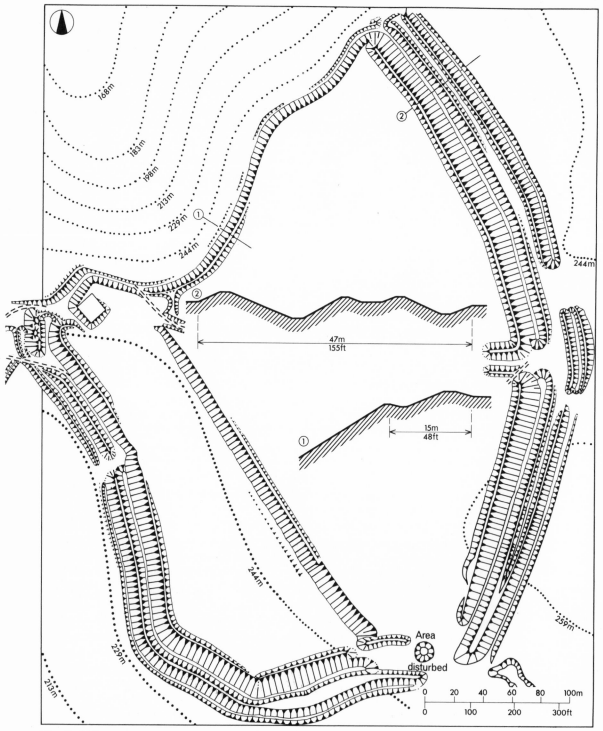

Fig.78. Oldbury, Wiltshire.

Fig.54

inner quarry ditch. There is a similar feature behind the system at Foel Fenlli. Of the two banks on the platform between the ditches at the eastern end of the site, the inner one is the smaller and is quite clearly the counterscarp bank to the main ditch. For most of the circuit it is covered by the bank associated with the outer ditch, but for about 91 m (300 ft) at the eastern end of the fort this bank swings out to leave the counterscarp bank visible immediately behind.

Fig.79
Pl.15

The last of the major variations on the two-ditch system involves the reversal of the outer bank and ditch so that the bank is the outermost part of the system. A good example is provided by the northern defences of Castle Rings (Staffs) where the arrangement consists of an inner bank and ditch separated by a berm, about 9 m (30 ft) wide, from the outer ditch, the material from which has been thrown outwards to form a bank on the counterscarp. The space between the two ditches looks in plan view, and to some extent in ground view, like a broad flat-topped bank, but this effect is due simply to the cutting of two ditches which isolate a strip of natural ground. Where there is a counterscarp bank associated with the inner ditch then this impression does not arise.

Fig.34a
Pls.21,22

On the north-eastern side of Eggardon (Dorset) there is a system of this type, some 70 m (230 ft) wide. It consists of an inner bank, ditch, and a massive counterscarp bank. About 10 m (35 ft) beyond the latter is the outer ditch with its associated bank on the outer edge. At the southern end of Caer Caradoc, Church Stretton (Salop), the outer ditch and bank are at the foot of a slope which runs down from the inner bank, ditch, and counterscarp bank. The intervening space varies from 6 to 18 m (20 to 60 ft). At Moel y Gaer, Llanbedr (Denb.), the corresponding space varies from 3 to 15 m (10 to 50 ft) in width. Other sites in this category include Kimsbury (Glos) and Pilsdon Pen (Dorset).

Fig.71

Fig.135

Fig.62

Fig.32

The remaining systems in Group 2 are those without ditches or those which have only one ditch, i.e. mixed systems. A good example of a two-bank system is provided by Maiden Castle (Ches.). Its defences on the eastern and southern sides consist of a bank about 1·8 m (6 ft) high and 12 m (40 ft) wide separated by a space of about 12 m (40 ft) from an outer bank of generally similar dimensions. The whole system is situated on a gentle slope and there is no indication of ditches. Two banks of smaller dimensions (about 3·6 m: 12 ft wide) are involved at Castle-an-Dinas, Ludgvan (Corn.). The space between is about 15 m (50 ft), so that questions of classification as single- or multiple-enclosure inevitably arise. On the north-east there is a third bank with an outer ditch, so that the system on this side belongs to the mixed category of Group 3.

There are a number of two-bank systems in Caernarvonshire. One of the best examples is found at Carreg y Llam where the stone-built inner bank is about 3·6 m (12 ft) thick. About 9 m (30 ft) beyond and in a slightly lower position is the outer bank, stone-built, about 2 m (7 ft) thick. The systems at Castell Odo, Conion, Pen-y-Gaer (Llanengan) and Carn Pentyrch have wider interspaces than Carreg y Llam, between 12 and 15 m (40 and 50 ft). At two other sites in this category, Meillionydd and Castell Caeron, the space between the inner and outer banks is in the region of 6 m (20 ft). In Cardiganshire Caerau Henllan and Cefn Blewog belong to the two-bank class, but in both cases the intervening space is such that they must also be considered under

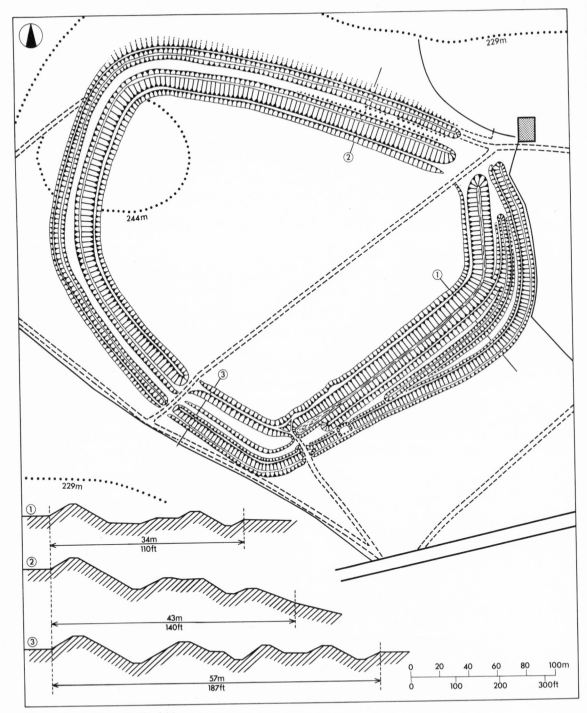

Fig. 79. Castle Ring, Staffordshire.

Fig.80. Combs
Moss, Derbyshire.

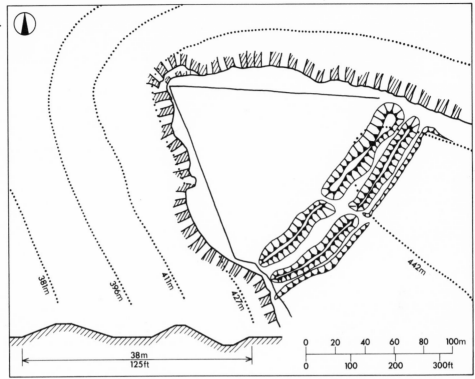

the heading of multiple-enclosure sites. In Glamorgan Y Gaer, Bonvilston,
now appears to be defended on the east by two banks or scarps about 12 m
(40 ft) apart, but this may be the result of the ditches being filled. On the west
there is a ditch associated with the outer bank, so that there the system appears
to be of the mixed type.

Fig.36   The defences at the southern end of Craigadwy Wynt (Denb.) are a good
example of a Group 2 mixed system. The defences for the greater part of the
site consist of a single stone-built rampart with no outer ditch. At the southern
end this is supplemented by an outer bank and ditch, so the arrangement is
bank, berm, bank, and ditch. There is a similar arrangement at the northern
end of the main enclosure at Pen-y-Corddyn (Denb.). The inner rampart,
derived from an inner quarry ditch, is separated from the outer bank and ditch
by a berm about 4·5 m (15 ft) wide. At Caer Bach (Caern.) the inner stone-built
rampart is 3·6–4·5 m (12–15 ft) thick. About 15 m (50 ft) beyond there is a
second bank, in this case accompanied by an outer ditch. Once again, because
of the size of the intervening space, the question of classification arises. There is
a mixed system on the north-western side at Carn Pentyrch (Caer.) although
the intervening space is only 6 or 9 m (20 or 30 ft) wide. This system forms part
of a multiple-enclosure site with an outer line of defence about 53 m (175 ft)
beyond to the north-west. Other systems in this category are found at Castell

155

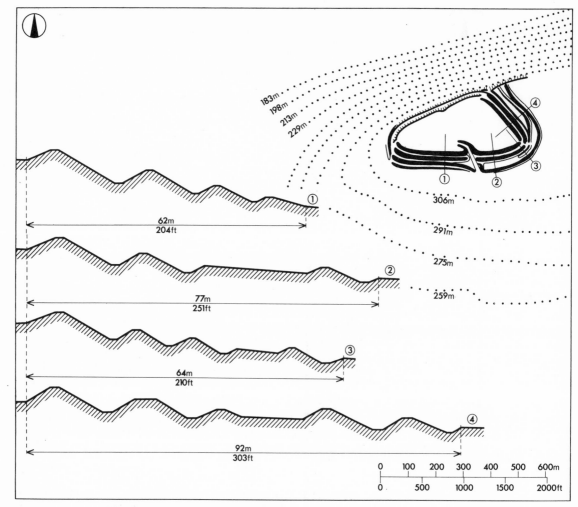

Fig.81. Wapley Camp, Herefordshire.

Fig.80

Grogwynion (Card.), Thornton Rath (Pemb), Llanmelin (Mon.), and Combs Moss (Derby.).

GROUP 3: THREE-DITCH OR THREE-BANK OR MIXED SYSTEMS

Three-ditch systems of the compact or separated type are comparatively few in number and occur in only about 10 per cent of all multivallate forts. The simplest form of the three-ditch system is a compact arrangement of three banks and three ditches. In Glamorgan there are three-ditch systems at Castle Ditches and The Bulwarks, Porthkerry, with widths of 53 and 46 m (175 and 150 ft) respectively. The defence system at Fan Camp (Breck.) would also appear to belong to this group. In a number of cases there is a counterscarp bank

156

Fig.82.
Llandewi Gaer,
Pembrokeshire.

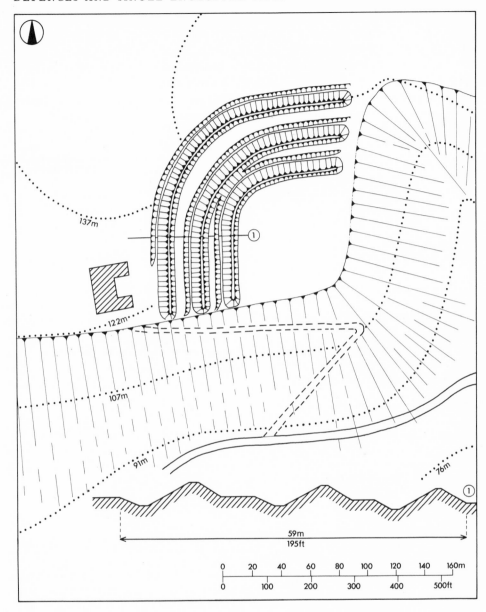

on the edge of the third ditch, making the system one of four banks and three
ditches. This is the pattern at Wapley Hill (Here.), on the south-west side,
where the system has an over-all width of about 61 m (200 ft). The south-
eastern section of the same site has two different versions of the three-ditch
system, while the eastern side has a four-ditch system which will be dealt with
under Group 4. Similar compact three-ditch systems with counterscarp banks
exist at Castle Ditches (Wilts.) and Old Oswestry (Salop), with over-all widths

Fig.81

Figs.89,91

157

Pls.3,14

in the region of 76 and 61 m (250 and 200 ft) respectively. At Old Oswestry the three-ditch system is, in fact, one of the simplest parts of the defence system. Other sectors are defended by four- and six-ditch systems.

Fig.82

As with the two-ditch systems the simplest variation from the compact form is the introduction of narrow berms. A system of this type forms the defences of Llandewi Gaer (Pemb.) on the north and west. On the south and east the steep natural slope provides adequate protection. The system is about 52 m (170 ft) wide over-all and the berms are between 4·5 and 6 m (15 and 20 ft) wide. There is a system of similar dimensions at Summer Houses (Glam.), on the western side near the cliff-edge. The system at the western end of the southern defences at

Fig.83a
Pl.41

Maiden Castle (Dorset) is of the same type but is on a very much larger scale, measuring 122 m (400 ft) over-all. The inner berm is about 9 m (30 ft) wide, the outer slightly less. In this case a fourth, counterscarp, bank is involved. In one or two places it is separated from the outer ditch by a third berm.

Fig.79
Pl.15

The three-ditch system on the south-eastern side of Castle Rings (Staffs) involves four banks, three ditches, and two spaces of berms. The inner part of the system consists of a bank, a ditch, and a counterscarp bank. About 3 m (10 ft) beyond is the second ditch, the earth from which has been thrown outwards to form the third bank. About 4·5 m (15 ft) beyond the latter is the fourth bank, derived from the third ditch, which forms the outer edge of the whole system. The over-all width is about 58 m (190 ft). There is a further variation at

Fig.31
Pl.25

the western end of Caer Caradoc, Clun (Salop), where the defences face level ground. As at Castle Rings the inner part of the system consists of a bank, ditch, and counterscarp bank. A few feet beyond the latter is a third bank, with the second ditch beyond. Beyond the second ditch is a space varying from 3 to 12 m (10 to 40 ft) in width, and then the outermost bank and ditch. The over-all width of the system is about 70 m (230 ft).

Fig.84
Pl.43

Most of the remaining sites in Group 3 involve wide spaces within the system, so that they will need to be considered again as multiple-enclosure sites. In a number of such sites only one wide space is involved. At Badbury Rings (Dorset) the inner part of the system is a compact two-ditch arrangement with two fairly massive banks (C/D verts. 8·2 and 6 m : 27 and 20 ft). About 18 m (60 ft) beyond is the smaller outer bank and ditch. There is a similar arrange-

Pl.19

ment at Flimston Bay promontory fort (Pemb). The banks forming the inner part of the system are smaller (C/D verts. c. 3 m : 10 ft), with the outer bank and ditch about 30 m (100 ft) beyond. At Camp Wood (Mon.) the space between the second ditch and the outer bank and ditch is about 37 m (120 ft). The inner part of the system consists of a bank (C/D vert. 6 m : 20 ft), a ditch, and a counterscarp bank, with a smaller bank and ditch immediately beyond.

Figs.30b,83b
Pl.20

At the south-eastern end of Hambledon Hill (Dorset) the wide space (about 37 m : 120 ft) is between the first and second ditches. The inner part of the arrangement consists of a massive bank (C/D vert. 9 m : 30 ft), a ditch, and a substantial counterscarp bank. Immediately beyond are what appear to be the remains of an unfinished bank and ditch. Beyond the wide space the outer part of the system consists of a compact arrangement of two banks and two ditches with a width of about 43 m (140 ft). The over-all width of the whole system is in

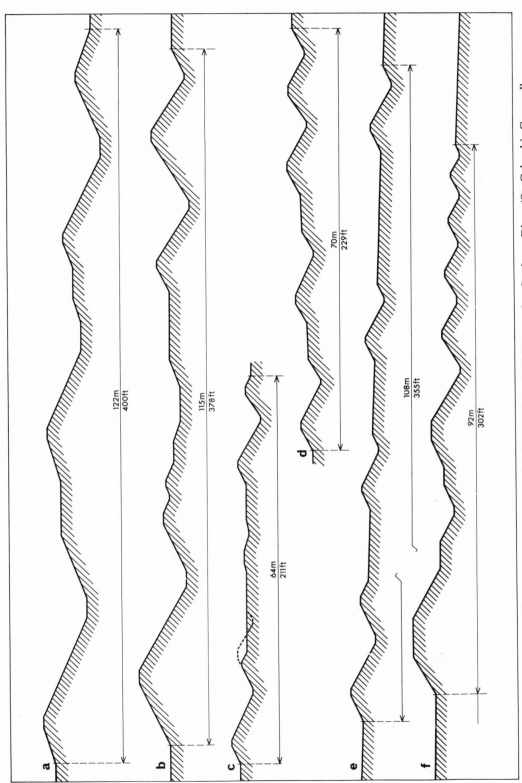

Fig. 83. Group 3 defence systems: 83a Maiden Castle, Dorset; 83b Hambledon Hill, Dorset; 83c Castle-an-Dinas (St. Columb), Cornwall. Group 4 defence systems: 83d Bulliber Camp, Pembrokeshire; 83e Symond's Yat, Gloucestershire; 83f Worlebury, Somerset.

Fig.84. Badbury
Rings, Dorset.

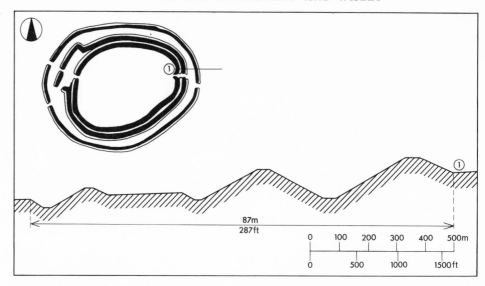

Fig.81

Fig.83c
Pl.7

Fig.92
Pl.50

Pl.39

the region of 122 m (400 ft). Wapley Camp (Here.) has a compact, two-ditch system separated by a 21-m (70-ft) space from the outer bank and ditch in the area to the east of the main entrance. The compact four-bank and three-ditch system to the west of the entrance was described earlier.

The last two sites to be considered in this particular group are Castle-an-Dinas and Warbstow Bury (Corn.). At Castle-an-Dinas, St. Columb, a maximum of four ditches are involved, although one of these, with its associated bank, is so flattened that it had probably gone out of use when the others were built. The inner part of the system consists of a bank, ditch, and a counter-scarp bank. In a number of places, however, this has been changed to a two-ditch arrangement by the addition of a ditch outside the counterscarp bank and the consequent increase in size of the latter. Between 9 and 14 m (30 and 45 ft) beyond the inner part of the system is the flattened bank and ditch, which is probably not contemporary with the other features. About 6 m (20 ft) beyond this again is the outer bank, ditch, and counterscarp bank. Excluding the flattened bank and ditch the whole system is of either the two- or three-ditch type. Including it, the systems involved are of the three- or four-ditch type. At Warbstow Bury the pattern is somewhat simpler. In the northern half of the site the arrangement is of the two-ditch type with an intervening space of about 37 m (120 ft). In the southern half, however, there is an additional bank and ditch separated from the inner ditch by a narrow berm. This bank and ditch, however, appear to be unfinished, so that in practice the system may never have been of the three-ditch type.

In many other three-ditch systems two wide spaces are involved. At White Sheet Castle (Wilts.) a simple version of such an arrangement forms the de-fences on the northern and eastern sides. The flat spaces between the three separate parts of the system are about 30 m (100 ft) wide and the over-all width is about 122 m (400 ft). A generally similar arrangement forms the main

Fig.85.
Danebury,
Hampshire.

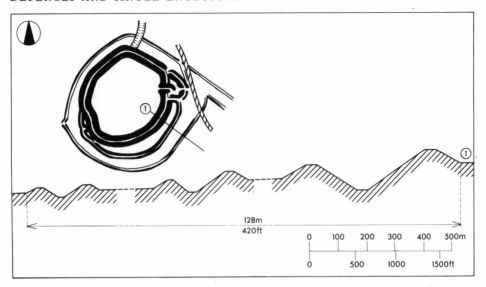

Fig.94

Fig.34a

Fig.85

Fig.104

defences at Milber Down (Devon), although a fourth bank and ditch is involved on one side and may have originally encircled the whole site.

In other wide-spaced three-ditch systems there are counterscarp banks associated with some or all of the ditches. At Westbury (Glos) the interspaces are about 15 m (50 ft) wide. The inner line consists of a bank and ditch, the middle and outer lines of bank, ditch, and counterscarp bank. The over-all width is about 85 m (280 ft). At the western end of Eggardon (Dorset) there are counterscarp banks with the inner and outer ditches but not with the middle ditch. The inner and outer spaces are 24·4 and 42·7 m (80 and 140 ft) wide respectively and the over-all width is about 122 m (400 ft). At Danebury (Hants) the over-all width is even greater, about 137 m (450 ft). Each of the three lines of defence consists of a bank, ditch, and counterscarp bank, the inner one on a very large scale (C/D. vert. *c.* 11 m : 35 ft) with a massive counterscarp bank. Both interspaces vary between 21 and 37 m (70 and 120 ft) in width. At Coxall Knoll (Here.) the inner bank is on an equally massive scale (C/D vert. *c.* 11·6 m : 38 ft), and is accompanied by a counterscarp bank. There is no counterscarp bank with the second line of defence although there is one with the outermost bank and ditch.

A good example of a three-bank system, i.e. a Group 3 system with no ditches, is provided by Warton Crag (Lancs). The remains of the three stone-built banks are spaced out at 61-m (200-ft) intervals so that once again the site will need to be considered under the heading of multiple enclosures. At Dinas, Llanfairfechan (Caer.), the spaces between the three stone ramparts on the south side are between 9 and 11 m (30 and 35 ft) wide. There were similar gaps at the northern end of Braich y Dinas in the same county, prior to the destruction of the site, although on the eastern side the interspaces were very much wider.

The last sites to be considered in Group 3 involve arrangements of the mixed

161

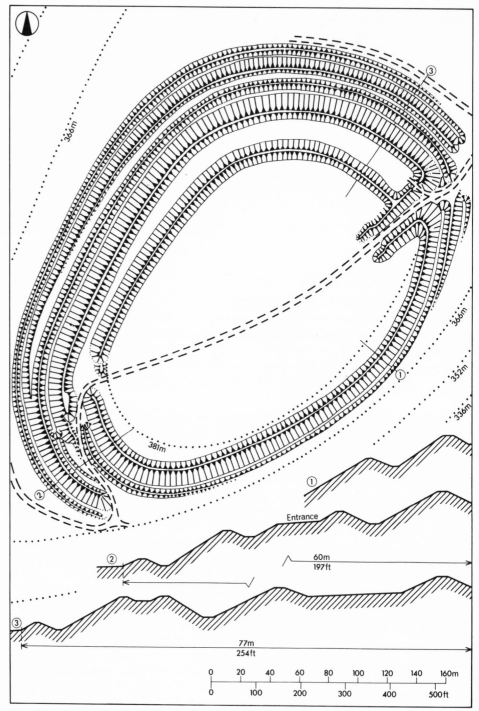

Fig.86. Bury Ditches, Shropshire.

Fig.86

type. Some of these are of the compact or separated type, others of the wide-spaced variety. A good example of the former is provided by the western defences of Bury Ditches (Salop). Five banks are involved in all, four of them associated with the two ditches present. The innermost bank (about 12 m: 40 ft wide) has no ditch. At a distance varying between 3 and 15 m (10 and 50 ft) beyond is the second bank with an outer ditch and a counterscarp bank (C/D vert. 8·5 m: 28 ft). Beyond a narrow berm is either a bank, ditch, and counter-scarp bank or simply a ditch and a counterscarp bank. The over-all width of this system is about 76 m (250 ft). A generally similar mixed system on a smaller scale, about 46 m (150 ft) wide, exists at Dinas Dinorwig (Caer.). The innermost feature is a stone rampart about 3·4 m (11 ft) thick without a ditch. About 3 or 3·5 m (10 or 12 ft) beyond is a compact arrangement of two banks, two ditches, and a counterscarp bank.

Fig.87

In other systems wide spaces are involved between the different parts of the defences. At Castle-an-Dinas, Ludgvan (Corn.), mentioned already under Group 2, there is a mixed Group 3 system on the north-eastern side. The inner part consists of two banks, without ditches, about 15 m (50 ft) apart. One or two metres beyond the outer bank is a third bank with an associated ditch. At Bosherston (Pemb) there is a similar gap between the inner and middle banks; the inner bank has no ditch. The outer part of the system consists of the middle and outer banks, with their associated ditches, in a compact arrangement. The over-all width of the system is about 46 m (150 ft). About 23 m (75 ft) behind the inner bank is what is presumed to be an earlier bank and ditch, so that four ramparts are involved in all, although they were probably not in use together. At The Breiddin (Montg.) the defences on the south-eastern side consist of two stone ramparts about 61 m (200 ft) apart, with an earthen bank and ditch immediately beyond the second bank.

Further examples of wide-spaced Group 3 systems will be covered in Chapter VI under the heading of multiple-enclosure sites.

GROUP 4: SYSTEMS WITH MORE THAN THREE DITCHES OR THREE BANKS

Only about 24 sites merit consideration in this group. About half the systems involved are of the compact or separated type. A good example of a compact four-ditch system is provided by Lodge Wood Camp (Mon.). Because of the vegetation the arrangement is not always easy to follow, but on the south the system can be seen to consist of four banks and four ditches in compact form. The two outer banks are very much flattened as compared with the inner banks. Four banks are involved also at Merrion Camp (Pemb), apparently in a compact arrangement. The three outer banks have been reduced by ploughing, so it is difficult to be absolutely certain of the original arrangement. The second bank may be simply a counterscarp bank to the inner ditch, so that the system may have been of the three-ditch type. An unequivocal example of a four-ditch system, with a counterscarp bank, is provided by Pen-y-Crug (Breck.): around the northern end and along the eastern and south-eastern sides there is a

Fig.88

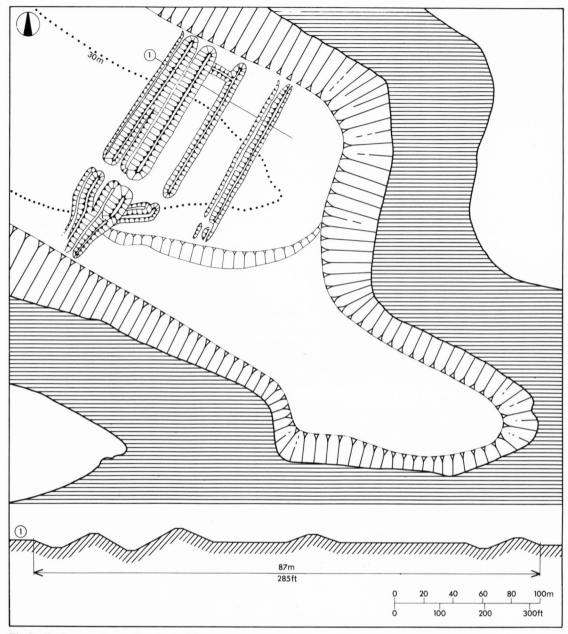

Fig.87. Bosherston Camp, Pembrokeshire.

Fig.88.
Pen-y-Crug,
Breconshire.

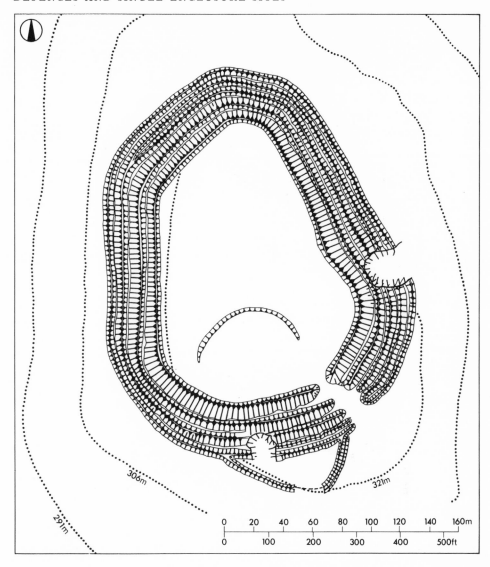

compact arrangement of five banks and four ditches with an over-all width of about 40 m (130 ft).

Fig.83d

At the eastern end of Bulliber Camp (Pemb) two narrow spaces or berms are introduced into the four-ditch system, between the inner ditch and the second bank and between the second ditch and the third bank. The third and fourth banks and their associated ditches form a compact arrangement. The over-all

Fig.81

width of the system is about 67 m (220 ft). At Wapley Camp (Here.) mentioned under Group 3, there are three variations of the four-ditch system at the eastern end of the site. In the simplest there is a berm about 6 m (20 ft) wide between the three compact inner banks and ditches and the fourth, outermost, bank and

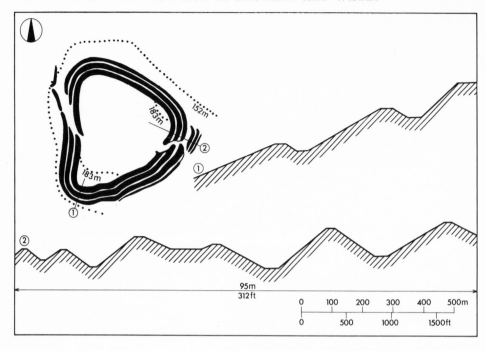

Fig.89. Castle Ditches, Wiltshire.

ditch. In an alternative version there is a single berm between the compact inner part of three banks and two ditches, and the outer part of two banks and two ditches. In a third version there are two berms. The inner part of the system, three banks and two ditches, is about 43 m (140 ft) wide. Beyond it there is a space about 15 m (50 ft) wide, with the third bank and ditch beyond. The second berm is somewhat narrower (about 12 m: 40 ft). Beyond it is the fourth bank and ditch. At Symond's Yat (Glos) three spaces are involved, the two inner ones about 12 m (40 ft) wide, the outer one about 23 m (75 ft) wide. The width of the system over-all is about 110 m (360 ft).

Fig.83e

There is a four-ditch system at the western end of Maiden Castle (Dorset) involving no less than seven banks. There are two spaces about 12 m (40 ft) wide within the system but these are, in fact, two of the roadways into the fort, so that the system is otherwise compact. It has an over-all width of about 198 m (650 ft). There is a somewhat similar arrangement at the eastern end of Castle Ditches (Wilts.). The inner part of the system is a compact arrangement of three banks and two ditches about 55 m (180 ft) wide. The outer part is a similar arrangement on a smaller scale, about 34 m (110 ft) wide. Between the two is a space about 6 m (20 ft) wide but, as at Maiden Castle, this forms the roadway into the fort.

Fig.83a
Pl.41

Fig.89

Most of the remaining four-ditch systems form part of multiple-enclosure sites. At Y Bwlwarcau (Glam.) the inner part of the system consists of two banks and two ditches, separated by a narrow berm. The outer part of the system is the same but is separated from the inner by a space between 30 and 61 m (100 and 200 ft) wide. At Gaer Fawr (Glam.) the inner part of the system consists of

Pl.45

Fig.94

a compact arrangement of three banks and two ditches. The third bank and ditch is 40 m (130 ft) beyond and the fourth a further 27 m (90 ft) away. The arrangements at Milber Down (Devon) have been referred to already under Group 3. The fourth bank and ditch is between 122 and 152 m (400 and 500 ft) beyond the rest of the defences on the western and south-western sides. The maximum width of the whole system is about 274 m (900 ft). The four-ditch arrangement at Wooston Castle (Devon) covers an even greater distance, about 335 m (1,100 ft), although whether this actually constitutes a defence system is open to doubt since the third and fourth lines are, in their present state, free-standing.

The system on the south side of Pen-y-Gaer, Llanbedr-y-Cennin (Caer.), is probably to be included in Group 4. The inner part of the system consists of a stone-built rampart about 4·5 m (15 ft) thick, without a ditch. About 3 or 4·5 m (10 or 15 ft) beyond is a compact arrangement of two banks and two ditches. About 15 m (50 ft) beyond is a third ditch with some indication of an associated bank on its inner edge. The unusual feature of this system is the fact that the 15-m (50-ft) space is occupied by a *chevaux de frise* of stones from 30 to 90 cm (1 to 3 ft) in length set on end in the ground at about 30-cm (1-ft) intervals. This occupies the full width of the 15-m (50 ft) berm and extends for about 91 m (300 ft). There is another, triangular area of *chevaux de frise* barring the direct approach to the western entrance. There is a similar use of *chevaux de frise* at Craig Gwrtheyrn (Carm.).

The few remaining systems in Group 4 involve arrangements even more complex than those just considered. Most of them are of the dispersed or wide-spaced type. On the western side of Clovelly Dykes, for example, there are five banks and five ditches spaced out over a distance of about 183 m (600 ft). The five banks and ditches at Burley Wood (Devon) are spaced out in a similar way over a distance of 244 m (800 ft). At Trevelgue promontory fort (Corn.) no less than nine banks are involved, although three, possibly four, of them are of the counterscarp type. The defences are in three groups. The inner group consists of a bank, a flat-bottomed ditch, and a short length of counterscarp bank. The second group, between 30 and 46 m (100 and 150 ft) beyond, consists of a compact arrangement of five banks and, probably, three ditches. The inner bank is separated from the remainder by a break in the cliffs that, in fact, transforms the outer part of the promontory into an island. This break is probably later than the defences and occupies the position of the inner ditch. The relatively small bank beyond is probably a counterscarp bank. Immediately beyond it is a massive bank and ditch with a smaller bank, ditch, and counterscarp bank immediately beyond in a compact arrangement. The third group consists of a bank and ditch with traces of a counterscarp bank running diagonally across the inner part of the promontory.

Pl.8

Fig.113
Fig.90

Pls.3,14
Fig.83f

The last two sites to be considered are Worlebury (Som.) and Old Oswestry (Salop). Worlebury has no less than eight banks, each with an outer ditch. Six of these are grouped to form the eastern defences of the main enclosure. The remains of the stone-built inner rampart are now about 21 m (70 ft) wide and 2·4–3 m (8–10 ft) high. There is a berm about 4·5 m (15 ft) wide separating it

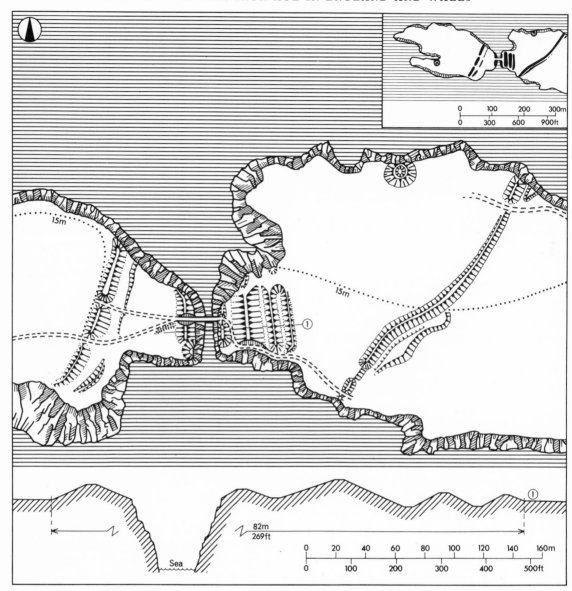

Fig.90. Trevelgue Head, Cornwall.

from a ditch about 9 m (30 ft) wide. Beyond the ditch is another berm about
3 m (10 ft) wide and then a compact arrangement of five banks and five ditches
covering about 55 m (180 ft). The banks become progressively smaller, the
outer one having a C/D vert. of only 1 or 1·5 m (4 or 5 ft). The width of the
system over-all is about 90 m (300 ft). About 20 m (70 ft) beyond the outer
ditch is a seventh bank and ditch, and a further 90 or 100 m (300 or 330 ft)
beyond is another.

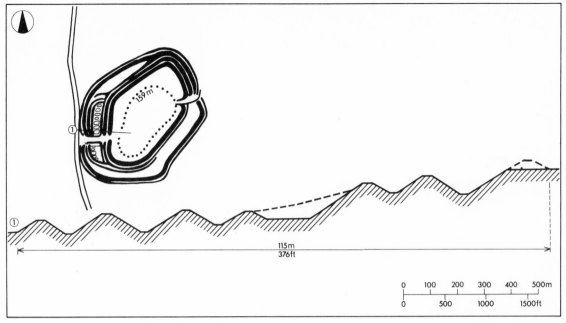

Fig.91. Old Oswestry, Shropshire.

Fig.91
Pl.14

Old Oswestry has fewer banks and ditches but incorporates one or two un-usual features on its western side where the defences are at their strongest. The inner part of the system is a conventional three-bank and two-ditch arrange-ment, both north and south of the main entrance. Beyond the counterscarp bank, however, there are differences between the two sections. To the south of the entrance there is a berm of natural ground about 7·6 m (25 ft) wide beyond the counterscarp bank and then a series of roughly rectangular quarry pits running along the back of the next, fourth, bank. This is one of a series of four closely-set banks, the outermost, the seventh, being of the counterscarp bank type. Whether both spaces, between banks four and five and between five and six, are also ditches is difficult to say. The fifth bank is noticeably smaller than the banks on either side and may be simply a counterscarp bank to the ditch associated with the fourth bank. The space between it and the sixth bank may be simply a narrow space of natural ground.

To the north of the main entrance the 7·6-m (25-ft) berm beyond the counterscarp bank is missing. Its place is taken by a series of rectangular com-partments which are presumably deeper versions of the rectangular quarry ditches to the south of the entrance. There has been considerable speculation about the nature and function of these compartments, but one thing is clear from ground examination: the compartments are, in fact, formed by excavation. The so-called banks between them are simply narrow undug sections of ground. The 'bank' at the outer edge is again simply the narrow strip of ground formed by the compartments on one side and the inner scarp of the third ditch on the

169

other. It may be that the area occupied by the compartments was originally a space or berm within the defence system. Its excavation in this particular way would have provided a series of compartments which could have been used for some specific purpose. Beyond the compartments the arrangement is more or less the same as to the south, a closely set series of banks and ditches with a width of about 58 m (190 ft). The over-all width of the whole system, both north and south of the entrance, is about 113 m (370 ft).

CHAPTER VI

Multiple-enclosure sites

The majority of Iron Age forts have only a single enclosure. There are other sites, however, accounting for about 15 per cent of the total, about 200 sites, in which the interior consists of two or more enclosures, and such sites form the subject of this chapter. In fact, the majority of multiple-enclosure sites consist of either two or three enclosures, sites with more being comparatively rare. Two of the principal arrangements found in multiple-enclosure sites, concentric enclosures and annexes, were described briefly in Chapter I and these must be considered now in more detail, together with other arrangements which come under the heading of multiple-enclosure sites.

Without anticipating the contents of Chapter IX the distribution of such sites can be indicated in broad terms. Multiple-enclosure sites are to a great extent a western and south-western phenomenon, the greatest numbers occurring in the western counties of Wales and the south-western counties of England. They are not, however, entirely absent from the remaining regions and are found, albeit in smaller numbers, in the south-east, in Wessex, in the Cotswolds, and in the Welsh Marches.

The four main types of multiple-enclosure site in south-west England, and the appropriate terminology, have been defined by Lady Fox[1] and this provides a basis on which all multiple-enclosure sites in England and Wales can be considered. The four groups are as follows: (a) concentric enclosures; (b) dependent enclosures; (c) annexed enclosures; (d) crossbank enclosures. Dependent and annexed enclosures define arrangements described so far as annexes, i.e. arrangements in which, broadly speaking, the enclosures are side by side, as opposed to concentric. Although in the south-west the differences between these two types are usually quite clear, this is not always so. In other regions it is often difficult to decide just how one enclosure is related to another. For this reason groups (b) and (c) will be considered together under the heading of 'annexes' and this term will be retained as a general designation, without prejudice to the continued use of the terms 'dependent enclosure' and 'annexed enclosure' where these are clearly applicable.

One other type of arrangement which can most conveniently be dealt with in this chapter is not present in the south-west and is not therefore covered by Lady Fox's terminology. Such an arrangement involves two enclosures which,

1. Fox, 'South-Western Hill-Forts', in Frere (ed.), *Problems of the Iron Age in Southern Britain* (1961), 35–60.

although not physically connected, are none the less so closely associated by their siting as to suggest that they formed a single unit. The subsidiary enclosures of such sites, usually, but not always, in the lower position, have been termed satellites.[2] Arrangements of this type will form the fourth group of multiple-enclosure sites to be considered here. The four groups will thus be as follows:

A. Concentric enclosures.
B. Annexes.
C. Crossbank enclosures.
D. Satellites.

Fig.37

Fig.105

While many multiple-enclosure sites belong exclusively to one or other of the four groups, there are others in which the subsidiary enclosures are of two or three different types. Tregeare Rounds (Corn.), for example, has three enclosures, the inner two of the concentric type, the third of the annexe type. Earl's Hill (Salop) has an annexe, a crossbank enclosure, and a satellite.

A. CONCENTRIC ENCLOSURES

As defined by Lady Fox, sites in this group 'consist of two or more lines of earthwork forming enclosures that are approximately concentric'.[3] In a number of sites the enclosures are both circular and concentric but in others, and more especially outside the south-west, the shapes and relative positions are less regular. As used here the term 'concentric' refers specifically to multiple-enclosure sites and it is the enclosures which are regarded as concentric rather than the defences. In a site such as Chun Castle (Corn.) the inner and outer defences are both circular and concentric, but as pointed out by Lady Fox the space between the two is only 6 m (20 ft) wide and is best regarded as a berm rather than as an enclosure. Chun Castle does not therefore qualify as a concentric site as defined here.

In the south-west about fifteen sites call for comment in the context of concentric enclosures, most of them in Cornwall. In nearly all of them the enclosures involved are, for all practical purposes, both circular and concentric. South-western multiple-enclosure sites have been listed by Lady Fox. Not included in the list is the smaller Castle-an-Dinas, Ludgvan, which would appear to qualify, if only just, by reason of the 15-m (50-ft) gap between its inner and outer defences. The inner enclosure is about 76 m (250 ft) in diameter and is defended by a bank about 3·6 m (12 ft) wide, without a ditch. Concentric with and about 15 m (50 ft) beyond this is a similar bank, again without a ditch. These two banks form the defences for about two-thirds of the circuit. On the east and north-east, however, where the approach is easier, there is a third bank, with an outer ditch, immediately beyond the second.

Fig.92

The defences of Castle-an-Dinas are on a modest scale. The defences of Warbstow Bury, on the other hand, are of impressive size, comparable with

2. Forde-Johnston, 'Earl's Hill, Pontesbury and Related Hillforts in England and Wales', *Arch. J.* 119 (1962), 76–77.　　　　3. Fox, op. cit. 37.

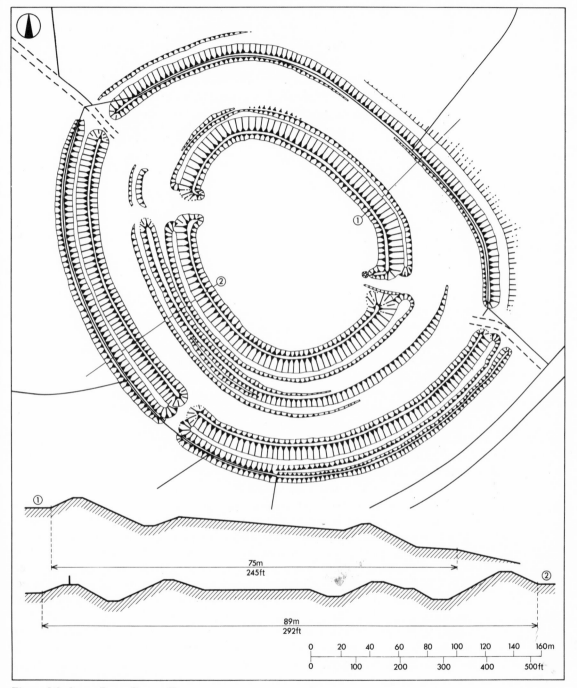

Fig.92. Warbstow Bury, Cornwall.

Fig.93. Castle
Killibury,
Cornwall.

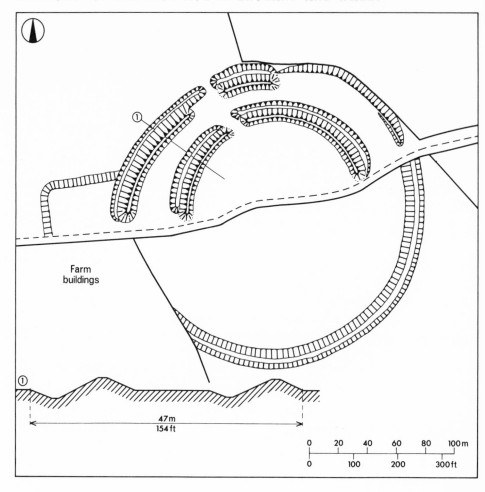

Farm
buildings

47m
154ft

0   20   40   60   80   100m
0   100   200   300ft

Pl.50

Iron Age forts in any area. The site is in a hill-slope position. The inner enclosure covers about 1 ha (3 acres) and is defended by a substantial bank and ditch
with a C/D vert. of over 6 m (20 ft). The outer defences are situated between
24 and 46 m (80 and 150 ft) beyond, and although on a smaller scale are still
impressive, with a C/D vert. of about 4·5 m (15 ft). On the south and west there
is a substantial counterscarp bank accompanying the bank and ditch. On the
same sides there are additional features between the main inner and outer
defences which have already been described (p. 160). Where best preserved
these consist of a bank and ditch a few feet beyond the edge of the inner ditch.
On the south-eastern side all that now remains is a single scarp about 15 m (50
ft) beyond the ditch edge. This third line of defence is on a smaller scale than
either the inner or outer defences, and may have been inserted between them.
It may, on the other hand, represent an attempt to strengthen the inner enclosure which was abandoned in favour of the existing outer defences.

Fig.83c

Castle-an-Dinas, St. Columb, occupies the summit of a rounded hill, with an

174

Plates 34–52

34 Spettisbury, Dorset, showing the 'humped' nature of the rampart on the north-eastern side, viewed from inside the fort. In a final stage the separate 'humps', each presumably representing a dump of material from the ditch, would have been smoothed out into a single level bank.

35 Castle Hill, Wiltshire, showing the flat-bottomed nature of the ditch, probably a result of ploughing. At Spettisbury (Plate 34) excavation has shown that a similar ditch was originally of the normal V-shaped type.

36 Dolebury, Somerset, showing the remains of the stone-built inner rampart on the north-west side of the site.

37 Carl Wark, Yorkshire, a well-preserved stone-faced rampart still standing some 3 m (10 ft) high, with a wedge-shaped supporting mass of earth behind. View from the south.

38 Bratton Castle, Wiltshire, viewed from the east. A multivallate site in a plateau-edge situation, defended by a compact arrangement of two banks and two ditches, with a box-like outwork at the entrance.

39 White Sheet Castle, Wiltshire, a multiple-enclosure site formed by three widely spaced ramparts. View from the north.

40 Old Sarum, Wiltshire. The massive outer defences, representing the original Iron Age fort, may owe something of their size to the builders of the later Norman castle which occupies the centre of the enclosure. View from the north-east.

41 Maiden Castle, Dorset, showing the formidable multivallate defences on all sides and the complex eastern and western entrances. View from the south-west.

42 Maiden Castle, Dorset. The multivallate defences in the south-western quarter of the fort.

43 Badbury Rings, Dorset. The inner defences, a compact arrangement of two banks and two ditches, are set back 18 m (60 ft) from the outer defence, a single bank and ditch. The main entrance has a box-like barbican formed by the divergence of the two parts of the inner defences. View from the north-east.

44 Buzbury Rings, Dorset, a multiple-enclosure site in a low-lying situation with few, if any, natural advantages. View from the south.

45 Y Bwlwarcau, Glamorganshire, a multiple-enclosure site with two inner concentric enclosures, and outer enclosures of the annexe type. View from the south.

46 Twyn y Gaer, Monmouthshire, a three-part multiple-enclosure site, two of the enclosures being the result of later subdivision. View from the east.

47 Castell Mawr, Pembrokeshire, a two-enclosure site formed by the sub-division of an original circular, single-enclosure site. View from the east.

48 Hardings Down, Glamorganshire, a complex of three separate but presumably related Iron Age enclosures, viewed from the north.

49 Cefn Carnedd, Montgomeryshire, a multiple-enclosure site with multivallate defences on the vulnerable side.

50 Warbstow Bury, Cornwall, a larger than usual example of a multiple-enclosure site of the concentric type. View from the north-west.

51 Foel Trigarn, Pembrokeshire, a site with three enclosures, two concentric and one of the annexe type, viewed from the north.

52 Uffington Castle, Berkshire, a univallate fort with an entrance of the out-turned type, viewed from the north-west.

34. Spettisbury,
Dorset

35. Castle Hill,
Wiltshire

36. Dolebury,
Somerset

37. Carl Wark,
Yorkshire

38. Bratton
Castle, Wiltshire

39. White Sheet
Castle, Wiltshire

40. Old Sarum,
Wiltshire

41. Maiden
Castle, Dorset

42. Maiden Castle, Dorset: the south-western defences

43. Badbury Rings, Dorset

44. Buzbury
Rings, Dorset

45. Y Bwlwarcau,
Glamorganshire

46. Twyn y Gaer,
Monmouthshire

47. Castell
Mawr,
Pembrokeshire

48. Hardings
Down,
Glamorganshire

49. Cefn
Carnedd,
Montgomery-
shire

50. Warbstow
Bury, Cornwall

51. Foel Trigarn,
Pembrokeshire

52. Uffington
Castle,
Berkshire

Pl.7

inner enclosure about 137 m (450 ft) in diameter. Its defence system was described in Chapter V (p. 160). The spaces between the various parts of the system are, in fact, reduced to two narrow strips, about 5·5 and 8 m (18 and 25 ft) wide. The significance of this in relation to concentric multiple-enclosure sites on the one hand and small, heavily defended sites on the other is discussed in Chapter X (pp. 284–5).

Both Warbstow Bury and Castle-an-Dinas are of the purely concentric type. At Tregeare Rounds and Killibury enclosures of the annexe type are involved

Fig.37

as well. Like Warbstow Bury, Tregeare Rounds is situated on sloping ground. The inner enclosure has a diameter of about 91 m (300 ft), with the outer defences between 24 and 30 m (80 and 100 ft) beyond. It is noticeable that the outer bank and ditch are on a larger scale than the inner defences, with a C/D vert. of approximately 3·9 m (13 ft) as opposed to 2·7 m (9 ft). The third enclosure, of the annexe type, is on the eastern and south-eastern sides. It is defined for the most part by a scarp running parallel to the outer bank and ditch for some 244 m (800 ft), forming an enclosure between 18 and 46 m (60 and

Fig.93

150 ft) wide. The pattern of two concentric enclosures at Killibury is very much the same, although in this case the site is on a hilltop, albeit a very slight one. The southern half of the site is virtually ploughed away with only faint traces of the outer ditch now visible. The third enclosure, on the west, is of the annexe type, although this too has been ploughed and is defined now by a scarp. Other concentric sites, consisting of either two or three enclosures are recorded at Bury Down, Kestle Rings, Blacketon Camp, and Caer Dane.

Fig.102

The last Cornish site to be considered in this context is Pencarrow Rings, which differs somewhat from the sites described so far, although it does qualify in that the outermost enclosure completely embraces the inner. The latter, consisting of three enclosures, will be described later. The outer enclosure concentric with it is very large and although not preserved on the north and east was probably in the region of 610 m (2,000 ft) long and 457 m (1,500 ft) wide. Attached to the north-western corner is a triangular annexe forming part of the entrance works.

Pl.8

In Devon the inner sections of the complex site of Clovelly Dykes also belong to the concentric type. In all, six enclosures are involved. The inner sub-rectangular enclosure covers about 1 ha (2½ acres) and was defended originally by a bank and ditch. Concentric with, and about 21 m (70 ft) beyond, these defences is a second stronger line of defence, forming a concentric enclosure of about 60 ares (1½ acres). The third line of defence completely embraces the second, but forms two additional enclosures of the dependent type rather than a third concentric enclosure. On the north and south the second and third lines have only berms or narrow spaces between them. On the east and west these broaden out to form enclosures, roughly semicircular on the east and triangular on the west. Beyond the latter to the west are two more enclosures of the annexe type. At Milber Down (Devon) the inner enclosure is similar in

Fig.94

size to the one at Clovelly, just over 80 ares (2 acres), and is defended by a bank and ditch. The defences of the second concentric enclosure are about 30 m (100 ft) beyond and are likewise of bank-and-ditch type. The third line of

Fig.94. Milber
Down Camp,
Devon.

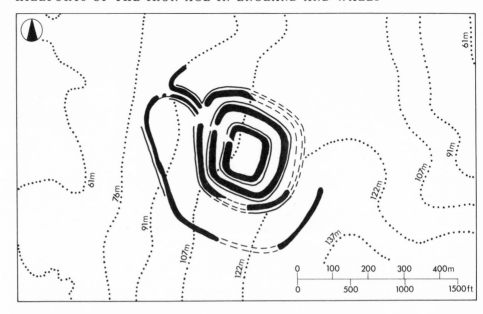

bank and ditch, now incomplete, does not, strictly speaking, define a third concentric enclosure. On the south-western side the space between the second and
third lines is too narrow to be regarded as an enclosure and must be treated
simply as a berm, although elsewhere the space is wide enough to qualify.
Between 91 and 152 m (300 and 500 ft) beyond the third line on the north-west,
west, south-west, south, and south-east is a fourth line forming a semicircle more
or less concentric with the other works.

Of the remaining Devonshire sites listed by Lady Fox only one belongs
unequivocally to the concentric category. Hunter's Tor, in a hilltop position,
consists of three concentric enclosures defended by stone-built ramparts. Lady
Fox lists Cold Rings, Ermington, as of either the concentric *or* annexed type. The
last site, Shoulsbarrow Castle, has natural defences to the south, so that the
outer enclosure embraces the inner on only three sides. In this it resembles two
other sites, The Bulwark, Cheriton (Glam.) and Foel Trigarn (Pemb). All three
sites, although not strictly concentric, are probably best dealt with under this
heading.

Fig.99

In Wessex five sites call for comment in the context of concentric enclosures.
Perhaps the most unusual is Buzbury Rings (Dorset), which, like some of the
south-western sites, is situated on sloping ground. The existing remains define
two enclosures with some slight suggestion of a third. The inner, roughly
circular, enclosure is about 122 m (400 ft) in diameter and is defended by a
single bank and ditch. The oval enclosure defined by the outer defences falls
somewhere between the concentric and the dependent enclosure types. On the
south the defences of inner and outer enclosures form a compact multivallate
system, but elsewhere they diverge to form a large outer enclosure. Where they
diverge on the west there is some evidence for a third bank, which may have

178

defined an additional enclosure between the two that exist now.

Fig.84
Pl.43

The near-by site of Badbury Rings has often been compared with Buzbury, but the two, in fact, have very little in common. The inner oval enclosure (6·8 ha: 17 acres) is defended for most of its circuit by a compact arrangement of two substantial banks with ditches (C/D verts. 8·2 m : 27 ft and 6 m : 20 ft). In the region of the main entrance, however, the outer bank and ditch turn outwards to define a rectangular enclosure some 152 m (500 ft) long and 30 m (100 ft) wide which, by definition, must be termed a dependent enclosure. The third bank and ditch, which are on a smaller scale, form a concentric enclosure. This is about 15 m (50 ft) wide for most of its circuit but on the west where the defences swing out to accommodate the entrance works it is considerably wider. A third Dorset site must also be classed as concentric. At Weatherby Castle the inner enclosure, about 2·4 ha (6 acres), is defended by a substantial bank (C/D vert. 7·3 m, 24 ft), a ditch, and in places a counterscarp bank. Completely embracing this is another enclosure, between 15 and 30 m (50 and 100 ft) wide, defined now by a bank about 15 m (50 ft) wide but probably in its original state by a bank and ditch.

Pls.31,32

In Wiltshire Figsbury Rings must also be considered as a concentric site. The inner circular enclosure is defined by the inner quarry ditch which is set back some 30 m (100 ft) from the main bank and ditch. It seems feasible to suggest that the need for an inner quarry ditch was taken as an opportunity for sub-dividing the interior of the univallate fort for some reason connected with its function. It is noticeable that the two causeways across the quarry ditch are immediately opposite the two entrances of the outer enclosure.

Fig.85

The last Wessex site in this category is Danebury in Hampshire, which occupies the summit of a hill with fairly steep slopes on the north and west, gentle slopes on the south, and a fairly easy approach from the east along a shallow ridge. The central, roughly circular, enclosure, about 4·8 ha (12 acres), is defended by a massive bank, ditch, and counterscarp bank (C/D vert. *c.* 10·6 m: 35 ft). This is flanked to the south and south-east by a long curving annexe defended by a smaller bank, ditch, and counterscarp bank. Completely embracing these two enclosures is a third, of the concentric type, defended by much slighter defences consisting of a ditch with a bank on the counterscarp, although in one or two places there is a slight inner bank as well. For most of its circuit this enclosure varies between 15 and 37 m (50 and 120 ft) in width, but in the region of the eastern entrance it is some 61 m (200 ft) wide. At this point the site is disturbed and difficult to interpret, but it seems clear that northern and southern sections of the outer defences did not actually meet. Instead they appear to have linked up with parallel earthworks about 30 m (100 ft) apart which define a sort of roadway running off for several hundred metres in a south-easterly direction.

Fig.95

In south-eastern England Goosehill Camp (Sussex) is of the concentric type and like a number of the south-western sites it is situated on sloping ground. The inner enclosure is oval in plan and is defended by a bank and ditch which take in an area of about 20 ares ($\frac{1}{2}$ acre). The defences of the outer enclosure, which is now incomplete, are between 24 and 37 m (80 and 120 ft) beyond and define

179

Fig.95. Goose
Hill Camp,
Sussex.

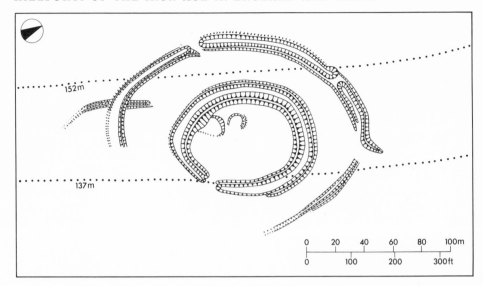

152m

137m

| 0 | 20 | 40 | 60 | 80 | 100m |

| 0 | 100 | 200 | 300ft |

an area which was probably in the region of 91 ares (2¼ acres). The only other south-eastern site which can be mentioned in this context is Witham (Essex). It consists basically of inner and outer oval enclosures linked in two places by crossbanks. The outer enclosure is about 366 × 305 m (1,200 × 1,000 ft) and the inner about 213 × 152 m (700 × 500 ft).

Only one site in the Cotswold region calls for comment in the context of concentric enclosures, and even that does not qualify as a multiple-enclosure site. Because of the small interval (between 4·5 and 7·6 m: 15 and 25 ft) between its inner and outer defences Cleeve Cloud must be placed in the same category as Chun Castle (Corn.), where the 6-m (20-ft) space involved was regarded as a berm rather than an enclosure. There are, however, two points about Cleeve Cloud which are worth noting. The first is that, like one or two of the sites in south-west England, the outer defences (C/D vert. 3·6 m: 12 ft) are larger than the inner (C/D vert. 2·7 m: 9 ft). This is a reversal of the normal pattern in compact and separated defence systems. The second point relates to the situation. Cleeve Cloud now appears to be a D-shaped cliff-edge site, but this is probably due to quarrying and erosion. The man-made defences face uphill, so that originally the site almost certainly stood on sloping ground and this again is characteristic of a number of south-western sites.

Most of the remaining concentric sites are in Wales. Two sites in Monmouth can be dealt with at the same time. The first of these, Tredegar Camp, has three enclosures, the outermost being of the annexe type. The site is in a semi-contour position facing an easy approach from the north-east. The inner sub-rectangular enclosure, about 1 ha (2½ acres), is defended by a bank, ditch, and in places a counterscarp bank.[4] The defences of the second enclosure are similar

Fig.77

Fig.96

4. In Savory's 'List of Hill-forts and other Earthworks in Wales: II. Monmouthshire', *Bull. Board Celtic Stud.* 13.4 (1950), 231–8, the inner enclosure at Tredegar is interpreted as part of a medieval earthwork. In the writer's view it forms part of the Iron Age fort, reused in a later period as the bailey of a medieval ring motte.

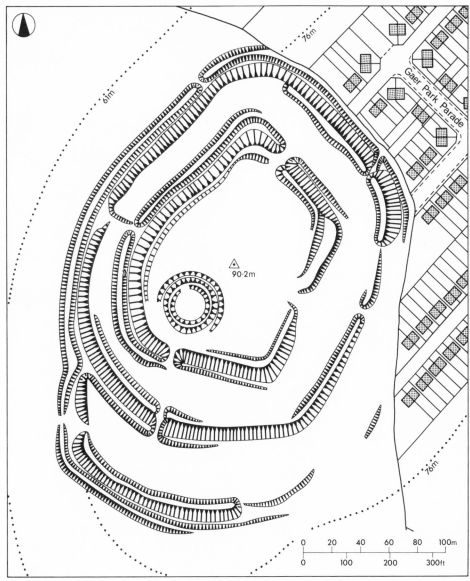

Fig.96. Tredegar Camp, Monmouthshire.

and are situated between 15 and 30 m (50 and 100 ft) beyond, taking in a further 1 ha (2½ acres). Flanking these concentric enclosures to the south-west is an annexe enclosing a further 60 ares (1½ acres). Gaer Hill Camp in the same county has only two enclosures. The small inner enclosure is sub-rectangular and is defended by a bank, ditch, and counterscarp bank. The outer enclosure concentric with it is much larger, but is defended by only a bank of no great strength.

In Glamorgan about 10 sites call for comment under the heading of con-

181

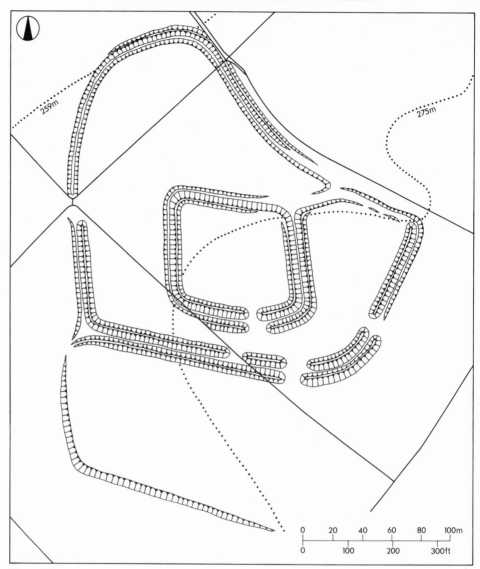

Fig.97. Caer Cwm Philip, Glamorgan.

Pl.45

centric enclosures. Bwlwarcau on Margam Mountain stands on sloping ground and involves no less than four enclosures. The inner sub-rectangular enclosure takes in about 26 ares ($\frac{2}{3}$ acre) and is protected by multivallate defences. For most of the circuit these are in separated form and consist of a bank, ditch, and counterscarp bank separated by a berm about 9 m (30 ft) wide—i.e. not wide enough to be regarded as an enclosure—from an outer bank, ditch, and counter-scarp bank. On the north-eastern side these merge to form a single system. Completely embracing this enclosure is a second enclosure with its defences, mainly a bank and ditch, about 55 m (180 ft) beyond. The third enclosure must be classed as of the dependent type since its defences and those of the second enclosure form a single multivallate system on the west. On the south and east they diverge to form an enclosure between 46 and 76 m (150 and 250 ft) wide. This enclosure is continued on the north although there the defences are formed by the natural slope to the river below. A large annexe on the western side may be a later feature.

Fig.97   About 2 km (1¼ miles) to the south-west Caer Cwm Phillip appears to be a simpler version of the Bwlwarcau arrangement. The inner, sub-rectangular enclosure is defended by a bank, ditch and counterscarp bank and measures internally 61 × 67 m (200 × 220 ft). This is embraced by the second enclosure (bank, ditch, and counterscarp bank) which takes in about 1·2 ha (3 acres). Between Bwlwarcau and Caer Cwm Phillip is a third site, Caer Blaen y Cwm, which is a simpler version again of the same general arrangement. It has a small sub-rectangular enclosure with outer defences about 46 m (150 ft) to the north and south. These, however, are not connected to form a complete enclosure and the site cannot, strictly speaking, be called concentric, although quite clearly it has very close links with the two concentric sites described already.

Of the remaining concentric sites in Glamorgan, Bonvilston Gaer, Castell Moel, and Maendy Camp are in hilltop positions and have two concentric enclosures each. At Bonvilston Gaer the oval inner enclosure, defended by a bank, measures about 55 × 40 m (180 × 130 ft) internally. It is placed within a sub-rectangular outer enclosure about 101 m (330 ft) in diameter. At Castell Moel only the inner enclosure is now preserved. The remains of the outer enclosure consist now of a bank about 30 m (100 ft) to the west. Maendy Camp differs somewhat from the other sites in the group but can be regarded as basically concentric. The inner enclosure, defended by a dry-stone rampart, measures about 37 × 43 m (120 × 140 ft). The defences of the outer enclosure are between 18 and 40 m (60 and 130 ft) beyond, except on the north where the

Fig.98   two lines come very close together. Llanquian Wood differs from the three sites just described in occupying a hill-slope position but conforms to the same over-all pattern, consisting of two concentric enclosures. The two sites on Harding's

Fig.111   Down listed by Savory[5] also occupy hill-slope positions but do not appear to qualify as concentric sites, although they are of the multiple-enclosure type.

Pl.17   At the Bulwark, Cheriton, the oval inner enclosure, about 122 × 91 m (400 × 300 ft), defended by a bank and ditch, has a steep natural slope to the north. The defences of the outer enclosure, up to 40 m (130 ft) beyond, embrace it on the three remaining sides. There are additional defences, of the crossbank type, to east and west. The last concentric site in Glamorgan is Gaer Fawr. The small inner enclosure, about 49 × 30 m (160 × 100 ft), is defended where best preserved by a compact arrangement of three banks and two ditches. About 40 m (130 ft) beyond is a single bank and ditch defining a second enclosure and a further 27 m (90 ft) beyond is another bank and ditch defining a third enclosure. The defences of the two outer enclosures appear to have been destroyed in the northern half of the site.

5. Savory, 'List of Hill-forts and other Earthworks in Wales: I. Glamorgan', *Bull. Board Celtic Stud.* 13 (1949), 152–61.

Fig.98.
Llanquian
Wood,
Glamorgan.

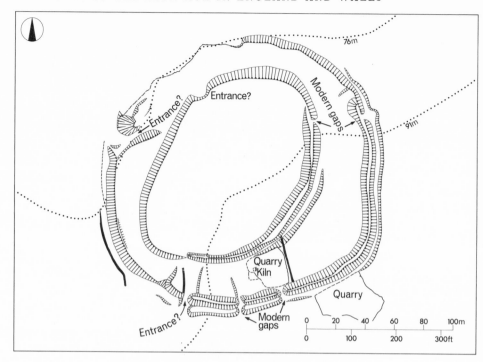

Section (f) of Savory's list of forts in Carmarthenshire[6] consists of 'Concentric or Segmented Hill-slope Enclosures' and includes 8 sites. Of these only 3 appear to be of the concentric type being considered here. Bignen and Plas earthworks, both of which have been very much disturbed, consist of two concentric lines of defence. Gelli Diogyn is described as having two weak outer banks on the north and one on the west and south. The remaining sites in Section (f), although of the multiple-enclosure type, do not appear to involve concentric arrangements.

Of the sites in Pembrokeshire only 4 need to be considered here. Caerau Moylgrove, involves three enclosures, all of the concentric type. The inner enclosure is some 110 m (360 ft) in diameter, about 80 ha (2 acres), and is defined now by a bank 1 or 2 m (3 or 6 ft) high. The middle and outer enclosures, 15 and 18 m (50 and 60 ft) wide respectively, are defended in the same way. The sites have been subjected to considerable ploughing, and the absence of ditches may be one of the results of this. If this is so then the original gap between the various lines of defence would have been less than stated above, by 3 or 4·5 m (10 or 15 ft), and less than the 15-m (50-ft) width which is regarded as the critical point between berms and enclosures. However, on the basis of its present appearance Caerau certainly belongs to the concentric multiple-enclosure category. If it did originally include ditches, then it would still constitute a closely allied type that would need to be noted here.

Keeston Castle is in a hill-slope situation. The inner enclosure, defended by a

6. Savory, 'List of Hill-forts and other Earthworks in Wales: V. Carmarthenshire', *Bull. Board Celtic Stud.* 16.1 (1954), 54–67.

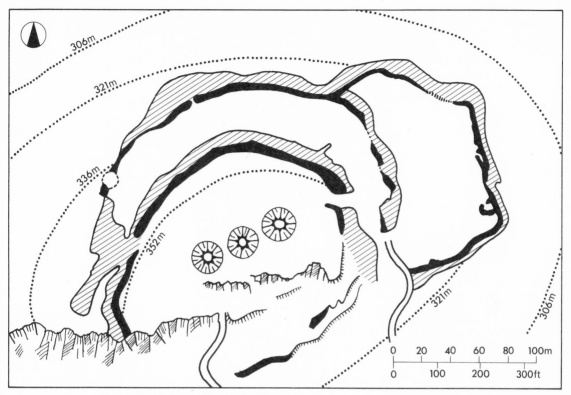

Fig.99. Foel Trigarn, Pembrokeshire.

bank and ditch, is about 46 m (150 ft) in diameter. The middle bank is about
11 m (35 ft) beyond and the outer bank, defining the second enclosure, a further
76 m (250 ft) away. The defences of both inner and outer enclosures have been
ploughed out on the south-eastern side. Summerton Camp also stands on
sloping ground and is generally similar in plan, although on a smaller scale.
The inner enclosure is about 46 m (150 ft) in diameter, the outer about 107 ×
91 m (350 × 300 ft). There is some suggestion of an annexe attached to the
southern side of the outer enclosure. Of the three enclosures involved at Foel
Trigarn the inner two form an arrangement which can best be described
as concentric. The stone ramparts involved are about 37 m (120 ft) apart on the
north, west, and east. On the south the inner defences are replaced by a steep
slope. There is some suggestion of an outer rampart about 46 m (150 ft) to the
south. The third enclosure, on the east, is of the annexe type.

Hogg[7] lists about 12 multiple-enclosure sites in Cardiganshire. Of these only
3 or 4 appear to be of the concentric type. This is consistent with the numbers in
Carmarthenshire and Pembrokeshire. Castellnadolig is one of the best examples
of the type, although the picture is confused by the modern field banks. The
arrangement involves two concentric oval enclosures. The inner enclosure is

7. Hogg, 'List of Hill-forts in Cardiganshire', ibid. 19.4 (1962), 354–66.

Fig.99
Pl.51

Fig. 100. Caer
Bach,
Caernarvonshire.

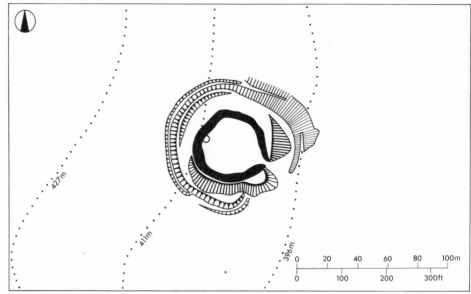

Fig. 100

some 122 × 61 m (400 × 200 ft) and the outer 244 × 183 m (800 × 600 ft). The whole site stands on gently sloping ground. The two enclosures at Cilcennin are also oval in plan. The inner enclosure measures about 107 × 61 m (350 × 200 ft) and is defended by a single bank. About 15 m (50 ft) beyond is the outer bank, defining an oval enclosure about 152 m (500 ft) long and 91 m (300 ft) wide. Other sites which are probably to be included in the concentric class are Gaer Pwntan and Cefn Blewog. At Castell Fflemish the space between the inner and outer lines of defence is too small to qualify as an enclosure and the site must be placed in the same category as Chun Castle (Corn.) and some of the concentric sites in Caernarvonshire to be described next.

The multiple-enclosure sites in Caernarvonshire include 6 or so sites of the concentric type together with 1 or 2 others which must be regarded as closely allied. At Dinas, Llanfairfechan, the inner enclosure, about 37 m (120 ft) in diameter, is defended by a stone rampart about 2·7 m (9 ft) thick. The space between the inner and outer defences varies between 9 and 21 m (30 and 70 ft) and the area enclosed is about 30 ares (¾ acre). On the east and south-east there are traces of a third rampart between 7·6 and 11 m (25 and 35 ft) beyond the second. At Caer Bach the inner enclosure is of similar dimensions and is defended by a rampart between 3·5 and 4·5 m (12 and 15 ft) thick. Concentric with, and about 15 m (50 ft) beyond this, is the outer line of defence consisting of a bank, ditch, and, in one section, a counterscarp bank.

At Carn Pentyrch the inner enclosure is only 24 × 27 m (80 × 90 ft) and is defended by a rampart between 3 and 4·5 m (10 and 15 ft) thick. This stands within another enclosure, oval in shape, defended on the north and north-west by a bank and ditch and elsewhere by a stone rampart. The gap between the inner and outer defences is for the most part about 18 m (60 ft), although on the

186

Fig.101.
Helsbury,
Cornwall.

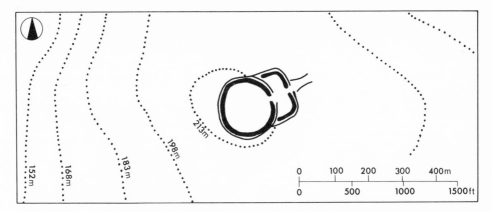

north-west it is reduced to as little as 4·5 m (15 ft). In addition to the concentric enclosures there is a third enclosure of the annexe type on the western and north-western sides, taking in a further 1 ha (3 acres).

The 3 concentric sites described so far have all been generally circular. At Carreg y Llam the inner and outer enclosures are elongated ovals. The inner enclosure is 36·6 (120 ft) long and 12 m (40 ft) wide and is defended by a stone rampart about 3·5 m (12 ft) thick. Between 7·6 and 15 m (25 and 50 ft) beyond is an outer rampart, also stone built, taking in another 1,349 sq m (1,613 sq yd). At the northern and southern ends there are additional enclosures of the cross-bank type.

In addition to the 4 sites just mentioned there are 5 other generally circular sites, with over-all diameters of between 61 and 91 m (200 and 300 ft), which have concentric defences. None of them, however, can be included in the multiple-enclosure category without qualification. In the case of Castell Caeron and Meillionydd the space between the inner and outer ramparts is only about 6 m (20 ft), so that it must be regarded as a berm rather than an enclosure. At Pen-y-Gaer, Llanengan, the defences are now only two scarps, but the gap between the two lines could not have been much greater than the two sites just mentioned. The two remaining sites, Castell Odo and Conion, come closest to qualifying for inclusion in the concentric multiple-enclosure category. In both cases there is an inner enclosure in the region of 46 m (150 ft) in diameter. Concentric with, and between 14 and 15 m (45 and 50 ft) beyond, it is the second line of defence, giving each site an over-all diameter of around 91 m (300 ft).

B. ANNEXES

In England and Wales as a whole the commonest type of multiple-enclosure site involves subsidiary enclosures of the annexe type, including under this heading both the dependent and annexed enclosures of Lady Fox's terminology. The sites in the south-west have been listed by Lady Fox.[8] Most of them

8. Fox, op. cit. 56–58.

Fig.101

are, in fact, of the annexed type. Helsbury (Corn.) has a circular inner enclosure, about 134 m (440 ft) in diameter, 1·41 ha (3½ acres), defended by a substantial bank and ditch, and stands in a hilltop position. To the east and north-east there is a roughly rectangular annexe, defended in the same way, taking in a further 60 ares (1½ acres). Access to the inner enclosure is via the annexe and the entrances to the two enclosures are in line. Castle Goff and Bury Camp are similar in arrangement, although on a smaller scale. At Castle Goff the bank and ditch enclose an inner area of less than 20 ares (½ acre). This is flanked to the north-west, west, and south-west by a D-shaped annexe taking in another 30 ares (¾ acre). At Bury Camp the inner enclosure is just under 40 ares (1 acre) in extent. The outer enclosure covers the northern, north-western, and western sides and takes in another 40 ares (1 acre).

The sites considered so far have all had roughly circular inner enclosures with D-shaped or lunate annexes on one side. Gearhill (Corn.) is less regular in plan and is on a very much larger scale. The main enclosure, defended by a bank and ditch, covers about 5 ha (13 acres). To the north-west, and defined now by a single scarp, is a large annexe taking in another 3 ha (7½ acres).

Fig.102

At Pencarrow, mentioned already under concentric enclosures, there is an enclosure of the annexe type attached to the outer bank and ditch on the western side, associated with an entrance. The annexe is triangular in plan, with maximum dimensions of 91 and 46 m (300 and 150 ft). There are also triangular

Fig.143

annexes at Blackbury Castle (Devon), associated with the main entrance, and these will need to be considered again in Chapter X.

In Devon Prestonbury consists of three enclosures, the outermost being of the crossbank type. The two inner enclosures conform to the general pattern of Helsbury, Castle Goff, etc. The innermost enclosure, in a hilltop position, is oval in plan and occupies an area of about 1·4 ha (3½ acres). To the east and north-east it is flanked by a lunate annexe taking in a further 80 ares (2 acres).

Fig.113

Burley Wood in the same county is much less regular in plan and involves no less than six enclosures, the outer three being of the crossbank type. The oval inner enclosure, defended by a bank, ditch, and in places a counterscarp bank, occupies about 1 ha (3 acres) in a semi-contour position. This is flanked on the southern, approach, side by two annexes, the smaller one occupying the north-eastern corner of the larger. There are also annexes associated with the con-

Figs.37,93

centric sites of Tregeare Rounds and Killibury in Cornwall.

Dependent enclosures are rather less numerous than the annexed enclosures just described. A classic example is provided by Castle Dore (Corn.). The inner circular enclosure, about 73 m (240 ft) in diameter, is defended by a bank and ditch, with a counterscarp bank on the annexe side. For about two-thirds of the circuit the inner and outer defences form a compact arrangement of two banks and two ditches, although the outer ditch is now almost completely filled on the western side. On the eastern side the inner and outer lines diverge to form a lunate enclosure with a maximum width of 30 m (100 ft). Access is via the dependent enclosure with the inner and outer entrances in line. Penhargard Castle and Nance Wood are basically of the same type. In Devon Denbury is a rather larger example of the same type of site. The inner oval enclosure, about

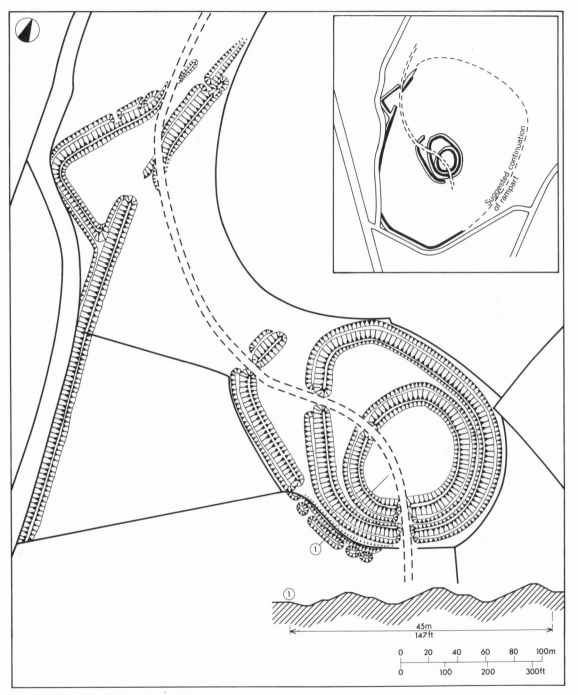

Suggested continuation of rampart

45m
147ft

| 0 | 20 | 40 | 60 | 80 | 100m |

| 0 | | 100 | | 200 | | 300ft |

Fig. 102. Pencarrow Rings, Cornwall.

1·8 ha (4½ acres) is defended by a substantial bank and ditch. On the south and east, and originally on the north, the inner and outer defences form a compact or separated two-bank and two-ditch arrangement. On the west, however, the outer defences swing forward to define a dependent enclosure about 152 m (500 ft) long and 91 m (300 ft) wide, taking in another 1 ha (3 acres).

At Hall Rings (Corn.) the arrangement falls somewhere between the dependent and annexed types. On the west and south-west the inner and outer defences form a compact arrangement. Towards the south-east they diverge in the manner of dependent enclosures. Where the outer defences rejoin the inner, however, they do so in the manner of annexed enclosures, that is, they stop short on the outer edge of the inner ditch. They do not continue around the site, nor do the compact defences on the western side. Largin Castle (Corn.) conforms very much to the classic pattern of Castle Dore, with an oval inner enclosure, about 107 × 76 m (350 × 250 ft), and a V-shaped outer enclosure on the uphill side. The crossbank enclosures associated with both of these sites will be considered later.

Fig.102

At Pencarrow (Corn.) no less than five enclosures are involved, the inner three of which need to be considered here. The large concentric enclosure and its annexe have been mentioned already. The core of the whole arrangement is a circular enclosure, about 61 m (200 ft) in diameter, defended by a bank and ditch. To the west and north-west is a second enclosure of the dependent type, so that the arrangement thus far follows the pattern of Castle Dore and Largin Castle. In addition to the inner and outer lines of defence, however, there is a third line, on the south and west. This may have been intended to form a second dependent enclosure. On the south, where it forms a compact arrangement with two inner banks and ditches, it appears to be unfinished, the ditch showing four undug causeways.

In Wessex about 12 sites have subsidiary enclosures which can be described as being of the annexe type. A number of these belong to Lady Fox's dependent-enclosure class. At Park Hill Camp (Wilts.) the sub-rectangular inner enclosure, about 80 ares (2 acres), is defended by a bank and ditch. The main outer enclosure is formed on the south-western side where the outer bank and ditch swing forward to leave an enclosure about 122 m (400 ft) long and about 30 m (100 ft) wide. There is a second smaller dependent enclosure on the south-eastern side as part of the entrance works. Two dependent enclosures are involved also at Rawlsbury (Dorset). Where the external slopes are steep the multivallate defences are compact, but elsewhere the inner and outer lines diverge to form two lunate enclosures with maximum widths of about 21 m (70 ft). In neither of these cases, nor in the case of the larger dependent enclosure at Park Hill Camp, is there any means of access so that the creation of these enclosures may be incidental to some other process.

Fig.34a
Pls.21,22

Eggardon (Dorset) and Bratton Castle (Wilts.) also involve enclosures of the dependent type. At the south-eastern end of Eggardon the inner and outer lines of the multivallate defences diverge to form a dependent enclosure about 137 × 30 m (450 × 100 ft). The section of the outer defences running across the ridge looks as if it were originally an independent cross-ridge dyke, and this

Fig.103.
Winkelbury,
Wiltshire.

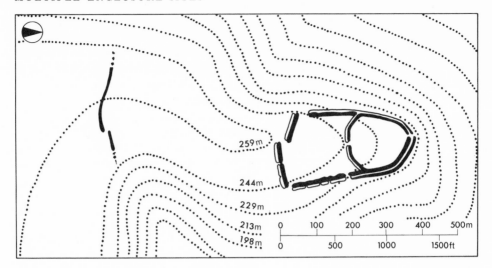

259m

244m

229m

213m

198m

| 0 | 100 | 200 | 300 | 400 | 500m |
| 0 | | 500 | 1000 | | 1500ft |

Pl.38

Fig.84
Pl.5

Fig.103

Pl.39

will be considered again in the next section. At the north-western end there is another dependent enclosure, about 152 × 30 m (500 × 100 ft), with a cross-bank enclosure beyond. At Bratton Castle two dependent enclosures are involved. At the north-eastern corner the inner and outer sections of the multi-vallate defences, basically two banks and two ditches, diverge to form a roughly rectangular enclosure about 91 × 61 m (300 × 200 ft). The second enclosure forms part of the entrance works. The area has been somewhat disturbed but the outer bank and ditch appear to swing forward from the line of the inner defences to define a generally rectangular area about 107 m (350 ft) long and 30 m (100 ft) wide. Like some of the sites in the south-west already described, access to the main enclosure is via this dependent enclosure, and such arrangements will need to be considered again in the chapter on entrances. There are parallels to the Bratton Castle entrance at Badbury Rings (Dorset) and Sidbury (Wilts.). These will be considered again in Chapter VII as entrance arrangements, although by definition they belong also to the dependent-enclosure category.

The remaining sites in Wessex have subsidiary enclosures that are best described simply as annexes. At Winkelbury (Wilts.) three enclosures are involved, the outermost being of the crossbank type. The second enclosure, which appears to be unfinished, may also have been originally of the crossbank type. Its southern defences consist of a free-standing cross-ridge dyke some 12 m (40 ft) beyond the southern ends of the unfinished eastern and western defences. It looks as if the intention were to form the three sides of an annexe by utilizing the existing cross-dyke and building new eastern and western defences. The inner enclosure at the outer end of the spur is roughly circular, about 2 ha 5 acres), and is defended by a single bank and ditch. Three enclosures are involved also at White Sheet Castle (Wilts.), a semi-contour site with an easy approach from the north-east and north-west. On these sides there are three lines of defence, each consisting of a bank and ditch, with interspaces of about 30 m

(100 ft) forming two curving annexes, each about 335 m (1,100 ft) long and about 1 ha (2½ acres) each.

The last annexe site to be considered in Wessex is Woolbury (Hants). The main enclosure, about 8 ha (20 acres), is defended by a bank and ditch and occupies the highest part of a ridge. On either side of the ridge to the south-west are slight defences in the form of scarps which start from the outer edge of the main ditch and continue for several hundred metres. Presumably at some point the enclosure was completed by a line of defence running across the ridge, but any such feature is now very difficult to trace on the ground. Because of this it is difficult to calculate the area of the annexe but it cannot be far short of the 8 ha (20 acres) occupied by the main enclosure.

In the south-east only Bigbury (Kent) and St. George's Hill (Surrey) qualify for inclusion in this section. Bigbury is a Large semi-contour site of 7·7 ha (19 acres) with the easy approach on the south-western side. On the northern side there is a deep indentation in the contours that gives the main enclosure an L-shaped plan. The angle of this is occupied by the annexe, the defences of which face north-west, north, and north-east. The area thus enclosed is about 2·4 ha (6 acres) and slopes down from south to north, so that the northern defences are in the region of the 46-m (150-ft) contour. The defences of the main enclosure follow the trend of the 61-m (200-ft) contour. St. George's Hill is also of the semi-contour type, in this case with the easy approach from the north-east. It is on this side that the annexe is situated. The main enclosure takes in about 5 ha (13 acres) and the annexe, which is D-shaped and defended by a bank and ditch, another 1 ha (3 acres).

In the Marcher region about 30 sites have subsidiary enclosures of the annexe type. At the southern end of the region there is a single site in the portion of Gloucestershire north-west of the Severn. Westbury is a semi-contour site with an easy approach on the southern side. The main sub-rectangular enclosure, about 1 ha (3 acres), is defended by a bank ditch, and in places a counterscarp bank. Flanking the southern and western sides is a long, narrow, L-shaped annexe enclosing a further 50 ares (1¼ acres). Beyond this again is a second annexe of similar size. The defences of both consist of a bank, ditch, and counterscarp bank. There appears to be an additional enclosure connected with the entrance works at the south-eastern corner of the site.

In Monmouth 6 sites fall into the annexe category. At Lodge Wood the inner enclosure is quite small, about 91 × 30 m (300 × 100 ft), and occupies the summit of a hill. To the east is a large annexe occupying about 1·6 ha (4 acres). Surrounding both enclosures is a complex arrangement of multivallate defences involving as many as four banks and four ditches. At Twyn y Gaer, also in a hilltop situation, three enclosures are involved. The strongest defences define an oval area of about 1·8 ha (4½ acres) with its long axis east and west. A crossbank divides this into two more or less equal parts and the western part is further subdivided into two smaller enclosures. Gaer Fawr, Pen Twyn, and Camp Wood are all of the semi-contour type. At Gaer Fawr the main enclosure, about 3 ha (8 acres), faces rising ground to the south. The annexe, to the north, takes in a further 60 ares (1½ acres). At Pen Twyn the main enclosure, about 80 ares (2

Pl.46

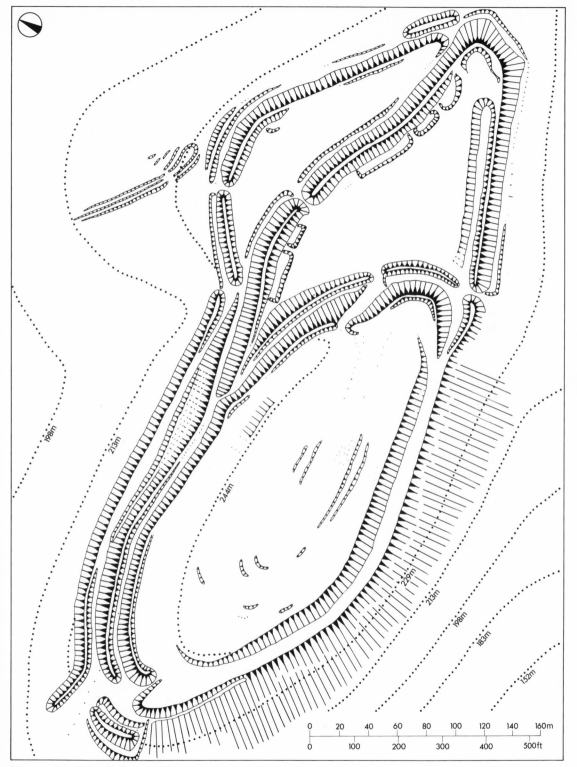

Fig.104. Coxall Knoll, Herefordshire.

acres), is defended by a bank and ditch. Beyond the ditch, to the south-east, is a second enclosure taking in another 1·4 ha (3½ acres). At Camp Wood the easy approach is on one of the long sides of an elongated oval enclosure, about 2·4 ha (6 acres). To the south, on the approach side, is a large annexe taking in another 1·6 ha (4 acres).

Fig.141

The annexes at Llanmelin differ somewhat from those described so far. They form part of an elaborate hornwork barring any direct approach to the entrance. Since there is no obvious access to the three enclosures involved they probably do not form annexes in the same sense as those described.

Fig.104

In Herefordshire Coxall Knoll and the Herefordshire Beacon each consist of three enclosures. At Coxall Knoll the main enclosure, about 3·4 ha (8½ acres), is oval in plan. To the east and north-east is a second triangular enclosure of 1 ha (3 acres) defended by a bank and ditch with an inner quarry ditch behind. On the northern side of this is a second annexe of about 40 ares (1 acre), defended by a bank, ditch, and in places a counterscarp bank. At the Herefordshire Beacon the two annexes are on opposite sides of the main enclosure which is oval in plan and encloses about 3 ha (8 acres). To the south and to the north-east are long spurs which are incorporated in the defence system. A single continuous bank and ditch embraces all three enclosures. The north-eastern enclosure has an area of 2 ha (5 acres) and the southern one an area of 3·6 ha (9 acres).

Fig.44b
Pl.27

Wall Hills, Ledbury, in the same county has only two enclosures. The main enclosure, about 4·5 ha (11 acres), defended by a bank and ditch, is of the pseudo-contour type. To the east, north-east, and north of this is a second enclosure of the annexe type, defended again by a bank and ditch enclosing a further 7·3 ha (18 acres).

The two remaining Herefordshire sites have subsidiary enclosures of the dependent type. At Risbury the inner enclosure of 3 ha (8 acres) is defended by a massive bank and ditch (C/D vert. 11 m : 36 ft). On the west and north-west these form a compact multivallate arrangement with the outer defences. On the remaining sides the two systems diverge to form what must be classed as a dependent enclosure with an area of about 2·4 ha (6 acres). Within the dependent enclosure there are features which are difficult to interpret but which may represent subdivisions of the area, of Iron Age date or later. At Wapley Camp the dependent enclosures, on the east and south-east, are relatively narrow with a maximum width of about 21 m (70 ft). Since they appear to have no means of access they may be simply a means of adding depth to the defence system.

Fig.81

In Brecon only a few sites can be attributed to the multiple-enclosure class and these are mostly of the annexe type. Hillis Camp is a 3·6-ha (9-acre) multivallate site in a hilltop position. Within, and presumably later than the multivallate defences, is a crossbank which divides the interior into two more or less equal parts. A similar process seems to have taken place at Castell Dinas. At Hillis Camp there is also an enclosure of the satellite type which will be considered later. The largest site in Brecon, Allt yr Esgair, involves three enclosures. The largest of these, about 3 ha (8 acres), occupies the northern slope of a long narrow hill aligned north and south. The second enclosure, on the

Fig.105. Earl's
Hill,
Shropshire.

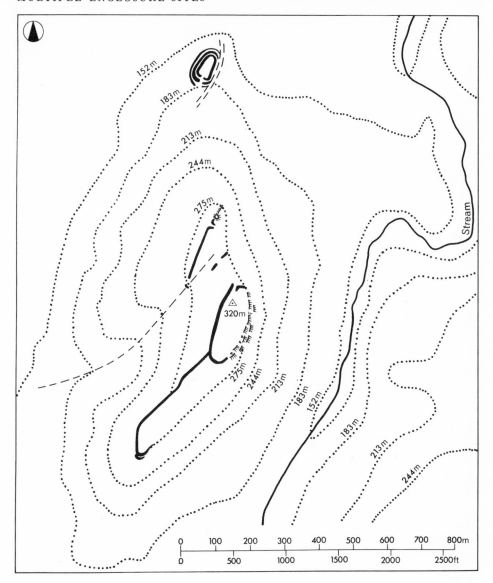

summit, takes in a further 1·6 ha (4 acres) and looks as if it is an extension of the
first. The third and smallest enclosure, about 50 ares (1¼ acres), looks like a
further extension and runs down the southern slope of the hill.

In Radnorshire Y Gaer, Llanddewi Ystradenny, appears to have a subsidiary
enclosure of the dependent type. The site is a multivallate contour fort. On the
north and east, however, there is wide interspace between the inner and outer
parts of the system, forming a second dependent enclosure.

In Shropshire The Wrekin bears some resemblance to the Herefordshire
Beacon. The main enclosure, 2·4 ha (6 acres), occupies the summit of a hog-

Fig.105

backed hill. This enclosure is embraced by the outer defences which diverge from the inner defences at the north-eastern and south-western ends to form two outer enclosures. The north-eastern enclosure covers about 1·6 ha (4 acres), the south-western about 1 ha (2½ acres). The main enclosure at Earl's Hill, 1·2 ha (3 acres), occupies the summit of a long narrow hill. The subsidiary enclosures present belong to a number of different types, but only the annexe will be considered here. This occupies a long narrow tongue of land to the south-west of, and just below, the main enclosure and takes in a further 1·6 ha (4 acres). At Caynham Camp there are traces of one, and possibly two, small annexes beyond the western end of the main enclosure.

Two of the Shropshire sites in this category are promontory forts with their annexes on the approach side. At Oliver's Point the inner enclosure, about 80 ares (2 acres), is defended by a bank, ditch, and counterscarp bank. Covering most of the approach side, on the east, is what is probably best interpreted as an annexe, defended in the same way, taking in a further 1 ha (2½ acres). This annexe is now completely open on the north side, but presumably in its original state it was completely embraced by man-made defences. Calcot Camp occupies a promontory defined by a U-shaped river bend. It is defended on the north and east by steep natural slopes and on the south and west by a bank and ditch. The inner enclosure covers about 1·6 ha (4 acres). Facing the level approach from the south-west are outer defences which define an annexe covering the full width of the promontory.

In Montgomeryshire 5 sites need to be considered under the general heading of annexes. Cefn Du occupies a long narrow hill with wide-spaced defences at the north-eastern and south-western ends forming small enclosures, two at the north-east, one at the south-west. The main enclosure in between covers about

Pl.49

20 ares (½ acre). At Cefn Carnedd, a site with an over-all area of about 10 ha (25 acres), the defences on the north-western side are of the separated multi-vallate type, consisting of three banks and three ditches with berms or narrow spaces between. On the south-eastern side there is only a single bank above a steep natural slope. The interior of the site is divided into two enclosures by a crossbank, cutting off the higher ground at the southern end.

Both Bryn y Saethau and Pen y Gorddin consist of small enclosures within larger ones, forming arrangements which fall somewhere between the concentric and the dependent types. At Bryn y Saethau the small inner enclosure, defended by a bank and ditch, is at the eastern end of the much larger oval enclosure where the two defence systems merge to become a single bank and ditch. Pen y Gorddin consists of a small oval enclosure, defended by rock scarps on the south and west and by a bank and ditch on the north and east, placed at the northern end of a large enclosure defended either by a bank and ditch or, on the west, by natural defences, in this case a steep fall to the river below. There are now no defences on the eastern side of the outer enclosure.

The last Montgomeryshire site in this category is Ffridd Faldwyn. Although the two main enclosures could be regarded as forming a dependent arrangement, the site in this respect is probably best classed as one of those in which earlier, abandoned defences are still visible, as for example at Yarnbury

Fig.36

(Wilts.). At the south-western end of the larger enclosure, associated with the main entrance, is another enclosure which must be classed as a dependent type.

At the northern end of the Marcher region Craigadwy Wynt (Denb.) consists of two enclosures, upper and lower, the upper one of the cliff-edge type, covering about 2·8 ha (7 acres). Beyond the cliff to the west is a second cliff forming a sort of step about 61 m (200 ft) wide, part of which is utilized as a second enclosure by means of ramparts running from the foot of the first cliff to the head of the second. This lower enclosure covers about 1·6 ha (4 acres) and has an inturned entrance at the northern end. Dinas Bran in the same county also consists of two enclosures in a rather different arrangement. On the northern side the defences are entirely natural: on the other three sides there are inner and outer lines of defence up to 46 m (150 ft) apart. The inner enclosure covers about 2·8 ha (7 acres), and the outer about 1·6 ha (4 acres) but as roughly half the latter consists of a fairly steep slope probably only 80 ares (2 acres) were of any practical use.

Moel Hiraddug (Flint.) consists basically of three enclosures, the largest of which occupies about 6·8 ha (17 acres). Parallel to and east of the southern half of this is a second enclosure taking in a further 2·4 ha (6 acres). To the south of these is the third enclosure, between the main inner and outer defences, occupying another 1·6 or 2 ha (4 or 5 acres).

In Caernarvonshire about a dozen sites have subsidiary enclosures which can be included under the heading of annexes. Among the largest and most complex are Garn Boduan, Carn Fadrun, and the now destroyed site of Braich-y-Dinas. All of these had large numbers of hut circles associated with them, as mentioned in Chapter IV. At Garn Boduan four enclosures are involved, the smallest of which (67 × 27 m : 220 × 90 ft) occupies the summit of the hill in the region of the 274-m (900-ft) contour. This is flanked on three sides, north, west, and south, by a very much larger enclosure covering some 10 ha (25 acres). On sloping ground to the south-east and to the west are two triangular annexes, the one on the west taking in a further 1·6 ha (4 acres). The general chronological relationship of these enclosures is known from excavation; the small summit enclosure is a late- or post-Roman feature. A generally similar arrangement is found at Carn Fadrun, with a small summit enclosure in the region of the 366-m (1,200-ft) contour and three larger enclosures below, covering in all some 11 ha (27 acres). There is a small enclosure on the summit at Conway Mountain also, within the much larger main enclosure to the east and north-east.

Braich-y-Dinas, now entirely destroyed, involved six enclosures. The main enclosure occupied the summit and southern and south-eastern slopes of a hill and covered about 1·6 ha (4 acres). To the north were two annexes, one beyond the other, each about 91 m (300 ft) long and 15 m (50 ft) wide. To the east of these three enclosures, on the long eastern slope of the hill, were three further enclosures of the annexe type occupying a further 2 ha (5 acres).

Since surveys of all the Caernarvonshire sites have been published in recent years the remaining sites will be dealt with only briefly. At Pen-y-Gaer, Llanbedr-y-Cennin, the lunate area west of the main enclosure must be classed

Fig.106. Pen
Dinas,
Cardiganshire.

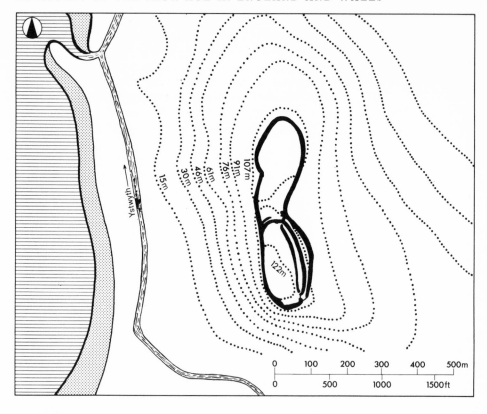

as of the dependent type since it is formed by the divergence of the inner and middle lines of defence. At Creigiau Gwineu two enclosures are formed by means of a crossbank cutting the interior into two more or less equal parts. At Moel y Gest the man-made ramparts define four enclosures with the natural rock scarps within the defences forming further subdivisions. In addition to these sites there are annexes of various types at Dinas Dinorwig, Pen-y-Castell, Cerrig y Dinas, and Carn Pentyrch. At Tre'r Ceiri there is a long annexe flanking the north-western side which is now open-ended but which may have originally been looped on to the main enclosure. The latter covers about 2 ha (5 acres) and the annexe a further 1·2 ha (3 acres).

Pl.30

Fig.106

In Cardiganshire Pen Dinas consists basically of northern and southern enclosures occupying the summit of a long narrow hill with the shape of an hourglass. The southern enclosure, about 80 ares (2 acres), has multivallate defences on the north, east, and south and slight defences on the west above the steep natural slope. Beyond the northern defences is a larger enclosure, about 2 ha (5 acres), with univallate defences.

Castell Grogwynion in the same county has natural defences on the north and east and its major man-made defences on the south and west, the two together defining an oval enclosure with a long axis running east and west. This enclosure is subdivided into eastern and western areas by a rampart running

198

Fig.107.
Cribyn Gaer,
Cardiganshire.

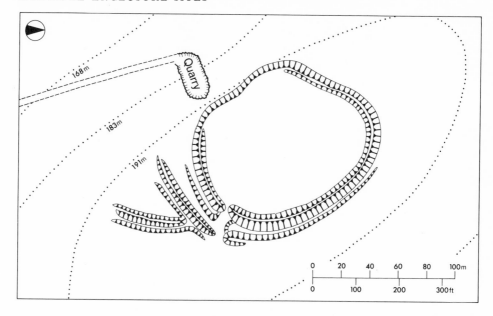

Fig.107

Fig.99
Pl.51

Fig.108

Fig.109

generally north and south. Castell Goetre is subdivided in a similar way. The main defences consist of a bank, ditch, and counterscarp bank, and the area thus defined is divided into two separate enclosures by a presumably later rampart. The only other Cardiganshire sites which can be mentioned in this context are Caer Argoed and Cribyn Gaer. Caer Argoed has a small annexe to the north-west of the main univallate enclosure. Cribyn Gaer has an outer enclosure to the south of the main entrance which falls somewhere between the annexe and the crossbank types. One end of the bank and ditch defining it is attached to the main defences in the normal annexe manner. The other end runs out to the head of the steep natural slope in the crossbank manner.

In Pembrokeshire about 20 sites merit consideration under the general heading of annexes. One of the sites involved, Foel Trigarn, has been mentioned already under concentric enclosures. The third enclosure, on the east, is of the annexe type. It is roughly rectangular, about 122 m (400 ft) from north to south and 61 m (200 ft) from east to west. There is an annexe of similar type but smaller dimensions on the western side of Scollock Rath. The main enclosure is roughly circular with a diameter of about 101 m (330 ft). It was defended by a bank and ditch, although the latter is now preserved only on the east. Attached to the western side is an annexe about 76 m (250 ft) long and 23 m (75 ft) wide, defended by a bank without a ditch. There are similar annexes at Plumstone Rath and Caerau, Aberpwll.

The annexe of Castell Gwyn is of a rather more unusual type. The site has been heavily ploughed but the over-all layout is still clear. The outer defences, a bank and ditch, are U-shaped in plan, with a steep natural slope running across the open end. Within the rounded end is a small circular enclosure, about 30 m (100 ft) in diameter, defended by a second bank and ditch. There

199

Fig.108.
Scollock Rath,
Pembrokeshire.

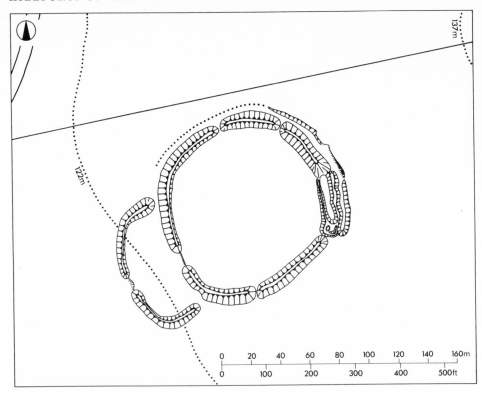

is a third, semicircular, bank and ditch between the circular enclosure and the
outer defences. Although in its present form it is of the annexe type, Castell
Gwyn bears some resemblance to the concentric forts described in the previous
section, particularly those which appear to have additional defences inserted
between pre-existing inner and outer defences.

Pl.47

At two other sites the annexes are presumably the result of subdividing a
pre-existing enclosure. Castell Mawr is a large oval enclosure, about 183×152 m
(600×500 ft), defended by a bank, ditch, and a substantial counterscarp bank.
The remains within the defences suggest that at a later date a crossbank was
inserted producing two roughly equal eastern and western enclosures. A similar
process seems to have taken place at another large oval site, West Pennar Rath,
again dividing the area into eastern and western enclosures.

Fig.110

At Caerau Gaer the main enclosure is oval in shape, about 91×61 m
(300×200 ft), and is defended where best preserved by a bank and ditch.
About 61 m (200 ft) to the north-east is an outer bank about 9 m (30 ft) wide
with a similar bank about 21 m (70 ft) beyond. These banks appear to run out
to the head of the south-eastern slope in the crossbank manner, but the opposite
end of the inner one at least appears to spring from the ditch of the main enclosure in the annexe manner. The relationship of the outer bank is obscured by
the road which flanks the site to the north-west.

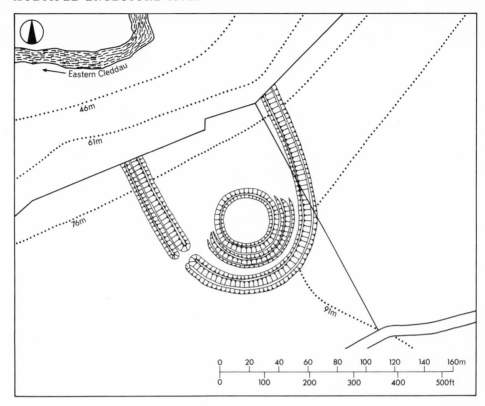

Fig.109. Castell Gwyn, Pembrokeshire.

The remaining annexe sites in Pembrokeshire can be dealt with only briefly. Castell Henllys has a univallate oval enclosure with traces of a crescent-shaped annexe on the western side. At Sealyham Rocks the annexe is on the south-western side of a main enclosure defended by a bank and ditch. Martin's Haven and Quoit's Wood are both plateau-edge sites with associated annexes on their north-western sides. Rickeston Rath has been ploughed but there are indications of an annexe to the north-west. Finally, crop marks at Slade Farm suggest that there was originally a large univallate enclosure with a crescent-shaped annexe to the south.

About half of the total of 20 or so multiple-enclosure sites in Carmarthenshire need to be considered under the heading of annexes. At Gaer Fawr the annexe flanks the long northern side of the main enclosure and is open-ended to the east. At Y Fan and Pen y Gaer, Meidrim, both hilltop situations, there are large annexes running down the western slopes. At Castell y Gaer a small enclosure about 91 × 61 m (300 × 200 ft) occupies the north-western corner of a larger oval enclosure defended by a bank and ditch and embracing about 3 ha (8 acres). At Llwyn Du the interior, about 1·8 ha (4½ acres), is subdivided into two enclosures by a substantial crossbank. The remaining sites are all of the hill-slope type. At both Y Gaer, Llanboidy, and Bwlch-y-Seiri there are suggestions of annexes on the eastern sides. The main enclosure at Castle Ely was,

Fig.110.
Caerau Gaer,
Pembrokeshire.

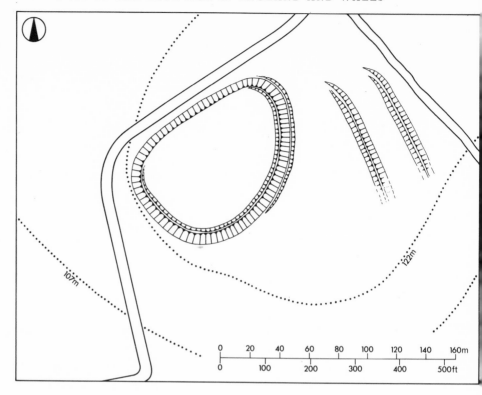

in its original state, a fairly large oval. It is flanked to the east by a much smaller sub-rectangular enclosure which may have formed an annexe. At Castle Hill, St. Clears, there is a wide space between the inner and outer defences on the west forming an annexe.

Pl.45

Fig.97

Fig.111
Pl.48

In Glamorgan there are annexes associated with two of the concentric sites mentioned in the previous section. At Bwlwarcau the annexe is formed by the divergence of two lines of defence on the southern and eastern sides. The outer one runs out to the head of the natural slope in the crossbank manner. At Caer Cwm Phillip the annexe is roughly rectangular in plan, about 183 × 91 m (600 × 300 ft), and flanks the outer concentric enclosure to the south. As mentioned earlier both sites on Harding's Down are of the annexe rather than the concentric type. Harding's Down West consists of an oval inner enclosure, about 91 × 61 m (300 × 200 ft) defended by a bank, ditch, and counter-scarp bank. The defences follow the contours on the north and west and cut across them on the south and east, just taking in the highest point of the hill on the south-east. The annexe is situated on the eastern and south-eastern sides. The strongest defences are on the south-east and consist of two banks and two ditches between 3 and 15 m (10 and 50 ft) apart. There is a 15-m (50-ft) gap between the end of the annexe defences and the defences of the main enclosure. The remains of Harding's Down East are not so well preserved but the site appears to consist of an oval main enclosure with an annexe on the lower,

Fig.111.
Harding's Down
West,
Glamorgan.

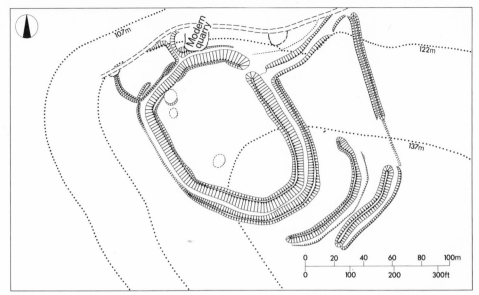

eastern, side. To the north of and roughly equidistant from both sites is a small circular enclosure about 37 m (120 ft) in diameter, defended by a bank and ditch which may form part of the same complex of earthworks.

Caer Ddynnaf stands in a cliff-edge situation with man-made defences on the west, south, and east. The main enclosure is some 274 m (900 ft) from east to west and 152 m (500 ft) from north to south. Flanking it on the west and south, and partly on the east, is a long narrow annexe with an average width of about 30 m (100 ft).

C. CROSSBANK ENCLOSURES

According to Lady Fox's definition crossbank enclosures 'consist of an inner zone which may be either a single or multiple enclosure . . . and an outer zone defended by one or more ramparts aligned across the spur or promontory'.[9] As in the case of annexes the enclosures are broadly speaking side by side, the chief difference being that normally two opposite sides of the crossbank enclosure are formed by natural features so that the crossbank itself has no physical connection with the defences of the main enclosure. It is for this reason that crossbank enclosures are found in promontory, semi-contour, and ridge-top situations. Included in this category are features usually termed cross-ridge dykes, since these, when associated with Iron Age forts, are deemed to form enclosures.

In the south-west crossbank enclosures have been mentioned already in the discussion of sites where more than one type of enclosure is present. These include Largin Castle and Hall Rings (Corn.), At Largin Castle there are two crossbanks, 274 and 549 m (900 and 1,800 ft) beyond the two dependent inner

9. Fox, op. cit. 43.

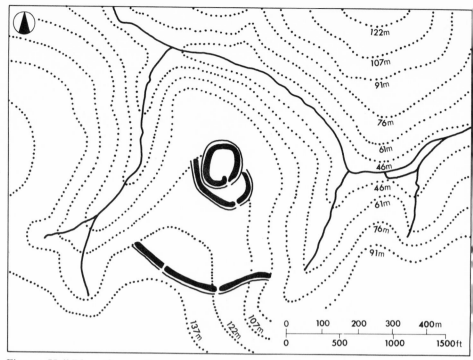

Fig.112. Hall Rings, Cornwall.

Fig.112

enclosures. The area defined by the outer crossbank on the south, the 91-m (300-ft) contour on the north, and the head of the natural slope to east and west is in the region of 36·4 ha (90 acres). At Hall Rings there is only one crossbank, 244 m (800 ft) beyond the dependent inner enclosures. The area defined is in the region of 12 ha (30 acres). The other Cornish sites in this category are Pencoose Castle, with a single crossbank, and Round Wood with two, covering the approach to an oval inner enclosure situated on a promontory end. Resugga Castle must also be mentioned here although its so-called crossbank does not form an enclosure. There are no natural slopes or other features to form the two remaining sides of an enclosure, and in its present form the site is something of a problem. Possibly it is an incomplete enclosure of the annexe type. Not included

Fig.90

in Lady Fox's list is Trevelgue promontory fort where the outermost bank running diagonally across the promontory is surely of the crossbank type, defining an outer enclosure of about 80 ares (2 acres).

In Devon Prestonbury and Burley Wood have also been mentioned previously. At Prestonbury the single curving crossbank is about 122 m (400 ft) beyond the annexe to the inner enclosure and adds another 4·8 ha (12 acres) or so to the

Fig.113

total area available. At Burley Wood there are no less than three crossbanks, at 21, 61, and 122 m (70, 200, and 400 ft) beyond the three inner enclosures. The total area defined by the outermost crossbank and the 213-m (700-ft) contour, which between them embrace all the enclosures, is about 6·4 ha (16 acres). At

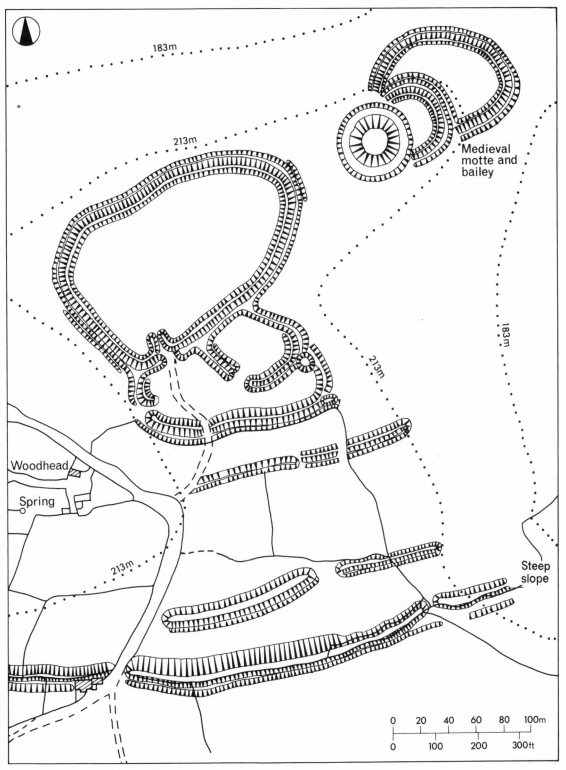

183m

213m

Medieval
motte and
bailey

213m

Woodhead

Spring

213m

Steep
slope

183m

0	20	40	60	80	100m
0		100	200	300ft	

Fig.113. Burley Wood Camp, Devon.

Castle Dyke (Chudleigh) the crossbank faces the easy approach from the south-west, about 213 m (700 ft) beyond the oval inner enclosure. The latter covers about 3·6 ha (9 acres); the outer, crossbank enclosure is less precisely defined but its area is at least half as much again, say 5·7 or 6·5 ha (14 or 15 acres).

Among the remaining sites in Devon, Voley Castle and Burridge Camp have single crossbanks and Noss Camp two. Hawkesdown Camp has an easy approach from the east. On this side a single crossbank cuts off about 1·2 ha (3 acres). Embury Beacon is a coastal site which has been subject to considerable erosion, but even in its original state it was probably of the crossbank type. The inner D-shaped enclosure, backed on to the cliff, is now only about 91 m (300 ft) long and 30 m (100 ft) wide. The outer enclosure, cut off by a bank and ditch about 366 m (1,200 ft) long, takes in roughly 2·8 ha (7 acres).

The last site to be considered in Devon is Wooston Castle which has points of resemblance to Resugga Castle, Largin Castle, and Hall Rings. In its siting it follows closely the pattern of the last two sites, with the inner enclosure of about 2 ha (5 acres) at the outer end of a falling spur, with a downhill approach from the south. At the root of the spur, about 61 m (200 ft) from the inner enclosure, is the first of three crossbanks, with its ends resting on the head of the natural slopes defining the spur. The two outer crossbanks are 122 and 183 m (400 and 600 ft) beyond, all three facing uphill. As at Resugga the ends of these two outer crossbanks end in mid-air and in their present form could hardly have performed any useful function.

In Somerset, west of the Parrett, four sites have subsidiary enclosures of the crossbank type. Ruborough Camp is a triangular univallate site in a semi-contour position with the easy approach from the west. The area enclosed is about 2 ha (5 acres). About 91 ha (300 ft) to the west is a crossbank cutting off a rectangular area of some 1·6 ha (4 acres). Bury Castle has the same general arrangement but is on a much smaller scale. The oval inner enclosure, about 52 × 43 m (170 × 140 ft), is in a semi-contour position with the easy approach again from the west. On this side and about 30 m (100 ft) beyond the inner ditch is a curving crossbank and ditch about 137 m (450 ft) long cutting off an area nearly twice the size of the inner enclosure. About 137 m (450 ft) beyond this again is a second, much longer, crossbank cutting off an even larger area. The main enclosure and first crossbank at Staddon Hill are of similar dimensions. Between 61 and 91 m (200 and 300 ft) beyond is the second crossbank running in a straight line east and west for some 122 m (400 ft). At Bat's Castle the main oval enclosure, defended by a bank, ditch, and counterscarp bank, covers about 1·4 ha (3½ acres). Between 122 and 152 m (400 and 500 ft) to the south-east is a bank and ditch of the crossbank type. It is unusual in plan running first south to north for 91 m (300 ft), then turning sharply to run south-east for 46 m (150 ft), and then turning less sharply to run north-east for 76 m (250 ft).

Fig.103   In Wessex about 6 sites have enclosures of the crossbank type. At Winkelbury (Wilts.), mentioned in the previous section, the second enclosure looks like a crossbank enclosure in process of conversion to an annexe. The third enclosure is undoubtedly of the crossbank type. It is of much slighter construction than the

Fig.34a
Pl.21

other earthworks and stands some 457 m (1,500 ft) in front of them, cutting off an additional 12 ha (30 acres). At Eggardon (Dorset) a similar process of conversion may have been carried a stage further. At the south-eastern end of the site the outer defences look very much as if they were originally a free-standing crossbank which had at a later stage been linked to the main defences to form a dependent enclosure.

Castle Rings (Wilts.) is situated on a ridge defined by the 213-m (700-ft) contours. About 91 m (300 ft) to the west of the main enclosure of about 4·8 ha (12 acres) is a crossbank and ditch running north–south across the ridge. There is a similar feature to the north-west of Rockbourne Knoll (Hants). The main enclosure of 1·4 ha (3½ acres) is in a semi-contour position with the easy approach from the north-west. About 40 m (130 ft) away on this side is a bank, ditch, and

Pl.6

counterscarp bank. Flower's Barrow (Dorset) also appears to have been a semi-contour site, although coastal erosion has now removed much of its southern side. On the easy approach, from the east, there is an outer bank and ditch about 122 m (400 ft) from the main enclosure. Other sites which can be mentioned in this context are Gorley Hill (Hants) and Grimsbury (Berks). The crossbanks to the south-east of Hambledon Hill (Dorset) have been shown by

Fig.30b

excavation to be of Neolithic date.[1] The existing outer defences on this side,

Fig.34a

however, may have been originally free-standing crossbanks which were later incorporated into the main defences, as was suggested for Eggardon.

Only two sites in south-east England have outer enclosures of the crossbank type. Chanctonbury (Sussex) is in a ridge-top position with the main oval enclosure of about 1·6 ha (4 acres) defended by a bank and ditch; about 336 m (1,100 ft) to the west along the ridge is an outer bank and ditch, now some 122 m (400 ft) long but probably longer originally. A similar distance to the south-east is another bank and ditch, in this case about 427 m (1,400 ft) long, with their ends resting on the 213-m (700-ft) contour lines which define the ridge top. At Wolstonbury in the same county there is only a single crossbank. The main enclosure stands at the end of a spur projecting northwards from the main line of the South Downs. A bank and ditch crossing the spur to the south define an outer enclosure of the crossbank type.

In the Cotswold region 4 sites belong to the crossbank enclosure category. The

Fig.83f

most extensive crossbanks are undoubtedly those associated with Worlebury (Som.). The site is of the semi-contour type with a level approach from the east. About 21 m (70 ft) beyond the outer edge of the elaborate eastern defences is a crossbank and ditch running generally north and south for over 305 m (1,000 ft) and in its original state probably longer. There is a second crossbank to the east of this, 91 m (300 ft) from the northern end and 183 m (600 ft) from the southern end, which is now about 366 m (1,200 ft) long. The area between the two is about 4·5 ha (11 acres). The southern ends of both crossbanks have been destroyed. On the north they run down the slope, dropping something like 61 m (200 ft) to end at the head of the cliffs bordering the Bristol Channel.

Fig.43e

Dolebury (Som.) also occupies a semi-contour position with a level approach

1. Excavated by Mr. D. J. Bonney. Report forthcoming.

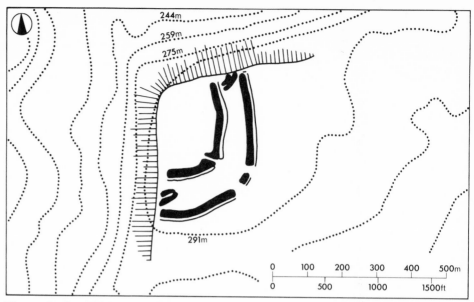

Fig.114. Bredon Hill, Worcestershire.

Pl.36

from the east. Just over 76 m (250 ft) away in this direction is a slight bank and ditch which does not now completely cross the ridge along which approach could be made.

At King's Weston Down three enclosures are involved. The presumed inner enclosure, about 40 ares (1 acre), has natural defences on the north and east and a bank and ditch on the south and west. About 107 m (350 ft) to the west is a circular enclosure some 55 m (180 ft) in diameter defined by a very slight bank and ditch. About 76 m (250 ft) west of this again and about 244 m (800 ft) from the first enclosure is a crossbank and ditch defining a third enclosure. At Fig.114 Bredon Hill (Worcs) the inner enclosure is defended on the south and east by a substantial bank and ditch. Between 52 and 91 m (170 and 300 ft) beyond is a second bank and ditch defining a second enclosure of the crossbank type.

As in Wessex and the Cotswolds crossbank enclosures in the Marcher region are few in number. In Herefordshire Croft Ambrey must be placed in this category since the outer defences are physically separate from those of the inner enclosure. The latter, a triangular area of about 3 ha (8 acres), is defended by natural slopes on the north and a compact arrangement of three banks and two ditches on the south and west. Between 61 and 91 m (200 and 300 ft) beyond the southern defences is a long crossbank, accompanied, where best preserved, by a ditch and counterscarp bank running from the head of the natural slope on the west for about 732 m (2,400 ft) until it fades into the natural slope on the east. This defines an outer enclosure of some 4.8 ha (12 acres).

Fig.105 In Shropshire Earl's Hill has an enclosure of the crossbank type in addition to enclosures of the annexe and satellite type. The crossbank stands at the outer edge of a platform between the slope defining the summit of the hill

208

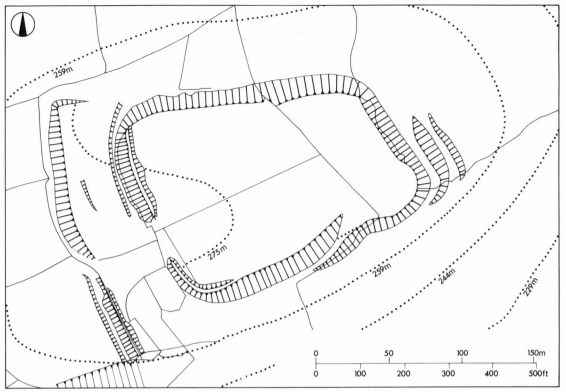

Fig.115. Pen y Foel, Montgomeryshire.

and the main slope to the west. As at Prestonbury (Devon) the crossbank has an inturned entrance. Within the area defined there are the unfinished remains of a presumably earlier crossbank.

Fig.115

In Montgomeryshire Pen y Foel is an almost classic example of a crossbank enclosure. The site has steep slopes on the north, east, and south and an easy approach from the west. The main enclosure of about 2 ha (5 acres) is defended on the approach side by a bank and ditch. Just over 30 m (100 ft) further west is a second bank and ditch running from the head of the natural slope on the north to the corresponding point on the south, a distance of about 183 m (600 ft). The area thus defined is about 60 ares (1½ acres). Pen y Clun in the same county also has its crossbank enclosure on the west. The main enclosure of about 80 ares (2 acres) is oval in plan and is defended by a bank, a ditch, and in places a counterscarp bank. Between 15 and 30 m (50 and 100 ft) beyond the western defences is a crossbank some 152 m (500 ft) long running from north-east to south-west. About 61 m (200 ft) from the south-western end is an entrance in line with the entrance to the inner enclosure.

At the northern end of the Marcher region only one site, Pen-y-Corddyn (Denb.), qualifies for inclusion in this category. The inner enclosure stands in a promontory position with natural defences on the west, south, and east and

209

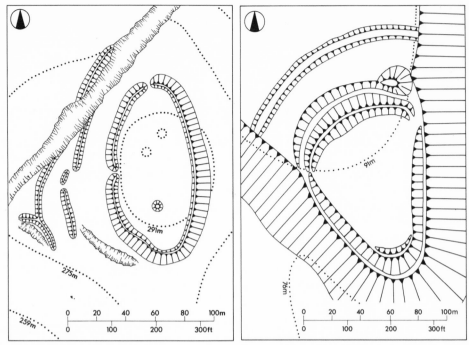

Fig.116. Daren Camp, Cardiganshire.   Fig.117. Hafod Camp, Carmarthenshire.

multivallate defences on the north. The area thus defined is about 9 ha (23 acres). Between 152 and 183 m (500 and 600 ft) beyond the multivallate defences is a single crossbank some 183 m (600 ft) long running from the head of the cliff on the west to a steep rocky outcrop on the east, and cutting off a further 4·4 ha (11 acres).

Further west, in Caernarvonshire, Pen-y-Gaer, Llanbedrog, has two parallel ramparts defending two sides of a small promontory fort. The inner rampart cuts off an area about 76×61 m (250×200 ft). About 24 or 27 m (80 or 90 ft) beyond there was originally a second rampart of the crossbank type, but this has been reduced by ploughing on the north and completely destroyed on the east. Nant y Castell follows a similar pattern but is on a much smaller scale. The inner rampart, covering the north and west, defends an area only 36·6 m (120 ft) long and 18 m (60 ft) wide. Parallel to and about 15 m (50 ft) beyond it is a second rampart cutting off a somewhat larger area. Carreg y Llam, mentioned already under concentric enclosures, has a third rampart of the crossbank type about 15 m (50 ft) to the south of the second enclosure. There is a fourth rampart to the north running from the concentric defences to the head of the cliff, so that the enclosure is somewhere between the annexe and the crossbank types.

Fig.116   In Cardiganshire the fort at Daren has an oval inner enclosure of about 107×52 m (350×170 ft) with crossbanks to the north-west and west. The first crossbank is between 15 and 23 m (50 and 75 ft) beyond the main enclosure. Beyond it at a distance of about 15 m (50 ft) is a second crossbank. At Caerau

210

Henllan there are natural slopes to the south and east, a rampart, and originally a ditch, to the north-west. About 46 m (150 ft) beyond is an outer rampart defining a crossbank enclosure some 122 m (400 ft) long and 46 m (150 ft) wide. At Castell-bach the main enclosure, about 76×46 m (250× 150 ft), has natural defences on the south and west and man-made defences on the north and east. About 107 m (350 ft) beyond to the north-east is a crossbank cutting off a much larger area. Esgair Nant-y-arian is described as having wide-spaced defences cutting off the end of an inland promontory, but whether the space between the defences is sufficient to form an enclosure it is not possible to say. The arrangement may well be the same as Old Warren Hill, where the space between the inner bank and ditch and the outer is 9 m (30 ft), i.e. too small to be regarded as an enclosure.

Pl.19

In Pembrokeshire Flimston Bay Camp, a coastal promontory fort, has a main enclosure defended on the approach side by a compact arrangement of two banks and two ditches. About 30 m (100 ft) beyond is an outer bank and ditch defining an enclosure of the crossbank type. At Popton Camp, another promontory fort, the inner defences consist of a bank and ditch about 61 m (200 ft) long cutting off the outer end of the promontory. About 30 m (100 ft) beyond is a crossbank and ditch about 122 m (400 ft) long, cutting off a second enclosure. Walwyns Castle may be of the same general type. Two crossbanks appear to

Fig.87

cut off two roughly equal areas, each about 76 m (250 ft) square. At Bosherston Camp three separate lines of defence run across the promontory. The innermost, however, seems to be an earlier feature, superseded by, rather than associated with, the two outer lines. The middle and outer lines are linked by flanking banks so that strictly speaking the space between, about 15 m (50 ft) in width, forms an annexe rather than a crossbank enclosure.

Fig.117

At Hafod Camp (Carm.) the triangular main enclosure is defended by scarped slopes on the east and south-west and by a curving bank and ditch on the easy approach side on the north. Parallel to, and about 24 m (80 ft) beyond the main defences is a crossbank about 137 m (450 ft) long running from scarp to scarp. The inner enclosure is about 91 m (300 ft) long and just over 61 m

Fig.24d

(200 ft) wide. At two other sites, Caer Blaen Minog and Allt y Ferin, the over-all situation is the same, that of a triangular promontory with man-made defences on the level approach side. In both cases, however, the additional feature crossing the promontory, a ditch, is within the enclosure and may simply be the remains of earlier, superseded defences. Gilman Camp appears to have a similar feature. At Pen y Gaer, Sarnau, and Caerau Clungwyn, crossbanks within the enclosures are probably secondary and possibly not Iron Age at all.

Fig.118

In Glamorgan the Knave, High Penard Camp, and Paviland Yellow Top are all clear examples of crossbank enclosures. At the Knave the southern and western sides are defended by natural features with man-made defences on the north and east. The inner bank and ditch is about 76 m (250 ft) long. About 18 m (60 ft) in front and parallel to it is an outer bank and ditch about 152 m (500 ft) long forming a second enclosure of the crossbank type. At High Penard there is a similar gap between the inner and outer defences, which each consist of a bank and ditch. The crossbank enclosure thus formed is about 46 × 18 m

Fig.118. The Knave, Glamorgan.

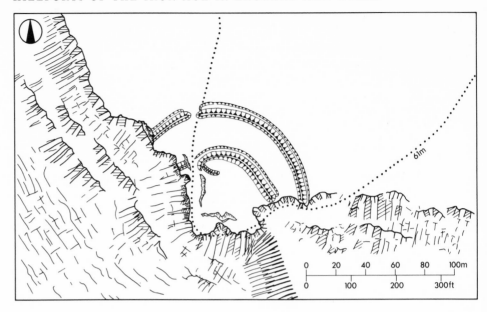

(150 × 60 ft). At Paviland Yellow Top the two crossbanks are about 24 m (80 ft) apart, with a possible third crossbank. At Danish Fort, Sully, the two crossbanks are described as widely spaced, although it is not stated whether the space involved is wide enough to be classed as an enclosure. The defences cut off the eastern end of Sully Island. Finally, there are what must be regarded as crossbanks to the east and west of The Bulwark, Cheriton, mentioned already under the heading of concentric enclosures.

D. SATELLITES

In the sites described in the previous sections the enclosures involved were adjacent to each other. In this section the enclosures, usually two in number, are quite separate. Their association as a single unit is suggested by their relative proximity, in most cases a matter of 183–457 m (600–1,500 ft), and by their siting. Quite clearly where no physical connection exists the chronological relationship must always be open to question.[2] None the less, associations of this type, usually consisting of a major and a minor enclosure, are sufficiently common to call for some explanation, even one which involves discarding the idea that the two enclosures are contemporary.

About 20 sites appear to have associated enclosures of the satellite type. Of these, 14 have been considered elsewhere[3] and the descriptive accounts given there need not be repeated here. One of the sites, Garn Fawr (Pemb.), appears to have an additional satellite on the western side as well as the one on the eastern side already described. About 457 m (1,500 ft) from and immediately below

2. Alcock, 'Hillforts in Wales and the Marches', *Antiquity*, 39 (1965), 185.
3. Forde-Johnston, op. cit. 66–91.

Fig.119.
Buckland Rings
and Ampress,
Hampshire.

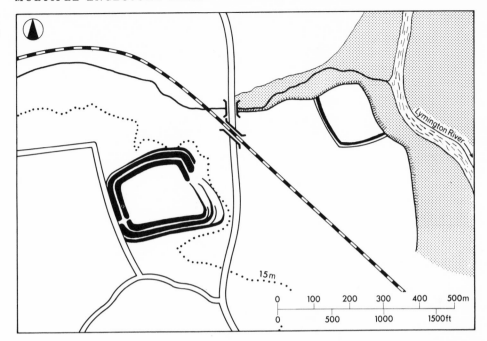

Garn Fawr is a tiny coastal promontory fort, Dinas Mawr. It is possible to suggest that this is associated with the main site in the same way as Gaer Fach which stands some 302 m (990 ft) to the east and that all three sites formed a single complex. The small coastal site is, in fact, included in Lluyd's plan reproduced in the Welsh Commission's inventory.[4]

Fig.119

In southern England the close association between Buckland Rings and Ampress Camp (Hants) was noted as early as 1789.[5] The main enclosure, Buckland Rings, is a multivallate semi-contour site standing on a small spur about 27 m (90 ft) above Lymington river. About 366 m (1,200 ft) to the east is Ampress Camp, standing just above river-level in the angle formed by the river and a small tributary running in from the west. In Wiltshire Martinsell

Fig.120

Hill also appears to have a smaller site associated with it. The main univallate enclosure occupies the eastern half of a flat-topped hill which rises to 288·6 m (947 ft). About 914 m (3,000 ft) to the south-west and about 46 m (150 ft) below is a small univallate semi-contour site, Giant's Grave, on a spur defined by the 244-m (800-ft) contour. A small circular enclosure about 457 m (1,500 ft) north of Yarnbury in the same county is shown on the Ordnance Survey's one inch to one mile map, and although it is not included on their Iron Age map,

Fig.41

nevertheless it merits at least a mention in this context. Dike Hills (Oxon.) and Sinodun (Berks) also call for some comment here. The low-lying situation of Dike Hills has been described already (p. 88). About 640 m (2,100 ft) to the south, on the opposite side of the Thames and about 122 m (400 ft) above,

4. R.C.A.M., *Pembrokeshire*, p. 187 and fig. 160.
5. Sumner, *The Ancient Earthworks of the New Forest* (1917), 15.

Fig.120.
Martinsell Hill
and Giant's
Grave, Wiltshire.

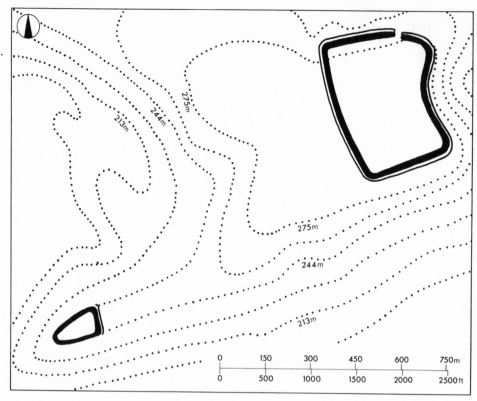

stands the univallate site of Sinodun in a hilltop situation. From it there is a
bird's-eye view back into Dike Hills, and the possibility that the two were
associated cannot be overlooked.

Two or three sites in the south-west seem to have smaller sites associated with
them in the satellite manner. Stockland Great Camp (Devon) was described
under hill-slope situations (p. 85). About 823 m (2,700 ft) to the north is
Stockland Little Camp, situated on a shallow spur. In Cornwall Gearhill Camp,
mentioned already under annexes, is situated in a semi-contour position with an
easy approach from the east. About 320 m (1,050 ft) to the south-east and separated from it by a small coomb is Caervallack, a Small multivallate fort. There
is a similar gap between another univallate site, Delinuth Camp, and Castle
Goff, which is again a Small multivallate site. Two other sites worthy of mention
are Ham Hill (Som.) and Lydney Park (Glos), in neither of which is there, in
fact, any visible satellites. They are mentioned here simply because in both cases
there is a hill immediately adjacent to the enclosure, providing the sort of situation in which satellite enclosures occur. In both cases these hilltops are occupied
by defence works of a later period.

The remaining sites to be considered are all in Wales. In Glamorgan the
multiple-enclosure, originally concentric, site of Gaer Fawr stands on the
north slope of Mynydd Gaer, straddling the 244-m (800-ft) contour. About

Fig.121.Castell
Mawr and
satellites,
Pembrokeshire.

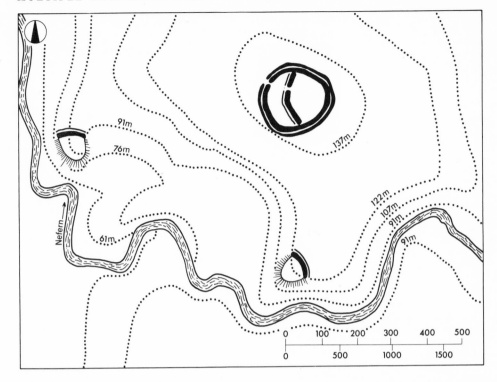

366 m (1,200 ft) to the south, on the crown of the hill at about 305 m (1,000 ft)
is a univallate single-enclosure site about 107 m (350 ft) in diameter, more or less
similar in size to the inner enclosure of the site below. In a number of the sites
dealt with in the paper mentioned earlier the subsidiary enclosures were in the
more elevated position. At Bwlwarcau, another concentric site, there is a small,
roughly circular enclosure, defended by a bank and ditch about 411 m (1,350 ft)
to the north. This is similar in size to the inner enclosure at Caer Blaen y Cwm,
about 549 m (1,800 ft, south-west of Y Bwlwarcau, and only slightly smaller
than the inner enclosure at Bwlwarcau itself. The small enclosure is shown on
the plan published by Sir Cyril and Lady Fox, but is omitted from the O.S.
Iron Age map.

Fig.97

At Caer Cwm Phillip, another concentric site a little further to the south-west,
there are at least one and possibly two associated enclosures. About 777 m
(2,550 ft) to the south-east there is a small circular univallate enclosure, Ton
Mawr, about 61 m (200 ft) in diameter. This is included on the O.S. Iron Age
map. About 160 m (525 ft) to the west of the main site, however, is another
small site which is not included. This is about 43 × 30 m (140 × 100 ft) internally
and appears to have something like an annexe on one side. Both of the associated
sites stand in plateau-edge positions where the ground falls away to the south
and west. There is also a small, roughly circular site equidistant and about

Fig.111
Fig.121

119 m (390 ft) from the east and west camps at Harding's Down.

Finally in Pembrokeshire there are 2 sites closely associated with Castell

Pl.47

Mawr which stands in a hilltop situation. About 320 m (1,050 ft) to the south on a promontory overlooking the river is a Small multivallate site, Pen-y-Benglog. About 411 m (1,350 ft) to the west is another Small fort, in this case univallate, in a similar situation. The two smaller sites are about 61 m (200 ft) below the level of the main enclosure. In Cardiganshire there is a Small site, Castell-bach, about 183 m (600 ft) north-east of Castell-mawr and another Small site about 411 m (1,350 ft) to the west of Cribyn Clota. The latter stands in a semi-contour position with the easy approach from the east and north-east. The associated site, Gaer Fach, is about 30 m (100 ft) lower on the western slope.

CHAPTER VII

Entrances

One of the difficulties of dealing with entrances is the question of classification. In many entrances, particularly those in multivallate forts, a number of distinct features are involved, inturned ramparts, looped ramparts, hornworks, etc., but these are not necessarily exclusive of each other. To classify entrances on the basis of such characteristics would be to produce an unacceptable degree of overlapping. Inturned ramparts in univallate forts, for example, are in most, but not all, cases exclusive of any other feature. In many multivallate forts, however, the inturned ramparts are simply two of a number of entrance features, so that to describe such entrances simply as inturned would be misleading.

To overcome this difficulty the defence principles involved will be considered rather than specific entrances. Thus inturned ramparts, rather than inturned entrances, will be considered as a single group wherever they occur, in univallate forts, in multiple-enclosure sites and in multivallate forts, and all other features will be treated in the same way. Entrance features will, therefore, be considered under the following headings: simple gaps; club-ended ramparts; inturned ramparts; out-turned ramparts; looped ramparts; overlapping ramparts; outworks. These features, either singly or in various combinations with each other, account for all the entrances to Iron Age forts.

Before dealing with features something must be said, if only briefly, about the original structure of entrances. The two main types of rampart, revetted and glacis, were described in Chapter I. In the simplest type of entrance, a simple gap, in a revetted rampart, the existing revetment is carried around the rampart end. In a glacis rampart, with no revetment, a special revetment has to be provided for the rampart ends which would otherwise spill down on to the roadway. In both cases, however, these end revetments produce a corridor, in length equal to the thickness of the rampart, through which anyone wishing to gain access to the fort had to pass, and this is one of the basic principles of Iron Age fort entrances. In most cases this constriction of access starts at the outer end of the causeway across the ditch and may extend for 15 or 30 m (50 or 100 ft) or more, depending on the respective dimensions of the bank, the berm, where one exists, and the ditch.

The short corridor produced by the end revetments provides the setting for the gate to the fort. It will be quite clear that the lengthening of this corridor will make access even more difficult for an attacker, and one of the simplest ways

Fig.122a

Fig.122b

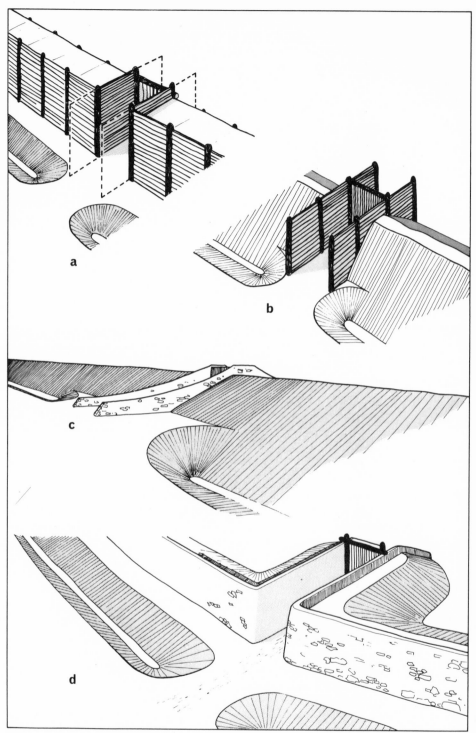

Fig.122. Entrances, original form: 122a with revetted ramparts; 122b and c with glacis ramparts; 122d with inturned ramparts.

Fig.122a

of doing this is to extend the revetments, either inwards or outwards, beyond the length necessary to revet the rampart ends. Such extensions need not necessarily be maintained at the maximum height of the rampart. Even at a height of 1 to 1·5 m (4 to 5 ft) they would act as an effective constriction of the roadway into the fort.

Fig.122d

The more common method of extending the entrance corridor, however, is by turning the ramparts inwards at right angles so that they run parallel to each other. The revetments forming the corridor are now solidly reinforced with the full weight and thickness of the inturned rampart behind them. The corridors or passages thus formed can be anything from 15 to 30 m (50 to 100 ft) long, and in one or two cases even longer. The gates to the fort are normally placed at or near the inner end of the inturns. Two other features can be mentioned here. Guard chambers, often in pairs, are sometimes found in the thickness of inturned ramparts, and the surface evidence for these will be considered later. The second feature, for which there is no surface evidence, is a bridge across the passageway, from one rampart crest to the other, under which attackers would have to pass to reach the gateway.

Intermediate between the simple gap and the inturned entrance is the club-ended or expanded-end rampart in which the entrance passage runs through a specially thickened section of rampart, thus increasing the length of the passage beyond the normal thickness of the rampart. In other entrances the ramparts are turned outwards, or one inwards and one outwards, to produce the requisite passage, and in others the passage is produced by the overlapping of the ramparts so that it is parallel to, rather than at right angles to, the main defences. In a much smaller number of cases constriction of access is produced by outworks projecting beyond the main line of the defences.

The arrangements outlined in this section account for virtually all of the entrances in univallate forts.

Entrances in multiple-enclosure sites are virtually a series of separate univallate entrances. Entrances in multivallate sites show a great deal of variation which arises to a great extent from the nature and complexity of the defence systems through which they pass. A common type in the commonest type of system, i.e. a two-ditch system, has a simple gap through the outer bank and ditch and an inturned arrangement for the inner bank.

SIMPLE GAPS

By far the commonest type of entrance is a simple gap in the rampart, with a corresponding causeway across the ditch, where one exists. In the 900 or so univallate forts in England and Wales, for example, between 85 and 90 per cent of all entrances are of this type. This means that something like 800 sites, or more than half of all Iron Age forts, have simple gap entrances. In addition to these there are multiple-enclosure sites where the entrances to the separate enclosures are of the simple gap type, and a number of multivallate sites where the entrances are a straight cut through whatever features, banks, ditches, berms, etc., are involved in the particular defence system.

219

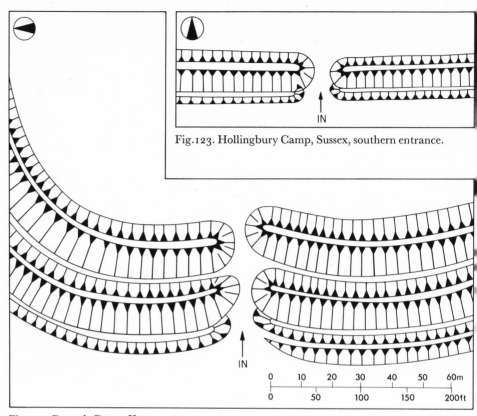

Fig.123. Hollingbury Camp, Sussex, southern entrance.

Fig.124. Caesar's Camp, Kent, entrance.

Fig.123   The eastern entrance at Hollingbury (Sussex) is as typical of simple gap entrances as any other. The causeway between the rounded ditch-ends is now about 4·8 m (16 ft) wide, although allowing for erosion it must have been somewhat wider originally, possibly as much as 8 m (25 ft). Its length, corresponding to the width of the ditches, is now between 6 and 8 m (20 and 25 ft), but again allowing for erosion, although this time with the reverse effect, its original length must have been in the region of 4·5 m (15 ft). The gap between the opposing rounded rampart-ends is 3 m (10 ft) at ground-level and about 11 m (35 ft) at the crests. The total length of the entrance, i.e. the combined widths of the existing bank and ditch, is about 15 m (50 ft). The original length must have been in the region of 9 or 11 m (30 or 35 ft). There are simple gap entrances both larger and smaller than Hollingbury but the basic pattern of a straight cut through the defences at right angles is repeated many hundreds of times. Since they form such a large proportion of the entrances in univallate forts simple gap entrances occur wherever such forts are found, which is virtually throughout the whole area of the survey. The entrances at Dungeon Hill (Dorset), Rame Head (Corn.), and Bodbury Ring (Salop), to mention only three widely scattered examples, are basically similar to Hollingbury and to the entrances in

Figs.64,24a
Fig.29

220

hundreds of other univallate sites. Such entrances tend to be overshadowed by the complexities of the entrances at Maiden Castle and Yarnbury, but they do represent the access arrangements at more than half of the Iron Age forts in England and Wales.

The entrances in many multiple-enclosure sites are virtually a series of two or more separate simple gap entrances. At Round Wood (Corn.), for example, there are three separate gaps through the defences of the inner oval enclosure and the two crossbanks to the west. All three entrances are in line and cover a distance of some 152 m (500 ft). At Coxall Knoll (Here.) the total distance involved is about 183 m (600 ft), again consisting of three separate gaps. In this case, however, the three gaps are not in line and several changes of direction are involved. After passing through the outer entrance it is necessary to veer to the left to reach the middle entrance, 61 m (200 ft) away, but the passage through this is at right angles to the approach because of the oblique axis of the entrance.

Access from the east to the innermost enclosure at Clovelly Dykes (Devon) is also via three separate gaps covering a distance of about 137 m (450 ft). The inner entrance is offset from the line of the other two by about 18 m (60 ft). At Milber Down in the same county the three inner gaps, which are in line, cover about 107 m (350 ft). The arrangements at White Sheet Castle (Wilts.) and Warton Crag (Lancs), in both of which three widely-spaced ramparts are involved, are of the same general type. At Park Hall Camp (Wilts.) and Carreg y Llam (Caer.) the arrangements consist of two gap entrances. At Park Hall Camp the inner gap is offset by about 30 m (100 ft) from the outer. At Carreg y Llam the two entrances are more or less in line, about 12 m (40 ft) apart, although the ground between them is quite steep.

The western entrance of Badbury Rings (Dorset) also needs to be considered in this context since it consists virtually of three separate gaps through three widely spaced lines of defence. The gap through the inner rampart is clearly original. The two gaps in line with it through the middle and outer ramparts are modern. The two original entrances in these ramparts are placed obliquely, to the south-west of the inner entrance. The total distance involved is about 152 m (500 ft). There are generally similar entrances at Bratton Castle and Sidbury (Wilts.), although in each case the third, outermost rampart is missing. All three entrances, however, can equally well be considered under the heading of outworks (p. 245), where further discussion of them will be found. Sites such as Castle Dore and Helsbury (Corn.) will need to be considered in the same context since the ramparts defining their outer enclosures could, with some justice, be regarded as outworks.

In a number of multiple-enclosure sites simple gaps are combined with other types of entrance. At Prestonbury (Devon), for example, the inner and middle entrances are simple gaps, some 61 m (200 ft) apart, while the outer entrance, another 137 m (450 ft) to the north-east, is of the inturned type. At Hall Rings (Corn.) the middle and outer entrances, 244 m (800 ft) apart, are simple gaps. The entrance to the inner oval enclosure has an inturned rampart on one side opposite a simple round-ended rampart on the other. Finally, at the eastern entrance of Badbury Rings (Dorset) there is a simple outer gap, offset to the

Fig.104

Fig.94
Pl.39

Fig.84
Pl.43

Pl.38
Pl.5

Fig.101

Fig.112

Fig.84

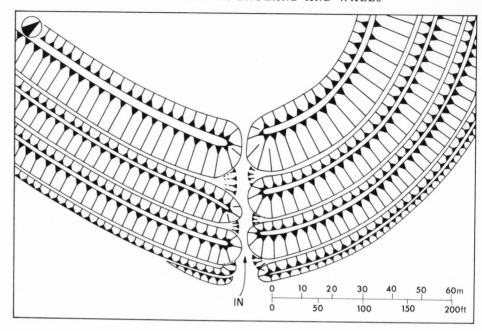

IN

south of the middle and inner entrances by about 30 m (100 ft). The middle and inner ramparts, with their ditches, form a compact two-ditch system. The middle rampart has a simple gap, while the two ends of the inner rampart have short inturns.

The simplest type of entrance in a multivallate site involves a straight cut through the defence system at right angles. The effect of this is to produce a narrow passage or corridor equal in length to the depth of the particular system so that, without any special entrance features, a long constricted approach to the interior is achieved. The entrance at the eastern end of Smalldown Camp (Som.), for example, is a compact series of simple gaps through an arrangement of two banks, two ditches, and a counterscarp bank, producing a passage about 29 m (95 ft) long. There is a similar entrance at the eastern end of Dolebury in the same county although there no counterscarp bank is involved. The length of the entrance passage is about 34 m (110 ft). In Cornwall Redcliff Castle, a small promontory fort, also has a straight cut through a compact arrangement of two banks and two ditches about 34 m (110 ft) long, and the inner part of the entrance at Rumps Point appears to belong to the same category, although there is, in addition, an outer entrance through a rampart set some 21 m (70 ft) in front of the main defences.

Most of the remaining sites in this category follow the same pattern, being set in compact two-ditch systems, with or without a counterscarp bank. At Caesar's Camp (Kent) the defences are very slightly indented on either side of the entrance, which is otherwise of the simple gap type. The entrances at Malwood Castle and the western end of Buckland Rings (Hants), if they are original

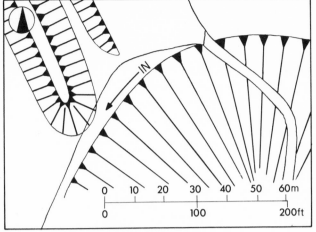

Fig.126. Kellsboro' Castle, Cheshire, entrance.

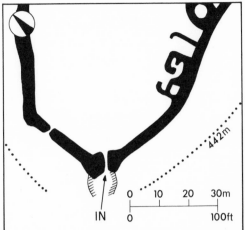

Fig.127. Tre'r Ceiri, Caernarvonshire, southern entrance.

Fig.43a

and not modern gaps, also belong to this group. Other sites which appear to belong include Pilsdon Pen (Dorset), Nottingham Hill and Bloody Acre Camp (Glos), Bulstrode Park (Bucks), Walterstone Camp (Here.), and Rushbury Ditches (Salop).

Fig.125

At Burrow Camp (Salop) the system through which the entrance passes involves four banks, although probably only two ditches, two of the banks being of the counterscarp type. The south-eastern entrance, described as a postern, is a straight cut through this system, producing a passage some 61 m (200 ft) long. There appear to be similar systems at Cherbury (Berks) and at Ebsbury and Hanging Langford Camp (Wilts.), in all of which there are entrances which rely on the depth of the defences for their effectiveness.

Fig.40

Fig.126

In addition to the entrances described so far there are also simple gap entrances in which one side of the gap is defined by a natural feature. The southern entrance at Oakmere (Ches.) is a simple example of this type. The single bank and ditch stop short about 4·5 m (15 ft) from the head of the low scarp which runs down to the edge of the mere, forming an entrance passage about 30 m (100 ft) long. There is a similar entrance at Kellsboro' Castle in the same county, between the eastern end of the bank and ditch and the natural slope defining the promontory.

Fig.82

Fig.74

Natural features are utilized in the same way in a number of multivallate forts. The promontory fort at Llandewi Gaer (Pemb) is defended on the north and west by a three-ditch multivallate system of the separated type, i.e. with berms between the three lines of defence, and by natural slopes on the south and east. The entrance is placed at the eastern end of the northern defences with the eastern slope defining one side of the entrance passage, which is about 52 m (170 ft) long. At Castell Pyr (Carm.) the entrance is at the northern end of a compact two-bank and two-ditch system with the northern side formed by the steep slope to the River Teifi below. There is a similar entrance at Bryn Alun

223

Fig.27

(Flint.). The entrance at Symond's Yat may also belong to this category. The defences involve four banks and ditches with spaces between 12 and 23 m (40 and 75 ft) wide between them. The very steep slopes on the eastern side of the promontory form one side of the entrance. The other appears to be formed by the ends of the four banks and ditches that draw closer together towards the eastern end although the intervening berms are still present. At Burrow Camp (Salop) one side of the south-western entrance is formed by the squared-off end of the multivallate system that runs in obliquely towards the head of the natural slope. The latter is surmounted by a rampart, so that the entrance passage is flanked on one side by a bank instead of the usual unprotected slope.

CLUB-ENDED RAMPARTS

Fig.127
Pl.30

Fig.20

In a number of cases it is clear from the surface remains that the entrance passage has been lengthened by increasing the thickness of the rampart in the entrance area. This can be seen very clearly in a number of stone-built forts in Caernarvonshire, especially Tre'r Ceiri, Conway Mountain, and Pen-y-Gaer. At Tre'r Ceiri the south-western entrance is markedly club-ended. On the western side the rampart proper is about 3·6 m (12 ft) thick and expands in the last 6 m (20 ft) or so to a knobbed end about 6 m (20 ft) thick. On the other side the rampart is narrower, about 2·4 m (8 ft), and the clubbed end about 4·8 m (16 ft) thick. The rampart-ends at the inner western entrance are also thickened but not to anything like the same degree. At Conway Mountain the stone ramparts begin to thicken at about 15 or 18 m (50 or 60 ft) from the entrances, from a width of about 3 m (10 ft) to a width of about 5·5 m (18 ft) flanking the entrance passages. On the southern side of the inner entrance at Pen-y-Gaer, Llanbedr-y-Cennin, the rampart expands to a thickness of about 9 m (30 ft) from a width, about 24 m (80 ft) away, of some 4·5 m (15 ft). In Denbighshire at Pen-y-Corddyn there are surface indications, confirmed by excavation, of a club-ended rampart at the southern entrance. In Montgomeryshire the rampart-ends defining the main entrance at Ffridd Faldwyn also belong to this group. The ramparts are at right angles to each other. About 30 m (100 ft) from the entrance the southern rampart begins to expand until it reaches a width of about 4·5 m (15 ft) at the crest. The expansion of the eastern rampart is even greater, reaching a maximum width of 9 m (30 ft) at the crest.

In the south-west the ramparts at Hawkesdown (Devon) also meet at right angles. About 46 m (150 ft) from its southern end the eastern rampart begins to expand until immediately overlooking the entrance it is about 6 m (20 ft) wide at the crest. At the multiple-enclosure site of Wooston Castle in the same county the entrance to the second enclosure has an inturned rampart on one side and a club-ended rampart on the other. At Resugga Castle (Corn.) both inner and outer entrances are flanked by club-ended ramparts. At Castle Dyke, Ugbrooke (Devon), the rampart-ends at both south-western and north-eastern entrances fall somewhere between the incipient inturned type and the expanded type. The western entrance at Bat's Castle (Som.) is similar. The rampart-ends appear to expand into triangular platforms about 9 m (30 ft) long and about

6 m (20 ft) wide at the crest. Most of the expansion takes place on the inner side, hence the similarity to incipient inturns. Other south-western sites which either certainly or possibly involve club-ended ramparts include Brent Knoll and Stokeleigh (Som.) and Prestonbury, Holne Chase Castle, and Cranbrook Castle (Devon).

In southern and south-eastern England there are only 3 or 4 sites which can be mentioned in this context. Probably the best example is Castle Hill (Hants), where the ends of the ramparts at both northern and southern entrances are wider and higher than elsewhere. At the eastern entrance of Old Winchester Hill (Hants) the southern rampart is club-ended while the one on the north is inturned. There are ramparts with expanded ends at two Sussex sites, Harrow Hill and Cissbury, although at the latter it is known from excavation that the expanded ends are post-Iron Age features.

Fig.63

INTURNED RAMPARTS

After simple gaps inturned ramparts represent the commonest type of entrance arrangement in Iron Age forts. They vary in length from what may be termed incipient types, projecting only one or two metres beyond the back of the rampart, to types up to and in some cases beyond 30 m (100 ft) long. For the most part inturned ramparts are associated with multivallate forts. Those associated with univallate forts tend to be of the short or incipient type, although it should be noted that these occur also in multivallate forts. For the purposes of this chapter the length of an inturn is interpreted as the distance it projects beyond the back of the rampart (i.e. beyond the foot of the rear scarp) towards the interior. The length of the passage thus produced is, of course, longer, the extra length being accounted for by the thickness of the rampart.

For convenience inturned ramparts can be divided into four groups on the basis of size. Under the heading of incipient inturns can be included those ramparts which project less than 4·5 m (15 ft) towards the interior of the fort. Because of this it is sometimes difficult to distinguish incipient inturns from some of the club-ended types dealt with in the previous section, particularly on the basis of some of the existing plans. However, the difference is usually visible on ground examination. In a true incipient inturn the whole rampart can be seen to turn towards the interior. A passage of the same length can be achieved by a club-ended rampart. In such a case, however, the rampart-end cannot be said to turn. At the crest it simply broadens out into a platform. In the corresponding part of the inturned rampart there is a definite change of direction, with a perceptible angle between the inturn and the rampart proper.

Fig.43e
Pl.36

Fig.25

Fig.71;Pl.13

A good example of incipient inturns is provided by Dolebury (Som.). At the western entrance, which passes through a two-ditch multivallate system, the ends of the inner rampart turn inwards, although only slightly, for about 3·6 m (12 ft). There are inturns of similar dimensions at the promontory fort of Linney Head (Pemb). At Cwm Castell (Card.) the inturns are even shorter, in the region of 2·4 or 2·7 m (8 or 9 ft). At Caer Caradoc, Church Stretton (Salop), there is a single inturn of the incipient type on the north side of the main

225

entrance; and a single incipient inturn forms the eastern side of the north entrance at Cadbury Camp, Tickenham (Som.). Other inturns in this group include Bevisbury (Hants), Nordy Bank (Salop), and Daren (Card.).

There is, of course, no hard line between incipient inturns and those in the next group, projecting between 4·5 and 9 m (15 and 30 ft) inwards, which may for convenience be classed as short inturns. The inturns at St. Catherine's Hill (Hants) are of this type, with the curving rampart-ends projecting inwards for about 6 m (20 ft). Excavation showed that in an early phase these short inturns provided the setting for twin guard-chambers, although there is now no surface evidence of these. At Badbury Rings (Dorset) there are short inturns, about 7·6 m (25 ft), to the inner of the three ramparts at the eastern entrance. At the concentric site of Warbstow Bury (Corn.) both the eastern and western entrances to the inner enclosure are of the short inturned type, the four inturns involved varying between 4·5 and 9 m (15 and 30 ft) in length. At Foel Fenlli (Denb.) the inturns at the main entrance at the western end of the site are about 7·6 m (25 ft) long. The rest of the arrangement comes under the heading of looped ramparts. At Gaer Fawr (Card.) both eastern and western entrances have inturns about 6 m (20 ft) long.

The third group to be distinguished on the basis of size embraces those inturns which project inwards between 9 and 15 m (30 and 50 ft) (medium-sized). These include the inturns at the univallate site at Beacon Hill (Hants) which project about 12 m (40 ft) inwards. They form part of a more elaborate arrangement which includes looped ramparts and twin hornworks. The medium-sized inturns at the north-eastern entrance at Hod Hill (Dorset) also form part of a more elaborate entrance, in this case of the overlapping type set in a multivallate system. Burley Wood (Devon) is of the multiple-enclosure type. Access to the main enclosure is by means of parallel inturns projecting about 12 m (40 ft) beyond the back of the rampart. The eastern entrance at Caer Caradoc, Clun (Salop), also belongs within this group, with inturns just over 9 m (30 ft) long, as does the south entrance at Midsummer Hill with inturns about 12 m (40 ft) long. The entrance of the multivallate site at Maiden Castle (Ches.) has inturned ends about 11 m (35 ft) long, to the inner rampart, with a simple gap in the outer rampart some 12 m (40 ft) away. At Moel y Gaer, Llanbedr (Denb.), both eastern and western entrances have inturns about 12 m (40 ft) long. The eastern inturns are the innermost feature of a multivallate overlapping arrangement.

Long inturns, i.e. those which project more than 15 m (50 ft) inwards, exist in smaller numbers. At Maiden Castle (Dorset) the inner part of the complex western entrance consists of twin portals about 30 m (100 ft) apart through the inner rampart, each flanked by long inturns. At the north portal the inturns are 21 and 24 m (70 and 80 ft) long, at the south portal 18 m (60 ft) each. At the equally complex eastern entrance at Yarnbury (Wilts.) the ends of the inner rampart are deeply inturned and on a massive scale. The northern inturn projects inwards about 29 m (95 ft), the southern about 24 m (80 ft). At Dumpdon Camp (Devon) the northern inturn is just 15 m (50 ft) long, but the southern one is somewhat longer, about 23 m (75 ft). In Herefordshire only the

Fig.116

Fig.21c

Fig.84
Pl.43
Fig.92
Pl.50
Fig.54

Fig.52
Pl.29

Fig.21a
Pl.23
Fig.113
Pl.25
Fig.31

Fig.23b
Fig.32

Fig.135

Fig.140
Pl.41

Pl.26

southern inturn at the south-eastern entrance at Thornbury Wall Hills belongs to this group, with a length of 24 m (80 ft). The northern inturn is only 12 m (40 ft) long.

Fig.86

At Bury Ditches (Salop) both inturns at the eastern entrance are 30 m (100 ft) long, with the northern inturn looped on to the second rampart. There are other long inturns at Hillis Camp (Breck.), Llantysilio Mountain (Denb.), and Borough Hill (Leics.).

Fig.30d

Fig.66

In most of the entrances considered so far the inturns have been more or less at right angles to the rampart proper. In some cases, however, the entrance passage cuts through the defences obliquely and the inturns reflect this arrangement. The south-western entrance at Mam Tor (Derby.) is of this type. The western inturn is at an angle of about 135° to the rampart. The angle between the eastern inturn and the rampart is narrowed in conformity with this to about 50°. In this case the oblique approach and inturns are dictated by the slope of the hill. An approach to the southern defences at right angles would have produced too steep an entrance. This cannot be the explanation for the oblique inturns at Eggardon (Dorset) since they are situated on virtually level ground. The entrance involves inner and outer portals in ramparts about 30 m (100 ft) apart. The two portals are not in line, the outer being offset to the south by about 61 m (200 ft). Its inturns are, however, so angled that they point directly towards the inner entrance. In any case right-angled inturns in this position would have led to the roadway they define ending virtually at the edge of the inner ditch. There is a good example of oblique inturns at the univallate site of Aconbury (Here.).

Fig.34a
Pl.21

Fig.81

A further variation on this theme involves curving inturns. An excellent example is provided by Wapley Camp (Here.), where the inturns are also very long: 30 m (100 ft) on the west, 64 m (210 ft) on the east. The curve is such that there is no unobstructed view through the passage between the inturns. The defences run east and west, with the approach from the south. Anyone entering the inturned section would gradually turn to the left until, on reaching the end of the passage and the enclosed area, he would be facing west. The inturns at Thornbury Wall Hills, mentioned earlier, also curve although not to anything like the same degree as at Wapley Camp. The two outer entrances at the multiple-enclosure site at Bredon Hill (Worcs) have inturns which are both long and curved. Because of erosion there is now a gap between them and the ramparts from which they sprang, but originally they must have been around 40 m (130 ft) long.

Fig.114

In a number of inturned entrances there are fairly clear surface indications that guard chambers existed, either singly or in pairs. There are about 15 such sites in England and Wales. The surface evidence takes a number of different forms. At Moel Arthur (Flint.) there is a noticeable hollowing on the inner side of each of the 14-m (45-ft) inturns so that they have a claw-like appearance. There is a very similar arrangement at Cadsonbury (Corn.) in the entrance on the eastern side. The evidence at two of the inturned entrances at The Wrekin (Salop) takes the same form, and in the case of one of them the surface evidence is supported by excavation evidence as well. At Bindon (Dorset) the ends of

Fig.128a
Pl.4
Fig.128b
Fig.128c

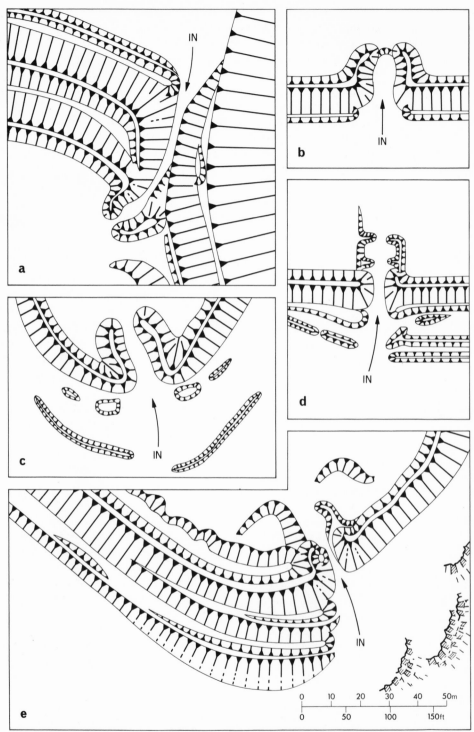

Fig.128. Inturned entrances with evidence of guard chambers: 128a Moel Arthur, Flintshire; 128b Cadsonbury, Cornwall; 128c The Wrekin, Shropshire; 128d Moel y Gaer (Rhosesmor), Flintshire; 128e Pen-y-cloddiau, Flintshire.

the 15-m (50-ft) inturns curve towards each other in claw-like fashion and suggest the possibility of guard chambers.

Fig.128d At other sites the evidence takes a slightly different form, best seen at Moel y Gaer, Rhoesmor (Flint.). The guard chamber on the north side is set beyond the end of the inturn proper. A low bank continuing the line of the inturn defines the back of the guard chamber. Two short banks at right angles to this define the two short sides. The fourth side is open to the roadway. These banks presumably define a rectangular guard chamber about 4.5×3 m (15×10 ft) attached to the end of the inturn rather than set into the thickness of it. The opposing guard chamber on the south side of the entrance is of the same type, although it appears to have been dug in part into the natural slope at this point. Fig.128e There is a guard chamber similar to the Moel y Gaer type at Pen-y-cloddiau (Flint.) on the eastern side of the south entrance. The guard chamber on the west is of the claw-type, as at Moel Arthur. There is a single guard chamber, again of the Moel·y Gaer type, at Castell Cawr (Denb.).

Fig.86 The evidence for guard chambers at Bury Ditches (Salop) differs from all the sites considered so far. The ends of the inturns are stepped out for the last 6 m (20 ft), so that they define two sides of a rectangle. These two sides are presumably two sides of a guard chamber set into the end of the rampart, with the two remaining sides free-standing. The arrangement, in effect, falls somewhere between the Moel Arthur type and the Moel y Gaer type. The guard chambers excavated at St. Catherine's Hill (Hants) were of the same type, with the back and one of the short sides set in the body of the inturn and the front and the other short side free-standing. There is surface evidence of guard chambers also at Plas Cadnant (Anglesey), Pen Dinas (Caer.), Caer Drewyn (Mer.) Pen- Figs.31,71 myarth (Breck.), and Caer Caradoc, Clun, and Caer Caradoc, Church Stretton (both Salop). There is a slight suggestion of guard chambers at the inner and middle entrances at Moel Hiraddug (Flint.) in addition to the one known from excavation at the north-west entrance. In Anglesey the southern inturn at the entrance of Parciau is longer than the one on the north and the back scarp curves round in a manner suggestive of a guard chamber.

Fig.70 In a few cases an inturned rampart is used in association with a natural feature. One of the best examples is provided by Helsby (Ches.). The entrance is at the south-west corner of the site where the man-made defences, a rampart without a ditch, run east and west. At the entrance the rampart turns inwards for about 15 m (50 ft), defining an entrance passage about 3 m (10 ft) wide Fig.60 between it and the cliff edge. There are generally similar arrangements at Bury Walls (Salop), and Croft Ambrey (Here.). At the latter the rampart turns inwards for about 27 m (90 ft), the first half of which is flanked by the natural Fig.129 slope. At Moel-y-Gaer, Bodfari (Flint.), the inner rampart on the north turns both inwards and outwards near the head of the natural slope, so that the narrow entrance passage is flanked for about 30 m (100 ft), half of which is accounted for by the inturn. There is a not dissimilar arrangement at Castell Pared Mawr (Caer.), with the rampart again turning both inwards and out-wards. At Garmsley (Worcs) the rampart turns inwards to run parallel to the head of the natural slope, which in this case is surmounted by a slight rampart.

Fig.129.
Moel-y-Gaer
(Bodfari),
Flintshire,
northern
entrance.

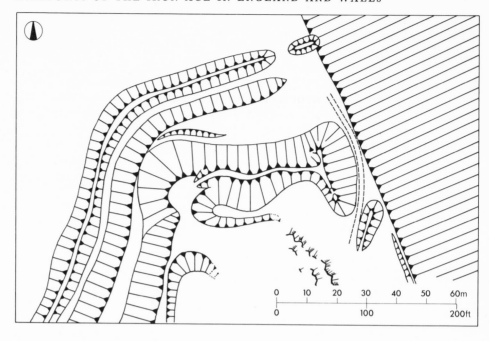

OUT-TURNED RAMPARTS

In a number of cases an entrance passage is produced by turning the rampart-
ends outwards instead of inwards or in a smaller number of cases by turning one
outwards and the other inwards. An example of an inturn/out-turn arrangement is provided by the entrance at the north end of the inner enclosure at Earl's
Fig.105   Hill, Pontesbury (Salop). On the eastern side of the entrance passage the
rampart is inturned, projecting about 12 m (40 ft) towards the interior. This
runs parallel to the out-turned rampart that forms the western side of the
entrance. This projects forward over the sloping ground, dominating the track
Fig.114   leading to the entrance like a bastion. The inner entrance at Bredon Hill
(Worcs) is also of the inturn/out-turn type. The ramparts on either side of the
entrance are at right angles to each other. The eastern rampart is sharply inturned. The southern rampart has a slight inturn but the dominant feature is
the out-turned portion which runs parallel to the opposing inturn.

Fig.129   At two sites mentioned in the previous section, Moel-y-Gaer, Bodfari (Flint.),
and Castell Pared Mawr (Caer.), the ramparts turned both inwards and outwards so that the ends were, in fact, T-shaped. The same is true of the rampart-
Fig.114   end at Bredon Hill mentioned in the previous paragraph, although there the
transverse section was not at right angles to the rampart proper. At Leckhampton (Glos), however, the entrance passage is formed between the T-shaped
ends of the ramparts to the north and south of the entrance. The entrance
belongs to both the inturned and out-turned category. The out-turns give the
impression of twin bastions dominating the immediate approach to the gateway.
The inturned portions are somewhat longer.

230

Fig. 130.
Hascombe
Camp, Surrey,
entrance.

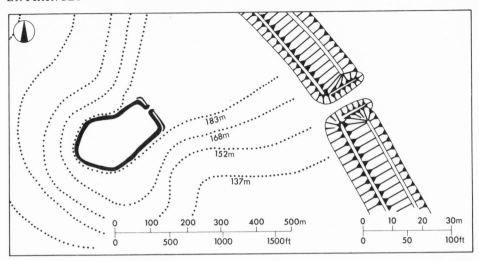

183m
168m
152m

137m

0   100   200   300   400   500m

0   500   1000   1500ft

0   10   20   30m

0   50   100ft

Fig. 130

Fig. 34c

Fig. 131

Fig. 27
Pl. 10

A straightforward example of out-turned ramparts in a simple univallate site is provided by Hascombe Camp (Surrey). At the eastern entrance the ramparts on the northern and southern sides turn outwards at right angles, passing the ditch-ends and projecting another 6 m (20 ft) or so beyond. The passage thus produced is about 24 m (80 ft) long. At the eastern entrance at Segsbury (Berks) the end of the out-turn has been destroyed by cultivation, but it is quite clear from what remains that the ditch turned outwards as well. There is no corresponding out-turn on the northern side. At Gorley Hill (Hants) there is likewise only one out-turn, on the western side of the entrance. This crosses the ditch-end and projects for about 24 m (80 ft). In all it flanks the approach for about 37 m (120 ft). At Maesbury (Som.) the out-turned portion of the inner rampart on the southern side of the western entrance has now been destroyed, but according to an early account it turned outwards for about 18 m (60 ft), crossing the end of its associated ditch.

At Weatherby Castle (Dorset) and Crickley Hill (Glos) the out-turned sections of rampart are curved, so that there is no direct run through the entrance. At Weatherby Castle the entrance is on the west. On the northern side the inner rampart turns outwards and curves around the ditch-end. The southern out-turn is considerably longer. It crosses the ditch-end and curves round to the north in conformity with the opposing out-turn. At Crickley Hill only one rampart is involved, facing east towards the level approach. The rampart on the southern side turns outwards accompanied by its ditch and then curves round towards the north. This curve embraces the very short curving out-turn on the northern side which, as at Weatherby, simply runs round the ditch-end.

At Bat's Castle (Som.) it is the ditches that turn outwards rather than the rampart. The defences consist of a bank, ditch, and couterscarp bank. When they reach the eastern entrance the ends of the rampart turn slightly inwards. The ditches, however, turn outwards at right angles, accompanied by the

231

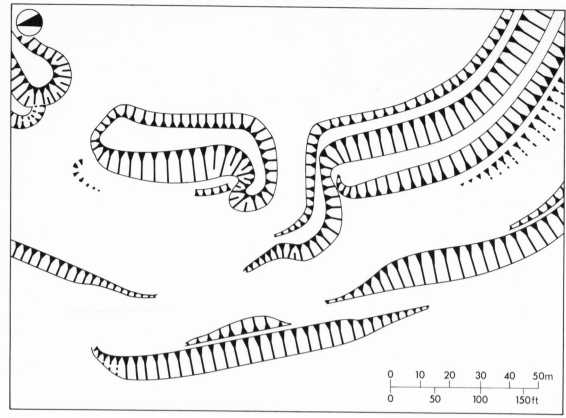

Fig.131. Weatherby Castle, Dorset, entrance.

counterscarp bank, and project for about 30 m (100 ft). The entrance passage is about 52 m (170 ft) long, running for the greater part of its length between parallel ditches with banks on their outer edges.

In Wales Gaer Fawr (Montg.), Pen-y-Gaer, Aberglaslyn (Caer.), and Gaer Fach (Carm.) all have entrances of the out-turned type. At the south-western entrance at Gaer Fawr the out-turned ramparts run parallel to each other for about 30 m (100 ft) down a fairly steep slope. The roadway thus defined makes a U-shaped turn around the end of the southern out-turn and runs along its southern flank to end at a point more or less opposite to, but much lower than, the inner part of the entrance. At Pen-y-Gaer the out-turn on the northern side of the entrance is a solid stone square-ended rampart about 1·5 m (5 ft) wide and projecting forward about 3 m (10 ft). The rampart on the opposite side also turns outwards, for a greater distance, of about 12 m (40 ft), and appears to form one side of a small rectangular enclosure. At Gaer Fach the stone ramparts at the eastern entrance turn outwards and run down a slope for about 61 m (200 ft), in the direction of the larger fort, Gaer Fawr, with which Gaer Fach is associated.

Fig.132

232

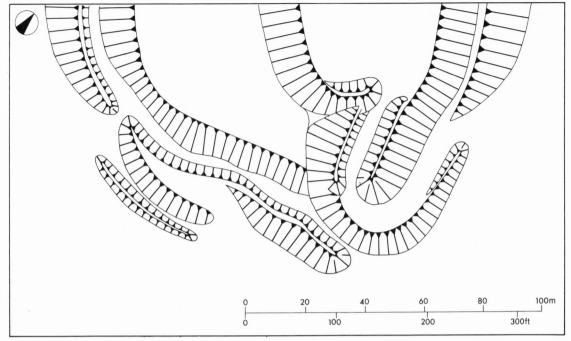

Fig.132. Gaer Fawr, Montgomeryshire, south-west entrance.

Fig.143

Other sites with some indication of out-turned ramparts include Old Sarum (Wilts.), Blackbury Castle (Devon), and Rawlsbury (Dorset).

LOOPED RAMPARTS

In entrances with looped ramparts the ends of the inner and outer ramparts are joined by ramparts which flank the roadway and prevent access to the ditch. A simple version of this principle can be seen in certain univallate systems with counterscarp banks. At both entrances of The Trundle (Sussex), for example, the counterscarp banks run round the ditch-ends and end at the front of the main rampart. The same thing happens at the inner entrance of Castle Dore (Corn.), at Crug Hywel (Breck.), and on the northern side of the entrance at Fig.54 Foel Fenlli (Denb.). On the southern side the ditch and its counterscarp bank swing about 9 m (30 ft) forward of the main rampart. The counterscarp bank turns round the ditch-end and crosses the intervening space to end again on the front of the main rampart. The two flanking banks are about 18 m (60 ft) apart at the outer end, narrowing to about 14 m (45 ft) at the inner end.

Fig.52
Pl.29

Two other univallate sites, Beacon Hill (Hants) and Uffington Castle (Berks) also belong to this group. At Beacon Hill the looping of the substantial counterscarp bank on to the main rampart produces a passage between flanking banks which is further prolonged by the inturned ramparts. In addition there are symmetrical hornworks springing from the counterscarp bank on either side

233

Fig.133. Norton
Camp,
Shropshire,
eastern and
south-eastern
entrances.

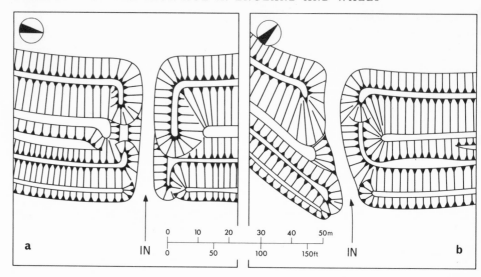

a   IN   b

0   10   20   30   40   50m
0   50   100   150ft

Fig.69
Pl.52

of the entrance. At Uffington Castle the counterscarp bank is large enough to be classed as a separate rampart. The looped principle is the only one involved. On the western side of the entrance the counterscarp bank is as big if not bigger than the main rampart, although because of the slope of the ground its crest is considerably lower. The flanking rampart is on the same scale. On the east side of the entrance the whole arrangement is on a somewhat smaller scale and the counterscarp bank dies out after about 30 m (100 ft). The entrance passage thus produced is about 37 m (120 ft) long.

Figs.35c,133

Apart from the sites just considered the looped rampart principle is best suited to multivallate systems, and is well illustrated by the two entrances at Norton Camp (Salop). The basic defence system consists of two banks and two ditches in either compact or separated form, the berm, where it exists, being from 3 to 9 m (10 to 30 ft) wide. Both entrances are on more or less level ground. On the eastern side of the western entrance the outer rampart turns inwards and comes to an end with its crest high on the slope of the inner rampart, but still slightly below the latter's crest. On the western side there is no corresponding loop, the inner rampart being out-turned, the outer club-ended. The entrance passage thus produced is in the region of 46 m (150 ft) long. At the eastern entrance the inner rampart on the eastern side turns outwards, its outer end looping on to the back of the outer rampart. The latter also turns outwards to flank the ditch-end. On the western side the inner and outer ramparts turn towards each other but do not meet at their existing level. The loop is completed by a flanking bank at a much lower level. The passage thus defined is again in the region of 46 m (150 ft) long.

The looped rampart principle is observable also in two other Shropshire sites (Rushbury Ditches and Bury Ditches), in Moel Arthur (Flint.), in Pen-y-Corddyn (Denb.), and in Dinas Dinorwig and Craig-y-Dinas (Caer.). At Bury Ditches the linking rampart on the north side of the eastern entrance is

Fig.86

234

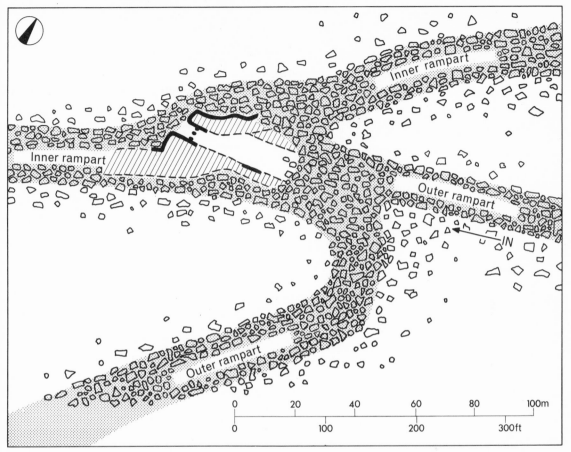

Fig.134. The Breiddin, Montgomeryshire, entrance.

prolonged by a very long inturn, so that the roadway is flanked for about 61 m (200 ft). At Moel Arthur likewise the looping is confined to one side of the entrance, in this case because most of the defence on the opposite side was provided by the natural slope. The same is true at the southern entrance of the promontory fort at Craig-y-Dinas where the narrow roadway between the ends of the inner and outer ramparts and the steep natural slope is flanked for about 40 m (130 ft) by a stone-built rampart. The looped ramparts at the north-western entrance at Pen-y-Corddyn are prolonged by the inturned ends of the inner rampart. The arrangement is symmetrical and the funnel-like passage produced is about 24 m (80 ft) long.

In southern England the looped principle can be seen at Danebury (Hants), Battlesbury (Wilts.), and Dudsbury (Dorset). At Danebury the final section of the entrance passage at the southern entrance is flanked by ramparts which cross the ditch-ends and project well beyond, particularly on the eastern side. It is only on this side that the arrangement can be described as looped. On the

Fig.128a

Fig.142

235

Fig.30c

Fig.35b

Fig.134

Fig.91
Pl.14

western side, although the rampart crosses the ditch-end it is not in fact looped on to anything since there is nothing immediately beyond the ditch at this point. At the eastern entrance at Battlesbury the arrangement is more or less symmetrical, the looped ramparts forming a passage about 34 m (110 ft) long. The entrance on the western side of Dudsbury also appears to involve the looped-rampart principle, although it is now difficult to be certain because of the construction of a modern drive-way and the vegetation on the south side.

The Breiddin (Montg.) and Old Oswestry (Salop) are both rather unusual examples of the looped-rampart principle. The main defences on the south-eastern side of The Breiddin consist of two stone-built ramparts on sloping ground about 61 m (200 ft) apart. Because of the slope the entrance roadway cuts obliquely across the defence system. The inner and outer ramparts are looped on to each other on either side of the roadway, the rampart on the southern side being some 152 m (500 ft) long. On the northern side of the entrance there are additional defences; bank, ditch, and counterscarp bank, and this bank is likewise looped on to the two stone ramparts, producing another flanking rampart in the region of 152 m (500 ft) long. However, the entrance passage thus produced is not of this length, since the flanking ramparts overlap rather than face each other directly. The overlap produces a passage about 91 m (300 ft) long.

At Old Oswestry (Salop) the looped-rampart principle is observable at both eastern and western entrances. At the eastern entrance the sloping roadway is flanked to the south by an earth bank which runs across the ends of the four banks on this side. The apparent height of the bank is increased by the hollowing of the roadway. There is no corresponding, flanking rampart on the northern side, the ditch-ends running right up to the road edge. At the western entrance the roadway is flanked on both sides by lengthwise ramparts, with their ditches on the inner side, i.e. away from the road. These ramparts appear to spring from the ends of the third bank, i.e. the counterscarp bank to the second ditch, and run forward past the compartments described in an earlier chapter (p. 169) to end abutting the outer band of defences. According to Varley's plan[1] the flanking rampart on the south is looped on to the sixth bank, and this was probably the original arrangement although there is now a break between the two.

OVERLAPPING RAMPARTS

In most of the entrances considered so far the entrance passage has cut through the defences more or less at right angles. In the entrances to be considered now the entrance passage, or part of it, is formed by the overlapping of two or more ramparts so that it is in line with the defences rather than at right angles to them.

There is a very simple example of this type of arrangement at the univallate fort of Slapton Castle (Devon). At the north-eastern end of the site the rampart-ends are offset from each other by about 18 m (60 ft) and overlap for a similar distance, thus forming an entrance passage of the type under discussion. Just

1. Varley, 'Hill-forts of the Welsh Marches', *Arch. J.* 105 (1948), 41–66.

inside the entrance there appears to have been a detached length of rampart forming another overlap which would have been squarely in the path of anyone passing through the main overlap and turning left towards the enclosed area. There is a generally similar arrangement at Burleigh Dolts in the same county and possibly at Stoke Canon, also in Devon, although there the evidence is less clear-cut. At another Devonshire site, Parracombe, the very simple entrance falls somewhere between the overlapping type and an incipient inturn/out-turn arrangement and this is true of a number of sites where the overlap is not very pronounced.

At Gaer Fach (Carm.), by contrast, the overlap is considerable, the stone ramparts running parallel to each other for over 61 m (200 ft). The site is a small univallate enclosure defended by a single stone rampart and stands as a lower camp or satellite to the much larger Gaer Fawr about 183 m (600 ft) away. The overlapping ramparts occupy most of the western side and give the appearance of a two-rampart multivallate system, but this is incidental to the main purpose of the arrangement which was to provide a long narrow entrance passage. An entrance passage of similar dimensions is provided on the eastern side of the same site by a different method, that of turning the rampart-ends outwards.

Fig.103

There are fairly simple overlapping arrangements at Hammer Wood (Sussex) and Winkelbury (Wilts.). At Hammer Wood the northern and southern sections of the inner bank and ditch overlap by about 15 m (50 ft), so that the entrance passage is between the ditch of the northern section and the bank of the southern. The gap through the outer bank and ditch is partially overlapped by an additional rampart running behind the northern section. At Winklebury the overlapping arrangement occurs in the middle rampart of the three-enclosure site and is generally similar to the inner entrance at Hammer Wood. The overlap is about 15 m (50 ft), and the passage thus produced between the ditch of the western portion and the bank of the eastern is about 15 m (50 ft) wide.

Fig.135

Moel y Gaer, Llanbedr (Denb.), Pen y Gaer, Llanbyther (Carm.), and Buckland Brewer (Devon) are slightly more complex than those just described. At the eastern entrance at Moel y Gaer three ramparts are involved, the middle and outer derived from ditches on their inner sides. These two ramparts overlap the inturned entrance through the inner rampart by about 30 m (100 ft). The whole entrance passage thus involves two right-angled bends, the middle section running in line with the defences, between the main rampart and the ditch on the inner side of the middle rampart. At Pen y Gaer only two ramparts are involved, each with an outer ditch. The inturned entrance through the inner rampart appears to have been overlapped for about 21 m (70 ft) by the outer bank and ditch, leaving an entrance passage some 5 m (16 ft) wide between the inner ditch and the outer bank. At Buckland Brewer the defences overlap for a distance of some 61 m (200 ft) at the north-western corner of the site.

Fig.21a
Pl.23

The overlapping entrances at the adjacent multivallate sites of Hod Hill and Hambledon Hill (Dorset) are strikingly similar. At Hod Hill the basic defence system consists of two banks and two ditches arranged in compact form. On the northern side of the north-eastern entrance the inner rampart turns

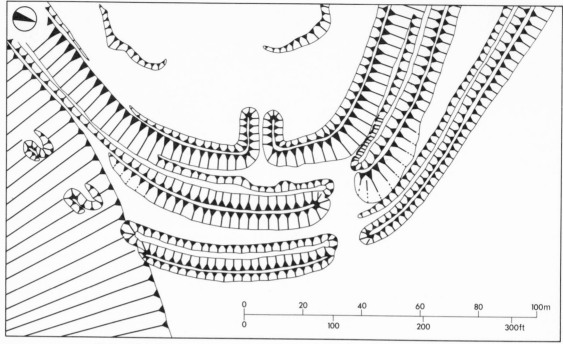

Fig.135. Moel y Gaer (Llanbedr), Denbighshire, eastern entrance.

Figs.30b,136
Pl.20

inwards while the outer bank and ditch and an accompanying counterscarp bank continue for a further 61 m (200 ft), overlapping the defences to the south of the inturned entrance. On this side the outer ditch stops short opposite the ends of the overlapping ramparts, so that the entrance passage, around 6 m (20 ft) wide, runs between the outer bank on the southern side, now without its ditch, and the continuation of the outer rampart from the northern side. At the south-western entrance at Hambledon Hill the pattern is the same, the only difference being that the overlap is in the opposite direction. The overlap, formed again by the outer bank, ditch, and counterscarp bank, is in the region of 76 m (250 ft) long and forms a roadway some 9 m (30 ft) wide. Such a striking degree of similarity at two adjacent sites suggests that a single mind was at work in the design and construction of these two entrances.

Fig.78
Pl.33

The eastern entrance at Oldbury (Wilts.) is closely akin to both Hod Hill and Hambledon Hill. The substantial inner rampart is deeply inturned, forming a passage about 30 m (100 ft) long. Direct approach to this is prevented by the overlap formed by the outer defences. Basically the eastern defences consist of a bank, ditch, and counterscarp bank, with a second bank and ditch immediately beyond. South of the entrance the outer defences begin to diverge from the inner until they assume a position about 8 m (25 ft) in front of them. This outer bank and ditch run squarely across the direct approach to the inturned inner rampart and come to an end about 30 m (100 ft) beyond. In the last 61 m (200 ft) or so they are accompanied by a counterscarp bank. On the northern

238

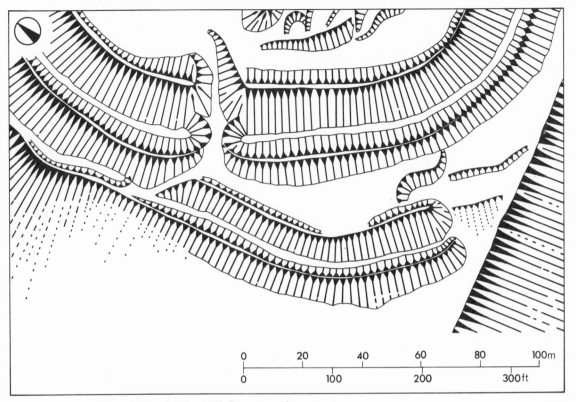

Fig.136. Hambledon Hill, Dorset, south-west entrance.

side the outer bank and ditch come to an end about 30 m (100 ft) from the opposing ends of the overlapping bank, ditch, and counterscarp bank. The cross-section just north of the inturned rampart is virtually identical to the cross-sections at Hod Hill and Hambledon Hill.

Fig.89

The eastern entrance at Castle Ditches, Tisbury (Wilts.), is a rather more elaborate version of the arrangements just described at Hod, Hambledon, and Oldbury. South of the entrance the defences now consist of three banks, three ditches, and a counterscarp bank in a compact arrangement. Cultivation may have destroyed a fourth ditch. There are three matching banks on the northern side, although the third ditch is replaced by the entrance roadway. The overlapping portion on the opposite side of the roadway also consists of a compact arrangement of two banks, two ditches, and a counterscarp bank. Because of a modern break it is now difficult to see exactly how these relate to the outer features south of the entrance of which they must be a continuation. In cross-section no less than six banks and four ditches are involved. Access to the interior involved passing between the ends of the overlapping defences and the natural slope, then turning sharply left into the passage formed by the overlap, and finally turning right to pass through the gaps in the three inner ramparts, a total distance of about 183 m (600 ft).

239

Fig.137.
Caesar's Camp,
Surrey,
entrance.

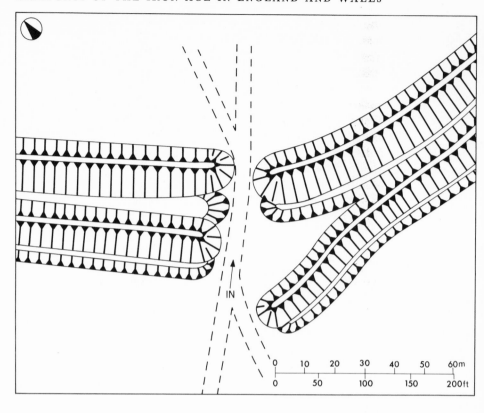

Fig.86

The western entrance at Bury Ditches (Salop) is another fairly elaborate example of the overlapping principle, the entrance passage running generally from south to north towards the interior of the fort. On the eastern side of the roadway the arrangement is fairly simple and consists of a bank, ditch, and counterscarp bank, the two latter features coming to an end about 21 m (70 ft) from the slightly out-turned end of the bank. This arrangement is overlapped on the west for about 91 m (300 ft) by a continuation of the complex system on the north-western side of the fort. Apart from the inner bank the remaining features, basically three banks and two ditches, sweep round in an arc, barring any direct approach to the inner entrance. The overlap formed by the inner of the three banks comes to an end after about 46 m (150 ft). Near its end it broadens out into a triangular platform about 14 m (45 ft) long and 4·5 m (15 ft) wide. It then continues at a lower level for about 24 m (80 ft) before fading out. The remaining features, two banks and two ditches, continue for a further 46 m (150 ft).

OUTWORKS

Under this heading are included those entrance features which, broadly speaking, project beyond the main line of the defences, excluding, of course, those

240

features dealt with already under out-turned ramparts and overlapping ramparts. The simplest outworks are single straight or curving hornworks springing from one side of the entrance and covering or restricting approach to it. Before dealing with these there are certain other arrangements, usually in multivallate forts, in which the same sort of effect is achieved.

Fig.137

At Caesar's Camp (Surrey) the defences on either side of the main entrance consist of a compact arrangement of two banks and two ditches. About 30 m (100 ft) from the entrance on the south-eastern side the outer bank and ditch swing away from the inner and curve forward, so that in effect they form a protective hornwork restricting the angle from which the inner part of the entrance can be approached. There is a very similar arrangement at Cadbury Camp, Tickenham (Som.). Again the outer bank and ditch, on the eastern side of the main entrance, swing forward in the manner of a hornwork, restricting the approach to the inner entrance. The same sort of thing happens at Embury Beacon (Devon), although there the defences are multivallate only on the hornwork side of the entrance.

Fig.25

At Linney Head (Pemb) it is the ditch on the eastern side of the entrance that curves across the direct approach and is accompanied by a counterscarp bank. The defences on this side are univallate, on the opposite, western, side multivallate. At Castle Hill (Hants) on the western side of the northern entrance the single rampart describes a quarter-circle covering the approach, but this is probably best classed as a curving out-turn rather than the type of hornwork just described. Finally, at the eastern end of Barbury (Wilts.) there is some form of protection for the entrance that may be of the type under discussion. On the northern side the counterscarp bank appears to swing away from the inner defences of two banks and two ditches compact, and acquire a ditch of its own. This third bank and ditch swing across 18 m (60 ft) in front of the direct approach to the eastern entrance and appear to curve round to end close to the second ditch to the south of the entrance, thus again acting as a protective hornwork.

Fig.36

As stated earlier the simplest type of outwork is the single hornwork. At Craigadwy Wynt (Denb.) this takes the form of a straight finger-like projection, about 21 m (70 ft) long, springing more or less at right angles from the rampart on the western side of the north entrance. The effect is to cut down the angle from which the entrance can be approached from 180° to about 90°. About 8 m (25 ft) to the west of one of the entrances at Conway Mountain there is a similar projection, in this case at an angle of about 45° to the rampart. The projection at the south-eastern entrance at Wall Hills, Thornbury (Here.), has been mentioned already as an out-turned rampart. It could equally well be classed as a single hornwork. Its effect is exactly the same, to cut down the angle of approach from 180° to about 90°. The hornwork at the eastern entrance of

Fig.138

Pen-y-cloddiau (Flint.) may have been designed as much to prevent cattle from straying into the gully immediately to the south as to prevent any hostile approach from this direction.

The straight finger-like hornworks described can be said, broadly speaking, to flank the direct approach on one side. Curving, single hornworks, on the

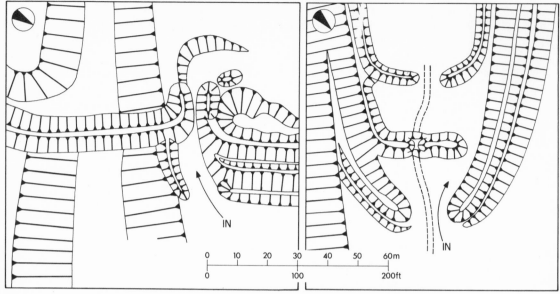

Fig.138. Pen-y-cloddiau, Flintshire, eastern entrance.

Fig.139. Caer Euni, Merionethshire, north-eastern entrance.

other hand, tend to cut across the direct approach. A very striking example of such a hornwork exists on the south-eastern side of the Roveries (Salop). From the western side of the entrance a massive hornwork swings round in a quarter-circle, completely inhibiting any direct approach to the inner part of the entrance. At Mortimer West End (Hants) the outwork is now detached from the main defences but may well have been originally of the curving hornwork type. A continuation of the present line would produce a hornwork some 46 m (150 ft) long, starting about 27 m (90 ft) north of the entrance gap and ending about 18 m (60 ft) in front of it. At Caer Drewyn (Mer.) the outwork at the eastern entrance may have been adapted at a later date for some other purpose, but originally there seems to have been a long hornwork starting about 61 m (200 ft) south of the entrance. This swings forward to end about 61 m (200 ft) in front of the entrance close to the edge of a rock scarp, the gap thus formed presumably forming the outer entrance. At Caer Euni in the same county the north-eastern entrance has both single and twin hornworks, the latter embracing the former.

All the hornworks considered so far have been fairly simple structures, involving a single bank, with or without a ditch, and of fairly modest dimensions. There are, in addition, one or two more complex entrances which are still basically of the hornwork type. In spite of its complicated surface remains the western entrance at Maiden Castle (Dorset) can be seen to consist of rather more elaborate versions of two of the types of hornwork considered so far. On the southern side of the double portals all the defences beyond the inner bank and ditch, consisting of three further banks and two ditches, form an enormous multivallate hornwork which crosses in front of the southern portal and stops short at the northern portal. To the north of the latter is a hornwork of the type

Fig.139

Fig.140
Pl.41

242

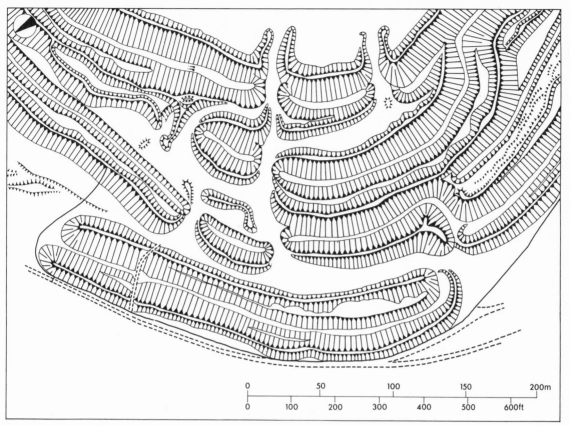

Fig.140. Maiden Castle, Dorset, western entrance.

described earlier at Caesar's Camp (Surrey), formed by the outer defences swinging away from the inner. Virtually the only other entrance feature is a detached length of bank, ditch, and counterscarp bank, nearly 305 m (1,000 ft) long which forms an overlapping arrangement with the two hornworks. The eastern entrance involves two such detached lengths of bank, ditch, and counterscarp and two hornworks formed by the divergence of inner and outer defences.

Fig.31
Pl.25

The single hornwork at the western end of Caer Caradoc, Clun (Salop), is less complex than the one in the corresponding position at Maiden Castle, but it still occupies most of the western end of the site. The main defences ·consist basically of two banks and two ditches. About 91 m (300 ft) south of the entrance an extra bank and ditch spring from the main defences and gradually diverge from them, eventually crossing the line of the direct approach to the entrance. Immediately opposite the end of the hornwork on the northern side of the entrance the outer bank is increased in height for about 18 m (60 ft), as if to form a sort of bastion at this point. At the eastern end of the site the outer defences on the northern side of the entrance form a sort of hornwork, even though the whole arrangement is still of the compact type.

243

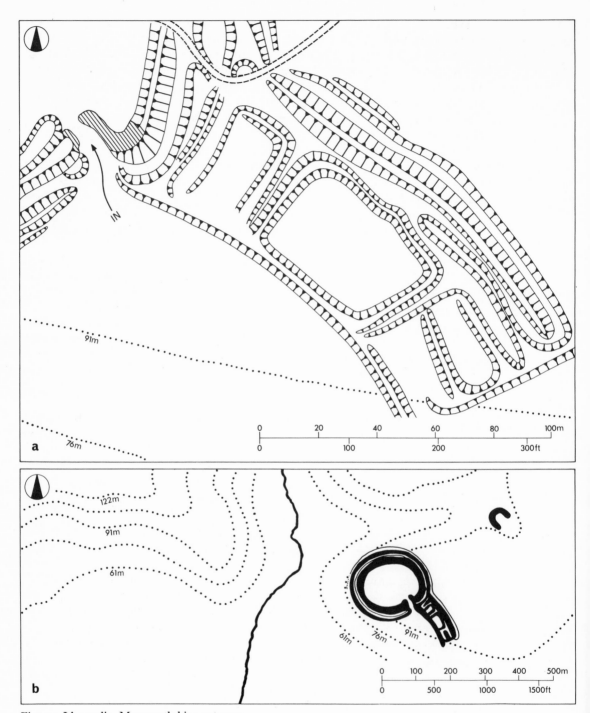

Fig.141. Llanmelin, Monmouthshire, entrance.

Fig.141

Whatever else they do the series of compartments associated with the entrance at Llanmelin also form an elaborate single hornwork. The whole feature springs from the main defences to the north of the entrance and runs off in a south-easterly direction, ending just short of the head of the natural slope. The effect is to block completely any direct approach to the entrance, the only alternative being the route around the end of the compartments, flanked on one side by the slope of the promontory on which the site stands. There is also a fairly elaborate hornwork at Ivington Camp (Here.).

Fig.50

Fig.52
Pl.29

Double or twin hornworks at Caer Euni (Mer.) have been mentioned already. Another site with the same features, also mentioned earlier under looped ramparts, is Beacon Hill (Hants). The hornworks, each consisting of a bank and ditch, spring from the counterscarp bank about 46 m (150 ft) on either side of the entrance. They curve forward and end about 9 m (30 ft) in front of the main defences and about 18 m (60 ft) from each other. The gap thus formed is more or less in front of the main entrance between the looped ramparts. There is a not dissimilar arrangement at Craig Gwytheyrn (Carm.), although there are no ditches involved. The inner part of the entrance appears to consist of looped inner and outer ramparts. Curving hornworks spring from the outer rampart about 61 m (200 ft) on either side of the entrance passage. In this case the gap between the ends of the hornworks is offset from the inner entrance by about 21 m (70 ft). A twin-hornwork effect is achieved at Maesbury (Som.) by the divergence of the inner and outer defences of a multivallate arrangement and a similar effect is achieved at Castle Dore (Corn.) and other south-western sites considered already under multiple enclosures.

Fig.142

The complex eastern entrance at Danebury (Hants) is also basically of the twin-hornwork type, although one side, the south, is complicated by earlier features. On the northern side a massive bank, ditch, and counterscarp bank spring from the counterscarp bank to the main ditch, about 30 m (100 ft) north of the entrance passage, and curve round to end in line with it. This embraces what is, in effect, an inner hornwork formed by an out-turned rampart. The southern hornwork also consists basically of a bank, ditch, and counterscarp bank, although it is L-shaped rather than curving, the southern part of it apparently consisting of the parallel inturns of an earlier disused entrance. The blocked western entrance may also at some stage of its history have involved twin curving hornworks.

Fig.84
Pl.43

The remaining outworks to be described are probably best dealt with separately since they do not, for the most part, fall into easily definable groups. Perhaps the only sites which can be included under one heading are those which have rectangular outworks. One of the best examples, Badbury Rings (Dorset), has been mentioned already in the section dealing with simple gap entrances in widely spaced defences. About 76 m (250 ft) north of the inner entrance the second bank and ditch turns outwards at right angles and then makes a second right-angled turn to run parallel to, and about 30 m (100 ft) in front of, the inner bank and ditch for a distance of about 152 m (500 ft). The existing gap opposite the inner entrance is modern. The original entrance through the second bank and ditch was at the south-west corner of the outwork where it

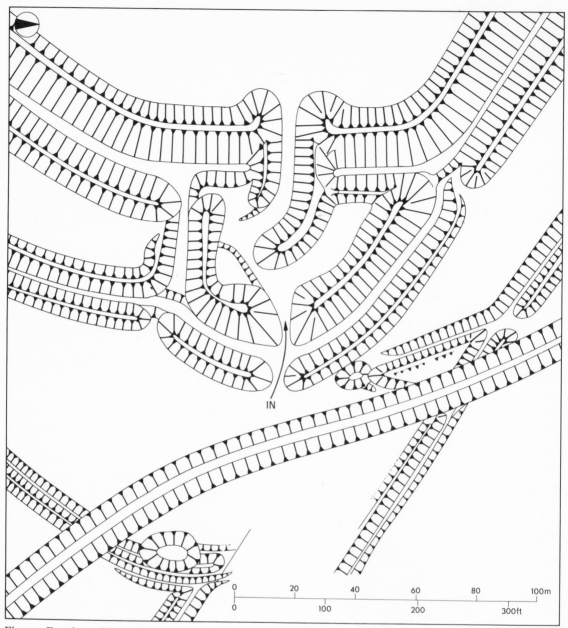

IN

| 0 | | 20 | | 40 | | 60 | | 80 | | 100m |

| 0 | | 100 | | 200 | | 300ft |

Fig. 142. Danebury, Hampshire, eastern entrance.

turns at rig⟨h⟩t angles again to resume its original line. The oblique approach is continued b⟨y⟩ the entrance through the third bank and ditch which is presumed to be a later addition. Whatever else it was intended to achieve, the outwork forms a rectangular enclosure some 152 m (500 ft) long and 30 m (100 ft) wide, very small in relation to its parent enclosure but very similar in size to the subsidiary enclosures at many of the south-western, multiple-enclosure sites.

Pl.38

The entrances at Bratton Castle and Sidbury (Wilts.) appear to be of the same general type, although at Bratton the outwork is considerably disturbed and it is difficult to be certain of the exact arrangement. On the eastern side the outer bank and ditch turn outwards at right angles, and there is a gap at the corner, as at Badbury, which is probably original. Directly in front of the inner entrance there is a gap and considerable disturbance in the outwork, but it is likely that originally the bank and ditch were continuous, again following the pattern of Badbury. The enclosure thus formed is about 107 m (350 ft) long and

Pl.5

up to 30 m (100 ft) wide. At Sidbury the corresponding enclosure is about 91 m (300 ft) long and between 15 and 23 m (50 and 75 ft) wide, and the over-all arrangement is more or less the same, with the outer entrance again situated in one corner of the outwork.

Pl.26

The outwork covering the eastern entrance at Yarnbury (Wilts.), unlike those just considered, is roughly semicircular in plan. Because of the disturbance at the northern end it is difficult to decide whether it is, in fact, an outwork of the type being considered here or simply an elaborate hornwork. Certainly the inner part of the work would appear to have existed originally as a simple hornwork, springing from the northern side of the entrance and curving round in a quarter-circle to bar any direct approach. This hornwork is incorporated in the later work which completely embraces it. This may likewise have been linked to the main defences on the north side, leaving the only access at the southern end. Between them the earlier and later works define a D-shaped enclosure about 91 m (300 ft) long and up to 37 m (120 ft) wide, comparable in size with the rectangular enclosures. Prior to modern ploughing there was a simple semicircular work covering the approach to the entrance on the eastern side of Chiselbury (Wilts.). Again, it is difficult to decide whether this was a hornwork anchored on one side of the entrance or something a little more elaborate. The area enclosed is about 49 m (160 ft) long and 21 m (70 ft) wide.

Fig.143

A further variation in shape is provided by Blackbury Castle (Devon) where the elaborate outwork is triangular in shape. It stands at the southern entrance of a Medium univallate site. About 52 m (170 ft) from the entrance on either side a bank and ditch spring from the main ditch at an angle of about 45°. They converge to form the outer part of the entrance about 61 m (200 ft) in front of the main defences. At this point the ditches turn inwards to run parallel towards the inner part of the entrance and the bank is placed on the opposite side, so that the entrance passage is between the two banks with the ditches on the outside. These outworks define two triangular enclosures about 40 × 37 m (130 × 120 ft). Access is from the inner end of the entrance passage between the ends of the parallel banks and ditches and the out-turned ends of the main rampart.

Fig. 143.
Blackbury
Castle, Devon,
southern
entrance.

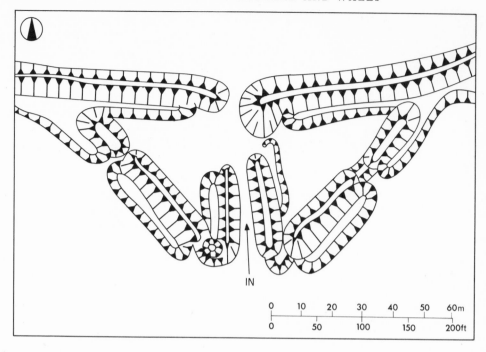

IN

| 0 | 10 | 20 | 30 | 40 | 50 | 60m |
| 0 | | 50 | | 100 | | 150 | 200ft |

Fig. 81

At Wapley Camp (Here.) only one side of the outwork is triangular, and this side is formed by the divergence of the outer bank and ditch from the remaining defences. About 61 m (200 ft) to the west of the entrance passage the outer third bank and ditch swing away from the remaining defences and end opposite the angle of the eastern inturn, leaving a triangular space inside. On the opposite side of the entrance the second ditch turns outwards at right angles and runs out for about 23 m (75 ft), but this, strictly speaking, does not form an outwork since it is completely embraced by the third outer line of defence that is set some 20 m (65 ft) in front of the remaining defences.

CHAPTER VIII

The typology of Iron Age forts

In the past Iron Age forts have been grouped in a number of different ways: on the basis of size (Large, Medium, or Small), situation (promontory, contour, etc.), defences (univallate, multivallate), or arrangement (single and multiple enclosures). Since these aspects are not mutually exclusive a very large number of so-called types would result if they were accepted as they stand. Such a typology would, however, be virtually meaningless. What is required is a more critical examination of the aspects so that a more objective typology can be established. Of the four aspects mentioned above that of arrangement seems the most fundamental. The size and defence aspects are probably best considered under the separate headings of single-enclosure and multiple-enclosure sites since they have rather different meanings in each case. Situation seems the least fundamental of the four aspects, for while certain situations, e.g. hill-slope forts, may be typologically significant, it seems unlikely that the differences between contour, semi-contour and promontory situations reflect, for the most part, anything other than differences in topography.

The present typological division of Iron Age forts is based on defences, univallate on the one hand, multivallate on the other, the latter embracing both compact multivallate forts and multiple-enclosure sites. Leaving the latter to one side for the moment, there remains a large number of single-enclosure sites, about 1,150, or 84 per cent of the total, divided into two groups because of differences in their defences. It is feasible to suggest, however, that these differences do not imply any difference in function, and that the whole range of univallate and multivallate defences represent variations in strength rather than anything more fundamental. A difference in function seems more likely to be implied by an alternative arrangement, for example two or more enclosures. It is suggested, therefore, that the first typological distinction to be made is between single-enclosure forts on the one hand and multiple-enclosure forts on the other. The single-enclosure sites can be further examined on the basis of size.

The three groups distinguished by the Ordnance Survey on the basis of size have no particular archaeological significance; they simply provide a convenient framework of reference to one aspect of Iron Age forts. It is quite clear, however, considering the full range of Iron Age forts, that size is in some measure significant. What needs to be examined here is the pattern of sizes within the group as a whole to see if, in fact, any distinguishable groups exist.

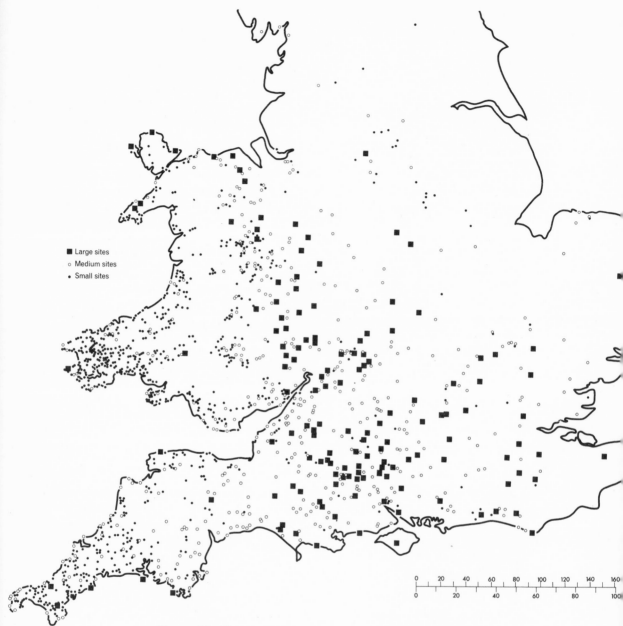

Fig. 144. Distribution of Large, Medium, and Small forts.

Large sites
Medium sites
Small sites

From the figures given in Chapter IV (pp. 93–97) it is quite clear that Iron Age forts enclosing more than 12 ha (30 acres) form only a very small group, about 3 per cent of the total, and can be left to one side for the moment. Most Large sites are between 6 and 12 ha (15 and 30 acres) and it seems very likely that, as far as size is concerned, they form a single group. Within the group no one fort is more than twice as large as any other and it would be dangerous to base any typology on such a relatively small difference. It would appear to be equally dangerous to try to distinguish between these sites and the larger sites of 4–6 ha (10–15 acres) in the Medium group. The question which must inevitably arise is at what point in the Medium range, if at all, does a difference in size become significant. The 4–12-ha (10–30-acre) group could probably be extended to include many more, possibly most, of the sites in the Medium range. This would suggest the existence, based on size, of a single group of Iron Age forts with internal areas from about 2 ha (5 acres) upwards, the vast majority being in the 2–12-ha (5–30-acre) size range.

Fig.144

Other types of evidence bearing on this point involve questions of distribution, layout, and defences. Distributionally the Large and Small forts virtually exclude each other. While the Medium forts occur with both groups most of them are, in fact, in or immediately adjacent to, the Large fort areas. It may, therefore, be suggested that because they occupy the same areas they are the same type of fort. These Medium sites are mostly of the single-enclosure type. By contrast, those which do occur in western regions are frequently of the multiple-enclosure type, linking them with the Small sites of the same type on grounds of layout. With regard to defences, the percentages of multivallate sites in the Large and Medium categories, 44 and 41 per cent, suggest that the two groups enjoyed the same experience with regard to multivallation, again, because they are the same type of site. The figure for Small sites, 28 per cent, indicates a different experience and suggests a separate group from the larger sites. All three types of evidence thus combine to suggest that the Large sites and most of the Medium sites form a single size-group, which can now be termed 'Standard', embracing all single-enclosure sites from the largest down to those of about 2 ha (5 acres). It seems unlikely that it will ever be possible to draw a precise line between Small and Standard sites on the basis of size alone. If they represent two separate traditions then there could well be some overlap in size, the Small sites at the upper end of the range, possibly now up to 2 ha (5 acres), being similar in size to the smaller Standard sites.

SINGLE-ENCLOSURE SITES

Standard single-enclosure sites have in the past been divided into univallate and multivallate types. Both, however, consist of single-enclosures so that it is feasible to suggest that they have a similar function. This does not necessarily preclude a cultural or chronological division based on defences. The main point to be considered is the significance, or otherwise, of multivallation. Is it, in fact, the new and clearcut defence technique so often suggested, or is it something less dramatic? Is there, in fact, such a clear division as the two categories, now so

Fig.145.
Theoretical
development of
single bank-and-
ditch to
multivallate form.

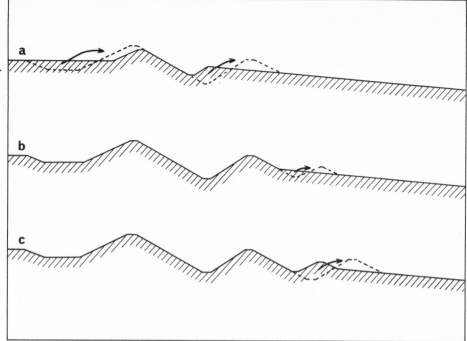

widely accepted, appear to suggest? Could it be that multivallation is no more than the result of strengthening defences, defences which can equally well be strengthened in other, less obvious ways, which in the present system do not lead to their inclusion in the multivallate category? One way of dealing with this question is to consider the processes by which multivallate defences could have evolved from univallate forms.

Fig.145a

Fig.145b

Fig.145c

The commonest univallate system is a single bank-and-ditch arrangement, sometimes with a small counterscarp bank. In any strengthening process the bank can be augmented from an inner quarry ditch and/or the ditch can be made wider and deeper. Since the inner edge of the latter is already occupied by the rampart the only way to throw the material is outwards. If the enlargement of the ditch is on a big scale then a large counterscarp bank will result, and this may be the explanation of the sites mentioned in Chapter V (pp. 135–7) which had outer banks sufficiently large to raise questions of classification, univallate or multivallate. In such banks (nearly always of simple dump construction), erosion will quickly smooth out the angle between the external ground surface and the sloping front, providing a ramp up which the momentum of an attacker will easily carry him. Something is needed to break up this momentum and the answer is another ditch, even if only a small one, with the material thrown inwards on to the associated bank or outwards to form a third, counterscarp, bank. Thus, theoretically at least, could be formed the commonest type of multivallate system, with two ditches and two, or three associated banks. Looked at in this way multivallation is the inevitable result of strengthening an existing univallate fort. It need not, on this basis, be regarded as a new and distinctive technique.

The structural sequence at Hod Hill provides a good example of this sort of development.[1] Richmond's stages I and IIA are straightforward univallate arrangements. In Stage IIB there is a considerable enlargement of the ditch, with the excavated material thrown outwards to form a substantial counter scarp bank. This would appear to be the final stage reached by a number of sites mentioned in Chapter V (pp. 135–7). In Stage III a ditch, apparently unfinished, is added immediately outside the latter. The end product, a compact two-ditch system is undoubtedly multivallate, but it is not easy to see at precisely which stage it became so. At no stage does it look as if a new defence technique has been introduced. In essence, it looks like the progressive strengthening of an original bank-and-ditch system as discussed above. This leads, almost incidentally, to a multivallate arrangement. This does not, of course, preclude the possibility of other sites being changed to the multivallate form in one step. This happens, for example, at Poundbury (Dorset) where in the second stage the original bank and ditch are reconstructed and a second bank and ditch are added outside to form a compact two-ditch system.[2]

One further point can be made on this topic. A V-shaped ditch would very quickly silt up and would need regular cleaning out to remain effective. This process alone could produce some sort of counterscarp bank, and if repeated often enough quite a substantial feature would result. This could then be seen as an additional defence feature, and once this was recognized the provision of a ditch in order to render its outer slope more effective could easily follow.

If Standard single-enclosure forts are not to be divided solely on the univallate/multivallate principle then other types of subdivision must be sought. That there are very noticeable variations within the group is apparent from even a cursory examination. There is a very considerable difference between a site such as Maiden Castle (Dorset) with its enormous multiple ramparts, complex entrances and large enclosed area, and a 3- or 4-ha (9- or 10-acre) single-rampart fort with a simple gap entrance; and between both of these and the very large sites mentioned in Chapter IV (pp. 93–97) with interiors of 40 ha (100 acres) or more. This suggests that at least three groups can be distinguished and these will be examined in turn, beginning with the largest group.

Illustrations of Type I: Figs.21b, 21c,22,23a,b, 24c,28,30d,34b, 34c,38a,39b,39d, 47,48,49a,52, 63,64,65,66,70

This group embraces the bulk of the sites distinguished as univallate in the old Large and Medium categories, and contains about 300 sites, ranging in size, for the most part, from about 2 ha (5 acres) up to about 12 ha (30 acres). They can all be included under the heading of Type I forts. They are defended by either a bank alone, a bank and ditch, or a bank, ditch, and small counterscarp bank. The ditched systems have C/D verts. of 4·5 m (15 ft) or less and the banks without ditches are of corresponding size, so that in neither case can defences be described as particularly strong. Entrances are usually simple gaps, incipient inturns or, in more limited areas, larger inturns. Such sites appear to correspond to the first phase, as revealed by excavation, of more complex, multivallate,

1. Richmond, *Hod Hill*, vol. ii (1968), 9–14 and fig. 66.
2. Richardson, 'Excavations at Poundbury, Dorchester, Dorset, 1939', *Antiq. J.* 20 (1940), 429–48.

sites, and it may be assumed that many of them represent a single structural phase. In the areas in which they occur they are the commonest type of Iron Age fort, outnumbering Types II, III, and IV combined.

Illustrations of Type II: Figs.26b, 27,35b,35c,39a, 39c,42,45,53, 54,60,72,73,77, 80,88
As far as is known at present all multivallate sites in Wessex, the South-east, the Cotswolds, and the Marches started as what have now been described as Type I sites. Such multivallate sites form the bulk of those included under the heading of Type II. Also included in this group are univallate sites with large counterscarp banks, as described in Chapter V, pp. 135–7, and those univallate sites in which the rampart is of large dimensions. About 150 sites are involved, the bulk of them of straightforward multivallate type. All three types are included under one heading since they are deemed to represent the strengthening, in various ways and to differing degrees, of original Type I sites.

Not included in Type II are certain multivallate sites, the outstanding example of which is Maiden Castle (Dorset). These are sites with very strong multivallate defences, complex entrances and, in many cases, interiors larger than those in the bulk of Type II sites. Again, as far as is known at present, they appear to have started life as Type I sites, but they also appear to have gone through the Type II stage to become something rather special in the way of Iron Age forts which can be included under the heading of Type III. Since the numbers involved are small, between 30 and 40 sites, each case for inclusion could, if required, be argued on its merits, but the list would certainly need to
Figs.43c,21a,30b, 84,34a,89,30c,78, 85,30a,43e,62
include the following: Maiden Castle, Hod Hill, Hambledon Hill, Badbury Rings, and Eggardon (Dorset); Yarnbury, Castle Ditches, Battlesbury, Bratton Castle, Oldbury, Sidbury, and possibly Ebsbury and Hanging Langford Camp (Wilts); Danebury (Hants), Cadbury Castle (Som.), and Hembury (Devon). In the Cotswolds area Dolebury (Som.), Kimsbury (Glos.) and one or two other sites may qualify. Most of the remaining Type III sites are in the Welsh Marches, where more cases may need to be argued separately. Sites are, on the whole, smaller than in Wessex although in many cases defence systems and entrances are no less complex. However, the comparison with Wessex is of less importance than the validity of the distinction between Types I, II, and III within the Marcher zone. Type III in the Marches is deemed to represent the same postulated process as Type III in Wessex, even if some of the sites and features involved are on a smaller scale. Among the sites which would
Illustrations of Type III in the Marches: Figs.91, 31,86,50,81,49b
appear to qualify for inclusion are Old Oswestry, Caer Caradoc, Clun, Bury Ditches and Burrow Camp (Salop), The Breiddin and Ffridd Faldwyn (Montg.), Wapley Camp and Ivington (Here.), and Burfa Camp (Rad.). The cases for other sites could be argued but at this stage the precise limits of the group seem less important than the recognition of its existence. Type III sites would appear to be very important Iron Age forts, developed beyond the Type II stage, with larger and more complex defences and, in most cases, with elaborate entrances.

Types I, II, and III account for the majority of the Standard single-enclosure forts. There remains one type of single-enclosure site which is distinguishable from the others by reason of its very large size, which may indicate some differ-
Illustrations of Type IV: Figs.41, 43a,b,58
ence in function. These very large sites (Type IV) include the 7 sites of over 40 ha (100 acres) mentioned in Chapter IV (pp. 93–97) and some, possibly all,

of the sites between 20 and 40 ha (50 and 100 acres). For the most part neither defences, entrances, nor siting are particularly striking so that size is the dominant aspect. About 20 sites are involved. It is feasible to suggest that because of their size such sites enjoyed a different function from Types I, II, and III, or at least a special version thereof.

All four types are found in the same areas, basically Wessex, Cotswolds, and the Marches. Types II and III would appear to represent the results of strengthening and developing certain Type I forts. Type IV would appear to be an enlarged, special, version of Type I and could well be broadly contemporary with it and its postulated development as represented by Types II and III. Certainly Type IV includes both simple bank-and-ditch defences and more complex, multivallate defences which can be presumed to have been originally simple.

Small, as opposed to Standard, single-enclosure sites with simple defences need to be considered next. These number about 500, each consisting at most of a bank, ditch, and counterscarp bank, and enclosing an area of less than 2 ha (5 acres), and in many cases considerably less. They can all be included

Fig.43f under the heading of Type V. One of the most noticeable characteristics of the group is the large number of sites which are circular in plan. Non-circular sites are, in many cases, of promontory or semi-contour type where the plan is dictated by the situation rather than by anything else. Circular sites are found in three types of situation, hill top, hill slope, and level ground. In a few cases the defences of hill-top sites follow the contours, but in most cases, because of the small size of the sites, the hill is very much larger than the enclosure, so that the situation is of the plateau type, with more or less level ground immediately outside the defences. This means that the shape of the enclosure is not dictated by the situation. The same is, of course, true of the hill-slope and the low-lying sites. In other words, the bulk of the Small circular sites are circular because their builders chose to make them so. Such a shape is in the long tradition of circular structures in prehistoric Britain: henges, barrows, huts, cemetery enclosures, etc., and it would, indeed, be surprising to find any other shape in circumstances where an arbitrary choice was involved. There would appear, then, to be no significant difference between circular sites and those other Small sites which, because of their situation, are of different and varying shapes.

Both circular and non-circular sites have what have been described as simple defences. In the same areas, however, are small numbers of sites, both circular and otherwise, with multivallate defences. These constitute Type VI, and account for about 70 or 80 sites. Perhaps the most striking aspect of many of these forts is that the area enclosed is sometimes very much less than the area

Fig.82 occupied by the defences. At Llandewi Gaer (Pemb), for example, an area only 61 m (200 ft) square is defended on the south and east by natural slopes and on the north and west by three substantial banks with ditches, with an over-all area nearly three times greater than that of the enclosure. At Bulliber Camp (Pemb) a small oval area is defended, where best preserved, by no less than four banks and ditches, the defences again being very much larger in area

Fig.73 than the area enclosed. Castell Pyr (Carm.) has an internal area of about 40 ares

255

(1 acre) with a defence system of two banks and two ditches occupying another 60 ares (1½ acres), and a similar pattern is observable in other Type VI sites such as Nant y Castell (Caer.) and Callow Hill and Robury Ring (Salop).

Illustrations of Type VII: Figs.5, 24b,25,27,90

One other type which needs to be considered is the coastal promontory fort, which is confined almost exclusively to those western areas where suitable cliff sites are available. Although it was suggested earlier that siting was not, in most cases, typologically significant, such sites may be exceptions. They may represent a deliberate choice of coastal situation for reasons of trade or economy. Many such sites are multivallate and may be connected with inland multivallate sites (Type VI). On the other hand, the promontory forts, both univallate and multivallate, may be simply coastal versions of the Small inland sites although it has to be admitted that they contain a markedly higher proportion of multivallate defences. It is also noticeable that they tend to be larger, having a higher proportion of sites formerly classed as Medium. This, however, may be of less significance since size in a promontory fort is often dictated by topography rather than anything else. Coastal promontory forts can be grouped under the heading of Type VII and account for between 70 and 80 sites.

MULTIPLE-ENCLOSURE SITES

Types I–VII embrace sites consisting of a single enclosure. The remaining sites to be dealt with here each consist of two or more enclosures. In Chapter VI all such sites, about 220 in number, were allocated to one or other of four groups according to the way in which the enclosures were arranged. In fact, some of the differences between the groups seem, on examination, to be comparatively slight. The difference between an annexe and a cross-bank enclosure, for example, would appear to be largely one of situation, the natural defences on two opposite sides of the latter making artificial defences unnecessary. In both cases an outer enclosure has to be traversed in order to reach the entrance of an inner one. The difference between concentric enclosures, apparently one of the most clear-cut types, and cross-bank enclosures such as Round Wood (Corn.) again would appear to be a difference of situation. In each case the inner enclosure is completely embraced by the outer. It is suggested, therefore, that differences between concentric, annexe, and cross-bank enclosures are, for the most part, differences of situation rather than anything more fundamental.

In looking at multiple-enclosure sites as a whole it is possible to distinguish three different types, based on the relative sizes of the enclosures involved. The largest group consists of those sites with enclosures between which there is no great disparity in size. The majority of such sites, about 90 in number, have in the past been classed as Small (i.e. based on the size of the innermost enclosure), so it follows that the additional enclosures are broadly within the same size range. Such sites can be included under the heading of Type VIII. In the second, much smaller group, probably embracing not more than 12 sites, the innermost enclosure, or nucleus, is again Small, but in this case it stands within a very much larger enclosure (Type IX). The third group, about 80 sites, embraces those with inner enclosures of Standard dimensions, i.e. from about

2 ha (5 acres) upwards, with any kind of additional enclosure (Type X). Each of these can be considered in more detail.

In discussing Type V (Small single-enclosure sites) it was noted that many of them were circular in plan. The same is true of the inner enclosures of many of the Type VIII multiple-enclosure sites. This is not to suggest that the outer enclosures represent a second structural phase, for at least some of the multiple-enclosure sites are known to have been built as such from the start, but the relationship is worth noting. Whatever their shape the inner enclosures of Type VIII sites range in size up to about 152 m (500 ft) in diameter, about 1·80 ha (4½ acres). Denbury (Devon) and Helsbury (Corn.) are both of this approximate size, with outer enclosures of about 1·2 ha (3 acres) and 60 ares (1½ acres) respectively. In both cases the *total* area involved is within the Standard rather than the Small range, so that a term such as Type VIII is preferable to 'Small multiple-enclosure site', in which the size indicated relates only to the inner enclosure. In concentric sites such as Tregeare Rounds or Killibury (Corn.) the nuclei embrace about 40 ares (1 acre) while the outer enclosures take in a further 1·2 ha (3 acres). In both cases there is a third enclosure of the annexe type, at Tregeare Rounds of about 60 ares (1½ acres), at Killibury of about 20 ares (½ acre). Warbstow Bury (Corn.), another concentric site, is on a bigger scale with an inner enclosure of about 1·2 ha (3 acres) and an outer of about 2 ha (5 acres). The combined acreage brings Warbstow Bury well within the Standard size range, and this is true also of 1 or 2 other sites which, however, must still be regarded as Type VIII because of the dimensions of the individual enclosures. Burley Wood (Devon), for example, has an oval inner enclosure of about 1·2 ha (3 acres) and five associated enclosures varying in size from about 20 ares to 1·4 ha (½ to 3½ acres). Clovelly Dykes and Milber Down (Devon) are of the same general type (pp. 177–8). It is possible that these are to be regarded as a special variant of Type VIII, although only a few sites are involved anyway, or as in some way intermediate between Types VIII and IX.

At the moment Type IX sites are classed as Small because of the size of their inner enclosures. Largin Castle (Corn.), however, has an external enclosure of some 34 ha (85 acres), defined by natural slopes on the north, west, and east and by a bank and ditch on the south. Thus, in spite of its classification, it is comparable in over-all size with the largest sites in Wessex and related areas. Hall Rings in the same county stands in a similar situation and is likewise classed as Small, although its outer bank and ditch and the natural slopes define an area of some 14 ha (35 acres), and Pencarrow Rings must originally have been in the region of 34 ha (85 acres), similar to Largin Castle. The inner enclosures of these sites could, by themselves, be included in Type V or Type VIII. They differ only in standing within very large outer enclosures. The latter, at least as far as size is concerned, would appear to have closer links with Wessex, in a number of cases with some of the very largest Type IV sites there. In the western regions in which they occur, however, they make a noticeable addition to the small number of sites, 7 only in the South-west, which embrace more than 6 ha (15 acres).

Type X multiple-enclosure sites are much more varied in their arrangement

Fig.101

Figs.37,93

Fig.92

Fig.113

Fig.94

Fig.102

Illustrations of
Type X: Figs.104,
105,114,115

than Types VIII or IX. Their inner enclosures have all the characteristics of Standard single-enclosure sites: the same size-range, from about 2 ha (5 acres) upwards, the same defences, univallate/multivallate, the same entrances and the same situations. It seems feasible to suggest, therefore, that they were originally of the single-enclosure type and advanced only later to the multiple-enclosure form.[3] In this they differ from the Type VIII multiple-enclosure sites, many of which, and possibly all, were built in this style from the beginning. The bulk of the Type X multiple-enclosure sites are of the annexe or crossbank type, and were described in Chapter VI (pp. 187–212). About 80 sites are involved in the group.

The last type of multiple-enclosure site to be considered differs from those described so far in that its enclosures are physically quite separate.[4] It consists of a parent enclosure and one or more smaller or satellite sites (pp. 212–16). The sites forming these groups are at present treated as independent units but they are here deemed to form a single site, of the multiple-enclosure type, and may

Illustrations of
Type XI: Figs.
119,120,121

all be included under the heading of Type XI. About 20 such sites are known, each consisting of two, or more rarely three, separate enclosures, i.e., about 40 sites under the present classification. Because they have no physical link the problem of the relationship between the enclosures is even more difficult than that which arises with the more conventional multiple-enclosure site. It could well be argued that the association is entirely fortuitous but in the writer's view the number of cases known makes it feasible to suggest that there is some sort of association which calls for an explanation. The explanation need not necessarily be the same as for other multiple-enclosure sites and, in chronological terms, may fall partly, or even entirely, outside the Iron Age; but an explanation needs to be sought and the search must start from within the Iron Age. Until a convincing alternative case is made out such sites will be treated here as a form of multiple-enclosure site under the heading of Type XI.

The eleven types of Iron Age fort classified in this chapter can be grouped again into what may be termed the 'Wessex tradition' and the 'Western tradition' (see p. 264). The characteristics of the groups are summarized as follows:

TYPE I

Fig.146

Single-enclosure sites of Standard size, i.e. mostly from *c.* 2 to 12 ha (5 to 30 acres), with simple defences: bank; bank-and-ditch; or bank, ditch, and counterscarp bank), C/D verts. up to 4·6 m (15 ft), and simple gap or inturned entrances.

Wessex tradition. No. of sites *c.* 300

3. A number of sites appear to have both Type III and Type X characteristics. They have quite clearly progressed beyond the Type II stage but this further elaboration involved also additional enclosures. Such sites may be simply a variation of the single-enclosure Type III sites and can be distinguished as Type III/X. The three most notable examples are Danebury (Hants) Eggardon (Dorset), and Wapley Camp (Here.).

4. Forde-Johnston, 'Earl's Hill, Pontesbury, and Related Hillforts in England and Wales', *Arch. J.* 119 (1962), 66–91.

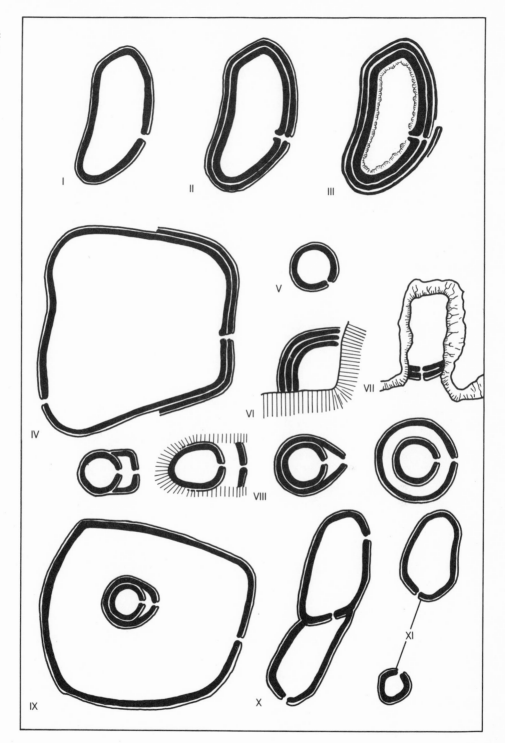

Fig. 146.
Diagrammatic
plans of Types
I–XI.

TYPE II

Fig.146

Single-enclosure sites of Standard size with stronger defences than above: massive bank-and-ditch; bank, ditch, and massive counterscarp bank; or, most commonly, two banks and two ditches, with or without a counterscarp bank. Entrances straight cut through defences, or inturned inner rampart.

Wessex tradition. No. of sites *c.* 150

TYPE III

Fig.146

Single-enclosure sites of Standard size and above, up to 20 ha (50 acres) in some cases, with very strong multivallate defences and elaborate entrances involving inturns, out-turns, overlaps, hornworks, and various kinds of barbican-like outworks.

Wessex tradition. No. of sites *c.* 40

TYPE IV

Fig.146

Single-enclosure sites of very large size, 23 ha (50 acres) and over, with both univallate and multivallate defences, but no other notable feature. Size appears to be the dominant aspect.

Wessex tradition. No. of sites *c.* 20

TYPE V

Fig.146

Single enclosure sites of Small size, i.e. less than 2 ha (5 acres), in many cases only *c.* 40 ares (1 acre), with simple defences: bank; bank-and-ditch; or bank, ditch, and counterscarp bank; C/D verts. *c.* 1·5–3 m (5–10 ft), and simple gap entrances. Apart from inland promontory and semi-contour positions, many are circular in plan.

Western tradition. No. of sites *c.* 500

TYPE VI

Fig.146

Single-enclosure sites of Small size with multivallate defences, sometimes with as many as four banks and ditches. Entrances straight cut through defences. Plans as for Type V.

Western tradition. No. of sites *c.* 80

TYPE VII

Fig.146

Coastal promontory forts, mostly in Cornwall and Pembrokeshire, many with multivallate defences. Size variable, according to situation.

Western tradition. No. of sites *c.* 80

TYPE VIII

Fig.146

Multiple-enclosure sites with all enclosures of Small size within any one site. Usually two or three enclosures. Entrances simple gaps. Plans concentric, annexe, or crossbank.

Western tradition. No. of sites *c.* 90

TYPE IX

Fig.146

Multiple-enclosure sites with very large outer enclosure, of Wessex-tradition dimensions. Inner enclosures of Type V or Type VIII. Entrances simple gaps.

Western tradition. No. of sites *c.* 12

TYPE X

Fig.146

Multiple-enclosure sites with nuclei of Standard size, with univallate or multivallate defences, and any sort of additional enclosure. Entrances as for Types I and II.

Wessex tradition. No. of sites *c.* 80

TYPE XI

Fig.146

Multiple-enclosure sites of two or more physically separate enclosures, i.e. main enclosure and satellite(s). Main enclosure usually of Wessex-tradition type, satellites often of Western, Small enclosure dimensions.

Wessex tradition. No. of sites *c.* 20

CHAPTER IX

Fig.2

Fig.147

Typological distribution

The number of forts in each of the counties of England and Wales is illustrated in Chapter I. The figures given there take no account of the areas of the counties involved, and a more objective basis of comparison is provided by the number of forts per hundred square miles. Wiltshire, for example, with an area of 1,345 sq miles and 49 forts has a density of 3·64 forts per 100 sq miles. In southern England there are broadly comparable densities in Hampshire (3·33), Wiltshire (3·64), Dorset (3·18), Somerset (3·90), and Devon (3·86). It is clear from this that the variations in Fig. 2 are a reflection of the areas of the counties as much as anything else. To the east and north-east densities are generally low, reflecting the low concentration of Iron Age forts. To the north-west, in Gloucestershire, there is a perceptible increase in density (4·78), while in the Marcher counties beyond the figures are generally similar to those in southern England: Herefordshire (3·32), Shropshire (3·20), Flintshire (2·73), and Denbighshire (2·84). This suggests that broadly speaking the nine counties had the same experience of Iron Age fort construction. However, the continuity of the figures is interrupted by Gloucestershire (4·78), where the higher density could be due to additional factors which did not affect the other counties. One such factor is the pattern of densities across south Wales, from Pembrokeshire to Monmouth, of which Gloucestershire is a continuation, so that it may well have been involved in both north–south and east–west density patterns. The densities in the counties on the western flank of the Marches are somewhat higher than the main Marcher counties and broadly comparable with the density in Gloucestershire.

The most striking density figures are in the three western extremities. There is a massive increase in density in Cornwall (13·57) as compared with Devon (3·86). There is another very marked difference between Pembrokeshire (23·61) and Carmarthenshire (8·92), and a less marked though still noticeable difference between the third extremity, Caernarvonshire (5·51) and its adjacent counties, Merionethshire (2·57), Anglesey (3·60), and Denbighshire (2·84). The similar geographical positions of Cornwall, Pembrokeshire, and Caernarvonshire make it feasible to suggest that their high densities stem from the same causes. Such marked increases in areas impinging on a recognized sea route suggest that a significant proportion of the Iron Age forts there are the result of arrivals by sea, via the western sea route. Such a striking pattern can hardly be the result of a landward movement from the opposite direction which would almost certainly have produced a different pattern.

Fig.147.
Density of forts,
by counties.

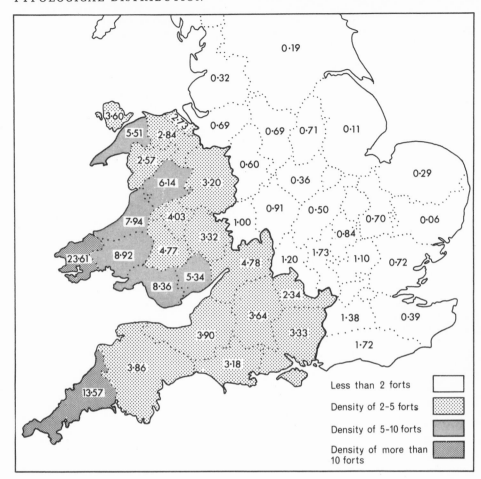

The most clearly marked frontier is between Cornwall and Devon in that the contrast in density between the two, about 3½ to 1, is greater than in the two other extremities. This suggests that there was less expansion from Cornwall than there was from Pembrokeshire. Two possible reasons may be suggested for this: first, the density in Cornwall is very much lower than in Pembrokeshire and there may have been far less pressure to expand; second, expansion from Cornwall could quite quickly have come up against expansion westwards from Wessex, bringing it to a halt. The territories adjacent to Pembrokeshire would certainly have been less densely occupied and expansion would have been much easier. In south-west England the densities in Devon and Somerset are marginally higher than the counties to the east and this small difference may represent the extent of expansion from Cornwall.

Pembrokeshire would appear to be the most important of the three western extremities. Its density is nearly twice that of Cornwall and more than four times that of Caernarvonshire. Its adjacent counties also have high densities, so that the contrast, about $2\frac{1}{2}$ to 1, is less than in the south-west and this suggests a greater degree of expansion. It looks as if Pembrokeshire was a major point of entry for large numbers of Iron Age forts which eventually expanded to occupy large areas of southern and western Wales.

The eleven types of Iron Age fort fall into two fairly clear groups, making it possible to formulate a concept of two separate traditions. As already indicated Types I–IV are found in the same areas: the south-east, Wessex, the Cotswolds, the Marches, and the area to the north and east. Types X and XI also occur in these areas and all six can be grouped together under the heading of what may be termed the Wessex tradition. This, in broad terms, embraces Standard forts in a series of variations: univallate, multivallate (both II and III), with additional enclosures (X), and with detached enclosures (XI).

The second group embraces sites beyond the Wessex tradition, in south-west England and in southern and western Wales, and may be termed the Western tradition, embracing Small univallate and multivallate forts (V and VI), coastal promontory forts (VII) and multiple-enclosure sites with Small nuclei (VIII and IX). With only a few exceptions these five types account for all the sites in the Western tradition area. The dividing line between the two traditions runs from somewhere in the Conway valley area in the north to the region of the Exe in the south. It is not suggested that each of these traditions is the result of a single event. It is for this reason that the term 'tradition', with its long-term implications, is used rather than terms such as 'style' or 'type'. Each tradition can be examined in more detail by considering the distribution of each of the eleven types.

As far as is known at present all multivallate forts in the Wessex tradition were built originally in univallate style, and became multivallate later as a result of further structural development. In other words, forts of Types II and III were originally of Type I and must be included in any consideration of its over-all distribution pattern. The same would appear to hold good for Types X and XI. This means that virtually all of the 600 or so sites in the Wessex tradition can be considered as a single group, made up of the existing Type I forts and the Type I stage of all the remaining forts. The extended Type I distribution area is formed by five of the seven regions defined in Chapter II (p. 21): South-east, Wessex, Cotswolds, Welsh Marches, and Chilterns, Midlands and North. Within this area there are considerable variations in

Fig.147

density. The highest concentrations are in the western part of the region. To the east densities fall away sharply and it is quite clear that in these areas there was a marked difference of experience. The western sector forms a wedge-shaped area extending from the south coast between the River Brit and Southampton Water to the north Wales coast between the Conway and the Dee. This area contains over 80 per cent of the extended Type I forts. The bulk of the remainder are located in south-eastern England with a thin scatter in the Midlands and the North.

Fig.148

From Beachy Head westwards as far as Land's End there is a continuous pattern of Iron Age forts on and behind the Channel coast. The sites in the western part of the area belong to the Western tradition and are not involved here. What has to be considered is how far to the west the Wessex tradition extended. The eastern end of what may be termed the front is clearly defined by Beltout Camp (Sussex), beyond which, to the east, there is nothing until the Thames and its associated sites are reached. In the west the front would appear to have extended into Devon, at least as far as the Exe, and possibly beyond, as far as Start Point or even the Tamar. The reason for this is that there are fairly large numbers of Medium-sized sites in the broad coastal zone to the east and south of Dartmoor. Some of these undoubtedly belong to the Western tradition, but their high proportion in relation to the area beyond the Tamar suggests that others may be attributable to the Wessex tradition. The front postulated above will, therefore, be regarded as extending from Beachy Head in Sussex to Start Point in Devon, about 370 km (230 miles) measured along the coast.

Behind this front and extending inland for varying distances is a continuous spread of Iron Age forts which would appear, at the extended Type I stage being considered here, to represent the results of a single event or of a series of very closely related events. The point of deepest penetration, some 113 km (70 miles) inland, forms the apex of a triangle with its base formed by the south coast from Southampton Water to the River Brit, about 113 km (70 miles), which contains the bulk of the sites under discussion. The sections of the front to east and west form, as it were, two wings to the main distribution involving much smaller numbers of sites and, apparently, less penetration inland from the coast. The triangular area consists mostly of chalk downland, drained by a series of rivers, Frome, Piddle, Stour, Avon, and Test, which seem likely to have played an important part in the movement of new arrivals into the area. Certainly the sites in Dorset, south Wiltshire, and south-western Hampshire are closely associated with rivers which flow to the south coast.

The eastern wing mentioned earlier is formed by the sites occupying the South Downs. In this case a direct movement across the coast and on to the immediately adjacent chalk downland seems the most likely. Further expansion is inhibited by the Weald, which effectively limits most sites to within about 16 km (10 miles) of the coast. The movement which produced the South Downs sites was almost certainly part of the same broad movement which produced the main Wessex distribution. The difference lies in the degree to which the hinterland was suitable for expansion and settlement.

In the west the sites between the Brit and the Exe could well be part of the movement directly across the coast, as in Wessex and Sussex. In the region beyond the Exe lateral expansion seems as likely an explanation, and this may apply to the Brit/Exe sites also.

In the southern part of the Wessex tradition area, therefore, there is a distribution pattern of extended Type I forts on a broad front from Beachy Head to Start Point, which extends inland to form the triangular distribution area defined above embracing Wessex, the South Downs and south-eastern Devon. Whether the sites involved were broadly contemporary or whether any degree of priority was implied by the shorter crossings at the eastern end of the front are matters which require the evidence of excavation.

To the north-east of Wessex, in the Thames Valley area, where much smaller

Fig.148. Distribution of Type I (extended) and Type IV.

numbers are involved, there is a string of sites following the main stem of the river and a concentration in the north Weald/North Downs area which would appear to suggest the Medway as a means of access. On the northern side of the Thames sites are more widely scattered, but are embraced by its pattern of tributaries. A handful of sites close to rivers flowing to the Essex coast, Crouch, Blackwater, and Colne, are probably to be associated with these. The whole distribution could well be the result of arrivals in the Thames estuary on a smaller scale than, but not necessarily at a different time from, the movement across the south coast into southern England.

Fig.148   Some of the more numerous sites to the north-west of Wessex in the Cotswold region, particularly those on the south-eastern flank, are probably due to expansion from Wessex; a similar expansion could account for some of the Thames Valley sites. Within the Cotswold group as a whole, however, the most striking pattern is formed by the sites along the north-western edge of the lime-stone escarpment. Some of these, again, are probably a result of expansion from Wessex. However, the same sites are closely related to the Bristol Channel, the major inlet on the western side of Britain, and it would be difficult to rebut the suggestion that some of the Cotswold sites are due to arrivals via this route. Quite clearly a much longer journey is involved than for either of the groups considered so far, but certainly not an impossibly long one, and not as long as the journey to south-west Scotland where some of the Iron Age people may be presumed to have arrived directly from the continent. In any journey around the south-west coast the Cotswold region would be the first to provide con-ditions generally similar to those in Wessex.

The Type I sites in the southern Marches, like those in the Cotswolds, must in part be the result of arrival via the Bristol Channel. Since the expansion from Wessex, postulated earlier, must be presumed to have continued into the same area, the Marcher sites, even at the Type I stage, cannot be attributed exclu-sively to either one or the other of these two sources. Both must be involved, even if to differing extents. From the Usk as far as the Leadon, about 64 km (40 miles) there is a series of rivers and associated tributaries providing access north and north-west into the heart of the Marcher zone. The Usk, the Wye, the Lugg, and their tributaries provide the setting for a pattern of sites which forms the southern half of the Marcher region, stretching over 80 km (50 miles) to the north. At least some of the sites beyond must be the result of expansion north-wards from the Lugg. However, many of them are associated with the Teme, which is itself a tributary of the Severn, and this raises the question of the part played by the Severn in the distribution of Marcher forts. Beyond the Leadon for some 80 km (50 miles) there is only a thin scatter of sites associated with the Severn, and only one site along the first 32 km (20 miles) of the Teme. How-ever, beyond this there is a pattern of tributaries joining it from the north, embracing a noticeable concentration of sites. In spite of the absence of inter-vening sites, the Teme, and therefore the Severn, still look the most likely means of access to this area of the Marches. Once having accepted the Severn/Teme route as viable it follows that the remainder of the middle Severn, giving access to the north Shropshire/Montgomeryshire area, is also likely to have been used.

Fig.148

This has the advantage that the route skirts around the Herefordshire/south Shropshire concentration, through which passage might have become difficult because of the existing Iron Age population.

Beyond Old Oswestry to the north there is a break in the pattern of Marcher forts, coinciding with a change in the river pattern. Instead of flowing generally southwards the trend is now in the opposite direction, with rivers running into the Dee and the Mersey and to the north Wales coast. It does not, of course, follow that the forts in the area came from the same direction. However, Iron Age forts in south-west Scotland suggest a coastal route up the western side of Britain and this must surely explain at least some of the forts at the northern end of the Marches.

In summary, it is suggested, therefore, that all the Type I forts considered above formed part of a single pattern of events, although not one which was necessarily concentrated in time. On grounds of accessibility Wessex, the South Downs, and possibly the Thames Valley, are likely to have been the first affected. Expansion north and north-west from Wessex must be invoked to explain at least part of the remaining Type I distribution; but alternative, if longer, routes must also be considered. With Wessex well occupied there might have been considerable difficulty for new arrivals trying to pass through the area, and an alternative route, via Land's End and the Bristol Channel, is a distinct possibility. Similarly the Severn route may have been used to bypass the southern Marches once these were well occupied, and the north Wales coastal route once the central and northern Marches likewise became too occupied for easy passage.

Fig.149

Something of the distribution pattern of Types II and III can be seen in the percentages of multivallate sites in each of the counties of England and Wales. There is a striking contrast between Surrey and Kent with 60 and 84 per cent respectively and the surrounding counties, and another marked contrast between Hampshire with 16 per cent and Dorset with 40 per cent. The most interesting pattern, however, is in the Marches and North Wales, where there is a high degree of uniformity: Monmouth (48 per cent) Hereford (53 per cent) Shropshire (53 per cent) Denbighshire/Flintshire (54 per cent) Anglesey/Caernarvonshire (54 per cent). To the west of the Marcher zone there is a gradual falling off in the percentage of multivallate sites, and a similar reduction in south-west England.

Fig.150

In the south the difference in the figures for Hampshire and Dorset suggests an east–west pattern centred approximately on the county boundary. An examination of the actual location of sites shows that virtually all the multivallate sites in Hampshire are in the western part of the county, beyond the Test, where they are continuous with those in Dorset. In this limited area they represent about 40 per cent of the total rather than the 16 per cent mentioned earlier. The lower figure is a result of the large number of univallate sites to the east of the Test. This pattern is continued by the univallate sites along the South Downs, so that there appears to have been an important difference of experience along the south coast, the area to the east of Southampton Water and the Test remaining at the Type I stage, the area to the west experiencing developments to the Type II and III stages in upwards of 40 per cent of its sites.

Fig.149.
Percentages of
multivallate
forts, by
counties.

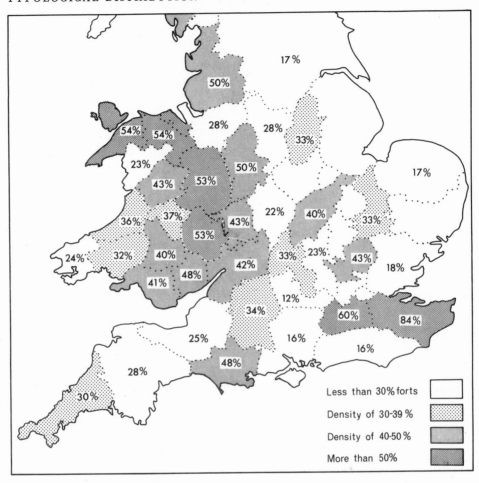

Fig.149

There is a less marked contrast between Wiltshire (34 per cent) and Dorset (48 per cent). Most of the multivallate sites in Wiltshire, however, are in the southern part of the county and, again, form a continuous pattern with those in Dorset. In the more limited area in which they occur the Wiltshire multi-vallate sites account for about 39 per cent of the total, very close to the figure for western Hampshire. There is a similar pattern in the areas of Somerset and Devon adjacent to Dorset. Out of 19 sites, 8 (42 per cent) are multivallate. There is, thus, in Wessex a pattern of Type I forts in the northern and eastern parts of the region and Types I, II, and III in the southern and western parts, and it is these areas which need to be looked at in more detail.

Its high percentage of multivallate sites suggests that Dorset formed a very important part of Wessex. Its southern flank, formed by the south coast, makes almost inevitable the suggestion that some movement from the continent was involved. This need not have been a single dramatic event. It could well have been spread over a considerable period, possibly a few generations, or an even longer period. Nor need it imply that the people involved were responsible for the appearance of multivallate defences. These could just as easily be explained by the reaction of the existing population to new arrivals. Whatever form it took, the movement seems to have been centred on Dorset. Beyond the county boundary percentages of multivallate sites are noticeably, although not dramatically, lower, being 40 per cent as compared with 48 per cent. The pattern formed is one of two triangles based on the coast. The inner triangle is formed by Dorset itself. The outer triangle embraces this and has its apex at Bratton Castle (Wilts.) and its base along the coast from Southampton Water to the Exe. The zone between the inner and outer triangles is less affected by multivallation, so that proximity to the coast would appear to be one of the factors involved. This could explain why Wiltshire, for example, has a lower percentage than Dorset. The over-all pattern in Wessex is thus one of three zones: Dorset, heavily affected by multivallation; the adjacent parts of Somerset and Devon, Wiltshire and Hampshire, less affected; and northern and eastern Wessex, virtually unaffected.

Fig.150

In the Thames Valley area the distribution of the main group of multivallate sites is compact and is confined to the north-western quarter of the Weald and the western sector of the North Downs. The factor which links virtually all the sites is the Medway, and its tributary the Eden, and it is difficult to suggest an alternative route for the arrival of whatever brought about the change from Type I to Type II. The sites in the Thames Valley proper and the area to the north seem to have remained largely unaffected.

The remaining multivallate sites in the Thames Valley area are much more widely distributed, but a fairly clear, if not easily explained, pattern is discernible. Beyond Holmbury (Surrey), the most westerly site in the last group discussed, there is a single line of multivallate sites stretching away to the north-west, through Caesar's Camp and Bullsdown (Hants) to Bussocks and Cherbury (Berks). On either side of this line there is a virtually unbroken pattern of Type I sites. From Cherbury the line continues, but now in an easterly direction through Dike Hills (Oxon.), Cholesbury (Bucks), The Aubreys (Herts.), to Wallbury and Witham (Essex). Again the sites on either side of this line are, with few exceptions, of Type I form. What is thus defined is a leaf-shaped area embracing the Thames and its tributaries and the associated Iron Age forts. Within this area the bulk of sites are of Type I. Type II sites form the edge of the leaf, with another spread of Type I sites beyond. One interpretation of this distribution is that it represents a reaction in the more elevated parts of the area against new arrivals in the Thames Valley.

Fig.150

Beyond Wessex to the north-west and centred more or less symmetrically on the Lower Severn, is a roughly circular area, about 56 km (35 miles) in diameter, which contains a very high proportion of multivallate sites (c. 64 per cent). This area is defined to the north-west of the Severn by Westbury (Glos) Little Doward (Here.), and Camp Wood and Tredegar Camp (Mon.), and to the south-east by Cadbury Camp (Som.) and Little Sodbury Camp and Nympsfield (Glos), and is surrounded on most sides by Type I sites, insulating it to a greater or lesser extent from other multivallate groups. This relative

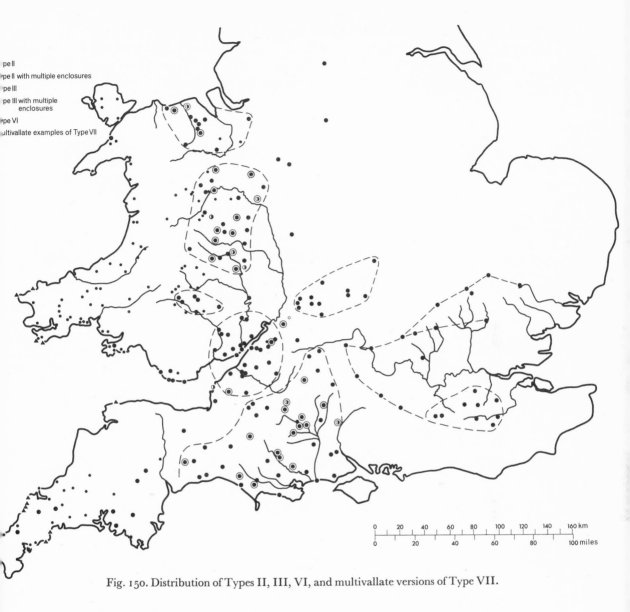

Type II
Type II with multiple enclosures
Type III
Type III with multiple
        enclosures
Type VI
Multivallate examples of Type VII

Fig. 150. Distribution of Types II, III, VI, and multivallate versions of Type VII.

isolation, and its disposition on either side of a major inlet, inevitably suggest arrival via the Bristol Channel. Such an area, where the Bristol Channel narrows rapidly to the Severn, would be one of the first to feel the impact of new arrivals and the dense concentration of multivallate sites could well reflect the reaction of the existing population.

To the north-east of this circle is a 32-km (20-mile) stretch of the Cotswold escarpment as far as Cleeve Cloud which, apart from Kimsbury, contains only Type I sites. Beyond, Cleeve Cloud forms one corner of a roughly rectangular area, further defined by Bredon Hill, Meon Hill, and Eubury, in which about 62 per cent of the sites are multivallate, similar to the percentage in the circular area, although much smaller numbers are involved. Being more remote from the presumed direction of arrival than the circular area, this group may well be later, but if it is, then it is difficult to explain why the 32-km (20-mile) stretch from Nympsfield to Cleeve Cloud remained virtually unaffected. The answer may be that the Cleeve Cloud group is the work of early arrivals who passed peacefully through the existing Type I forts to the south-west. At a later stage the people in the latter area, possibly alarmed by the increasing numbers of migrants, could well have reacted by strengthening the defences of their own forts.

Fig.150

At the south-western end of the Cotswold region there is another small group of Type II sites in and around the Mendips. These are separated from the circular area by a spread of about a dozen Type I forts running in an east–west band from Wains Hill on the coast to Bathampton Camp, some 40 km (25 miles) away. The bulk of these Type I forts are isolated from the coastal zone by the concentration of multivallate sites at the mouth of the Avon and this may well explain why they remained at the Type I stage when virtually everything around them advanced to Type II. The Mendip multivallate sites may well be explained in the same way as the Cotswold sites; they could, on the other hand, be derived from north-west Wessex. The multivallate sites there, from Bratton Castle to Cadbury Castle, form a link between the Mendips and the remainder of Wessex which may be significant. Across the Bristol Channel multivallate sites along the Glamorgan coast, built in Wessex-tradition style, may well be involved in whatever processes were responsible for the Mendip sites.

Beyond the Severn, the north-western half of the circular area forms the first of four groups of Type II forts which can be distinguished in the Marches. To the north-west is a second small group around Brecon which appears to be closely associated with the Usk and its tributaries, and it is difficult to suggest any other arrival route than the Usk and therefore participation in the events which embraced the Lower Severn area.

Fig.150

The most striking distribution pattern in the Marches is in the Herefordshire/south Shropshire area, and involves two clearly defined sectors, south-eastern and north-western. The south-eastern sector is, with few exceptions, occupied by Type I forts, the north-western mostly by Type II; the 'frontier' between is very clearly defined. On the Type I side it is marked by a line of forts running from Chesterton Walls south-west to Abdon Burf, south to Clee Burf, Titterstone Clee, Garmsley Camp and Wall Hills (Thornbury) and then south-west again through Sutton Walls and Credenhill to Poston, a distance of some 89 km (55 miles). To the north and west is the great concentration of Type II forts in the central Marcher zone, covering an area about 80 km (50 miles) long and about 48 km (30 miles) wide. On its southern and eastern sides it is defined by a string of Type II forts which face, at a distance of a few miles, the string of Type I forts just mentioned: The Wrekin, Rushbury Ditches, Nordy Bank, Caynham Camp, Bach Camp, Risbury Camp, and Ivington Camp. The northern and western edges are less strikingly but none the less clearly defined. The whole area contains about 90 sites of which about half are of Type II, with a scatter of Types X and XI. It is noticeable that the Type I sites are mostly in the northern and western areas, well away from the frontier zone. The areas immediately behind the frontier are occupied almost exclusively by Type II sites.

The difficulty in interpreting this central Marcher group arises from the lack of access routes other than through, presumably undisturbed, Type I areas. This latter point may be the key to the problem. It may be that the whole of the undisturbed Type I area was taken over in a fairly quick movement by incoming peoples, and that only in regions further to the north and west was there time for refortification, producing the frontier-like pattern described above. Such an explanation implies a fairly massive movement at one time, a single event, something approaching an invasion, although such a term should be used with caution, rather than the more gradual folk movements generally envisaged. Another possibility is that refortification was due to internal rather than external factors. Localized warfare and the need to balance the deterrent effect of an enemy's strengthened multiple ramparts, with similar features of one's own, could well have played some part in producing the dense pattern of multivallate sites in the central Marches. Outside factors may have played only a small part in the process.

If neither of the above explanations is correct then the people responsible for the multivallate forts either passed through the univallate area, leaving no mark of their passage, or they went round it. One way of doing this would be via the middle Severn which passes for the most part to the east of the univallate area. This could account for the multivallate sites in the northern half of the central zone, but would still leave the multivallate sites associated with the Teme and the Lugg to be explained. The Teme sites could represent, at least in part, an expansion southwards from the upper Severn area. The alternative is to suggest that they came via the Teme from the middle Severn, passing through the area of univallate forts which at this point is not particularly dense. The sites associated with the Lugg and its tributaries could be part of the same pattern.

A movement bypassing the univallate area to the west is also a possibility. A close link between the lower Severn multivallate sites and the Brecon group has already been suggested. A further link may exist between the latter and the multivallate sites at the southern end of the central zone, a link which skirts the univallate area to the west. There is a further possibility to be considered. In a region such as the Marches with coastal access at both northern and southern ends, movement is possible in both directions. Apart from a scatter of univallate sites in the upper Dee area the pattern of multivallate sites is virtually continuous from the Lugg to the north Wales coast. There is no major obstacle to a spread southwards from this coast, certainly nothing to compare with the barrier which appears to be imposed by the spread of Type I forts to the south and east of the central zone.

Beyond the central zone to the north there is a scatter of about a dozen univallate sites along the upper Dee and its tributaries, and beyond this again a final concentration of multivallate sites in and around the Clwyd valley. It seems feasible to suggest that these represent arrivals via the north Wales coast. The upper Dee univallate sites may well mark the southern limit of their spread, but they do not form an impenetrable barrier and the possibility, already suggested, of a spread further to the south, into the northern part of the central zone, must be kept in mind.

The distribution of Type III has not so far been considered separately from that of Type II. The number of sites involved is only about 40, so that no striking distribution pattern is to be expected. In fact, Type III forts are found, broadly speaking, throughout the Type II area; that is, in the western part of Wessex, in the Cotswolds, and in the Marches, with one or two possible sites in the south-east. If they do represent a special development of Type II, as suggested earlier, then this is the sort of distribution to be expected.

In summary, the distribution of Types II and III can be seen to fall into a relatively small number of fairly well-defined geographical groups. The majority of sites are embraced by the three major groups, in western Wessex, the lower Severn circular area and the central Marches. These are flanked by five smaller groups, two to the east (Medway and north-east Cotswolds), two to the west (Mendips and Breconshire), and one to the north (Clwyd valley). Outside these eight groups there is only a scatter of Type II and III sites.

The number of Type IV sites is only about 20. Unlike the Type III, however, they are not confined to the Type II area. They can be said, broadly speaking, to be scattered throughout the Wessex tradition area so that their original association would be with Type I. Since they now have both Type I and Type II defences, they would appear to have undergone the same changes as the Standard forts which progressed from Type I to Type II. On this basis it looks as if the difference between them and other Wessex tradition forts was simply one of size, together with whatever that implies in terms of function.

Fig.2

Fig.151

Type V sites, i.e. Small, with simple defences, form the largest single group of Iron Age forts, about 500 in number. About two-thirds of the group occur in only five counties: Pembrokeshire, 100; Carmarthenshire, 53; Cardiganshire, 32; Cornwall, 108; and Devonshire, 38. This is very clearly a western distribution with a marked emphasis on the two westernmost counties, Cornwall and Pembrokeshire. In south-west England the greatest concentration is in western Cornwall, and is separated from similar sites in the east by a north–south band of mostly multiple-enclosure sites. The distribution of the Type V sites in the west suggests that their builders could have arrived equally well by either the north or south coast of the county. In the eastern half of the county, however, the distribution suggests that the emphasis is on the north rather than the south coast. The same is true beyond the Tamar, in Devon. In the southern and south-eastern parts of the county there is a scatter of Type V sites, but beyond the Exe they are few and far between. They occur very occasionally as far east as the South Downs, but such sites may be simply small versions of Type I sites, with little or no connection with the south-west. If, as seems likely from the density figures, Type V sites originated in Cornwall, then the impetus behind their expansion along the south coast would not appear to have carried much beyond the Tamar and to have virtually ended at the Exe. Along the north coast, on the other hand, there is a fairly regular pattern of Type V sites as far as the River Parret in Somerset. Beyond the Parret there is a further scatter of sites along the Cotswolds as far as the Frome. Beyond this point, and beyond the Wye, on the opposite side of the Severn, there are virtually no Small univallate sites.

Fig.151

In south Wales, in Carmarthenshire and Pembrokeshire, there is a concentration of Type V sites closely associated with rivers flowing into the Bristol Channel. The importance of this coast is further emphasized by the distribution of other types of site which tend to occur there rather than on the north Pembrokeshire/Cardiganshire coast. Beyond the Tywi to the east there is a pattern of Type V sites very similar to the one on the facing coasts of Devon and Somerset. This pattern continues as far as the Wye, more or less opposite the limit of such sites in the Cotswolds. As far as Type V is concerned the pattern in the Bristol Channel region consists of major concentrations in the western extremities, with smaller concentrations along the inward-facing coasts as far to the east as the Wye and the Frome, thus penetrating to some extent into a Wessex tradition area. The spread of Type V sites along the north Pembrokeshire/Cardiganshire coast is much thinner than on the inward-facing coasts and matches the equally thin spread in south-east Cornwall and southern and south-eastern Devon. In Cardigan Bay they extend as far as Barmouth Bay, beyond which they are few and far between.

This accounts for nearly 400 of the 500 or so Type V sites. The bulk of the remainder are found on the western flank of the Marcher zone, from Brecknockshire to the Clwyd valley. On the southern and western sides of the Brecknock group there is a spread of about 20 Type V forts which seems best interpreted as part of an expansion eastwards and north-eastwards from Pembrokeshire. Further north, beyond a scatter of sites in Radnorshire, there are about 24 Type V sites in western Shropshire and eastern Montgomeryshire, on and just beyond the north-western edge of the central Marcher group. Again these seem best interpreted as part of the pattern of Type V sites based ultimately on Pembrokeshire. Northwards again there is a scatter of sites in the upper Dee/Clwyd area.

Fig.151

The distribution of the 70 or 80 Type VI forts, i.e. Small enclosures with multivallate defences, is less easy to define than that of Type V. Sites are scattered throughout western regions, although some do occur in the Wessex tradition area, these possibly being nothing more than small versions of Type II sites. There appear to be fewer Type VI sites in south-west England than there are in Wales, where they occur mainly in Pembrokeshire, Cardiganshire, Carmarthenshire, Brecknockshire, Radnorshire, and eastern Montgomeryshire. In the latter three counties they are in contact with the Wessex tradition, and this could be

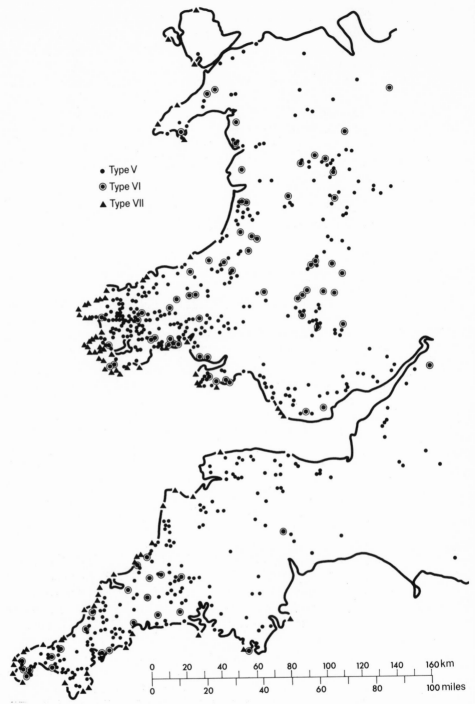

Fig.151. Distribution of Types V, VI, and VII.

the clue to their existence. They may well represent the influence of the Wessex-style multivallate defences on the builders of the Small forts, an influence which spread eventually, although not on a large scale, throughout the Western tradition area.

Coastal promontory forts are confined to western regions. About three-quarters of them, around 60 sites, occur in only two counties, Cornwall and Pembrokeshire, with the bulk of the remainder in the immediately adjacent areas. Some of them may be only Type V or Type VI sites which happen to be located on coastal promonotories. However, in an area where there was probably a great deal of activity on and along the coasts it is feasible to suggest that some Type VII sites formed a separate group. Their coastal situation may reflect not so much the exploitation of a defensible position as their involvement in trade, or a maritime economy, either of which would tend to differentiate them from inland communities.

Virtually all the sites considered so far have been of the single-enclosure type. The remaining types (VIII–XI) involve sites with two or more enclosures. The first two belong to the Western tradition, while Type X and XI form part of the Wessex tradition.

Fig.152 Type VIII sites, i.e. enclosures of Small size, occur within the areas embraced by Type V, but their distribution is rather more restricted. In south-west England most of them are concentrated in the central north–south band in Cornwall, referred to already, with mostly Type V sites in the areas to east and west. Within this central band the majority of the Type VIII sites are associated with the Camel and its tributaries, and this is in keeping with the generally greater emphasis, in the south-west, on the north as opposed to the south coast. In the south-west Type VIII forts are found only in small numbers outside Cornwall, mostly in south Devon, where they could well represent an extension eastwards from central Cornwall. As far as Type VIII is concerned, and in contrast to Cornwall, the south coast of Devon appears to be more important than the north where multiple-enclosure sites are few and far between. However, sites of any sort are few in the north Devon area, so that this may not mean very much. In the south-west as a whole, however, it is quite clear that the key area for Type VIII multiple-enclosure sites is the central north–south band in Cornwall.

Most of the remaining Type VIII sites are located in southern and western Wales. From Pembrokeshire, in south Wales, they extend as far east as the Wye, and are situated, for the most part, within a few kilometres of the coast. This is probably less significant than might at first appear since, apart from Pembrokeshire and western Carmarthenshire, there are few sites of any sort at any distance from the coast. The pattern does, however, contrast with that on the opposite shore of the Bristol Channel where, apart from the area of the River Camel, there are few multiple-enclosure sites. This contrast is further emphasized by a noticeable group of Type VIII sites in Glamorgan, opposite the virtually blank area of north Somerset. Beyond Pembrokeshire to the north-east there is a scatter of Type VIII sites in Cardiganshire, as far as the Dyfi, with the remaining sites in the Lleyn peninsula in Caernarvonshire.

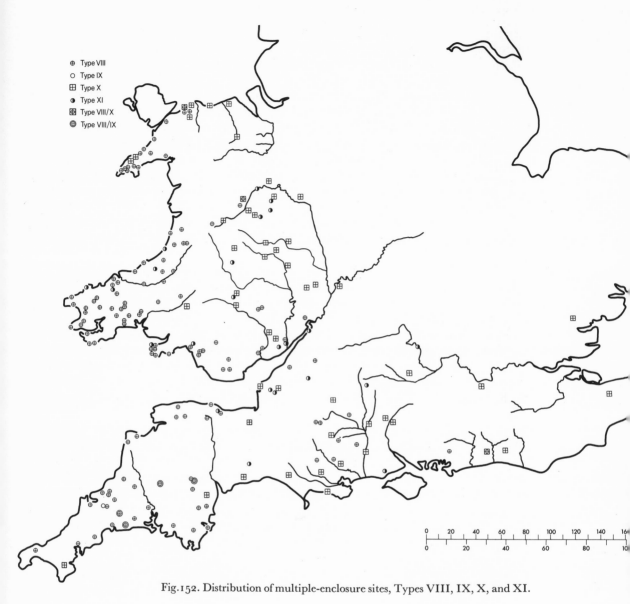

Fig.152. Distribution of multiple-enclosure sites, Types VIII, IX, X, and XI.

Fig.152

Type IX sites, i.e. Small enclosures within much larger enclosures, are few in number, involving only about 12 forts, and appear to be a south-western feature, confined to Cornwall and south Devon. In other words, they fall within the distribution area of Type VIII, and perforce of Type V. Their central features or nuclei are, in fact, of these two types (V and VIII) and considered alone, without their outer, Wessex-style enclosures, they would fall quite neatly into one or other of these two categories. Type IX sites are located in the same general area as 5 out of the 7, presumably Wessex tradition, Large (old terminology) sites in the south-west and may be complementary to their distribution.

Fig.152

Type X multiple-enclosure sites form part of the Wessex tradition. They are not, however, spread evenly throughout the Wessex-tradition area. Although there are exceptions, broadly speaking they are found on its western flank, on or close to the junction with the Western tradition. In Wessex they occur in central and west Dorset and in south-west Wiltshire. From here the pattern extends north and west as far as the north Wales coast. It embraces the south-western half of the Cotswold region, Monmouthshire, Brecknockshire, and the western part of the central Marcher zone, with a few sites carrying the distribution into north Wales. Throughout this area are scattered some 70 or 80 sites, nowhere sufficiently concentrated to form a group but occurring with sufficient regularity to constitute a noticeable pattern. Inevitably, their proximity to the Western-tradition area suggests that the idea of subsidiary enclosures was derived from there.

The last type of Iron Age fort to be considered is Type XI. Each of these consists, in fact, of two, and in some cases three, physically separate sites which are deemed to constitute a single unit, thus forming a variant of the multiple-enclosure type. The distribution of most of these has been illustrated elsewhere.[1] A few additional sites recognized since 1962 do not substantially change the over-all pattern which extends from the central Marches to the south and south-west, with sites in Shropshire, Radnor, Brecknockshire, Monmouthshire, Glamorgan, and Pembrokeshire. With only 20 or so sites involved the pattern is inevitably thin but it does appear to be more or less evenly divided between the Wessex- and the Western-tradition areas, and, as was suggested for Type IX, both traditions may be involved. There may, in fact, be a closer link between the two. Their distributions are broadly complementary, so that differences between them may be regional rather than anything more fundamental. This will be discussed further in the next chapter.

1. Forde-Johnston, 'Earl's Hill, Pontesbury, and Related Hillforts in England and Wales', *Arch. J.* 119 (1962), 66–91.

CHAPTER X

Discussion and conclusions

The 1,366 existing Iron Age forts mentioned in Chapter I (p. 11) are unlikely to represent the total number originally built. Allowance must be made for the destruction of sites in the intervening 2,000 years, particularly of those in the Small, univallate category. Many of these, although still visible, are in a poor state of preservation and will eventually disappear completely. Many must have done so already. By the same token, because they are so often poorly preserved, many Small univallate forts must have been overlooked in field survey and still remain to be discovered. The original number of Iron Age forts can never be precisely ascertained, but making some allowance for increased numbers in other categories as well, a total of around 1,600 may be suggested, and this is probably a conservative estimate.

Recent research has shown that a number of sites on the O.S. Iron Age map now appear not to be Iron Age forts at all. These include Hulberry (Kent)[1] and Carshalton (Surrey)[2] in the Large multivallate class and Ranscombe (Sussex)[3] in the Large univallate category. The elimination of the first two leaves the North Downs virtually free of forts, although flanked to north and south by the Thames Valley and north Weald groups respectively. Two other sites which probably can be eliminated are Buckton Castle (Lancs)[4] and Berry Cliff (Devon). Although both of them are defensive enclosures of a sort, from ground examination they do not appear to belong to the Iron Age fort category.

Three sites not included on the Iron Age map but which nevertheless appear to be Iron Age forts are Oakmere (Ches.), Camp Hill (Lancs), and Carl Wark (Yorks). Oakmere, in a low-lying, waterside situation, is a perfectly good enclosure of the type under consideration. Camp Hill, in the grounds of Camp Hill Estate, Liverpool, is almost completely destroyed, but it is still just possible to identify a scarp representing the western defences. There is documentary evidence as to the former appearance of the site,[5] and the digging of a section in 1960 uncovered a tumbled mass of sandstone blocks consistent in volume

1. Feachem, 'Ordnance Survey: Archaeological Report, 1', *Antiquity*, 40 (1966), 145.
2. *Surrey Arch. Coll.* 60 (1963), 50.
3. Burstow and Holleyman, 'Excavations at Ranscombe Camp, 1959–1960', *Sussex Arch. Coll.* 102 (1964), 55–67.
4. Forde-Johnston, 'The Iron Age Hillforts of Lancashire and Cheshire', *Trans. Lancs. and Ches. Antiq. Soc.* 72 (1962), 11.
5. Eyes, MS. Survey, 1835.

with the sort of rampart which would have defended such a site.[6] Carl Wark (Yorks.) is a perfectly straightforward promontory fort, defended on the approach side by a well-preserved, stone-fronted rampart, still standing to a height of 3 m (10 ft). By any account it must be included as an Iron Age fort. In addition to the sites just mentioned there are almost certainly others awaiting discovery or reappraisal as a result of more intensive fieldwork.

In Chapter II the existence of quite extensive areas of chalk downland where Iron Age forts do not exist was noted, both for Wessex and the south-east (pp. 23, 27–28). Along the North and South Downs and in much of Hampshire this may simply be a reflection of the size of the population. In Wessex, however, these blank areas are adjacent to areas which are, in terms of forts, fairly densely occupied. It may be that there was some economic relationship between the two in that the blank areas may have been some sort of communal territory, or open range, on which, by agreement, enclosures were not built, these being grouped close-by in the adjacent territory. It may be that two different types of economy were involved, one pastoral, calling for enclosures, the other arable, having no need of such structures. If this is not the explanation and if the unoccupied downland was available for forts, but not used, then any suggestion of population pressure would appear to be unlikely. The explanation of this particular pattern in the chalk regions might well provide the answer to the function, or one of the functions, of Iron Age forts.

The problem of blank areas was linked with another problem, that of grouping (pp. 23, 28), the solution of which could be equally illuminating from the point of view of function. Along the South Downs the blank areas separate groups of 2, 3, and 4 sites, and the same pattern is observable, if in slightly less striking form, in other areas. In fact, throughout the Wessex tradition area a considerable number of sites form small groups, of 2–4, with noticeable gaps between them and the neighbouring groups. The same pattern does not obtain in the Western tradition where the pattern of distribution is, on the whole, more even. It is possible that the existence of such groups can be explained on purely chronological grounds, no more than one or two sites out of the group being in use at any one time. The alternative explanation is that the sites in each group are contemporary, in which case it may be that a series of enclosures, rather than a single one, was required to serve the needs of a community in a particular area. The space between the sites in each group, often about 3–8 km (2–5 miles), makes it feasible to suggest, for example, that the reason for the series of enclosures was to avoid driving cattle long distances in order to impound them each night. A series of enclosures carefully spaced around the area which the community used would reduce any single journey to 3–5 km (2 or 3 miles) at most. Alternatively a series of contemporary enclosures might have been required for a range of different functions, perhaps as defended villages, as well as cattle pounds, or some other as yet undetermined function. Possibly the answer to the problem of these blank areas lies in a combination of such explanations.

One of the topics dealt with in Chapter III was altitude. Although only a few

6. Forde-Johnston, op. cit. 12–13.

sites are situated at or near sea-level, there are many others which are equally low-lying locally, whatever their elevation in absolute terms. The best examples of this are coastal promontory forts. Whatever their elevation above the sea, on the landward side they are frequently at exactly the same level as their surroundings. The same is true of many inland sites. This frequently means that most of the advantage of height is lost. The interesting aspect of all this is the number of sites involved. Some 60 per cent of all Iron Age forts (Groups II–VII) have a level approach on one or more sides and are, therefore, low-lying in relation to part of their immediate surroundings. If defence needs were paramount then one would expect to find some compensation for the lack of natural defences on these sides. In some sites such compensation is evident in the form of multivallate defences, but in others the defences are no stronger on the approach sides than they are on the remainder of the circuit. This suggests that pure defence is not always the dominant aspect. Quite clearly defence of a sort is involved, but not to the extent of overriding other considerations, possibly of an economic or social nature.

The defence aspect of hill-slope forts would appear to be even slighter than some of the sites considered already. Evenly sloping ground is not normally the first choice for a defence work of any sort. It may be, however, that a free choice was not involved. There is no reason why an open, undefended settlement should not be on sloping ground. If and when the need for defence arose then a choice would be involved, either to put the defences around the existing village or to build a new, defended village somewhere else. It is feasible to suggest that in some cases people chose to defend what they had, rather than abandon it in favour of a new village. The same explanation could, of course, be invoked for other situations which are not particularly strong in terms of defence. An alternative explanation for hill-slope sites is that the enclosures were placed in a position convenient to the best available pasture which, incidentally, was on sloping ground.

Apart from pre- and post-Iron Age structures (pp. 103–5) the internal features of Iron Age forts consist of abandoned defences and hut remains. The former (pp. 105–8) indicate an enlargement of the enclosure leaving some or all of the original defences within the new defence system. This may represent a straightforward structural development with no chronological break involved. On the other hand, it is feasible to suggest that the new defences did not immediately follow the old. There could well have been an intervening period when, presumably, a defence enclosure was not required. This could imply some fluctuation in political conditions, rather than a steady progression from peaceful to troubled times. Certainly at Ffridd Faldwyn (Montg.)[7] the smaller, earlier fort had ceased to have any defensive function by the time the larger, later fort came to be built, and the same may be true of some of the other sites which show evidence of earlier defences.

Perhaps the most interesting aspect of interiors is the question of huts, which are always circular in plan. There is no surface evidence for rectangular huts in

7. O'Neil, 'Excavations at Ffridd Faldwyn Camp, Montgomery, 1937–9', *Arch. Camb.* 97 (1943), 15.

any of the forts in England and Wales, except for some in north-west Wales which are almost certainly post-Iron Age. The circular form is in marked contrast to the Continental tradition of rectangular huts, and make it difficult to suggest that they, like the enclosures within which they stand, are derived from the mainland of Europe. It seems much more likely that they represent a continuation of the native Bronze Age tradition, in which case it would appear that however large the migration which ushered in the Iron Age, it did not involve a complete replacement of the existing population. The persistence of the native tradition, in this and in other ways,[8] brings into question the whole size and nature of the migration into Britain at the beginning of the Iron Age. On the basis of such survivals it is feasible to suggest that the arrival of the Iron Age people was a slow, gradual process; an infiltration rather than an invasion, which only slowly changed the material culture and way of life of the native population, introducing, among other things, the methods of Hallstatt fortification.

The small proportion of forts with surviving hut remains, about 5 per cent, (p. 109) makes it difficult to assess the extent of their function as habitation sites, since this figure certainly does not represent the original proportion. It may well be that every Iron Age fort at one time enclosed huts, in greater or lesser numbers, but if this was so then it seems likely that a much higher proportion would have survived. On the other hand, it does seem likely that the figure was higher than 5 per cent. Presumably, however, this forms some sort of sample of the original patterns of occupation. At one end of the scale there are sites with hundreds of hut circles, and at the other sites with only one or two. In between there are groups ranging from about 12 to 36. There is, of course, no certainty that the huts and defences, even if both are of Iron Age date, are contemporary, but in the absence of evidence to the contrary it is assumed that they are.

The two outstanding examples of forts with large numbers of huts, Hod Hill and Hambledon Hill, Dorset, are of Type III and it may well be that they are representative of the whole group. Assemblages of this size must be regarded as urban centres and this function would appear to be associated with Type III, rather than the Types I or II. There is no evidence of sites at the Type I or Type II stage with corresponding numbers of huts. There is, on the other hand, some evidence in such sites of smaller communities, represented by groups of 10–40 huts. At the lower end of the scale this could be the accommodation for a single, extended family group, given that some of the huts could be for farm purposes and not simply for human occupation. The location of the huts within fairly elaborate defences, such as at Abbotsbury, Dorset, makes it feasible to suggest that, in some cases at least, they were intended for a chief and his family living permanently within the enclosure which was used also as a refuge in times of danger by the whole community. At the upper end of the scale the larger groups of up to 40 huts could be the remains of genuine villages, the occupants of which worked the surrounding lands but for reasons of security built and lived within a defended enclosure. Such groups of huts could, with increasing pros-

8. Hodson, 'Cultural Grouping within the British Pre-Roman Iron Age', *Proc. Prehist. Soc.* 30 (1964), 104.

perity and normal population growth, have developed to the larger, urban-type groups as seen in Hod Hill and Hambledon Hill.

In Chapter V Iron Age forts were considered on the basis of their defences which, in some cases, appear to be unfinished. Either these forts were overtaken by the danger which they were designed to prevent, or the danger never materialized, causing the construction to be abandoned. In either case this would suggest that they were built, at least in some cases, to meet particular circumstances, *ad hoc*, and were not enclosures kept in a permanent state of readiness. The fact that some of the unfinished defences are in univallate sites and others in the outer line of multivallate sites, may again suggest a pattern of fluctuating circumstances, at least in certain areas.

Of the various features, banks, ditches, berms, etc., which make up defence systems those ditches which are now flat-bottomed (p. 128), as opposed to the normal V-shaped section, call for some comment. Flat-bottomed ditches, i.e., flat-bottomed as originally dug, are a Belgic feature and the remains at sites such as Spettisbury Rings (Dorset) make it feasible to suggest a Belgic origin. However, it has been shown that the existing remains at Spettisbury do not reflect the nature of the original ditch. Excavation[9] has shown that the original ditch bottom is at least 3 m (10 ft) below the existing flat-bottomed ditch and is almost certainly V-shaped like other Iron Age fort ditches. The same would appear to be true for the other flat-bottomed ditches in Wessex and the Cotswolds. The most likely explanation is that regular ploughing or some other agricultural activity in the ditch has steepened the sides and broadened and gradually flattened the bottom, producing the profile now visible. The widely scattered nature of the distribution pattern would, in any case, argue against an interpretation in cultural terms, except in the south-east where there is excavation evidence for the Fécamp-style ditch.[1]

The strong defences of some sites in western regions need to be looked at in the light of evidence from certain multiple-enclosure sites. At the concentric site of Warbstow Bury (Corn.; p. 172), the intervening space for about half of the circuit is occupied by an unfinished bank and ditch. In this particular case the remaining space is still wide enough to qualify the site for inclusion in the multiple-enclosure category. But it can readily be seen that if the intervening space had been narrower, then the insertion of additional defences would have transformed the site from a multiple-enclosure site to a single-enclosure site with very strong defences. Castle-an-Dinas, St. Columb, (Corn.), another concentric site (p. 174) also has evidence of an unfinished attempt to reinforce the inner enclosure. In this case, however, in one sector of the site, the reduction of the intervening space is such that it falls below the limit set for multiple-enclosure sites. Because the space is wider in other sectors the whole site can still be classed as multiple-enclosure, but it is clear that defence requirements have overridden the economic need represented by the outer enclosure, the usefulness of which

9. Forde-Johnston, 'A Note on Excavations at Spettisbury Ring', *Proc. Dorset Nat. Hist. and Arch. Soc.* 80 (1958), 108.

1. Ward-Perkins, 'Excavations at the Iron Age Hill-fort of Oldbury, near Ightham, Kent', *Archaeologia*, 90 (1944), 137 and pl. xxxi.

must have been reduced by this move. In both of these cases it is quite clear that utilization of the intervening space is regarded as the obvious means of strengthening a multiple-enclosure fort where this is called for. It is equally clear that if the space is fully utilized in this way then the site ceases to be a multiple-enclosure site and becomes a strongly defended, single-enclosure, Small site, in the terminology now adopted; a Type VI Iron Age fort. The Type VI fort at Llandewi Gaer (Pemb.; p. 158) may have evolved in this way. It is noticeable that the inner and outer ramparts are parallel to each other, at a distance of about 24 m (80 ft). The middle rampart runs between, leaving berms 4·6–6 m (15–20 ft) wide, except at the north-west angle where it cuts across the corner, coming very close to the outer edge of the inner ditch. This may indicate that it was inserted between two widely spaced pre-existing ramparts. Without the middle rampart Llandewi Gaer is of Type VIII; with it, it is quite clearly of Type VI. The implication of all this is that at some stage in the history of the Western tradition the need for additional defence was felt sufficiently strongly for some Type VIII sites to give up their outer enclosures to new ramparts, thus reducing them in area or, in some cases, entirely eliminating them.

On the question of entrances (Chapter VII), inturned ramparts are, for the most part, associated with the Wessex tradition. Although they are found in western regions, they do not occur in any great numbers, the majority of entrances being of the simple gap type. Within the Wessex tradition their distribution is further restricted. They are not found in any great numbers in Wessex itself, and where they do occur it is usually in multivallate sites, many of them of the more elaborate Type III sites. Many other Wessex sites, both univallate and multivallate, have entrances of the simple gap type. On this basis it looks as if inturned ramparts are late rather than early in the Iron Age fort sequence in Wessex. The same would appear to be true for the Cotswold region. It is only in the Marcher region that inturned ramparts can be said to become common, occurring in both univallate and multivallate sites. If the Marcher sites, either wholly or in part, are to be derived from the Wessex/Cotswold region then it looks as if this took place at or about the time that inturned ramparts were introduced into Wessex which, as suggested above, would appear to have been fairly late in the Iron Age fort sequence there. It is, however, possible to suggest that inturned entrances were derived, either from Wessex or elsewhere, separately from the enclosures to which they were subsequently attached. The entrance is the most vulnerable part of any defence work and is one which is likely to be elaborated, even if the rest of the site remained unchanged. Thus univallate Marcher forts with inturned entrances are not necessarily tied to the date of such entrances. The enclosure itself could be earlier. The fact that inturned entrances occur in both univallate and multivallate sites does not necessarily prove that the two types of site were in use together. Given that all multivallate forts had an earlier univallate stage, once the latter had adopted the inturned entrance this would inevitably still be present in the multivallate stage. This, if anything, would suggest that in the Marches inturned entrances predated multiple-ramparts.

The simple gap entrance is common to both Wessex and Western traditions, although this is probably not of any great significance. Given that an enclosure needs an entrance, a straight cut through the defences is the minimum provision which can be made. Also common to both traditions are annexes in the form of what may be termed entrance enclosures. In the west, where Helsbury (Corn.) may be regarded as the type site, the annexe or entrance enclosure and main enclosure are comparable in size. In Wessex, on the other hand, at sites such as Badbury Rings (Dorset) and Bratton Castle (Wilts.) the entrance enclosures, although of the same size as those in western regions, are very small in relation to the enclosures to which they are attached. The question which arises is whether these annexes perform the same function in the two traditions. It may well be that there is little or no connection between the two, but this is unlikely. In Wessex they would appear to be part of the entrance defences, a form of barbican, possibly without any economic function. In the Western tradition, on the other hand, their size relative to the main enclosure makes a purely defensive function less likely and an economic one more probable. On the question of priority, in the Wessex tradition such entrance enclosures appear to be secondary features, associated with the reconstruction and stengthening of the site. In the west, on the other hand, they appear to be primary, the whole site, main enclosure and annexe, apparently being built at one time. This could indicate that the Western sites are earlier, with the Wessex sites derived from them at a time when they were under reconstruction, i.e., not in the earliest part of the Iron Age fort period. Distribution lends some slight support to this suggestion. The pattern in the south-west is, on the whole, more compact, indicating a fairly well-established tradition. In Wessex, on the other hand, such sites tend to be scattered and this may be an indication of sporadic derivation from some outside source, presumably in the south-west.

Two other topics, origins and functions, need to be considered, if only in broad terms. The extent to which the question of origins can usefully be discussed in this survey is limited, but a few general points can be made. Leaving the separate types to one side for the moment, the two traditions, Wessex and Western, if they have any validity, are likely to have had links with different parts of Europe, the Wessex tradition with the area from the Cherbourg peninsula to the Rhine mouth and beyond, the Western tradition with Atlantic Europe. Although this whole region falls within the range of Celtic civilization the different parts of Europe inevitably produced different faces of the basic Hallstatt culture, the various pre-existing regional cultures playing no little part in this process. It will be clear that the local Hallstatt culture of northern France and the Low Countries would be noticeably different from that of Atlantic Europe. If, as suggested, these two regions provide the sources of the two traditions, then it is not surprising to find that the two groups of Iron Age forts are so different from each other.

It is not, however, necessary to invoke a continental source for every one of the eleven types distinguished here. Certain types may be regarded as basic, or primary, and others, developments thereof, as secondary, although doubts exist in a number of cases. Within the Wessex tradition Type I must be regarded as primary, and linked with an influx, large or small, of people from the Continent at a date yet to be determined, although it does not necessarily follow that forts were built immediately on arrival. Types II and III may be regarded as secondary, since they are known to have had earlier Type I structural phases, so that the question of continental origins may not be involved. The reasons for their structural elaboration, and possibly for the development of Type I itself, may be internal rather than external, the result of factors which, possibly after an initial phase when no forts were required, produced first Type I, then Type II, and ultimately Type III, although factors other than straightforward defence may have been involved in the latter. If migration from the Continent played a greater part than suggested here, then both the original construction and the subsequent refortification could still be interpreted as the reaction of the native population against new arrivals rather than the work of the new arrivals themselves.

The remaining Wessex-tradition types (X and XI) can also be regarded as secondary in the sense that they usually involve nuclei of Standard size which probably represent the first structural phase. The additional enclosures indicate a link with the Western tradition, with the balance of probability favouring the priority of the latter, unless both traditions were influenced at more or less the same time from some third source. By the same token no question of priority need necessarily be involved between southern England and northern France with regard to Type I. Given that there was continuing contact during the early part of the Iron Age, the need for defended enclosures could well have arisen in both areas at the same time, more or less in parallel. The implication of all this is that native development played a much bigger part than continental influence or migration, except possibly for the basic Type I. Once this had been established here then all the developments represented by Types II, III, IV, X, and XI could have followed with little or no external stimulus. Types X and XI may represent continental influence at second hand, via the Western tradition, the origins of which must be considered next.

In the Western tradition Type V must be regarded as primary. Both density and distribution indicate migration via the western seaway and presumably, therefore, from somewhere on the Atlantic coast of Europe. Again, questions of priority do not necessarily arise, particularly between Brittany and Cornwall. Some of the remaining Western-tradition sites can be interpreted as secondary, but the pattern is not so clear-cut as it apparently was for the Wessex tradition. Type VI is probably best interpreted as a development of Type V, but for the remaining types reservations must be made. If the coastal promontory forts (Type VII) do form a separate group then they must be regarded as primary here, even if in parallel with similar sites in Atlantic Europe, notably in Brittany. While Type VIII could be interpreted as a development of Type V, its fairly compact distribution in the south-west suggests that it too could well be primary. There are, moreover, acceptable prototypes in the Iberian peninsula. Type IX, which involves only a very small number of sites anyway, is probably not primary in the sense of having a continental origin, although its outer enclosure may be derived from outside the Western-tradition area, namely from Wessex. The over-all pattern in the Western tradition then would appear to involve rather more continental influence and rather less native development than in the Wessex tradition. This is not surprising in view of the geographical pattern, in which the separate parts of western Britain are always more accessible by sea than the more compact Wessex-tradition area where the southern flank, once occupied, would tend to form a barrier to the admission of new peoples and new ideas.

The question of function can be finally answered only with the aid of excavation evidence, but again some general points can be made. Whatever else excavation evidence may indicate it seems unlikely to point to a single function covering the wide variety of types and sizes outlined in the survey. It seems safe to assume, even at this stage of our knowledge, that Iron Age forts enjoyed a number of different functions, although not necessarily at the same time or in the same areas.

One of the functions traditionally attributed to Iron Age forts is that of temporary refuges in times of danger, and this may well be so, although even with the aid of excavation evidence such a function would be difficult to prove. Presumably one of the reasons for this interpretation is the location of the enclosures on hills, spurs, promontories, ridges, etc., the assumption being that permanent, peacetime quarters would be in more sheltered situations below. But the same pattern of elevated enclosures and low-lying permanent occupation could just as easily suggest seasonal use. It is feasible to suggest, therefore, that some of these enclosures were connected with the exploitation of elevated areas, and this exploitation is most likely to have been the pasturing of livestock in the spring and summer months. The scale and nature of the defences surrounding the enclosures may simply indicate how much of the community's wealth was tied up in livestock. The siting of many forts in the Wessex-tradition area certainly does not argue against such an interpretation. As noted in Chapter III, many Iron Age forts, whatever their elevation face level ground on one or more sides, and this level ground, often of considerable extent and forming a high plateau, would in many cases provide excellent summer pasture so that cattle could be kept on it for considerable periods. This being so, some means of protecting the cattle would be required and this could have been provided by the enclosures which we call forts.

Quite clearly, however, neither this interpretation, nor that of temporary refuges, holds good for all Iron Age forts. Two groups at least call for alternative explanations: Type III, Maiden Castle-type forts, and Type V, Small single-enclosure sites in the Western tradition. The complexity of the former and the extreme simplicity of the latter make it unlikely that both occupied the same position in Iron Age civilization. With regard to the Maiden Castle types we know, both from observation and excavation, that some of them had reached the status of defended towns or villages by the end of the Iron Age, whatever else they were in their earlier structural phases. The same explanation may, of course, hold good for less complex sites where the evidence can be revealed only by excavation, so that there may well be a class of Iron Age forts which were, in fact, defended towns and villages, at least during the later stages of their existence. It may well be that such a class of forts occupies a larger place in the

Iron Age than has hitherto been allowed. The absence, in so many cases, of any surface evidence of occupation has perhaps led us to postulate functions other than straightforward habitation. In fact, defended villages may represent a standard type of Iron Age settlement, although not necessarily throughout the full extent of the period or in every region.

For reasons of size alone this sort of explanation will not hold good for Type V sites. At best they might be interpreted as defended hamlets, but if due allowance is made for the sort of space, and buildings, required by a farming community, then even this explanation seems unlikely. The social unit represented is more likely to be a family or an extended family group. In other words, Type V sites, and Type VI as well, could be defended homesteads or farms and this, among other things, may explain their less dramatic siting than some of the larger Iron Age forts. They may well represent in western regions what Little Woodbury, with its unfinished defences, represents in Wessex. This again may provide an explanation for the striking concentrations of Iron Age forts in western regions, concentrations made up largely of Type V sites. In comparing densities in Wessex and Pembrokeshire, for example, we are not comparing like with like, since the Wessex forts are so very much larger than those further west. If the suggestions made above are correct then the differences go beyond those of mere size. Types V and VI may represent the sum total, or at least the bulk, of Iron Age habitation sites in western regions, sites which were, as a matter of course, defended. As such they are currently included in distribution maps of Iron Age forts. However, sites in Wessex which may be functionally similar, such as little Woodbury, are not included, because they are not normally defended. What we may be comparing at the moment is a limited number of rather special, defended sites, whatever their precise function, in Wiltshire, with the bulk of the run-of-the-mill habitation sites, incidentally defended, in Pembrokeshire, and quite clearly such a comparison is meaningless. Until we have much more information about the functions which Iron Age forts fulfilled we cannot make any worthwhile comparisons between different areas, and we cannot place too much reliance on distribution maps which do not acknowledge differences in either nature or function.

In a sense the conclusions appropriate to a survey based on surface evidence have already been given in Chapters VIII and IX. Having established, or at least suggested, a basic typology and its associated distribution pattern, the point has been reached at which fieldwork gives way to excavation. Ideally such a survey would have been carried out before any excavation was attempted so that a rational excavation programme could have been worked out, involving, initially, the investigation of say, one of each of the eleven types. In fact, some 200 sites have already been excavated with little or no reference to any over-all plan, and it is quite clear, from even a cursory investigation, that there is an unacceptable degree of imbalance in the pattern of excavation as carried out over the last half-century or so. This imbalance manifests itself in a general way in the geographical pattern of excavated sites and in a more particular way in their number within each of the eleven types distinguished here.

In geographical terms the number of sites excavated in the Wessex-tradition area is much greater than the number in the Western area, even though the latter contains a larger number of sites over-all, so that the proportional difference is even greater than the number of excavations alone would indicate. The same percentage (15 per cent) applied equally to both Wessex and Western traditions would produce figures of about 90 and 110 excavations respectively, but, in fact, the true figures are, in round numbers, 160 and 40 excavations. These represent a sample of around 26 per cent for the Wessex tradition and only 5 per cent for the Western tradition. Quite clearly until some sort of balance between the two is restored any assessment of Iron Age forts in general, or of the relationship of the Wessex and Western traditions in particular, must be suspect. There is a further degree of imbalance within the Wessex tradition, many more sites in Wessex itself, and in the south-east, having been excavated than in the regions to the north and north-west, in the Cotswolds and Welsh Marches.

The imbalance demonstrated by the geographical pattern is further emphasized by considering the pattern within the typological scheme. Again, a cursory examination shows that the emphasis in excavation has been placed, on the whole, on the larger and more spectacular sites, leaving the simpler, but more numerous, sites poorly represented. According to the 15 per cent formula Type V (Small, single-enclosures) should be represented by about 75 excavated sites, and such a number would go a long way towards answering many of the questions about the Western tradition. In fact, only a handful of such sites has been excavated. The same formula applied to the Wessex tradition indicates that excavated sites should be twice as numerous in Type I as in Type II, but, in fact, the reverse is almost true, the more so if Type III is included with Type II, demonstrating again the neglect of the simpler site in favour of those with more complex defences and entrances. By far the biggest number of excavations have been carried out in such sites, and these constitute Types II and III of the basic typology. Much of the interpretation of Iron Age forts, and of the Iron Age itself, has been based on the evidence from these sites, but Types II and III represent less than 15 per cent of the total and may be a very special development of the Iron Age fort tradition.

There is no point in pursuing this question further. Enough has been said to show how wide is the discrepancy between the ideal and the actual. The first conclusion which must, therefore, be drawn is that to a considerable extent we have been digging the wrong sites. Over-all, the 15 per cent sample is more than adequate; 10 per cent would have been sufficient, but it has not been taken equally from each of the eleven types involved. It is, in fact, an average, made up of a wide range in sample levels, high for the more complex sites, low for the simpler sites. The only way now to achieve a satisfactory sample throughout the full range of Iron Age forts is to bring the lower percentages closer to, but not necessarily right up to, the higher percentages. This will mean a great deal of excavation in Types I and V, but this has a very considerable advantage. Because they are relatively simple these sites can be completely excavated. This is particularly important with regard to the interiors since it is here that evidence of the social and economic aspects is likely to be found and until we know a great deal more about these than we do at present we cannot claim to know anything about Iron Age forts. The Type I stage of Type II and III forts, buried as it is beneath the later structures, can rarely, if ever be fully investigated; but since this is the base on which everything else develops it needs to be investigated in its own right in the undeveloped Type I state. Samples in those types which have thus far been neglected would produce an enormous amount of new evidence which would probably go a long way towards solving the problems of Iron Age forts and of the Iron Age itself.

One conclusion which can be drawn from the over-all pattern of Iron Age forts is the wide variety of experience enjoyed by different parts of the survey area. Not the least interesting part of this pattern is the eastern area of England where forts are virtually nonexistent. Their absence is not to be explained by the absence of Iron Age culture, so that some other reason must be sought. This Eastern tradition, as it may be termed, forms one of three facets of the same problem, the other two being the Wessex and Western traditions with their differences in distribution, types, origins, etc. But even within these traditions very considerable differences of experience are represented. In wide areas in the Wessex tradition forts seem to have remained at the Type I stage while in adjacent and clearly defined regions most of the forts are of Types II or III. In parts of the Western tradition the simple Type V forts are dominant, while in others there is a variety of types. This all suggests a fairly complex geographical pattern, and it may be that a geographical approach to the problems of the Iron Age would provide better results than a purely chronological attempt. Certainly in those areas of the Wessex tradition mentioned already not very much is implied in chronological terms by the existence of, presumably, one phase Type I sites; and if, as suggested earlier, Types II and III developed only gradually from Type I then such developments may be difficult to pinpoint chronologically, so that clear-cut stages may always be difficult to establish. In Hodson's attempted alternative to the ABC system[2] clear-cut horizons are clearly hard to find and this difficulty may reflect the true nature of the Iron Age in southern Britain. Certainly on present evidence the geographical pattern is the dominant one and this may be the indication of the way in which the problems of the Iron Age, or at least the problems of Iron Age forts, should be tackled.

The remaining conclusions will be concerned with an attempt to reconstruct, as far as is possible with surface evidence alone, the sequence and chronology of the events which eventually produced the full pattern of Iron Age forts, beginning with the Wessex tradition. What may be termed the first event in this is represented by Type I, extended as described on p. 264. Involving as it does some 600 sites, spread over a very wide area this event is likely to have extended over a period of time and to be susceptible of subdivision on a geographical basis. Four overlapping geographical zones can be distinguished, based on the means of access involved: the South Coast, the Thames estuary, the Bristol Channel, and the north Wales coast. The South Coast must be deemed to represent the means of access of the people responsible for the 200 or so Type I

2. Hodson, op. cit. 107.

forts in the roughly triangular area formed by Wessex itself, the South Downs to the east and the south Devon coast to the west. These people may be presumed to have originated in the area behind the facing coast of northern France. Eventually—and the mechanics of this movement and the time involved are matters beyond the scope of fieldwork—they came to occupy the area just mentioned. Eventually, too, there appeared in the same area the 200 or so Type I forts under discussion. Exactly when forts began to be built in relation to the actual arrival of people is as yet unknown. People might have settled over the whole area before the need for forts arose. Alternatively, their first act on arrival, whenever that was, might have been to proceed with construction. The duration of the period during which Type I forts were built in the south is likewise as yet unknown. Part of the answer to this problem may be that not all forts were in use together, so that collectively they cover a much longer period than the history of any one site. The question of chronology will be further commented on below.

Because it is on one of the two coasts which face the Continent the Thames estuary may have been penetrated as early as the South Coast. On the other hand there is no evidence, at least in terms of forts, of any sizeable movement on to the east coast from the facing continental coast and it may be that the people who entered the Thames estuary came from the same area as those who crossed the South Coast. If early migrants exploited the shortest crossing, to the Dover region, then voyages along the coast, in both directions, would almost inevitably have led to movement into the Thames Valley, so that south and south-east coasts may be part of a single pattern.

The Cotswolds and Welsh Marches are accessible from Wessex, but they are accessible also from the Bristol Channel and it is hard to escape the conclusion that this major inlet was the means by which some, possibly a great part, of the Iron Age population responsible for Type I forts in the area arrived. Involving as it does a very much longer voyage around the south-western peninsula this route could well be one which was forced upon later migrants by resistance to further movement into Wessex. The same sort of process may have taken place at the northern end of the Marches with access via the north Wales coast when the central and southern Marches had become fully occupied, again implying a certain time lag.

The process by which the full pattern of Type I forts was formed is thus envisaged as involving three or four stages, with an implied time lag after the first two, the South Coast and Thames estuary, which could well be contemporary or at least very close in time. This interpretation, however, involves the assumption that the pattern of migration was what may be termed progressive. This is still the most likely explanation but it is worth considering the possibility that it was on a much more massive scale and more concentrated in time, affecting all four regions at more or less the same time. This is not to suggest that Iron Age forts were built at the same time or in a concentrated period. However the pattern of settlement was formed, either progressively or quickly, the building of forts could well have been subsequent to the complete diffusion of Iron Age people throughout the Wessex tradition area. Nor need it have followed the same pattern. If forts were not an immediate result of the arrival of Iron Age people then presumably some additional stimulus, after the settlement pattern was formed, led to their construction in a chronological and geographical sequence unaffected by the original pattern of migration.

Both in numbers and in geographical extent Type I forts are the most important event in the Wessex tradition and the one on which all subsequent developments would appear to depend. In which case it is obviously very important to try to establish first of all the over-all chronological limits within which Type I forts were built, and then the relative chronologies of the regional groups, assuming that any degree of priority was involved. If it was, then it is possible that the Type II and III developments in the south were contemporary, in part at least, with the later Type I stages in more northerly regions. The establishment of a clear chronology for Type I should be one of the main aims of future excavation and one which should have priority over any other project in the Wessex tradition. The results of such an investigation would probably tell us more about the nature of the Iron Age, particularly in its earlier stages, than any other piece of research.

The second major event in the Wessex tradition is the development of about one-third of the total of extended Type I forts to the Type II stage, including in the latter those forts which, later again, progressed to the Type III stage, the whole group being embraced by the term extended Type II. The inclusion of these sites under a single heading, as one event in the terms being used here, does not mean that the Type II stage was reached as a result of a single structural development. It is known from excavation that in many cases two, three, and sometimes more, structural phases were involved. It is likely, however, that some, possibly many, of these phases are purely local, and are perhaps even confined to a particular site, so that it would be unwise to interpret such changes in terms of national or even regional events. This being so, and since such refinements cannot be perceived from surface evidence alone, all single-enclosure sites in the Wessex tradition which are not Type I will be included under extended Type II as the result of a single event. What we are in a sense dealing with in the Wessex tradition is undeveloped Type I on the one hand and developed Type I, in however many stages, on the other.

One immediate conclusion which can be drawn from the distribution pattern of extended Type II forts is that the factors which gave rise to refortification were confined to a number of clearly defined regions, leaving a large area of the Wessex tradition unaffected. Leaving the central Marcher group to one side for the moment, the other Type II areas are all easily accessible from the sea, either directly or via major rivers, and it is difficult to escape the conclusion that outside factors were involved in the appearance of multivallate forts. This is not irreconcilable with the idea that the change from Type I to Type II was a gradual one, nor need it imply that the more complex forts were the work of new arrivals. Given that Type I forts existed already the threat represented by new arrivals could very well have induced the existing population to strengthen its defences. This implies that a slow migratory process rather than an invasion was involved, and that multivallation was not a new, imported military tech-

293

nique but rather a gradual process, in some cases involving several structural phases, carried out by the native population to meet a growing threat.

The following may be suggested as a possible pattern of events. At some time after the appearance of Type I throughout the Wessex tradition area there appears to have been a further series of migrations, following the routes suggested earlier for the later stages of Type I. These, while not necessarily absolutely contemporary with each other, are probably part of a single broad pattern, probably resulting from some development on the Continent. Only limited areas of the Wessex tradition were affected, the resultant pattern reflecting possibly the economic desirability of the area or the part of the Continent from which the migrants came, or a combination of the two. The migrations were probably not isolated single events. They are morely likely to have had a gradual but perceptible build-up through one or two generations, or possibly even longer, accompanied by gradually increasing apprehension on the part of the native population, resulting in the refortification of the Type I forts in the area.

One of the most striking groups of extended Type II forts is in the central Marcher zone. This is much less easy of access than the two other major groups and is flanked to the south and east by a broad spread of Type I forts. If the process just outlined obtained here also then the new arrivals must have bypassed the Type I area, and the obvious way to bypass it is via the Severn and it is difficult to escape the conclusion that this was the route by which much of the additional population arrived, producing the same reaction as elsewhere. Again, the date and duration of Type II are as yet unknown.

It is perhaps worth stating again the possibility that in some Type II sites structural changes are unrelated to outside events. Inter-tribal or intercommunal squabbling, cattle-raiding, etc., could easily have given rise to situations in which a single fort might be damaged sufficiently to require reconstruction. It is not necessary to see every structural phase in every site in terms of national or even regional events. Aggressive and/or acquisitive neighbours from the next hill or valley could provide as many entries in the archaeological record as any long-distance migrants from the continent.

Given the small numbers involved, about 40, and their characteristics, large size, strong defences, elaborate entrances, it is hard not to conclude that Type III represents a rather special form of Iron Age fort. At the Type I and Type II stages nothing more than straightforward defence need be involved. At the Type III stage, however, and given the circumstances of increasing internal pressure caused by new immigrants, something more than straightforward communal defence would seem to be involved. Political and economic factors must be considered as possible elements in the picture. Internal conflicts could well have led to struggles for power in areas where previously little or no political structure had existed, so that eventually those who were victorious emerged as political leaders, consolidating their positions in powerful Iron Age forts. Economic factors could have contributed to the same result, creating the need for market centres where agricultural products could be exchanged for the goods and services of non-productive sections of the community. Such centres would lead almost inevitably to the accumulation of wealth, and wealth, inevitably to power, consolidated again in the Type III forts under consideration. The most likely circumstances would involve a complex interplay of both political and economic factors.

Types I, II, and III represent the mainstream of development in the Wessex tradition. The progressive increase in complexity is matched by a noticeable reduction in numbers, the 600 or so extended Type I sites being reduced to about 200 at the extended Type II stage and to only about 40 at the Type III stage, the latter having assumed, it is suggested, a rather more specialized function involving political and economic factors. It may well be that at each stage only one type was in use, so that at the end of the process only Type III forts remained. The 20 or so examples of this type in Wessex would fit in very well with the 20 *oppida* captured by Vespasian in his advance to the west, which would suggest that the type persisted down to the Roman conquest.

Of the remaining Wessex tradition types Type IV can be disposed of quite quickly. Because they are found in both univallate and multivallate style it seems reasonable to conclude that they developed in parallel with Types I and II and they may simply be larger versions of these, either serving the needs of large communities or fulfilling some more specialized function which demanded greater space than was normally provided in a Standard-sized fort.

Type XI (satellite sites) were treated as a special version of the multiple-enclosure arrangement. Since they straddle the frontier between the Wessex and Western traditions they may well represent a fusion of the two, falling, typologically, somewhere between Type X multiple-enclosure sites (those with Standard nuclei) and Type IX (Small nuclei in very large outer enclosures). They are, in any case, a numerically small group and can be considered as interesting rather than important. Their chronology is probably to be included within that of Type X, the last Wessex tradition type.

In spite of having distinguished multivallate sites (Types II and III) from multiple-enclosure sites, in this case Type X, it is noticeable that for the most part they are found in the same areas within the Wessex tradition. Thus in a sense they can all be included under one heading as sites which have been elaborated from the Type I stage. But closer examination shows that something other than parallel, alternative development is involved. In the case of multiple-enclosure sites the nuclei are in some cases of Type I and in others of Type II. The conclusion which must be drawn is that the addition of enclosures is some other type of development, superimposed on the Type I/Type II process, whatever that represents. The further conclusion which can be drawn is that either this feature came in at a time when the transition from Type I to Type II was taking place, or that Types I and II existed side by side over a considerable period and that the practice of building on additional enclosures was applied indifferently to both. The fact that the multiple-enclosure sites are, on the whole, on the western flank of the Wessex tradition suggests some link with Western-tradition multiple-enclosure sites, although just what form this link took, chronologically or otherwise, is something which can be decided only by excavation.

In the Western tradition the striking concentrations of Type V sites in the western extremities lead almost inevitably to the conclusion that they are the result of migration by sea, presumably from some part of western Europe, possibly Brittany or north-west Spain. While they obviously form a very important part of the Western tradition their chronological position is much less clear than the position of Type I in the Wessex tradition. Because of their sheer numbers it seems reasonable to assume, in the present state of our knowledge, that Type V as a whole, although not necessarily individual sites, had a long life span. Because of their simplicity and this postulated life span it seems reasonable to assume further that they began earlier than any other Western type. There is, in fact, no reason why they cannot have been as early as Type I in the Wessex tradition, the two types developing in response to the same basic stimulus, whatever that was, but, because of environmental, economic, social differences, etc., developing in two separate size ranges, Standard and Small.

Although there does not appear to be, in the Western tradition, a sequence similar to Wessex Types I, II, and III, Type V is incorporated, in one form or another, in many, if not most of the remaining Western tradition sites. Type VI is exactly the same sort of enclosure, except that it has multivallate rather than univallate defences. In Type VII, more particularly in south-west Wales, many of the enclosures are similar in size and defences to Types V and VI. Type V appears again as a nucleus in Type VIII, and Type VIII itself as a nucleus in Type IX so that the Small enclosure, either independently or incorporated in other types, is a basic element in, and presumably therefore a link between, all the Western-tradition forts. Just what form that link took, either culturally or chronologically, can be decided only by excavation, but certain broad conclusions can be drawn from surface evidence and from a few sites which have already been excavated.

The known relationship between Types I and II is suggestive of a similar relationship between Types V and VI in the Western tradition. In the absence of any evidence to the contrary it seems not unreasonable to assume, at least for the moment, that this is broadly true. The scattered pattern of these multivallate sites as compared with the concentrated, compact groups in Wessex and the Marches would appear to indicate that they were derived from the Wessex tradition, rather than the reverse. It may well be that in western regions the idea was taken over fully formed so that new, Small sites were built from the beginning in multivallate, Type VI form. Such a pattern may have less chronological significance than in Wessex; fashion, wealth, and power may be involved, with Types V and VI as contemporaries, at least in part.

Many of the enclosures in Type VII forts are larger than those found in the bulk of Types V and VI, but size is of less significance in a promontory fort where the best and most economical line of defence frequently takes in more space than is actually needed. Some of these sites are probably simply coastal versions of Types V and VI, but others could well represent a separate economic group, specifically sited on the coast with an eye to trade. In which case they are likely to be subsequent to rather than earlier than or contemporary with the bulk of the inland sites. Most western coastal promontory forts are so bleak and exposed that they seem unlikely to represent the establishments of the earliest arrivals. Given a free choice these would probably have moved inland to more sheltered locations, leaving the coastal positions to those to whom they were an advantage, if not a necessity. The occupation of the coastal promontories could then have been subsequent to the build-up of the inland population as represented by Types V and VI.

For Type VIII there is both surface and excavation evidence. The surface evidence in some cases suggests that two phases were involved. In Cornwall the smaller scale of the inner defences as compared with the outer at the concentric sites of Killibury and Tregeare Rounds (p. 177) would appear to indicate that the latter were a later addition. This suggests that some Type V sites became Type VIII as a result of a structural addition. On the other hand, excavation evidence at other Type VIII sites, Castle Dore (Corn.) and Milber Down (Devon), for example, indicates that some Type VIII sites were built from the beginning in the multiple-enclosure style. The two types of evidence together suggest the probability that Type VIII developed out of Type V by structural addition and that subsequently, with such sites as models, certain sites were built from the beginning in the Type VIII style. The alternative is that the Type VIII style of fort arrived fully formed from an outside source and as a result of its influence certain existing Type V sites were altered to conform with the multiple-enclosure layout. This is possible, but less likely. The fact that the inner enclosures of Type VIII coincide so closely with Type V enclosures suggests a much closer link than would exist if the more complex sites were introduced from outside. In any case, whichever interpretation is correct, Type VIII would appear to be later than Type V and to be contemporary only with the latter part of its period of use.

The most logical explanation of Type IX would appear to be that it represents a further extension, in a limited number of sites, of the process just outlined; in other words, that the Large outer enclosures are subsequent additions to inner enclosures of Type V or Type VIII forms. The alternative explanation is that the inner enclosures were inserted into pre-existing Large enclosures. What does seem unlikely is that any Type IX site was built from the beginning in the form in which it now appears. The dimensions of the outer enclosures suggest links with the Wessex tradition, and it may be that such sites represent a fusion of the two traditions. It is noticeable that, as far as can be ascertained, the inner enclosures are of Type V or Type VIII, but not of Type VI, which may indicate that development, if that is what is involved, of Type V to Type VI had not yet taken place. This would be in keeping with the broad pattern of Type I/II in the Wessex tradition. The Large outer enclosures of Type IX are, in fact, simply Type I sites, or in some cases Type IV, which now embrace a Western-tradition site. The development of Type V to Type VI would, in the interpretation adopted here, be consequent on the development of Type II in the Wessex tradition.

So far no attempt has been made to attribute dates to the events outlined in these conclusions. Any detailed chronology is, in any case, the province of excavation evidence and as such is outside the scope of this survey. However, some attempt to indicate, if only very approximately, when certain main events are thought to have taken place, would appear to be desirable, even if such an attempt reflects no more than conventional thinking on the subject. In fact, an alternative to the current, generally accepted chronology, will be suggested, covering a much longer period of time so that the term long, as opposed to the existing short, chronology is appropriate.

The current, short chronology is enshrined in the ABC system, and can be outlined very briefly.[3] The first effects of continental Hallstatt Iron Age culture are dated 'before 600 (B.C.)'. These are followed by the colonizing era, (from about 550 to 350 B.C.) which brought Iron Age A culture, but as yet no Iron Age forts, to southern and eastern England. Only in the period of Iron Age B culture, from about 300 B.C. onwards, do the first forts appear, built by the inhabitants as a defence against new immigrants rather than by immigrants themselves on arrival. Outside southern and eastern England the date of the first forts is seen as nearer 200 rather than 300 B.C. Multivallate forts in Wessex, the south-east, and south-west begin around 150 B.C. and somewhat later in other regions. This is the essence of the short chronology, which may well be correct. Certainly it is in keeping with the view that the chronology of Iron Age forts was essentially compact, in the sense that once they came into use they continued so until the end of the Iron Age. This is part of the pattern suggested earlier (p. 287) in which, after a peaceful period without forts, there was a period of Type I fort building, followed by progressively stronger defences (Types II and III). An interpretation on progressive lines is certainly feasible and may well be correct, at least for certain regions. However, the existence of unfinished univallate sites (p. 120), of unfinished outer defences in multivallate sites (p. 122), and of sites in which there are earlier, abandoned, and later, outer defences (pp. 105–8), suggest the possibility of a fluctuating rather than a progressive development, again at least in certain areas. The suggestion of alternating periods of peace and fortification argues against a compact chronology, although not necessarily against a short one; it does, however, open up the possibility mentioned earlier, of a long chronology, of use over a much longer period of time than has hitherto been visualized.

It should be emphasized at the outset that the long chronology is a hypothesis rather than a securely based scheme, based on evidence which, so far, is suggestive rather than conclusive. Nonetheless it appears to meet the needs of the last millennium B.C. as well as, if not better than, the short chronology.

One of the first points to be made is that the existence of a large number of sites of the same type is always susceptible of two interpretations. One of these is that large numbers of people were involved, and, it follows, in a relatively short period of time. The alternative is that there were smaller numbers of people, the large number of sites being the result of construction over a long period of time. The 600 or so extended Type I sites are susceptible of such an explanation and something along these lines has already been suggested (p. 268). In the Western tradition the Type V sites, about 500 could also be

3. Hawkes, 'The ABC of the British Iron Age', *Antiquity*, 33 (1959), 170–82, reprinted in Frere (ed.), *Problems of the Iron Age in Southern Britain* (1961), 1–16.

explained in this way. The implications of such an interpretation are twofold. First, it could push back the beginning of fort building beyond the conventional date (*c.* 350 B.C.) to some unspecified date within the first millennium B.C., as far as the generally accepted dates for the beginning of the Iron Age proper (*c.* 500 B.C.) or even the earliest Iron Age incursions (*c.* 650 B.C.), and possibly even beyond the latter, regardless of whether such an extension is Late Bronze Age or earliest Iron Age. Second, if the earlier dates, 650 B.C. and beyond, have any validity then there may not have been the great influx of Iron Age A people so generally invoked to populate south-eastern Britain and to mark the beginning of the full Iron Age.

In relation to these postulated early dates the evidence of some continental forts is of no little interest. Although the situation in northern France and the Low Countries with regard to chronological evidence is generally similar to the position here, in Germany Iron Age (so-called) forts appear to have a life-span more than sufficient to accommodate even the earliest date envisaged for the British Isles, and one, moreover, which goes back beyond the Iron Age into the preceding Bronze Age period. The practice of building forts appears to have begun as early as 1200 B.C. Given such a date it is, in fact, surprising that, on the short chronology, the building of forts did not begin in Britain until *c.* 350 B.C., a time lag of over eight centuries. This, of course, is no proof of an early date here, but taken in conjunction with what was said in the last paragraph it may be said to add somewhat to such a possibility. Perhaps of even greater interest than the date of 1200 B.C. is the Late Bronze Age context in which forts first appear in Germany. The possible significance of this for British chronology in the last millennium B.C. will be further commented on below, but it does indicate that forts of the types under discussion need not necessarily be confined to the Iron Age period, whatever dates in years are attributed to it.

The possibility of envisaging a long chronology arises largely out of the drastic reorganization of the British Bronze Age chronology carried out over the last decade or so and recently summarized by Burgess.[4] One of the results of this was to remove the Deverel-Rimbury culture from the Late Bronze Age and place it firmly in the Middle Bronze Age between 1200 and 1000 B.C. Also removed, in this case to the Early Bronze Age, were the traditional Late Bronze Age pottery types. This wholesale evacuation of the period left a large and embarrassing chronological gap, with very little to occupy it, between 1000 B.C. and the traditional dates for the beginning of the Iron Age. Part of the gap could be filled by the continuation, envisaged by Burgess, of the Deverel-Rimbury culture after 1000 B.C., but this could hardly be carried beyond 800 B.C. at most, and probably 850 B.C. would be a more realistic date. This being so, and in the absence of other evidence, it seems feasible to suggest that the remainder of the gap, or some part of it was filled by the earliest forts which, by implication, may not be Iron Age at all, but Late Bronze Age, and by an earlier Iron Age than hitherto envisaged.

Apart from simply eliminating an awkward chronological gap, however,

4. Burgess, 'Chronology and Terminology in the British Bronze Age', *Antiq. J.* 49 (1969), pt. 1, 22–29.

there are more compelling reason for bringing the Deverel-Rimbury culture and Iron Age culture and/or forts closer together in any chronological scheme. Hodson[5] has listed a number of features which occur in both Late Bronze Age and Iron Age contexts and which, he suggests, indicate a surviving native Bronze Age contribution to Iron Age culture. Most of the 'Late' Bronze Age contexts were, in fact, Deverel-Rimbury and while the culture was regarded as Late Bronze Age Hodson's suggestion made a great deal of sense. The removal of the Deverel-Rimbury culture to the Middle Bronze Age, to the years 1200–1000, however, at one stroke interposed a considerable gap between two groups of material which displayed very close resemblances. Such a situation would mean envisaging the persistence virtually unchanged, of certain types of artefact—ring-headed pins and weaving combs, for example—throughout a period of some seven centuries (1200–500 B.C.). This seems very unlikely, and since Deverel-Rimbury now appears to be well-anchored chronologically, the only logical solution would appear to be an early date for the Iron Age and an even earlier one for Iron Age forts (c. 850 B.C.). This assumes, as suggested earlier, that the Deverel-Rimbury culture did continue until such a date. If it did not, then perhaps even earlier dates need to be envisaged. What does seem unlikely is that there was any substantial chronological gap between Deverel-Rimbury and later contexts in both of which the same types of artefact appear, or that such types persisted over a matter of six or seven centuries. Even if there were some, as yet unperceived, Late Bronze Age culture, intermediate between Deverel-Rimbury and the Iron Age, the span of time just mentioned would still appear to be too long, so that the beginning of the Iron Age, and to an even greater extent the date of the first forts, would still need to be put back well beyond the traditional dates.

The C14 evidence from Grimthorpe and Almondbury (Yorks) and Mam Tor (Derby.) could well be of great significance in this context. Radiocarbon measurements on two groups of animal bone from the ditch of the Iron Age fort at Grimthorpe[6] have produced dates (B.P.) of 2640±130 and 2920±130 which indicate date ranges of 820–560 B.C. and 1100–840 B.C. respectively. Even the lowest date (560 B.C.) is very high in terms of current Iron Age chronology. However, both dates must be treated with some reserve because of the known difficulties in dating specimens of bone. Another difficulty is the lack of any overlap between the two dates. The difference may have been caused by humic acids, in which case the sample from the lower level giving the older date, 1100–840 B.C. is more likely to be correct. At Almondbury[7] Phase III has produced a C14 date of 550 B.C.±50. Allowing a century for the two preceding phases the earliest fort on the site could have been as early as 700, or at least within the seventh century B.C. The C14 date from Mam Tor is earlier than both of these (c. 1130 B.C.).[8] The dates from all three sites would fit in very

5. Hodson, op. cit. 104 and fig. 1.
6. Stead, 'An Iron Age Hill-Fort at Grimthorpe, Yorkshire, England', *Proc. Prehist. Soc.* 34 (1968), 190.
7. Almondbury, *publication forthcoming*.
8. Mam Tor: for this information in advance of publication I am indebted to Mr. D. G. Coombs, Department of Archaeology, Manchester University.

well with the suggested long chronology but it must be emphasized again that the evidence cannot as yet be regarded as conclusive.

At Rainsborough (Northants)[9] the excavators concluded that not only was the original fort built at an early date, within the fifth century B.C., but also that it was built from the beginning in multivallate style. Such a date is well outside the short chronology for Iron Age forts, particularly for a multivallate structure. Leaving the type of structure to one side for the moment the date would fit in well with the long chronology in which forts would be built, in small numbers at any one time, over a long period from about 850 B.C. onwards. The excavators suggest that Rainsborough 'is not likely to have been the earliest (fort) built' so that quite clearly they visualize their use during the previous century at least, back to 600 B.C., and possibly beyond.

With regard to structure it has been stated earlier (p. 264) that all Wessex-tradition multivallate forts started life as univallate. In this respect Rainsborough is unusual, if the excavators' suggestion 'that Rainsborough was multivallate from phase 2' is accepted. However, they do concede that the first outer bank and ditch may be slightly later than the inner defences, which would bring Rainsborough back in line with all other multivallate sites. In fact, there appears to be no stratigraphical connection between the inner and outer defences and therefore no reason why the relationship should be any different from the normal Wessex-tradition pattern. This embraces the common practice of adding an outer bank and ditch to pre-existing inner defences and also the less-common practice, exemplified at Wandlebury (Cambs) of placing the additional defences *inside* the existing ones which thus become the outer line of defence. If this happened at Rainsborough then it is possible to suggest an earlier date than the fifth century for the first fort which would have consisted solely of the first phase of the outer bank and ditch. This could take the fort back into the sixth century B.C., well in keeping with the long chronology. It would still mean, however, that the multivallate stage at Rainsborough was reached in the fifth century B.C., some three centuries earlier than is allowed in the short chronology.

While one cannot as yet put forward a conclusive case for a long chronology there does seem to be sufficient suggestive evidence to warrant the formulation of a working hypothesis which can be summarized as follows. In the Wessex tradition the earliest (Type I) forts were built, if in only small numbers, as early as 850 B.C., in which case they are Late Bronze Age rather than Iron Age. They need not have been built in what have been traditionally regarded as the earliest fort areas (Wessex and the South Downs), but in the Thames Valley/East Anglian region, including the Chilterns. This area is open to access from the Rhine via which the practice of fort building could have come directly from Germany at an early date. It may be that a Late Bronze Age group of forts here was confined to a particular region, namely the one just suggested. This would allow the South Downs/Wessex forts to be both later and/or Iron Age. On the other hand there is no reason why some forts in the southern areas

9. Avery, Sutton, and Banks, 'Rainsborough, Northants., England: Excavations, 1961–5', *Proc. Prehist. Soc.* 33 (1967), 291–2.

should not likewise be as early as 850 B.C. The traditional method of dating forts has been largely self-defeating. The pottery found in excavation is labelled Iron Age because it occurs in a (so-called) Iron Age fort, and forts are Iron Age because they have Iron Age pottery. In many cases this is the only evidence and it is quite clearly not good enough for a sound chronology.

It is suggested that from the postulated date of 850 B.C. Type I forts continued to be built until at least the fifth century B.C. Presumably during this time they spread gradually over the whole of the Wessex tradition area. This does not mean that any one fort remained in use for as long as three or four centuries. The generally simple nature of the forts involved makes a protracted period of use unlikely. What is suggested is that the practice of building forts was of long standing, with some forts being built, used, and abandoned long before others had been begun. At any one time only a proportion of the 600 or so, extended Type I forts were in use. At some time during this period, possibly towards the end (*c*. 500 B.C.) Type IV forts would have come into use.

If the Rainsborough evidence is correct then by some date in the fifth-century multivallate forts (Type II) were already in existence. Again, there is no reason why Rainsborough should be regarded as earlier than all other sites so that the date for the beginning of multivallation would need to be around 500 B.C., if not earlier. The reduction in numbers, from about 600 extended Type I to about 200 Type II, may be the result of strengthening only those forts which were still in use, the remainder having long since been abandoned. Because of the very distinct geographical pattern in univallate/multivallate distribution this would suggest that in certain areas forts had gone out of use completely by the time multivallation began in other areas. Again because of the length of time involved, from *c*. 500 B.C. on, it is unlikely that all mutivallate forts lasted for a matter of four or five centuries each. It is much more likely that their duration was less, perhaps one, two, or three centuries, but that collectively they cover the longer period just mentioned. This would imply that there was a considerably overlap in time of Types I and II. The refurbishing of already abandoned Type I forts in the multivallate fashion must also be envisaged, as must the advance of the univallate Type IV sites to the same state during this period. Since Type X forts have both Type I and Type II nuclei the addition of the extra enclosures would appear to have taken place during the overlap period, from 500 B.C. down to 400 or possibly 350 B.C. The same sort of dating would apply to Type XI.

This leaves only the rather special Type III sites to be dealt with in the Wessex tradition. Some of these must be anchored chronologically at one end to A.D. 43, but not necessarily all of them, although it is less likely that such sites went out of use in the same way as Types I or II. The chances are that all such important sites remained in use until the Roman conquest. This being so, it is difficult to suggest more than a century and a half, or at most two centuries, for their period of use. This would indicate a date of 150 B.C. at the earliest, and more likely nearer to 100 B.C., for the development of a limited number of Type II forts to the Type III stage. Such a date is, in fact, very much in keeping with conventional chronology, so it could be that the greater part of the chronological expansion needed is in the earlier part of the fort period, involving Type I particularly, and Type II. Towards the end both long and short chronologies come into step, and both must, in any case have the same terminal date of A.D. 43.

In the Western tradition the large numbers of Type V may represent, as suggested for Type I in the Wessex tradition, a longer period of use and an earlier date than hitherto suggested. Assuming that events in Atlantic Europe, from which region the Western tradition is presumed to have been derived, were somewhat later than in regions further to the east, a later initial date than 850 B.C. may be suggested. It seems unlikely, however, that events in the two traditions can be separated by any substantial chronological gap and a date of between 750 and 700 B.C. is suggested for the earliest Type V forts in the west. If compact multivallate defences are a feature derived from Wessex, then Type VI must be later than the date suggested for the development of this feature in the Wessex tradition (*c*. 500 B.C.), and a date of *c*. 400 B.C. can be suggested. Again the process was probably a slow one, although because of the smaller numbers involved and the widely scattered distribution the pattern is not comparable with the Type I/II pattern in the Wessex tradition. Type V could and probably did continue alongside Type VI and probably survived it, perhaps continuing until late in the Iron Age, or to the end of it.

Type VII, i.e. coastal promontory forts, may also be affected by this dating. If the numerous multivallate forts in this group have earlier univallate stages then these could well be contemporary with Type V, but probably nearer 400 B.C. than 750 B.C. They would then have proceeded to the multivallate stage after 400 B.C., along with the Type VI sites. Even if they were built from the beginning in multivallate style the same sort of dating would probably apply.

The two remaining types (VIII and IX) have multiple enclosures. In the Wessex tradition these are deemed to have originated during the Type I/II overlap, between 500 and probably *c.*400–350 B.C. If they are derived from the Western tradition then a date in the first half of the fifth century can be suggested for Type VIII between 500 and 450 B.C. Since sites of this type appear as nuclei in the much larger Type IX sites the date of the latter ought to be somewhat later, say *c*. 400 B.C., although if the outer, large enclosure already existed then there is no reason why Type VIII sites should not have been built inside them at the same time as they were being built independently, i.e. between 500–450 B.C. The outer enclosures could have been part of the Type I (or Type IV) development between 850 and 500 or 400 B.C., representing the extension from Wessex into the Western tradition area of about 20 sites, mostly Large, as suggested earlier (p. 279). Any greater extension to the west may have been inhibited by the presence there already of Iron Age and/or fort-building people, which would suggest that the two fort-building traditions are broadly contemporary.

The persistence of Type V to the end of the Iron Age has been suggested above, which means that it could have spanned the whole fort building period in the west. If this is so then the other four Western-tradition types could have survived also, since they all have close links with Type V. This contrasts with a suggestion made earlier (p. 295) for the Wessex tradition that there was a progressive decrease in numbers as forts became more complex, so that possibly by the end of the Iron Age only Type III was in use. This could be so, but the alternative pattern suggested for the Western tradition is also a possibility. In other words, although they begin at different dates (c. 850 and 500 B.C.) Types I and II, or some of them, could have persisted to the end of the Iron Age alongside Type III. This implies that the practice of building the simple Type I forts could have continued even after some of them had been developed to Type II, and the practice of building both types could have continued after a small number of Type II had developed to Type III. On the whole, however, this seems less likely than a pattern intermediate between the two extremes, in which Type I overlaps Type II for a longer period than suggested earlier, persisting as late as 300 or 250 B.C., and some Type II sites continuing until the end of the Iron Age, in the latter part of which, from 150 to 100 B.C. on, they were contemporary with the third stage in the Wessex-tradition development, Type III, the Maiden Castle type, and the culmination of Iron Age fort building.

The reorganization of Late Bronze Age chronology mentioned earlier left the period with one very substantial remnant, the Late Bronze Age hoards. What these represent in either cultural or chronological terms is still something of a puzzle, but their broad distribution at least is relatively clear. For the most part they occur in the eastern regions of southern Britain, coinciding, if only approximately with the Eastern tradition mentioned earlier (p. 291), where forts are few and far between. In other words, their distribution is in some way complementary to the distribution of forts in the Wessex and Western traditions. The question which follows almost inevitably from this is whether the existence there of a Late Bronze Age culture, of which the hoards are at present the only evidence, was the reason why so few forts appear in eastern regions. If this is so it could be intepreted as suggesting that forts on the one hand, and hoards on the other, are different regional aspects of a southern British Late Bronze Age.

These conclusions have now reached, if indeed they have not already passed, the point beyond which it is not legitimate to proceed purely on surface evidence. In an ideal archaeological environment the time would now be ripe for an ambitious excavation programme. However, as indicated earlier, the formulation of this typology has, in fact, been overtaken by the excavation of some 15 per cent of all Iron Age forts. One of the first jobs to be tackled, in consequence, although one which is beyond the scope of the present work, is to apply the large body of evidence resulting from these excavations to the typology and the hypotheses arising therefrom which form the conclusions of this survey. This has been done in some small degree already in the present work (in the relationship between Types I and II, for example), but this is one of the more obvious results of evidence derived from excavation, and the whole, now considerable, body of excavation evidence needs to be looked at in much more detail in the light of the typology proposed here.

With regard to the future quite clearly some attempt must be made to redress the marked discrepancy between the various types as far as excavation is concerned. The over-all figure of 15 per cent means that in certain types the percentage is, in fact, much higher, probably well over 20 per cent. To bring the lowest percentages up to the highest would involve an enormous excavation programme which would be both expensive and time-consuming. This sort of programme applied to a large group such as Type V could well produce duplication of evidence and could not be justified. What is required, however, is a sample, by excavation, of the size mentioned earlier, around 10 per cent. Even this would produce a very considerable programme. Applied to Type V for example it would mean the excavation of some 50 sites, less those few which have been dug already. Considering the fairly wide area over which Type V appears this would, in fact, mean an average of only 6 or 7 sites for each of the counties mainly involved in their distribution. This is not by any means an impossible programme and would go a long way towards solving some of the problems of the Iron Age in western regions. Apart from Type V substantial excavation programmes are needed for Types I, VIII and X. These four represent the greatest part of the problem. Smaller numbers are involved with the remaining types and a more modest excavation programme would meet the needs of Types IV, VI, IX, and XI. Of all of these probably the greatest need is for a detailed investigation of the Western tradition's Type V which, after all, represents some 37 per cent of all Iron Age forts.

In looking beyond the excavation programme at the wider problems of the Iron Age and of Iron Age forts it needs to be emphasized that the conclusions presented here are, in a sense, misnamed. They are interim, temporary rather than final, simply one stage in a long archaeological process. With the aid of excavation evidence they can be either accepted, modified, or rejected, but they do represent the essential starting point, in the shape of hypotheses rather than final conclusions, formulated out of all the evidence which can be gleaned from surface examination. In this sense, the final section of this work is much less the end of one piece of archaeological work than the beginning of another. The conclusions (so-called) of any piece of fieldwork must look forward rather than back. In presenting such conclusions as are outlined here the author is deeply conscious of their vulnerability to excavation evidence. Nonetheless such conclusions must be attempted, if only to provide a target at which to aim; and even if, in the process of scoring, the target is entirely destroyed, the new target will, one presumes, be the stronger and more substantial for the process. If as a result of future excavation, the typology and other hypotheses advanced here are abandoned, either partially or entirely, in favour of a new, well-founded, and more substantial framework it will occasion little or no regret in their author. The process of stimulation, even to opposition, is no small part of any endeavour and is one which has occupied an important place in archaeological research. To have provided this stimulation, should such an advance in our knowledge occur, would be regarded by the author as a more than adequate reward for such efforts as were involved in this survey.

Select bibliography

ALCOCK, L. A. (1960). 'Castell Odo: An Embanked Settlement on Mynydd Ystum, near Aberdaron, Caernarvonshire', *Arch. Camb.* **109**, 78–135.

—— (1965). 'Hillforts in Wales and the Marches', *Antiquity*, **39**, 184–95.

—— (1967). 'A Reconnaissance Excavation at South Cadbury Castle, Somerset, 1966', *Antiq. J.* **47**, 70–76.

—— (1968). 'Excavations at South Cadbury Castle, 1967: A Summary Report', ibid. **48**, 6–17.

—— (1969). 'Excavations at South Cadbury Castle, 1968: A Summary Report', ibid. **49**, 30–40.

—— (1970). 'Excavations at South Cadbury Castle, 1969: A Summary Report', ibid. **50**, 14–25.

ALLCROFT, A. H. (1908). *Earthwork of England* (London).

ANDREW, C. K. C. (1949). 'Trevelgue Hillfort', *Arch. News Letter*, **2.** 7, 111.

ANGLESEY. *An Inventory of the Ancient Monuments in Anglesey*, by the Royal Commission on Ancient Monuments (Wales and Monmouth) (H.M.S.O., 1937, reprinted 1960).

ANTHONY, I. (1958). *The Iron Age Camp at Poston, Herefordshire* (Hereford: Woolhope Club).

APPLEBAUM, E. S. (1949). 'Excavations at Wilbury Hill, an Iron-Age Hill-Fort near Letchworth, Hertfordshire, 1933', *Arch. J.* **106**, 12–45.

APSIMON, A. M. (1957). 'Portishead Camp, Somerset', *Proc. Univ. Bristol Spelaeol. Soc.* **8. 1**, 40.

—— (1957). 'Excavations at Burledge Camp, Somerset', ibid. **8. 1**, 40.

ARMITAGE, E. S., and MONTGOMERIE, D. H. (1912). 'Ancient Earthworks', *V.C.H. Yorks.* **2**, 1–71.

AVERY, M., SUTTON, J. E. G., and BANKS, J. W. (1967). 'Rainsborough, Northants., England: Excavations, 1961–5', *Proc. Prehist. Soc.* **33**, 207–306.

BAYNE, N. (1957). 'Excavations at Lyneham Camp, Lyneham, Oxon.', *Oxoniensia*, **22**, 1–10.

BARING-GOULD, S., BURNARD, R., and ENYS, J. D. (1899). 'Exploration of the Stone Camp on St. David's Head', *Arch. Camb.* 105–31.

—— —— and ANDERSON, I. K. (1900). 'Exploration of Moel Trigarn', ibid. 189–211.

BIRCHALL, ANN (1965). 'The Aylesford-Swarling Culture: The Problem of the Belgae Reconsidered', *Proc. Prehist. Soc.* **31**, 241–367.

BOTHAMLEY, C. H. (1911). 'Ancient Earthworks', *V.C.H. Somerset*, **2**, 467–532.

BOWEN, A. R. (1952). 'The Hillforts of Worcestershire and its Borders', *Trans. Worcs. Arch. Soc.* **29**, 33–37.

BOYDEN, J. R. (1956). 'Excavations at Goosehill Camp, 1953–5', *Sussex Arch. Coll.* **94**, 70–99.

—— (1958). 'Excavations at Hammer Wood, Iping: 1957', ibid. **96**, 149–63.

BRADFORD, J. S. P. (1940). 'The Excavations at Cherbury Camp, 1939', *Oxoniensia*, **5**, 13–20.

—— (1942). 'An Early Iron Age site at Blewburton Hill, Berks.', *Berks. Arch. J.* **46**, 97–104.

BRAILSFORD, J. W. (1947). 'Excavation at the Promontory Fort near Okehampton Station', *Proc. Devon Arch. Explor. Soc.* **3**, 86–91.

BROOKS, R. T. (1964). 'The Rumps, St. Minver: Interim Reports on the 1963 Excavations', *Cornish Archaeology*, **3**, 26–34.

—— (1966). 'The Rumps: Second Interim Report on the 1965 Season', ibid. **5**, 4–10.

—— (1968). 'The Rumps, St. Minver: Third Interim Report, 1967 Season', ibid. **7**, 38–39.

BRUCE, J. R. (1921). 'Pen y Gaer, near Llangollen', *Arch. Camb.* 115–42.

BIBLIOGRAPHY

BULLOCK, J. D. (1956). 'The Hill-Fort at Helsby, Cheshire', *Trans. Lancs. and Ches. Antiq. Soc.* **66**, 107–12.

BURROW, E. J. (1919). *The Ancient Entrenchments and Camps of Gloucestershire* (Cheltenham and London).

—— (1924). *The Ancient Earthworks and Camps of Somerset* (Cheltenham and London).

—— (1925). 'Excavations on Leckhampton Hill, Cheltenham, during the summer of 1925, 1926', *Trans. Bristol and Glos. Arch. Soc.* **47**, 81–112.

BURSTOW, G. A., and HOLLEYMAN, G. A. (1964). 'Excavations at Ranscombe Camp, 1959–1960', *Sussex Arch. Coll.* **102**, 55–67.

BUSHE-FOX, J. P. (1915). *Excavations at Hengistbury Head, Hampshire, 1911–12* (London: Society of Antiquaries).

CAERNARVONSHIRE. *An Inventory of the Ancient Monuments in Caernarvonshire*, **1–3**, by the Royal Commission on Ancient Monuments (Wales and Monmouth) (H.M.S.O., 1, 1956; 2, 1960; 3, 1964).

CARMARTHENSHIRE. *An Inventory of the Ancient Monuments in Carmarthenshire*, by the Royal Commission on Ancient Monuments (Wales and Monmouth) (H.M.S.O., 1917).

CHANCELLOR, E. C. (1944). 'Badbury Rings Reviewed', *Proc. Dorset Nat. Hist. Arch. Soc.* **66**, 19–30.

CHATWIN, P. B. (1927). 'Excavations on Corley Camp, near Coventry', *Trans. Birmingham Arch. Soc.* **52**, 282–7.

CLARK, J. G. D. (....). *Prehistoric England* (London: Batsford).

CLARKE, R. R. (1960). *East Anglia* (London: Thames & Hudson).

CLIFFORD, E. M. (1937). 'The Earthworks at Rodborough, Amberley and Minchinhampton, Gloucestershire', *Trans. Bristol and Glos. Arch. Soc.* **59**, 287–307.

—— (1961). *Bagendon, a Belgic Oppidum* (Cambridge: Heffer).

CLINCH, G. (1905). 'Ancient Earthworks', *V.C.H. Sussex*, **1**, 453–80.

—— (1908). 'Ancient Earthworks', *V.C.H. Bucks.* **2**, 21–35.

—— and MONTGOMERIE, D. H. (1912). 'Ancient Earthworks', *V.C.H. Surrey*, **4**, 379–405.

COLLINS, A. E. P. (1947). 'Excavations on Blewburton Hill, 1947', *Berks. Arch. J.* **50**, 4–29.

—— (1953). 'Excavations on Blewburton Hill 1948 and 1949', ibid. **53**, 21–64.

—— and COLLINS, F. J. (1959). 'Excavations on Blewburton Hill, 1953', ibid. **57**, 52–73.

COLVIN, H. M. (1959). 'An Iron Age Hill-Fort at Dover?', *Antiquity*, **33**, 125–7.

COOMBS, D. (1967). 'Mam Tor', *Derby. Arch. J.* **87**, 158–9.

CORNISH, J. B. (1906). 'Ancient Earthworks and Defensive Enclosures', *V.C.H. Cornwall*, **1**, 451–73.

COTTON, M. A. (1954). 'British Camps with Timber-laced Ramparts', *Arch. J.* **111**, 26–105.

—— (1959). 'Cornish Cliff Castles', *Proc. West Cornwall Field Club*, **2**, 113.

—— (1961). 'Observations on the Classification of Hill-forts in Southern England,' in Frere (ed.), 61–68.

—— (1962). 'Relationships between Iron Age Earthworks in France and Britain', *Arch. News Letter*, **7**. 7, 147–52.

—— (1962). 'Berkshire Hillforts', *Berks. Arch. J.* **60**, 30–52.

—— and FRERE, S. S. (1968). 'Ivinghoe Beacon Excavations, 1963–5', *Records of Bucks*, **18**, 187–260.

—— and WOOD, P. (1960). 'Alfred's Castle', *Berks. Arch. J.* **58**, 43–48.

COX, J. C. (1905). 'Ancient Earthworks', *V.C.H. Derby.* **1**, 357–96.

CRAWFORD, O. G. S. (1924). *Air Survey and Archaeology* (H.M.S.O.).

—— (1953). *Archaeology in the Field* (London: Phoenix House).

—— and KEILLER, A. (1928). *Wessex from the Air* (Oxford: Clarendon Press).

CROFTS, C. B. (1955). 'Maen Castle, Sennen: the Excavation of an Early Iron Age Promontory Fort', *Proc. W. Cornwall Field Club*, **1**. 3, 93–108.

CROOK, M., and TRATMAN, E. K. (1954). 'Burledge Camp, Somerset', *Proc. Univ. Bristol Spelaeol. Soc.* **1**. 7, 39–41.

CROSSLEY, D. W. (1963). 'List of Hill-forts and other Earthworks in Pembrokeshire', *Bull. Board Celtic Stud.* **20.** 2, 171–203.

CROW, D. A. (1930). 'Excavations at Ditchling Beacon', *Sussex Arch. Coll.* **71**, 259–61.

CUNLIFFE, B. W. (1966). 'Stoke Clump, Hollingbury and the Early Pre-Roman Iron Age in Sussex', ibid. **104**, 109–20.

—— (1973). *The Regni: Peoples of Roman Britain* (London: Duckworth).

—— (1974). *Iron Age Communities in Britain* (London: Routledge & Kegan Paul).

CURWEN, E., and CURWEN, E. C. (1927). 'Excavations in the Caburn, Near Lewes', ibid. **68**, 1–56.

—— —— (1930). 'Thunderbarrow Hill', ibid. **71**, 258–9.

CURWEN, E. C. (1929). 'Excavations in the Trundle, Goodwood, 1928', ibid. **70**, 33–85.

—— (1930). 'Wolstonbury', ibid. **71**, 237–45.

—— (1931). 'Excavations in the Trundle. Second Season, 1930', ibid. **72**, 100–50.

—— (1932). 'Excavations at Hollingbury Camp, Sussex', *Antiq. J.* **12**, 1–16.

—— (1933). 'Excavations on Thundersbarrow Hill, Sussex', ibid. **13**, 109–33.

—— (1937). *Archaeology of Sussex* (London: Methuen, 1937; 2nd edn., 1954).

—— and ROSS-WILLIAMSON, R. P. (1931). 'The Date of Cissbury Camp', *Antiq. J.* **11**, 14–36.

DANIEL, G. E. (1943). *The Three Ages* (Cambridge University Press).

DAVIES, E. (1929). *Prehistoric and Roman Remains of Denbighshire* (Cardiff).

—— (1949). *Prehistoric and Roman Remains of Flintshire* (Cardiff).

DAVIES, G. H. (1956). 'Bedfordshire Earthworks: No. 1. Maiden Bower, near Dunstable (Pt. II)', *Beds. Archaeologist*, **1.** 3, 98–100.

DAVIES, J. A., and PHILLIPS, C. W. (1926). 'The Percy Sladen Memorial Fund Excavations at Bury Hill Camp, Winterbourne Down, Gloucestershire, 1926', *Proc. Univ. Bristol Spelaeol. Soc.* **3.** 1, 8–24.

DENBIGHSHIRE, *An Inventory of the Ancient Monuments in Denbighshire*, by the Royal Commission on Ancient Monuments (Wales and Monmouth) (H.M.S.O., 1914).

DE QUINCY, A. B. (1969). 'A Promontory Fort at Parc Cynog, Carmarthenshire', *Arch. Camb.* **118**, 73–85.

DOBSON, D. P. (1931). *The Archaeology of Somerset* (The County Archaeologies) (London: Methuen).

DORSET, *An Inventory of the Historical Monuments in Dorset*, **1–3**, by the Royal Commission on Historical Monuments (England), (H.M.S.O., 1, 1952; 2, in three parts, 1970; 3, in two parts, 1971).

DOWDEN, W. A. (1957). 'Little Solsbury Hill Camp. Report on excavations of 1955 and 1956', *Proc. Univ. Bristol Spelaeol. Soc.* **8.** 1, 18–28.

—— (1962). 'Little Solsbury Hill Camp, 1. Report on Excavations of 1958', ibid. **9.** 3, 177–82.

DOWNMAN, E. A. (1906). 'Ancient Earthworks', *V.C.H. Northants.* **2**, 397–419.

DUNNING, G. C. (1931), 'Salmonsbury Camp, Gloucestershire', *Antiquity*, **5**, 489–91.

—— (1947). 'Chillerton Down Camp, Gatcombe, Isle of Wight,' *Proc. Isle of Wight Nat. Hist. and Arch. Soc.* **4.** 2, 51–56.

DYER, J. F. (1955). 'Maiden Bower, nr. Dunstable', *Beds. Archaeologist*, **1.** 2, 46–52.

—— (1961). 'Bedfordshire Earthworks: No. 1, Maiden Bower', *Beds. Magazine*, **7.** 56, 320–4.

—— (1961a). 'The Hill-forts of Bedfordshire', ibid. **8.** 59, 112–18.

—— (1962). 'Ravensburgh Castle—Observations on its Construction', *Beds. Arch. J.* **1**, 77–78.

DYMOND, C. W., and TOMKINS, H. G. (1886). *Worlebury: An Ancient Stronghold in the County of Somerset* (2nd edn., 1904).

DYMOND, D. P., and STEAD, I. M. (1959). 'Grimthorpe: A Hillfort on the Yorkshire Wolds', *Antiquity*, **33**, 208–13.

ELGEE, F. (1930). *Early Man in North-East Yorkshire* (Gloucester: Bellows).

FALCONER, J. P. E., and ADAMS, S. B. (1935). 'Recent Finds at Solsbury Hill Camp, near Bath', *Proc. Univ. Bristol Spelaeol. Soc.* **4.** 3, 183–222.

Farrar, R. A. H. (1955). 'An Early Iron Age Fort on Shipton Hill, Shipton Gorge', *Proc. Dorset Nat. Hist. and Arch. Soc.* **77**, 135–6.

Feachem, R. W. (1966). 'Ordnance Survey: Archaeological Report, 1', *Antiquity*, **40**, 145.

Fell, C. I. (1953). 'Hunsbury Hill', *Arch. J.* **110**, 212–13.

—— (1961). 'Shenberrow Hill Camp, Stanton, Gloucestershire', *Trans. Bristol and Glos. Arch. Soc.* **80**, 16–41.

Field, L. F. (1939). 'Castle Hill, Newhaven', *Sussex Arch. Coll.* **80**, 263–8.

Flintshire. *An Inventory of the Ancient Monuments in Flintshire*, by the Royal Commission on Ancient Monuments (Wales and Monmouth) (H.M.S.O., 1912).

Forde, C. D., *et al.* (1963). 'Excavations at Pen Dinas, Aberystwyth', *Arch. Camb.* **112**, 125–53.

Forde-Johnston, J. (1958). 'A Note on Excavations at Buzbury Rings', *Proc. Dorset Nat. Hist. and Arch. Soc.* **80**, 107–8.

—— (1958a). 'A Note on Excavations at Spettisbury Ring', ibid. 108.

—— (1962). 'The Iron Age Hillforts of Lancashire and Cheshire', *Trans. Lancs. and Ches. Antiq. Soc.* **72**, 9–46.

—— (1962a). 'Earl's Hill, Pontesbury, and Related Hillforts in England and Wales', *Arch. J.* **119**, 66–91.

—— (1963). 'Field work on the Hillforts of North Wales', *J. Flints. Hist. Soc.* **20**, 1–20.

—— (1963a). 'The Hillforts of Staffordshire', *Arch. J.* **120**, 262–3, 288–9, 299–300.

—— (1965). 'The Hillforts of the Clwyds', *Arch. Camb.* **114**, 146–78.

Fowler, P. J. (1960). 'Excavations at Madmarton Camp, Swalcliffe, 1957–8', *Oxoniensia*, **25**, 3–48.

—— and Rahtz, P. (1970). 'Cadcong 1970', *Current Archaeology*, **23**, 337–42.

Fox, Lady (Aileen). (1952). 'Hill-Slope Forts and Related Earthworks in South-West England and South Wales', *Arch. J.* **109**, 1–22.

—— (1957). 'Hembury Hill-fort', ibid. **114**, 144–7.

—— (1961). 'South-Western Hill-forts', in Frere (ed.), 35–60.

—— (1964). *South-West England* (London: Thames & Hudson).

—— *et al.* (1950). 'Report on the Excavations at Milber Down, 1937–8', *Proc. Devon Arch. Explor. Soc.* **4.** 2–3, 27–65.

Fox, C. (1923). *The Archaeology of the Cambridge Region* (Cambridge University Press).

—— (1936). 'Caer Dynnaf, Llanblethian', *Arch. Camb.* 20–24.

—— and Fox, A. (1934). 'Forts and Farms on Margam Mountain, Glamorgan', *Antiquity*, **8**, 395–413.

—— and Hemp, W. J. (1926). 'Two Unrecorded Hillforts on Llanymynech Hill, Montgomeryshire, and Blodwell Rock, Shropshire, and their Relation to Offa's Dyke', *Arch. Camb.* **81**, 395–400.

Fox, N. P. (1957). 'An Interim Note on the Excavation of Caesar's Camp, Keston', *Arch. Cant.* **71**, 243–5.

—— (1970). 'Excavation of the Iron Age Camp at Squerryes, Westerham', ibid. **85**, 29–34.

Frere, S. S. (ed.), (1961). *Problems of the Iron Age in Southern Britain* (Institute of Archaeology, Occasional Papers, no. 11).

Gardner, E. (1911). 'The British Stronghold of St. George's Hill, Weybridge', *Surrey Arch. Coll.* **24**, 40–55.

Gardner, W. (1904). 'Ancient Earthworks', *V.C.H. War.* **1**, 345–406.

—— (1906). 'Note on the Defences of Pen y Gaer', *Arch. Camb.* 257–67.

—— (1908). 'Ancient Earthworks (South of the Sands)', *V.C.H. Lancs.* **2**, 507–54.

—— (1910). 'Excavations at Pen-y-Corddyn, Denbighshire', *Arch. Camb.* 79–156.

—— (1921). 'The Ancient Hillfort on Moel Fenlli, Denbighshire', ibid. 237–52.

—— (1922). 'The Ancient Hill Fort known as Caer Drewyn, Merionethshire', ibid. 108–25.

—— (1926). 'The Native Hillforts of North Wales and their Defences', ibid. 221–82.

—— (1932). 'Craig Gwrtheyrn Hill Fort, Llanfihangel yn Arth, Carmarthenshire', ibid. 144–50.

309

—— (1932a). 'Ffridd Faldwyn Hill Fort, near Montgomery, ibid. 364–71.

—— (1934). 'Caer y Twr, a Hill Fort on Holy Island, Anglesey', ibid. 156–73.

—— (1935). 'The Bulwarks: A Promontory Fort at Porthkerry, Glamorgan', ibid. 135–40.

—— (1937). 'Y Gardden Hill-fort, Ruabon, Denbighshire', ibid. **92**, 151–8.

—— (1947). 'Dinorwig Hill-fort, Llanddeiniolen, Caernarvonshire', ibid. **99**, 231–48.

—— and SAVORY, H. N. (1964). *Dinorben* (Cardiff: National Museum of Wales).

GELLING, P. S. (1959). 'Excavations at Caynham Camp, near Ludlow. First Interim Report',
Trans. Salop Arch. Soc. **56.** 2, 145–8.

—— (1960). 'Excavations at Caynham Camp, near Ludlow. Second Interim Report', ibid.
56. 3, 218–27.

—— (1963). 'Excavations at Caynham Camp, near Ludlow, ibid. **57.** 2, 91–100.

—— (1965). 'Excavations at Pilsdon Pen, 1965', *Proc. Dorset Nat. Hist. and Arch. Soc.* **87**, 90.

—— (1966). 'Excavations at Pilsdon Pen, 1966', ibid. **88**, 106–7.

—— (1967). 'Excavations at Pilsdon Pen, 1967', ibid. **89**, 123–5.

—— (1968). 'Excavations at Pilsdon Pen, 1968', ibid. **90**, 166–7.

—— (1969). 'Excavations at Pilsdon Pen, 1969', ibid. **91**, 177–8.

GLAMORGANSHIRE. *An Inventory of the Ancient Monuments in Glamorganshire*, **1**, by the Royal Commission on Ancient Monuments (Wales and Monmouth) (H.M.S.O., 19—).

GORDON, A. S. R. (1940). 'The Excavation at Gurnard's Head, an Iron Age Cliff Castle in
Western Cornwall.' *Arch. J.* **97**, 96–111.

GOULD, I. C. (1903). 'Ancient Earthworks', *V.C.H. Essex*, **1**, 275–314.

—— and DOWNMAN, E. A. (1908). 'Ancient Earthworks', *V.C.H. Heref.* **1**, 199–262.

—— —— (1908a). 'Ancient Earthworks', *V.C.H. Kent*, **1**, 389–445.

GRANT KING, D. (1961). 'Bury Wood Camp, Report on Excavations, 1959', *Wilts. Arch. Mag.*
58, 40–47.

—— (1962). 'Bury Wood Camp, Report on Excavations, 1960', ibid. 185–208.

—— (1967). 'Bury Wood Camp, Excavations in the Area of the South-West Opening', ibid.
62, 1–15.

—— (1969). 'Bury Wood Camp, Excavations in the North-East and North-West Areas', ibid.
64, 21–50.

GRAY, H. ST. G. (1903). 'Excavations at Castle Neroche, Somerset, June–July 1903', *Proc.
Som. Arch. and Nat. Hist. Soc.* **49**, 23–53.

—— (1904). 'Excavations at Smalldown Camp, near Evercreech, 1904', ibid. **50**, 32–49.

—— (1913). 'Trial Excavations at Cadbury Castle, South Somerset, 1913', ibid. **59**, 1–24.

—— (1922). 'Trial Excavations at Cadbury Camp, Tickenham, Somerset, 1922', ibid. **68**, 8–20.

—— (1924). 'Excavations at Ham Hill, South Somerset. Pt. I', ibid. **70**, 104–16.

—— (1925). 'Excavations at Ham Hill, South Somerset. Part II', ibid. **71**, 57–75.

—— (1930). 'Excavations at Kingsdown Camp, Mells, Somerset, 1927–9', *Archaeologia*, **80**,
59–98.

—— (1933). 'Trial-excavations in the So-called "Danish Camp" at Warham, Norfolk',
Antiq. J. **13**, 399–413.

GRESHAM, C. A. (1943). 'Multiple Ramparts', *Antiquity*, **17**, 67–70.

GRIFFITHS, W. E., and HOGG, A. H. A. (1956). 'The Hill-fort on Conway Mountain, Caernarvonshire', *Arch. Camb.* **105**, 49–80.

GRIMES, W. F. (1945). 'Maiden Castle', *Antiquity*, **19**, 6–10.

—— (1951). *The Prehistory of Wales* (Cardiff: National Museum of Wales).

—— (1962). 'Moel Trigarn', *Arch. J.* **119**, 341.

GRINSELL, L. V. (1957). 'Enclosures and Hill-forts', *V.C.H. Wilts.* **1**, pt. 1, 261–71.

—— (1958). *The Archaeology of Wessex* (London: Methuen).

—— (1970). *The Archaeology of Exmoor* (Newton Abbott: David and Charles).

GUTHRIE, A. (1960). 'Bosigran Cliff Castle', *Proc. W. Cornwall Field Club*, **2.** 4, 151–3.

HALDANE, J. W. (1966). 'Stokeleigh Camp, Somerset', *Proc. Univ. Bristol Spelaeol. Soc.* **11.** 1,
31–38.

HANNAH, I. C. (1932). 'Philpots Camp, West Hoathly', *Sussex Arch. Coll.* **73**, 157–67.

HARDING, D. W. (1972). *The Iron Age in the Upper Thames Basin* (Oxford: Clarendon Press).

—— (1974). *The Iron Age in Lowland Britain* (London: Routledge & Kegan Paul).

HARFIELD, M. (1962). 'Cadbury Castle', *Proc. Som. Arch. and Nat. Hist. Soc.* **106**, 62–65.

HARTLEY, B. R. (1956). 'The Wandlebury Iron Age Hill-Fort, Excavations of 1955-6', *Proc. Camb. Antiquarian Soc.* **50**, 1–27.

HAWKES, C. F. C. (1931). 'Hill-Forts', *Antiquity*, **5**, 60–97.

—— (1935). 'Excavations at Buckland Rings, Lymington, Hants', *Proc. Hants Field Club*, **13**, 124–64.

—— (1940). 'Excavations at Quarley Hill, Hants', ibid. **14**, 136–94.

—— (1940*a*). 'Excavations at Bury Hill, 1939', ibid. **14**, 291–337.

—— (1950). 'Pilsdon Pen Camp', *Arch. J.* **107**, 91–92.

—— (1959). 'The ABC of the British Iron Age', *Antiquity*, **33**, 170–182, reprinted in Frere (ed.), (1961).

—— MYRES, J. N. L., and STEVENS, C. G. (1930). 'St. Catherine's Hill, Winchester', *Proc. Hants Field Club*, **11**.

HAWKES, J. (1940). 'Excavations at Balksbury, 1939', ibid, **14**, 338–45.

—— (1951). *A Guide to the Prehistoric and Roman Monuments in England and Wales* (London: Chatto & Windus).

HAYES, P. (1957). 'Moel y Gaer, Llanbedr', *Flints. Hist. Soc. Publications*, **17**, 88–89.

—— and EVANS, J. S. (1960). 'Hope: Hill Fort of Caer Estyn', ibid. **18**, 171–5.

HAZZLEDINE WARREN, S. (1928). 'Loughton Camp, Loughton, Essex', *Essex Naturalist*, **22**, 117–38.

HEMP, W. J. (1943). 'A Hill-fort Problem', *Arch. Camb.* **97**, 93–75.

HENCKEN, H. (1932). *The Archaeology of Cornwall and Scilly* (London: Methuen).

HENCKEN, T. C. (1938). 'The Excavation of the Iron Age Camp on Bredon Hill, Gloucestershire, 1935–1937', *Arch. J.* **95**, 1–111.

HILL, D., and JESSON, M. (eds.) (1971). *The Iron Age and its Hillforts*, University of Southampton, Monograph Series no. 1.

HODSON, R. (1960). 'Reflections on "the ABC of the British Iron Age" ', *Antiquity*, **34**, 138–40.

—— (1964). 'Cultural Grouping within the British Pre-Roman Iron Age', *Proc. Prehist. Soc.* **30**, 104.

HOGG, A. H. A. (1958). 'The Secondary Iron Age in Britain', *Antiquity*, **32**, 189–90.

—— (1960). 'Garn Boduan and Tre'r Ceiri, Excavations at two Caernarvonshire Hillforts', *Arch. J.* **117**, 1–39.

—— (1962). 'List of Hillforts in Cardiganshire'. *Bull. Board Celtic Stud.* **19.** 4, 354–66.

—— (1965). 'Early Iron Age Wales', in Foster and Daniel (eds.), *Prehistoric and Early Wales*, 109–150 (London: Routledge and Kegan Paul).

HOLLEYMAN, G. (1937). 'Harrow Hill Excavations, 1936', *Sussex Arch. Coll.* **78**, 230–52.

HOULDER, C. H. (1961). 'Rescue Excavation at Moel Hiraddug: 1. Excavations in 1954–55', *Flints. Hist. Soc. Publications*, **19**, 1–20.

HUGHES, H. (1906). 'The Exploration of Pen-y-Gaer, above Llanbedr-y-Cenin', *Arch. Camb.* 241–56.

—— (1906*a*). 'Pen-y-Gorddyn or Y Gorddyn Fawr', ibid. 268–72.

—— (1907). 'Report on the Excavations carried out at Tre'r Ceiri in 1906', ibid. 38–62.

—— (1912). 'Prehistoric Remains on Penmaenmawr', ibid. 169–82.

—— (1913). 'Prehistoric Remains on Penmaenmawr', ibid. 353–66.

—— (1915). 'Prehistoric Remains on Penmaenmawr', ibid. 17–39.

—— (1922). 'Prehistoric Remains on Penmaenmawr (known as Braich y Dinas)', ibid. 346–59.

—— (1923). 'Prehistoric Remains on Penmaenmawr (known as Braich y Dinas)', ibid. 243–68.

—— and LOWE, W. B. (1925). 'Dinas, Llanfairfechan', ibid. 343–64.

HUGHES, I. T. (1924). 'Excavations conducted on Midsummer Hill Camp', *Trans. Woolhope Naturalists Field Club*, 18–27.

HUME, C. R., and JONES, G. W. (1959). 'Excavations on Nesscliff Hill', *Trans. Salop Arch. Soc.* **56**, 125–8.

HUNT, J. W. (1959). 'Banwell Camp. Report on Excavation by the Banwell Society of Archae-ology', *Notes and Queries for Somerset and Devon*, **27.** 270, 238–9.

JACK, G. H., and HAYTER, A. G. K. (1925). 'Excavations on the Site of Caplar Camp', *Trans. Woolhope Naturalists Field Club*, 23–28.

JESSUP, R. F. (1930). *The Archaeology of Kent* (London: Methuen).

—— (1970). *South East England* (London: Thames & Hudson).

JONES, G. D. B., and THOMPSON, F. H. (1965). 'Excavations at Mam Tor and Brough-on-Noe, 1965', *Derby. Arch. J.* **85**, 123–6.

KENDRICK, T. D., and HAWKES, C. F. C. (1932). *Archaeology in England and Wales, 1914–1931* (London).

KENYON, G. H. (1954). 'Piper's Copse, E.I.A. Camp', *Sussex Notes and Queries*, **14.** 3–4, 59–60.

KENYON, K. M. (1942). 'Excavations on the Wrekin, Shropshire, 1939', *Arch. J.* **99**, 99–109.

—— (1953). 'Excavations at Sutton Walls, Herefordshire, 1948–51', ibid., **110**, 1–87.

—— and PHILLIPS, J. P. (1950). 'Excavations at Breedon-on-the-Hill, Leics.', *Trans. Leics. Arch. Soc.* **26**, 17–82.

LANE, H. C. (1969). 'Markland Grips Iron Age Promontory Fort', *Derby. Arch. J.* **89**, 59–67.

LEEDS, E. T. (1927). 'Excavations at Chun Castle, in Penwith, Cornwall', *Archaeologia*, **76**, 205–40.

—— (1931). 'Chastleton Camp, Oxfordshire, a Hillfort of the Early Iron Age', *Antiq. J.* **11**, 382–98.

LETHBRIDGE, T. C. (1948). 'Further Excavations at the War Ditches', *Proc. Camb. Antiq. Soc.* **42**, 117–27.

LIDDELL, D. M. (1930). 'Excavations at Hembury Fort, Devon', *Proc. Devon Arch. Explor. Soc.* **1**, 40–63.

—— (1931). 'Excavations at Hembury Fort, Devon', ibid. 90–120.

—— (1932). 'Excavations at Hembury Fort, Devon', ibid. 162–90.

—— (1935). 'Excavations at Hembury Fort, Devon', ibid. **2**, 135 ff.

LINDLEY, E. S. (1957). 'Brackenbury Ditches', *Trans. Bristol and Glos. Arch. Soc.* **76**, 150–6.

LLOYD, J. C., and SAVORY, H. N. (1958). 'Excavations at an Early Iron Age Hill-Fort and a Romano-British Iron-Smelting Place at Gwernyfed Park, Aberllynfi, in 1951', *Brycheiniog*, **4**, 53–71.

LOWTHER, A. W. G. (1945). 'Report on Excavations at the Site of the Early Iron Age Camp in the Grounds of Queen Mary's Hospital, Carshalton, Surrey', *Surrey Arch. Coll.* **49**, 56–74.

—— (1945a). ' "Caesar's Camp", Wimbledon, Surrey: The Excavations of 1937', *Arch. J.* **102**, 15–20.

LYNHAM, C. (1908). 'Ancient Earthworks', *V.C.H. Staffs.* **1**, 331–79.

MARSHALL, G. (1935). 'Excavation of an Iron Age Camp at Poston, Vowchurch, Hereford-shire', *Trans. Woolhope Naturalists Field Club*, 89–99.

MEPHAM, W. A. (1930). 'Prittlewell Camp. Report on Excavations, 1929', *Trans. Southend-on-Sea and District Antiq. and Hist. Soc.* **2**, no. 1, 29–48.'

MERIONETHSHIRE. *An Inventory of the Ancient Monuments in Merionethshire*, by the Royal Commis-sion on Ancient Monuments (Wales and Monmouth) (H.M.S.O., 1921).

MITCHELL, G. S. (1910). 'Excavations at Chanctonbury Ring, 1909,' *Sussex Arch. Coll.* **53**, 131–7.

MONEY, J. H. (1941). 'An Interim Report on Excavations at High Rock, Tunbridge Wells, 1940', ibid. **82**, 104–9.

—— (1960). 'Excavations at High Rock, Tunbridge Wells, 1954–1956', ibid. **98**, 173–221.

—— (1968). 'Excavations in the Iron Age Hill-fort at High Rocks, near Tunbridge Wells, 1957–1961', ibid. **106**, 158–205.

MONTGOMERIE, D. H. (1908). 'Ancient Earthworks', *V.C.H. Herts.* **2,** 103–27.

—— (1924). 'Ancient Earthworks', *V.C.H. Worcs.* **4**, 421–34.

—— (1947). 'Old Sarum', *Arch. J.* **104**, 129–39.

MONTGOMERYSHIRE. *An Inventory of the Ancient Monuments in Montgomeryshire*, by the Royal Commission on Ancient Monuments (Wales and Monmouth) (H.M.S.O., 1911).

MORGAN, C. L. (1908). 'Note on the Clifton, Burwalls and Stokeleigh Camps', *Proc. Clifton Antiq. Club*, **5**, 8–24.

MORGAN, W. L. (1911). 'Cil Ivor Camp', *Arch. Camb.* 43–53.

—— (1920). 'The Classification of Camps and Earthworks', ibid. 201–23.

MORRIS, B. (1958). 'Hen Castell, a Re-discovered Hill-slope Earthwork in Gower', *Trans. Cardiff Naturalists Soc.* **87**, 23.

MOSS-ECCARDT, J. (1964). 'Excavations at Wilbury Hill, Herts., 1959', *Beds. Arch. J.* **2**, 34–46.

MUSSON, R. C. (1950). 'An Excavation at Combe Hill Camp, near Eastbourne, August, 1949,' *Sussex Arch. Coll.* **89,** 103–16.

NASH-WILLIAMS, V. E. (1933). 'An Early Iron Age Hill-Fort at Llanmelin, near Caerwent, Monmouthshire', *Arch. Camb.* **88**, 237–346.

—— (1939). 'An Early Iron Age Coastal Camp at Sudbrook, near the Severn Tunnel, Monmouthshire', ibid. **94**, 42–79.

—— and SAVORY, H. N. (1949). 'Map of Wales showing Hill Forts and other Earthworks', *Bull. Board Celtic Stud.* **13**, 152.

NEWCOMB, R. M. (1970). 'The Spatial Distribution of Hill Forts in West Penwith', *Cornish Arch.* **9**, 47–52.

O'NEIL, B. H. St. J. (1933). 'The Promontory Fort on Keston Common', *Arch. Cant.* **45**, 124–8.

—— (1934). 'Excavations at Titterstone Clee Hill Camp, Shropshire, 1932', *Antiq. J.* **14**, 13–32.

—— (1934a). 'Excavations at Titterstone Clee Hill Camp, Shropshire, 1932', *Arch. Camb.* **89**, 83–111.

—— (1937). 'Excavations at Breiddin Hill Camp, Montgomeryshire, 1933–35', ibid. **92**, 86–128.

—— (1943). 'Excavations at Ffridd Faldwyn Camp, Montgomery, 1937–9', ibid. **97**, 1–57.

ORDNANCE SURVEY (1962). *Maps of Southern Britain in the Iron Age* (H.M.S.O.).

—— (1963). *Field Archaeology.* O.S. Professional Papers, N.S. no. 13 (H.M.S.O.).

PEAKE, H. (1931). *The Archaeology of Berkshire* (London: Methuen).

PEMBROKESHIRE, *An Inventory of the Ancient Monuments in Pembrokeshire*, by the Royal Commission on Ancient Monuments (Wales and Monmouth) (H.M.S.O., 1925).

PETER, T. C. (1895). 'Carn Brea', *J. R. Inst. Cornwall*, **13**, pt. 1, 92.

PHILLIPS, C. W. (1948). 'Ancient Earthworks', *V.C.H. Cambridge and the Isle of Ely*, **2**, 1–47.

PIGGOTT S. (1931). 'Ladle Hill—An Unfinished Hill Fort', *Antiquity*, **5**, 474–85.

—— (1947). 'Plan of Yarnbury Castle'. *Arch. J.* **104**, 31, fig. 2.

—— and PIGGOTT, C. M. (1943). 'Winkelbury', *Proc. Hants Field Club*, **15**, 53–56.

—— —— (1940). 'Excavations at Ram's Hill, Uffington, Berks.', *Antiq. J.* **20**, 465–80.

PITT-RIVERS, L. (1888). 'Excavations in Winkelbury Camp', *Excavations in Cranbourne Chase*, **2**, 233–87.

PLAYNE, G. F. (1877). 'On the Ancient Camps of Gloucestershire', *Proc. Cotteswold Naturalists Field Club*, **6**, 202–46.

POTTS, W. (1907). 'Ancient Earthworks', *V.C.H. Oxon.* **2**, 303–49.

POWELL, T. G. E. (1933). 'Oxenton Hill Camp', *Trans. Bristol and Glos. Arch. Soc.* **55**, 383–4.

—— *et al.* (1963). 'Excavations at Skelmore Heads, near Ulverston, 1957 and 1959', *Trans. Cumb. and Westmld. Antiq. Soc.* **63**, 1–30.

PRESTON, F. L. (1950). 'Hillforts in S.W. Yorkshire', *Trans. Hunterian Arch. Soc.* **6**. 3, 85–94.

—— (1954). 'The Hillforts of the Peak', *Derby. Arch. J.* **74,** 1–31.

PRICE, J. E. (1882). 'On Excavations in the Camp, the Tumulus, and Romano-British Cemetery, Seaford, Sussex', *Sussex Arch. Coll.* **32**, 167–200.

RADFORD, C. A. R. (1947). 'Stoke Hill Camp', *Proc. Devon Arch. Explor. Soc.* **3**, 24–32.

—— (1951). 'Report on the Excavations at Castle Dore,' *J. R. Inst. Cornwall*, N.S. **1**, Appendix 1–119.

—— and COX, J. (1955). 'Cadbury Castle, South Cadbury', *Proc. Som. Arch. and Nat. Hist. Soc.* **99–100**, 106–13.

RADNORSHIRE. *An Inventory of the Ancient Monuments in Radnorshire*, by the Royal Commission on Ancient Monuments (Wales and Monmouth) (H.M.S.O., 1913).

RAHTZ, P. A. (1957). 'Kings Weston Down Camp, Bristol, 1956', *Proc. Univ. Bristol Spelaeol. Soc.* **8**. 1, 30–38.

—— (1969). 'Cannington Hillfort 1963', *Proc. Som. Arch. and Nat. Hist. Soc.* **113**, 56–68.

—— and BARTON, K. J. (1963). 'Maes Knoll Camp, Dundry, Somerset. I: Trial Excavations, 1958', *Proc. Univ. of Bristol Spelaeol. Soc.* **10**. 1, 9–11.

—— and BROWN, J. (1959). 'Blaise Castle Hill, Bristol, 1957', ibid. **8**. 3, 147–71.

RAMM, H. G. (1957). 'A Survey of the Combs Moss Hill-fort', *Derby. Arch. J.* **77**, 49–53.

RICHARDSON, K. M. (1940). 'Excavations at Poundbury, Dorchester, Dorset, 1939', *Antiq. J.* **20**, 429–48.

—— (1957). 'Blackbury Castle,' *Arch. J.* **114**, 165–6.

RICHMOND, I. A., *et al.* (1968) *Hod Hill*, **2** (London: Trustees of the British Museum).

RIVET, A. L. F. (1961). 'Some of the Problems of Hill-Forts', in Frere (ed.), 29–34.

ROYAL COMMISSIONS: ON ANCIENT MONUMENTS, ON HISTORICAL MONUMENTS. *See under* county names.

SAUNDERS, A. D. (1961). 'Excavations at Castle Gotha, St. Austell, Cornwall: Interim Report', *Proc. West Cornwall Field Club*, **2**. 5, 216–20.

—— (1963). 'Excavations at Castle Gotha: Second Interim Report', *Cornish Arch.* **2**, 49–51.

SAVORY, H. N. (1949). List of Hill-forts and other Earthworks in Wales: I. Glamorgan', *Bull. Board Celtic Stud.* **13,** 152–61.

—— (1950). 'List of Hill-forts and other Earthworks in Wales: II. Monmouthshire', ibid. **13.** 4, 231–8.

—— (1950a). 'List of Hill-forts and other Earthworks in Wales: III. Brecknockshire', ibid. **14**, 69–75.

—— (1951). 'Excavation at the "Gaer", Aberllynfi (Breek.)', ibid. **14**, 251–2.

—— (1952). 'List of Hill-forts and other Earthworks in Wales: IV. Radnorshire', ibid. **15**, 73–80.

—— (1953). 'List of Hill-forts and other Earthworks in Wales and Monmouthshire. Additions and Corrections to Sections I–III', ibid. **15**, 228–31.

—— (1954). 'List of Hill-forts and other Earthworks in Wales: V. Carmarthenshire', ibid. **16.** 1, 54–67.

—— (1954a). 'The Excavations of an Early Iron Age Fortified Settlement on Mynydd Bychan, Llysworney (Glam.), 1949–50. Part I', *Arch. Camb.* **103**, 85–108.

—— (1955). 'Prehistoric Brecknock: The Early Iron Age', *Brycheiniog*, **1**, 116–25.

—— (1956). 'The Excavation of an Early Iron Age Fortified Settlement on Mynydd Bychan, Llysworney (Glam.), 1949–50. Part II', *Arch. Camb.* **104**, 14–51.

—— (1958). 'Excavations at Dinorben Hill-fort, Abergele (Denb.), 1956–7', *Bull. Board Celtic Stud.* **17.** 4, 296–309.

—— (1958*a*). 'Caer Drewyn', *Arch. Camb.* **107**, 135–6.

—— (1959). 'The Excavations at Dinorben Hill-fort, Abergele, 1956–9', *Trans. Denb. Hist. Soc.* **8**, 18–39.

—— (1961). 'Twyn-llechfaen Hill-fort Excavations, 1959', *Bull. Board Celtic Stud.* **19,** 173.

—— (1965). 'Recent Archaeological Excavation and Discovery in Glamorgan: I, Prehistoric Periods', *Morgannwg*, **9**, 88–91.

SCOTT-GARRETT, C. (1958). 'Littledean Camp', *Trans. Bristol and Glos. Arch. Soc.* **77**, 48–60.

SEABY, W. A. (1950). 'The Iron Age Hill-fort on Ham Hill, Somerset', *Arch. J.* **107**, 90–91.

SIMMONS, B. B. (1963). 'Iron Age Hill Forts in Nottinghamshire', *Trans. Thoroton Soc.* **67**, 9–20.

SIMMS, B. B. (1932). 'Recent Investigations of the Hillfort and Camp at Maer', *Trans. North Staffs. Field Club*, **66**, 91.

SMALLCOMBE, W. A. (1949). 'Notes on Excavations on Blewburton Hill, Berks.', *Antiquity*, **92,** 208–11.

SPURGEON, C. J. (1963). 'Two Pembrokeshire Earthworks', *Arch. Camb.* **112,** 154–8.

STANFORD, S. C. (1967). 'Croft Ambrey Hill-fort—Some Interim Conclusions', *Trans. Wool-hope Naturalists Field Club*, **39**, 31–39.

—— (1970). 'Credenhill Camp, Herefordshire: An Iron Age Hill-fort Capital', *Arch. J.* **127**, 82–129.

—— (1974). *Croft Ambrey* (Hereford: privately printed for the author).

STANLEY, J. (1954). 'An Iron Age Fort at Ball Cross Farm, Bakewell', *Derby. Arch. J.* **74**, 85–99

STANLEY, M. and STANLEY, B. (1959). 'The Defences of the Iron Age Camp at Wappenbury,' Warwickshire', *Trans. Birmingham Arch. Soc.* **76**, 1–9.

STAPLETON, P. (1909). 'Exploration of Moel-y-Gaer, Bodfan', *Arch. Camb.* 232–8.

STEAD, I. M. (1968). 'An Iron Age Hill-Fort at Grimthorpe, Yorkshire, England', *Proc. Prehist. Soc.* **34**, 148–90.

STEVENSON, W. (1906). 'Ancient Earthworks', *V.C.H. Notts.* **1**, 289–316.

STONE, J. F. S. (1958). *Wessex before the Celts* (London: Thames & Hudson).

SUMNER, H. (1913). *The Ancient Earthworks in Cranbourne Chase* (London: Chiswick Press).

—— (1917). *The Ancient Earthworks of the New Forest* (London: Chiswick Press).

—— (1931). *Local Papers* (London: Chiswick Press).

TEBBUTT, C. F. (1970). 'Garden Hill Camp, Hartfield', *Sussex Arch. Coll.* **108**, 39–49.

—— (1970*a*). 'Dry Hill Camp, Lingfield', *Surrey Arch. Coll.* **67**, 119–20.

THOMAS, A. C. (1965). 'The Hill-Fort at St. Dennis', *Cornish Arch.* **4**, 31–35.

THOMAS, N. (1959). 'The Excavations at Conderton Camp, Bredon Hill, 1958–9', *Proc. Cotteswold Naturalists Field Club*, **33**, 100–6.

—— (1960). *A Guide to Prehistoric England* (London: Batsford).

THOMAS, S. (1965). *Pre-Roman Britain* (London: Studio Vista).

THREIPLAND, L. M. (1956). 'An Excavation at St. Mawgan-in-Pyder, North Cornwall', *Arch. J.* **113**, 33–81.

TRATMAN, E. K. (1959). 'Maesbury Castle, Somerset', *Proc. Univ. Bristol Spelaeol. Soc.* **8**, 172–8.

—— (1963). 'Maes Knoll Camp, Dundry, Somerset', ibid. **10.** 1, 11–15.

TURNER, D. J. (1963). 'Excavations at Carshalton 1961', *Surrey Arch. Coll.* **60**, 50–53.

TYSON, N., and BU'LOCK, J. D. (1957). 'The Iron Age Fortifications at Planes Wood, Whalley', *Trans. Lancs. and Ches. Antiq. Soc.* **67**, 115–17.

VARLEY, W. J. (1935). 'Maiden Castle, Bickerton: Preliminary Excavations, 1934', *Liverpool Univ. Annals of Arch. and Anthrop.* **22**, 97–110.

—— (1936). 'Further Excavations at Maiden Castle, Bickerton, 1935', ibid. **23**, 101–12.

—— (1948). 'Hill-forts of the Welsh Marches', *Arch. J.* **105**, 41–66.

—— (1950). 'Excavations of the Castle Ditch, Eddisbury, 1935–38', *Trans. Hist. Soc. of Lancs. and Ches.* **102**, 1–68.

WACHER, J. S. (1958). 'Breedon-on-the-hill. Interim Report', *Trans. Leicester Arch. and Hist. Soc.* **34**, 79–80.

WAILES, B. (1963). 'Excavations at Castle-an-Dinas, St. Columb Major: Interim Report', *Cornish Arch.* **2**, 51–55.

—— (1964). 'Castle-an-Dinas, St. Columb Major', ibid. **3**, 85.

WAINWRIGHT, G. J. (1967). 'The Excavation of an Iron Age Hillfort on Bathampton Down, Somerset', *Trans. Bristol and Glos. Arch. Soc.* **86**, 42–59.

—— (1969). 'The Excavation of Balksbury Camp, Andover, Hants', *Proc. Hants Field Club.* **26**, 21–56.

—— (1967). *Coygan Camp* (Cardiff: Cambrian Archaeological Association).

WALL, J. C. (1906). 'Ancient Earthworks', *V.C.H. Devon.* **1**, 573–630.

—— (1907). 'Ancient Earthworks', *V.C.H. Leics.* **1**, 243–76.

—— and DOWNMAN, E. A. (1908). 'Ancient Earthworks', *V.C.H. Salop.* **1**, 351–413.

WARD-PERKINS, J. B. (1939). 'Excavations on the Iron Age Hill-fort of Oldbury, near Ightham, Kent', *Arch. Cant.* **51**, 137–81.

—— (1944). 'Excavations on the Iron Age Hill-fort of Oldbury, near Ightham, Kent', *Archaeologia*, **90**, 127–76.

WATTS, S. (1957). 'Creech Hill Camp, Milton Clevedon', *Proc. Univ. Bristol Spelaeol. Soc.* **8**, 42–43.

WHEELER, R. E. M. (1925). *Prehistoric and Roman Wales* (Oxford: Clarendon Press).

—— (1939). 'Iron Age Camps in North-western France and South-western Britain', *Antiquity*, **13**, 58–77.

—— (1943). *Maiden Castle, Dorset* (Reports of the Research Committee of the Society of Antiquaries of London, no. XII).

—— (1944). 'Multiple Ramparts: A Note in Reply', *Antiquity*, **18**, 50–52.

—— (1949). 'Earthwork since Hadrian Allcroft', *Arch. J.* **106** (Supplement), 62–83.

—— (1952). 'The Herefordshire Beacon Hill Fort', *Arch. J.* **109**, 146–8.

—— (1953). 'An Early Iron Age "Beachhead" at Lulworth, Dorset', *Antiq. J.* **33**, 1–13.

—— and WHEELER, T. V. (1932). *Report on the Excavation of the Prehistoric, Roman, and Post Roman Site in Lydney Park, Gloucestershire* (Reports of the Research Committee of the Society of Antiquaries of London, no. IX).

WHIMSTER, D. C. (1931). *The Archaeology of Surrey* (London: Methuen).

WHITE, D. A. (1963). 'Excavations at the War Ditches, Cherry Hinton, 1961–2', *Proc. Cambridge Antiq. Soc.* **56–57**, 9–29.

—— (1963*a*) 'Excavations at the War Ditches, Cherry Hinton, 1949–51', ibid. 30–41.

WHITLEY, M. (1943). 'Excavations at Chalbury Camp, Dorset, 1939', *Antiq. J.* **23**, 98–121.

WHYBROW, C. (1967). 'Some Multivallate Hill-forts on Exmoor and in North Devon', *Proc. Devon Arch. Explor. Soc.* **25**, 1–18.

WILKERSON, J. C., and CRASTER, M. D. (1959). 'Excavations at Whiteley Hill, Barley, Herts.', *Proc. Cambridge Antiq. Soc.* **52**, 2–5.

WILLIAM, H. W. (1902). 'The Exploration of a Prehistoric Camp in Glamorganshire', *Arch. Camb.* 252–60.

WILLIAMS, A. (1939). 'Excavations at the Knave Promontory Fort, Rhossili, Glamorgan', ibid. **94**, 210–19.

—— (1940). 'The Excavation of Bishopston Valley Promontory Fort, Glamorgan', ibid. **95**, 9–19.

—— (1941). 'The excavation of High Penard Promontory Fort, Glamorgan', ibid. **96**, 23–30.

—— (1945). 'A Promontory Fort at Henllan, Cardiganshire', ibid. **98**, 226–40.

—— (1952). 'Clegyr-Boia, St. David's (Pemb.): Excavation in 1943, ibid. **102**, 20–47.

WILLIAMS-FREEMAN, J. P. (1915). *An Introduction to Field Archaeology as Illustrated by Hampshire* (London: Macmillan).

BIBLIOGRAPHY

WILSON, A. E. (1938). 'Excavations in the Ramparts and Gateway of the Caburn, August–October 1937', *Sussex Arch. Coll.* **79**, 169–94.
—— (1939). 'Excavations at the Caburn, 1938', ibid. **80**, 193–213.
—— (1940). 'Report on the Excavations on Highdown Hill, Sussex, August 1939', ibid. **81**, 173–204.
—— (1950). 'Excavation on Highdown Hill, 1947', ibid. **89**, 163–91.
WINBOLT, S. E. (1930). 'Excavations at Saxonbury Camp', ibid. **71**, 223–36.
—— (1930a). 'Excavations at Holmbury Camp, Surrey', *Surrey Arch. Coll.* **38**, 156–70.
—— (1932). 'Excavations at Hascombe Camp, Godalming, June–July 1931', ibid. **40**, 78–96.
—— (1936). 'An Early Iron Age Camp in Piper's Copse, Kirdford', *Sussex Arch. Coll.* **77**, 245–9.
—— and MARGARY, I. D. (1933). 'Dry Hill Camp, Lingfield', *Surrey Arch. Coll.* **41**, 79–92.
WITTS, G. B. (1883). *Archaeological Handbook of the County of Gloucester*, 2 vols. (Cheltenham).
WOOD, P. (1954). 'The Early Iron Age Camp on Bozedown, Whitchurch, Oxon.', *Oxoniensia*, **19**, 8–14.
—— (1959). 'The Early Iron Age Camp called Grimsbury Castle, near Hermitage, Berks.', *Berks. Arch. J.* **57**, 74–82.
WOODARD, P. (1951). 'Excavations on Wolstonbury Hill, 1950', *Sussex Notes and Queries*, **13.** 6, 131–4.

YOUNG, A., and RICHARDSON, K. M. (1955). 'Report on the Excavations at Blackbury Castle', *Proc. Devon Arch. Explor. Soc.* **5.** 2–3, 43–67.

Index